Mary Virginia Robinson
— January 1989.

GREAT LEADERS OF THE CHRISTIAN CHURCH

Copyright © 1988 The Moody Bible
Institute of Chicago

Except where noted otherwise, all
Scripture quotations in this book are
from the Holy Bible, New International
Version © 1973, 1978 by the
International Bible Society.

Library of Congress Cataloging in
Publication Data

Great leaders of the Christian church.

  1. Christian biography.
I. Woodbridge, John D., 1941-
BR1700.2.G74 1988   270′.092′2 [B]
87-34974
ISBN 0-8024-9051-4

Designed and produced for Moody
Press by Three's Company,
12 Flitcroft Street, London
WC2H 8DJ, England
Editor: Tim Dowley, BA PhD
Design: Peter M Wyart, MSIAD
Typesetting: Watermark, Watford,
Hertfordshire
Worldwide co-edition organized and
produced by Angus Hudson Ltd,
London

Moody Press, a ministry of the Moody
Bible Institute, is designed for
education, evangelization, and
edification. If we may assist you in
knowing more about Christ and the
Christian life, please write us without
obligation: Moody Press, c/o MLM,
Chicago, Illinois 60610 U.S.A.

1 2 3 4 91 90 89 88

Great Leaders of the Christian Church

John D. Woodbridge
General Editor

MOODY PRESS
Chicago

Contents

Contributors

David W. Bebbington Ph.D., Lecturer in History, University of Stirling, Scotland. *Elizabeth Fry, C.H. Spurgeon.*

Gerald L. Bray D.Litt., Lecturer in Systematic Theology, Oak Hill Theological College, Southgate, London, England. *Tertullian, Athanasius.*

Geoffrey W. Bromiley M.A., Ph.D., D.Litt., Senior Professor of Church History, Fuller Theological Seminary, Pasadena, California. *Ulrich (Huldrych) Zwingli, Karl Barth.*

Harold O.J. Brown S.T.B., Th.M., Ph.D., Professor of Biblical and Systematic Theology, Trinity Evangelical Divinity School, Deerfield, Illinois. *Boniface, Bernard of Clairvaux.*

F.F. Bruce D.D., F.B.A., Formerly Rylands Professor of Biblical Criticism and Exegesis, University of Manchester, England. *Paul.*

D.A. Carson M.Div., Ph.D., Professor of New Testament, Trinity Evangelical Divinity School, Deerfield, Illinois. *Peter.*

Robert G. Clouse B.D., M.A., Ph.D., Professor of History, Indiana State University, Terre Haute, Indiana. *Gregory the Great, Thomas Becket.*

Arnold A. Dallimore D.D., Retired Baptist Minister and Writer, Cottam, Ontario, Canada. *George Whitefield.*

Cyril J. Davey Retired Minister and Writer, Bristol, England. *George Müller.*

Kenneth R. Davis M.A., Ph.D., Vice President, Academic Dean, and Professor of Religious Studies and History, Trinity Western University, Langley, British Columbia, Canada. *Menno Simons.*

Lyle W. Dorsett B.A., M.A., Ph.D., Director of the Marion E. Wade Center and Professor of History at Wheaton College, Wheaton, Illinois. *C.S. Lewis*

J.D. Douglas *M.A., B.D., S.T.M., Ph.D., Writer and Editor, St. Andrews, Scotland. John Knox.*

C. Stephen Evans M.PHIL., Ph.D., Professor of Philosophy and Curator of the Howard and Edna Hong Kierkegaard Library at St. Olaf College, Northfield, Minnesota. *Søren Kierkegaard.*

Everett Ferguson Ph.D., Professor of Church History, Abilene Christian University, Abilene, Texas. *Irenaeus, Jerome, Leo the Great.*

W. Robert Godfrey M.A., M.Div., Ph.D., Professor of Church History, Westminster Theological Seminary in California, Escondido, California. *Martin Luther.*

Paul Helm M.A., Reader in Philosophy, University of Liverpool, England. *Jonathan Edwards.*

Thomas Kay M.A., Ph.D., Professor of History, Wheaton College, Wheaton, Illinois. *Pope Innocent III.*

A.N.S. Lane M.A., B.D., Lecturer in Historical Theology at London Bible College, London, England. *John Wyclif, John Hus, William Tyndale.*

Robert D. Linder M.R.E., M.Div., M.A., Ph.D., Professor of History, Kansas State University, Manhattan, Kansas. *Columba, Ignatius Loyola, Francis Xavier.*

Caroline T. Marshall Ph.D., Professor of History, James Madison University, Harrisonburg, Virginia. *Patrick, Bede, Catherine of Siena, Teresa of Avila.*

H. Dermot McDonald Ph.D., formerly Vice Principal and Senior Lecturer, History of Doctrine and Philosophy of Religion, London Bible College, London, England. *Anselm of Canterbury, Thomas Aquinas.*

Leon Morris Ph.D., formerly Principal of Ridley College, Melbourne, Australia. *John.*

Ronald H. Nash M.A., Ph.D., Professor of Philosophy, Western Kentucky University, Bowling Green, Kentucky. *Augustine of Hippo.*

Roger Nicole M.A., Th.D., Ph.D., D.D., Professor of Theology Emeritus, Gordon-Conwell Theological Seminary, South Hamilton, Massachusetts. *B.B. Warfield.*

James I. Packer D.Phil., Professor of Systematic and Historical Theology, Regent College, Vancouver, Canada. *John Calvin.*

James H. Pain B.D., S.T.M., D.Phil., Pfeiffer Professor of Religion, The Graduate School, Drew University, Madison, New Jersey. *Alcuin, Peter Abelard.*

Rodney L. Petersen B.D., Ph.D., Assistant Professor of Church History, Trinity Evangelical Divinity School, Deerfield, Illinois. *Francis of Assisi.*

Richard V. Pierard M.A., Ph.D., Professor of History, Indiana State University, Terre Haute, Indiana. *Dietrich Bonhoeffer.*

John C. Pollock M.A., Writer, South Moulton, Devon, England. *William Wilberforce, D.L. Moody, Billy Graham.*

Roger Pooley M.A., Ph.D., Lecturer in English, University of Keele, England. *John Bunyan.*

David Porter Writer, Greatham, Nr. Liss, Hampshire, England. *Francis Schaeffer.*

Arthur O. Roberts B.D., Ph.D., Professor of Philosophy and Religion, George Fox College, Newberg, Oregon. *George Fox.*

Garth M. Rosell M.Div., Th.M., Ph.D., Vice President of Academic Affairs, Professor of Church History, Gordon-Conwell Theological Seminary, South Hamilton, Massachusetts. *Charles Grandison Finney.*

Robert V. Schnucker Ph.D., Professor of History and Religion, Northeast Missouri State University, Kirksville, Missouri. *Origen.*

Ian Sellers M.A., M.Litt., Ph.D., Minister, United Reformed Church of England, Warrington, Cheshire, England. *Phillip Jakob Spener.*

Michael A. Smith M.A., Dip.Th., Minister of Golcar Baptist Church, Huddersfield, Yorkshire, England. *Cyprian of Carthage, Basil the Great.*

Brian Stanley M.A., Ph.D., Lecturer in Church History, Spurgeon's College, London, England. *David Livingstone.*

Peter Toon Th.D., Ph.D., Director of Post-Ordination Training, Diocese of St. Edmundsbury, England. *Thomas Cranmer, Blaise Pascal, John Owen.*

Ruth Tucker M.A., Ph.D., Visiting Professor of Missions, Trinity Evangelical Divinity School, Deerfield, Illinois. *William Carey.*

A. Skevington Wood Ph.D., Fellow of the Royal Historical Society, formerly Principal of Cliff College, Sheffield, England. *John and Charles Wesley.*

David F. Wright M.A., Senior Lecturer in Ecclesiastical History, University of Edinburgh, Scotland. *John Chrysostom.*

Edwin M. Yamauchi Ph.D., Professor of History, Miami University, Oxford, Ohio. *Ignatius of Antioch, Justin Martyr.*

Introduction

Throughout the centuries millions of persons have identified themselves as Christians – the followers of Jesus Christ. For some that identification cost them their lives. From the stoning of Stephen recorded in Acts 7 to the murder of Jim Elliot and his missionary colleagues in Ecuador, thousands of Christians have died as martyrs. Other Christians did not make that momentous sacrifice. Nonetheless they demonstrated their stout commitment by the way they lived as Christ's disciples in the face of rude taunts, testings, and temptations. Still others wore their Christianity lightly by putting it on simply as a cloak of social convention.

A cobbler, a king, a charwoman, a queen – Christians have stepped forth from all social classes to follow this Jesus who died on a cruel cross only to be miraculously resurrected from the dead on the first Easter morning. Many of them who called themselves Christians believed that He was "truly God and truly man," the Word become flesh. He had died for their sins to bring them salvation; they responded by believing in Him and following His teachings. He was their Lord and Savior. Moreover this Jesus had promised that He would come again for His church. After He left, the Holy Spirit came to comfort and empower Christians in their mission. And they had much to do before He returned. He had commanded them to love God with all their hearts, souls, and minds, and their neighbors as themselves. He had also commissioned them to preach the gospel, making disciples and baptizing new converts.

So epochal was the life of Jesus that it changed the way His followers thought about history: they would often describe themselves as living "in the year of our Lord ..." (anno Domini : A.D.).

Forgotten Saints

The memory of millions of those Christians has long since vanished from the collective consciousness of humanity, forgotten by succeeding generations. Allusions to many of them do not appear in the pages of extant texts available to us. Of their joys, acts of kindness done in imitation of their Master, and their pluck in Christian witness, we know nothing. Their difficulties and troubles have also been largely forgotten. The old spiritual captured well the plight of some: "Nobody knows the trouble I've seen, nobody knows but Jesus." The belief that Jesus knew and understood, even if no one else knew or seemed to care, was often their only comfort. Those believers who peopled many cultures and the color of whose skins covered the spectrum red, brown, yellow, black, and white, constitute the host of the now silent heroes and heroines of the Christian church.

By contrast, the names of other Christians can still be heard. Many of these names are picked up only as vague whispers; other names still resound like trumpet blasts. The Christians were noted in manuscripts or books or in oral traditions that have been preserved until our day. Their ranks include pastors, social reformers, church officials, apologists, theologians, missionaries, evangelists, philosophers, scientists, writers, artists, musicians, merchants, farmers, and others from different walks of life. A select number of them were those we would call today Christian leaders.

Great Leaders

The present volume focuses on the lives and contributions of a choice group of these leaders of the Christian churches. Although not all these individuals were necessarily the most spiritual Christians of their day, many of them were expressly that. A few were considered leaders principally because they exercised political and ecclesiastical power. Still others provoked controversial theological reflection in the Christian churches, which reflection, even if not fully evangelical, cannot be ignored and should be evaluated. But more generally, many of the leaders discussed in this book have been remembered because their deeds gave evidence of the stamp of Christ upon their lives. Their teaching and spiritual modeling were deeply appeciated and even emulated by large numbers of Christians.

Each discussion of a "great" leader opens with a brief chronology of the person's life (if such can be established). Thereafter follows an introduction that assesses the featured person's place in the history of the Christian church. A more extended text then relates many of the most important activities, writings, and spiritual insights of the leader. And finally, the graphics facilitate a more comprehensive understanding of the life and times of the leader.

This volume, then, serves as a ready-made reference tool concerning some of the most important leaders of the Christian church. The articles possess a certain authority because many of the distinguished contributing writers are themselves among the leading experts in the Christian world regarding the individuals they discuss. Indeed, whatever merits this volume possesses are due to the skills of these authors who participated so graciously in a project that brought scholars from several lands into a co-operative effort.

But this book is more than a resource

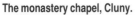

The monastery chapel, Cluny.

tool for the classroom, the church, or the home. By reading its pages, readers will discern recurring and important themes in some of the leaders' lives: a remarkable willingness to serve Christ, no matter what the cost; a trust in the truthfulness and promises of Holy Scripture; a love for the church; an affection for other Christians; a concern to meet the needs of down-and-outers and up-and-outers.

A rich heritage

Our increased familiarity with the thinking and spiritual insights of these leaders may help us to understand better the dynamics of the Christian faith itself – that faith which so captured their hearts, minds, and imagination.

We should also come to a greater awareness of the great heritage which is ours who name the name of Christ. In various ways we are debtors to the men and women who served Jesus Christ faithfully in generations before our own.

The specific list of great leaders discussed in this book was drawn up by Dr. Tim Dowley and the editor in consultation with several colleagues. Only limitations of space determined that a larger number

of worthy candidates could not be included in this volume. For example, living Christian leaders were specifically excluded, with the exception of Billy Graham. It is also to be supposed that a volume written from the vantage point of fifty years hence would include more women and persons from the Third World.

So enter now into the instructive and inspiring stories of those men and women whom the Christian churches have generally recognized as great leaders, while recalling that millions who are great in God's eyes were unknown servants. But as it turns out, many of the great leaders themselves were largely prompted by a spirit of Christian servanthood.

Jesus' words underscore the paradox of the Christian's life so frequently, as evidenced in this book: " whoever wants to become great among you must be your servant, and whoever wants to be first must be your slave – just as the Son of Man did not come to be served, but to serve, and to give his life as a ransom for many" (Matthew 20: 26b-28).

John D. Woodbridge

Peter
?-*c.*A.D. 65

The death, resurrection, and ascension of Jesus Christ left the newborn church without the physical presence of its head. To an onlooker, the church was leaderless. Yet, prepared by temperament and calling, tempered by failure and shame, Peter stepped into the breach. A contemporary of Jesus, one of his first disciples, and a frequent spokesman for them, Peter survived his Master by almost three and a half decades, until he was martyred, probably in Rome about A.D. 65.

Even before the first Pentecost, Peter assumed leadership and appealed to Scripture in his bid to find a replacement for Judas Iscariot. When the Holy Spirit fell on the little band of 120 believers on the day of Pentecost, it was Peter who preached, resulting in 3,000 converts. His preaching was simple, direct, passionate; and so far as the records go, he repeatedly rose to the occasion when there was a sudden crowd or an outbreak of opposition and persecution.

But Peter's importance extends beyond these points to two further issues. He was the first, so far as we know, to insist on the sufficiency *and exclusiveness* of Jesus to provide salvation (Acts 4:12). At that point the people of "the Way" (as Christians were then sometimes known) became a threat to the established Jewish authorities. More important, to Peter was confided the vision of the sheet,

Peter: mosaic from a baptistery in Ravenna, Italy

and the lesson that what God makes clean we are not to regard as unclean. The vision paved the way for the first official evangelization undertaken among Gentiles (Acts 10-11); more, it contributed to Peter's firm grasp of the principle that Gentiles do not have to become Jews before becoming Christians. They do not have to promise to obey the Mosaic law before they can put their faith in the Jewish Messiah. Without Peter's public insistence

on this principle, the church could not have become the multi-cultural, multi-racial institution it rapidly became, nor could the New Testament Scriptures have been written. In short, Peter was not only the first great leader of the church, but the crucial transitional figure who helped to establish the missionary and theological basis on which the church was built and the New Testament was written.

Peter

and the Founding of the Church

D. A. Carson

Peter's life and work

The name Peter, given by his parents, was apparently the Hebrew "Simeon" (Acts 15:14; 2 Peter 1:1) or "Simon," though his brother Andrew was given a Greek name. This diverse linguistic heritage is not surprising: "Galilee of the Gentiles" (Matthew 4:15), Peter's home territory, boasted a rich mix of Greek and Aramaic, of Jews and Gentiles. To Jerusalem ears, Peter's spoken Aramaic was so accented as to identify his origins (Mark 14:70).

Reared in a fishing family, Peter left his home town of Bethsaida (John 1:44) to settle in Capernaum (Mark 1:21, 29). Both towns were located on the shores of Galilee. Of the details of his upbringing, age and education, we know nothing; but although he received no formal training in the law (see Acts 4:13, which does not mean Peter was illiterate), he certainly inherited the piety and customs of his people, and continued them well into his Christian years (Acts 10:14). Married by the time he started to follow Jesus (Mark 1:30; with what family we do not know), Peter later chose to bring his wife with him on some of his journeys as an apostle (1 Corinthians 9:5).

According to John, at least Andrew and perhaps Peter himself were disciples of John the Baptist before they became disciples of Jesus. Indeed, it was the Baptist who pointed Jesus out to them as the promised Messiah (John 1:35-42). This initial transfer of allegiance to Jesus helps to explain the promptness of Peter's and Andrew's response when Jesus subsequently called them by the lake (Mark 1:16-18). The constitution of the more restricted and intimate circle of apostles apparently came still later (Mark 3:16ff.).

At their first meeting (John 1:35-42), Jesus gave Peter the Aramaic name *Kepha*, rendered "Cephas" in most of our Bibles. The Greek equivalent was *petros*, "Peter." Whether in Aramaic or Greek, the word simply means "rock," and (so far as our sources go) was unknown as a personal name before this time. There is no good reason for thinking that Peter was first given that name only at Caesarea Philippi (Matthew 16:18).

Peter during the ministry of Jesus

When the portrayals of Peter in each of the four gospels are compared, notable differences emerge. In Mark, Peter is portrayed with more negative overtones than in the other three; but the same is true of all the apostles, whose failure to understand the nature and work of Jesus Messiah Mark takes pains to highlight. Peter crops up more frequently as a spokesman in Matthew. Luke makes no mention of Jesus' sharp rebuke of Peter (9:20-22) and generally presents Peter's failures in milder guise; for his attention is turned less to apostolic misunderstanding than to the developments then taking place in the history of redemption, including the role Peter himself must play in it–all in anticipation of the second part of Luke's two-volume work, the book of Acts. Peter retains his prominence in John, who includes some episodes not recorded by the synoptic evangelists (for example, the call of Andrew and Peter in John 1:35-42; Peter's reaction to Jesus' washing of his feet, 13:6-11).

But despite minor differences in emphasis, the composite picture of Peter that emerges from the four gospels is remarkably stable. Peter always stands first in the list of disciples; indeed, he was one of the three who formed an inner ring (Mark 5:37; 9:2; 14:33). If he sometimes appears as spokesman for the Twelve, it is partially in function of an energetic, impetuous nature that dares to say what others think. If on the night Jesus is betrayed it is Peter who emphatically insists he will never disown his Master, the other disciples soon voice their agreement (Mark

Remains of the building at Capernaum believed to be Peter's house.

14:31). If the Twelve sometimes find Jesus' words hard, Peter speaks for all of them when he refuses to defect: "Lord, to whom shall we go? You have the words of eternal life. We believe and know that you are the Holy One of God" (John 6:68-69).

About ten episodes in which Peter plays a prominent role are recorded during the period of Jesus' ministry, before the passion; and another dozen are linked with the passion and resurrection of Jesus. The former include Peter's walk on the water and subsequent loss of faith (Matthew 14:22-31), and the great catch of fish (Luke 5:1-11), with its impact on Peter's commitment. But the event that stands out most sharply in his own mind is the transfiguration of his Master (Matthew 17:13); for he himself alludes to it in his epistles (1 Peter 5:1; 2 Peter 1:16-18).

The Passion and Resurrection

Those events that link Peter to Jesus' passion and resurrection reveal Peter at his best and his worst. His courage in vowing never to disown his Lord was doubtless honest and well-intended; but his vile oaths when he denied he knew Him were as inexcusable as they are understandable. His alertness and boldness when he unsheathed his sword and sliced off Malchus's ear (doubtless Peter was aiming at his neck!) testified to his devotion to Jesus; but he still had no comprehension of a Messiah with Jesus' formidable powers who would *choose* ignominy, pain, and death. So he fled with the rest, skulked behind the crowd on the way back to the high priest's residence, and tarnished his courage with the deepest shame. But no thoughtful Christian today wants to point an accusing finger; for the depth of Peter's shame was matched by the depth of his repentance when he wept bitterly at the crowing of the rooster.

The Peter who joined the others in tremulous fear, behind locked doors, during those wretched hours when Jesus lay in the tomb and hope lay in ashes, was graciously marked out by the risen Lord by the announcement of the resurrection (Mark 16:7). Joining his close associate John in a race for the empty tomb (John 20:3-9), Peter found his hope rekindled. First among the Twelve to witness the resurrected Christ (Luke 24:34; 1 Corinthians 15:5), publicly reconciled to his

Master and commissioned to tend the flock of God (John 21), Peter learned that his own vaunted strength and resolve were far less important than the Lord Jesus' forgiveness and commission. Doubtless this is the origin of the utterly different strength, the strength of brokenness and meekness, that so profoundly characterizes his two epistles.

Peter's confession and commission

Few passages have occasioned more debate in the history of the church than the three synoptic texts that record Peter's confession of who Jesus is, and Jesus' commission in return (Matthew 16:13-20; Mark 8:27-30; Luke 9:18-21). The Roman Catholic church has often appealed to these verses as the foundation of the papacy; in reaction, Protestants have too frequently imposed on the same verses an assortment of interpretations scarcely less fanciful. Among the disputed points that deserve brief comments are:

1. John's gospel finds Peter and Andrew confessing Jesus as the Messiah in the first chapter. Why then do the synoptic gospels, especially Matthew, treat this confession of who Jesus is as such a major turning point? This is one reason some scholars think John is hopelessly anachronistic. Nevertheless, the two stances need not be set at odds. What John describes in his first chapter is intrinsically likely; for after all, what could have induced the brothers Peter and Andrew to leave the Baptist at the peak of his popularity and go over to Jesus unless they perceived Him to be *greater* than the Baptist?

But Jesus turned out to be a Messiah quite different from any of the contemporary expectations, including those of His disciples. Jesus' claims were often ambiguous, His stance was not aggressive, He displayed no eagerness to set up David's throne and throw the Romans out of the land, and He seemed more interest-

The Sea of Galilee from its western shore.

ed in preaching, healing the sick, and eating with harlots and other public sinners than in setting up a messianic administration. The crowds were therefore ambivalent about Jesus. Even they could perceive His greatness and thought Him at least a prophet (Matthew 16:14); but it took nothing less than special revelation from God to perceive that Jesus really was, despite the evidence apparently to the contrary, the promised Messiah (Matthew 16:16-17). That Peter's grasp of this revelation was still deficient is made clear in the ensuing verses when he insists that Jesus could not possibly be killed (Matthew 16:21-27). Aided by divine revelation, he might be prepared to accept this meek leader, Jesus, as the Messiah; he was not yet prepared to accept a crucified Messiah.

2. Many have argued that "this rock" on which Jesus will build His church is not Peter but Peter's faith, or the confession Peter has just enunciated that Jesus is the

Remains of the third-century synagogue at Capernaum.

Banias (Caesarea Philippi), site of Peter's confession.

Christ. After all (it is argued), the word for "rock" is *petra*, the feminine form of *petros*, from which we derive "Peter." And does not Peter himself elsewhere insist that *Jesus* is the rock (1 Peter 2:5-8)? But metaphors can be applied in different ways in the New Testament. For instance, here Jesus builds His church, whereas in 1 Corinthians 3:10 Paul is the builder; in 1 Corinthians 3:11, Jesus is the church's foundation, whereas in Ephesians 2:20 the foundation is "the apostles and prophets"; in John 9:5, Jesus is the light of the world, but in Matthew 5:14 His disciples are the light of the world. Moreover the difference between *petra* and *petros* is in the nature of a pun; and the pun connects Jesus' saying with Peter, with the very name that Jesus Himself had given him. Jesus is saying that Peter is the rock on whom the church will be built. This is consistent with the first half of the book of Acts.

3. The promise of the keys and of the "binding and loosing" (Matthew 16:17-19), first given to Peter, is later extended to the other apostles (18:18). Probably they are related to church discipline, based on the authority of the gospel itself.

4. Even if it could be demonstrated that the bishops of Rome were the direct successors of Peter (and it cannot be), it does not follow that whatever is promised to Peter in these verses will also be transferred to them in some exclusive way. Jesus says nothing of the sort. Peter's *distinctive* role is as the "foundation" of the church a role which by its very nature cannot be transferred to others.

Many in the Western, Latin church have rightly labelled Peter *primus inter pares*, "first among equals." There is no evidence Peter was set over the other apostles; indeed, at one point the apostles *sent* Peter and John on a mission (Acts 8:14). But there is ample evidence that Peter achieved a certain founding preeminence, what some have called "a salvation historical primacy," that can be traced out in the early years of the church.

Peter in the early church

Like the other apostles and the initial group of 120 believers, Peter remained in

Jerusalem after the ascension, waiting for the promised Spirit. Even before Pentecost, however, Peter emerged as the leader who prompted the newborn church, on the basis of Scripture, to appoint a replacement for Judas Iscariot (Acts 1:15-26).

On the day of Pentecost, all of those first believers declared "the wonder of God" (2:11) in tongues; but it was Peter who preached and saw 3,000 converts. The heart of his message was simple: the phenomena of Pentecost are nothing other than what the Old Testament Scriptures anticipated when they looked forward to the messianic age when the Spirit would be poured out. Jesus Himself inaugurated that age; for the Scriptures, rightly understood, declare not only that "great David's greater Son" had to suffer, but that He would not see corruption. Rising from the dead, He would be exalted to the right hand of God, as Lord and Christ. The appropriate and urgent response of the people must be to repent and be baptized in the name of Jesus Messiah so as to receive forgiveness of sins and the gift of the Holy Spirit.

Among miracles, rising persecution, growing ability to cite the Old Testament, a difficult case of church discipline, multiplying numbers, and the need for administrative helpers, Peter remained the dominant figure, grasping each opportunity. What must have appeared to outsiders as a Jewish sect was a body of Spirit-filled believers eager to devote themselves to the apostles' teaching. As early as Acts 4, Peter insisted that the Jesus he preached could not be reduced to one option among the various strands of Judaism: "Salvation is found in no one else, for there is no other name under heaven given to men by which we must be saved" (4:12). When the Samaritans were evangelized by Philip (Acts 8), it was Peter and John who were sent to examine the situation; and they served as the agents who mediated the Holy Spirit to the Samaritans, thereby ensuring that the Jewish believers in Jerusalem and the Samaritan half-breed believers farther north would begin on the same footing and belong to the same body.

Jews and Gentiles

Even after the conversion of Saul (Acts 9; c. A.D. 33), the church lacked any profound grasp of the conditions of entrance into the church, the messianic community, by Gentile Christians. A substantial number of Jewish believers held that Gentiles had to become Jews first and commit themselves to observing the law of Moses before they could legitimately accept the Jewish Messiah. By miraculous means, Peter learned that what God makes clean – whether of foods the Old Covenant considered unclean, or principally of non-Jewish peoples – is clean (Acts 10). The resulting conversion of Cornelius and his household, and the descent of the Spirit on them, even though they had not pledged themselves to live as Jews, is so crucial a turning point in the history of the church that Luke devotes a large amount of space to the episode (Acts 10-11). When Peter returned to Jerusalem to face hostile questions from fellow Jewish Christians, Luke records Peter's answer at length, even though it is largely repetitious of the previous chapter; for the church's principal acceptance of Peter's conclusion (11:18) bore far-reaching results. Not only did it stimulate Gentile mission, but it laid the basis for new and complex theological relationships between the New Covenant and the Old, relationships that forever removed the possibility that Christianity would degenerate into a relatively obscure Jewish sect.

This does not mean that controversy on these points was silenced. By A.D. 49 or 50, similar issues had again become so central in the wake of Paul's multiplying Gentile ministry that a council was held in Jerusalem (Acts 15). Peter again played a crucial role (15:6-11). Referring afresh to the conversion of Cornelius and the events that surrounded it, he concluded with language that is very nearly Pauline: "Now then, why do you try to test God by putting on the necks of the disciples a yoke that neither we nor our fathers have

Interior, St Peter's, Rome.

been able to bear? We believe it is through the grace of our Lord Jesus that we are saved, just as they are" (Acts 15:10-11).

Peter and Paul

These crucial convictions of the apostle Peter must be borne in mind when the clash with Paul in Antioch (Galatians 2) is assessed. True, Paul did publicly rebuke Peter; but the rebuke was not sparked by fundamental disagreement over the nature of the gospel, but over Paul's perception that Peter was failing to live up to the gospel Peter himself preached. There seems little evidence to support the theory of some scholars that Peter and Paul represent not merely different emphases in the early church, but thoroughly antithetical theological systems. Peter's failure in Antioch was almost certainly a well-motivated but ill-judged step aimed at keeping peace in Jerusalem, without adequate reflection on the damage he was doing to Gentile believers.

Peter's movements after the death of Stephen can be sketched in only roughly; after the Jerusalem Council, they are certainly obscure. We find him, before Acts 15, in Joppa, Caesarea Maritima, Antioch, and elsewhere. This suggests he embarked on missionary work in Palestine (as it was later called) and Syria. Presumably his absence from Jerusalem contributed to the assumption of leadership in Jerusalem by James, the half-brother of Jesus. After a miraculous escape from prison (Acts 12), Peter apparently undertook missionary journeys of greater scope. There is reason to think he ministered for a while in Corinth (1 Cor. 1:12); his first epistle suggests close links with believers in Asia Minor and other Roman provinces of what is now called Turkey.

Peter's death

There is no evidence that Peter founded the church in Rome; but there are good reasons for thinking he ministered there. He may well have written his first epistle while residing in that city. The story of his death in the apocryphal *Acts of Peter* cannot be credited: we are told that he was martyred under Nero, but asked to be crucified upside down because he was not worthy of suffering death on the cross in an upright position as his Master had done. But however poorly attested this tradition is, we can well believe that at the end Peter was deeply concerned to glorify God by his death (compare John 21:18-19). Probably both Peter and Paul were martyred under the same persecuting outburst; but under what circumstances, we cannot now be sure.

Peter's epistles

It is more than a little ironic that Peter's first canonical epistle should be devoted to informing believers how to live with Christian hope, fidelity, and integrity in the midst of suffering and opposition. The apostle who had disowned his Lord with oaths in order to escape detection had been so transformed by the grace of God

Opposite: Statue of Peter, St Peter's, Rome.

operative in his life over three decades that he could write a profound tract on suffering.

The second epistle of Peter has often been judged inauthentic. Arguments based on the differences in style between the two epistles are inconclusive: Peter may have used different amanuenses (stenographers) and in any case the differences in style are no greater than those between 1 Timothy and Titus, where unity of authorship is almost universally acknowledged. Certainly the themes are very different: 2 Peter is designed to warn the reader against a false teaching, and Peter appeals to the return of Christ as an incentive to faithfulness and a threat to the ungodly. However, 2 Peter can refer to itself as the second letter (3:1) and makes mention of its author's presence at the transfiguration; so it is hard to avoid the conclusion that if Peter did not write it, the pseudonymous writer was self-consciously trying to deceive his reading audience. In fact the evidence against the traditional authorship is not as strong as sometimes thought, and it seems simpler to accept the letter's ascription of itself to Simon Peter (1:1). The substantial overlap of material between 2 Peter and Jude is no impediment; for even if 2 Peter borrowed from Jude (currently the majority view), given the frequency of copying others' work in the ancient world it is hard to see how any jeopardy to apostolic authorship exists.

Peter's literary remains cannot compete in number or depth with those of Paul. But his Spirit-anointed courage, preaching, and leadership brought the church through the first years of its life. His sure grasp of the sufficiency and finality of the revelation of God in Christ Jesus, especially in the cross and resurrection, helped bring the church to self-conscious awareness of its own identity. His frequent citation of Scripture, his appeal to Christ's teaching, and his unswerving commitment to the lessons learned in the Cornelius episode prevented a major split in the early church and paved the way to the rich theological formulations of the apostle Paul.

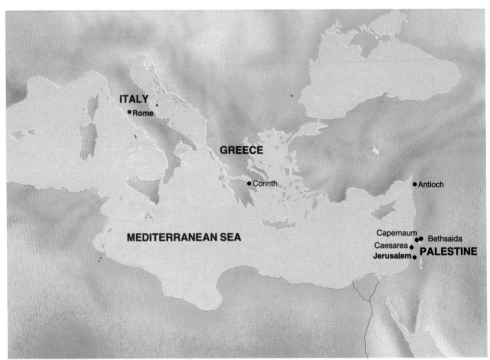

Paul

c. A.D.1-?65

"Saul, who is called Paul," the chosen instrument in the hand of the risen Lord, occupies a unique place at the threshold of the church's history. He was not the first person to preach the gospel; he was not even the first to preach it to Gentiles; but when once he was called and commissioned, he "worked harder than all of them" (1 Corinthians 15:10). In less than thirty years he established the Christian presence along the main roads and in the chief cities from Antioch to Rome. To him above all, under God, is due the firm rootage of Christianity in the Gentile world.

In addition to his activity as gospel preacher and church builder, Paul must be recognized as the church's first great theologian. His letters were not written as essays in systematic theology; they addressed themselves to urgent situations in the life of the churches. But they contain a wealth of teaching about the profoundest implications of the gospel; the being and purpose of God, the Person and work of Christ, the ministry of the Holy Spirit, the way to get right with God, the basis of Christian ethics, the hope of the people of God, and the destiny of the created universe. His exposition of these themes is unsurpassed and permanent in its relevance.

Above all, Paul is the great champion of Christian freedom.

He was aware of the propensity of many Christians to submit to spiritual guidance so absolute that it becomes spiritual dictatorship. Against legalism in any form he steadfastly set his face, urging his converts to stand firm in the liberty with which Christ had set them free. Repeatedly, great liberation movements in the life of the church have been due to the rediscovery and renewed proclamation of Paul's message of freedom in Christ.

Street in the old city, Damascus.

The Life of	
Paul	
*c.*A.D.1	Birth in Tarsus, Cilicia.
*c.*33	Called and commissioned by Christ on the Damascus road.
35-45	Evangelization in Syria and Cilicia.
45-47	Ministry with Barnabas in Antioch.
47	Famine relief visit to Jerusalem.
47-48	Evangelization with Barnabas in Cyprus and central Asia Minor.
48 or 49	The Apostolic Council at Jerusalem.
49-50	Evangelization of Macedonia.
50-52	Evangelization of Corinth and the province of Achaia.
52-55	Evangelization of Ephesus and the province of Asia.
56	"Illyricum" (Romans 15:19).
56-57	Winter in Corinth; letter to the Romans written.
57	Last visit to Jerusalem.
57-59	In custody in Caesarea.
59-60	Voyage to Italy, including winter in Malta.
60-62	In custody in Rome.
?65	Execution in Rome.

Paul

and the Missionary Enterprise

F. F. Bruce

The early expansion of Christianity

Christianity from the first was a missionary enterprise; otherwise it would not have lasted more than a generation. In the spring of A.D. 30 its founder was publicly executed, and His followers were dispersed. His cause, it seemed, had collapsed; it was impossible, by all natural reckoning, that it could ever survive the scandal of the cross. No one, surely, would accept a crucified man as teacher, leader, or savior.

Yet the impossible happened. Not more than twenty years after His death, the proclamation of His message caused commotion in the Jewish communities of Alexandria, Thessalonica, and Rome. Moreover, His way of life was being accepted by Gentiles throughout the Roman Empire. Thirty years after His death, Christianity had been firmly established in the provinces of Syria, Cilicia, Galatia, Asia, Macedonia, and Achaia; and in Rome itself His Gentile followers outnumbered those of Jewish birth.

The impossible happened because Jesus, the crucified one, rose from the dead on the third day, appeared to His disciples, filled them with new hope and power, and recommissioned them to be His witnesses. Nor was it only to His former disciples that He appeared in resurrection. He appeared to one man in particular, Saul of Tarsus, with such compelling grace that He transformed him on the spot from a fierce persecutor of Jesus' followers into the most devoted champion of the faith he had tried to exterminate.

Paul's life and work

Saul was his Jewish name; he is better known by his Roman name, Paul. He was born to a threefold inheritance.

By ancestry he was a Jew; by inclination and training he was dedicated to the maintenance and propagation of the religious traditions of his nation, an upholder of the sacred law of Israel, a member of the party of the Pharisees.

By environment he was a Hellenist. Tarsus, his native place, was a center of Greek culture, "no mean city,"as he called it himself (Acts 21:39). Yet he was not educated in Tarsus but in Jerusalem, at the school of Gamaliel, the most eminent rabbi of his day. Nevertheless, he was familiar with the Greek way of life, and Greek was no acquired language for him; he spoke and wrote it fluently.

Third, he was a Roman citizen. By the time of Paul's birth, Roman power was securely established in western Asia. He was born in the Roman province of Cilicia; better still, he was born a Roman citizen. Roman citizenship was a privilege sparingly bestowed on provincials; Paul's father or grandfather must have rendered some signal service to the Roman cause to be honoured in this way. Once Roman citizenship had been granted to a man, his family inherited it.

This rich heritage was, to use one of Paul's characteristic expressions, brought into captivity to the obedience of Christ. The obedience of Christ meant for Paul that, from the moment Christ called him on the Damascus road to be His apostle to the Gentiles, this was his purpose in life: "this one thing I do" (Philippians 3:13). He knew himself to be conscripted into the service of Christ; yet never was there such a willing conscript.

Paul and Jerusalem

As compared with those who were apostles before him, those who had been Jesus' companions during His earthly ministry, Paul was odd man out. No one could challenge the validity of *their* commission; but Paul's credentials were repeatedly challenged. He claimed to have

Opposite: Mosaic of Paul from a baptistery in Ravenna.

been commissioned by the risen Christ, but he could not substantiate his claim by an appeal to witnesses. How, then, did he substantiate it? By the energy with which he worked for Christ; by the number of churches he planted; better still, by the quality of his converts' lives. He knew that his own ministry would be judged by the character of his converts – judged not only by his fellow-Christians but preeminently by the Lord Himself on the day of final review. When he was called upon to render an account of his apostolic stewardship, Paul would be content if he could point to his converts, his "joy and crown" (Philippians 4:1), and invite the Lord to assess his work by what He found in them.

Although Paul did not lack detractors, even within the Christian fellowship, the leaders of the Jerusalem church acknowledged that he had been called and empowered to evangelize his fellow Jews. Paul carefully maintained his independence of the Jerusalem authorities; he was responsible to Christ alone. Yet he was equally careful to discharge his ministry in fellowship with Jerusalem.

Paul's apostolic career

About three years after his conversion Paul returned to Cilicia (administratively united at that time with the neighboring province of Syria) to preach the gospel there. In the early 40s he accepted an invitation from Barnabas to join him in caring for the young church of Antioch and directing its evangelistic activity. Later, the church of Antioch released him and Barnabas to undertake missionary outreach in Cyprus and Asia Minor. At that time were founded the churches of Galatia to which, not long afterwards, the letter to the Galatians was sent.

About A.D. 50, after the Council of Jerusalem, he parted company with Barnabas and moved west, evangelizing the provinces of Macedonia and Achaia (the main parts of modern Greece). There he preached the gospel and planted churches in Philippi, Thessalonica, Berea, Corinth, and elsewhere. He was prevented from staying long in any of the Macedonian cities, but the churches planted during his brief visits to them were among the most stable and encouraging in his whole mission field. In Corinth, the chief city of Achaia, he spent eighteen months. Christianity was firmly planted during that period in Corinth and in other parts of Achaia. While he was in Corinth, Gallio, member of an influential Roman family, arrived as proconsul of Achaia. Since his proconsulship can be dated rather precisely in A.D. 51-52, this gives us a fixed date in the chronology of Paul's career. An attempt was made to prosecute Paul before Gallio for propagating an illegal religion. Gallio decided that, whatever Paul was preaching, it was some variety of the Jews' religion, which was protected by Roman law, and he had no desire to adjudicate between rival interpretations of Judaism. Gallio's ruling, in fact, was helpful; it meant that Paul's preaching did not contravene Roman law, provided it caused no breach of public order.

Evangelization of Asia

Paul's next base was across the Aegean, in Ephesus, where he spent nearly three years. This was one of the most fruitful phases of his apostleship. Thanks to his witness and that of his colleagues, the whole province of Asia was thoroughly evangelized and remained for centuries a principal bastion of Christianity in the Mediterranean world. During those years, too, the necessity of dealing with continuous problems among his converts in Corinth taught him what was involved in "the care of all the churches."

During those years, too, Paul organized among his Gentile churches a special collection in aid of the church in Jerusalem. This was not only a charitable gesture; Paul intended it to constitute a bond of closer unity between the Jewish Christians of the mother church and the Gentile Christians of his mission field. When he took the proceeds of this collection to Jerusalem, accompanied by delegates from the contributing churches, he hoped

The Roman aqueduct, Caesarea.

that sufficient evidence would be provided of divine approval of his apostleship.

When this responsibility had been discharged, he planned to leave the eastern Mediterranean and evangelize Spain, visiting Rome on the way. To prepare the Roman Christians for his visit, he sent them a letter just before he set out for Jerusalem. In this letter he presented the Roman church – a church he had never seen – with a statement of the gospel as he understood and proclaimed it; and he evidently had a clear picture in his mind of the important part that the Roman church could play in the furtherance of this gospel in the world.

Prisoner of Rome

His plan did not work out as he had hoped. In Jerusalem he was taken into protective custody by the Roman authorities and transferred to Caesarea for his greater safety. The Jewish leaders charged him with violating the sanctity of the Temple and, in general, with being a disturber of public order. After several appearances before Felix, procurator of Judea, and his successor, Festus, he exercised the privilege of a Roman citizen by appealing to have his case referred to the judgment of the emperor in Rome. There, he was confident, he could expect a more impartial hearing than was possible in Judea; moreover, in this way he made sure of getting to Rome.

In Rome he spent two years under house arrest, waiting for his appeal to be heard. His presence there, despite his inability to move around freely, brought great encouragement to the Christian cause in the capital. The gospel became a talking point in the praetorian guard and in the imperial civil service, and the Christians in Rome eagerly exploited this interest so as to bear more energetic witness. Paul reckoned therefore that, whether the emperor's verdict was favorable or adverse, the progress of the gospel was promoted by his coming to Rome.

Because the narrative of Acts ends before Paul's appeal is heard, we cannot be sure of its outcome. Nor can we be sure if, in the event of his being acquitted, he ever

Paul's Journeys

First Journey

Second Journey

Third Journey

Journey to Rome

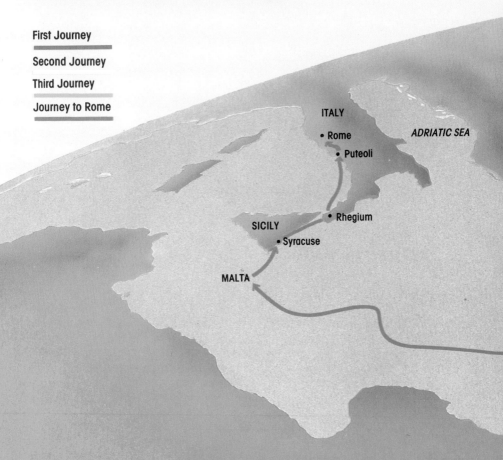

ITALY

• Rome

• Puteoli

ADRIATIC SEA

SICILY

• Rhegium

• Syracuse

MALTA

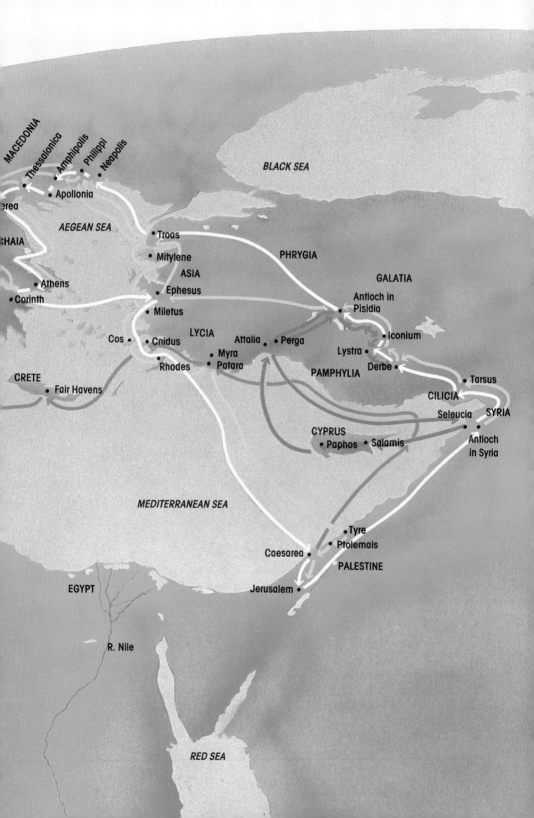

MACEDONIA

Thessalonica • Amphipolis • Philippi • Neapolis

• Apollonia

erea

BLACK SEA

AEGEAN SEA

CHAIA

• Troas

• Mitylene

PHRYGIA

ASIA

GALATIA

• Athens

• Ephesus

Antioch in
Pisidia

• Corinth

• Miletus

• Iconium

Cos •

LYCIA

Attalia • Perga

• Cnidus

Lystra •

• Myra

Derbe •

• Tarsus

Rhodes • Patara

PAMPHYLIA

CILICIA

CRETE

Seleucia

SYRIA

• Fair Havens

CYPRUS

Antioch
in Syria

• Paphos • Salamis

MEDITERRANEAN SEA

• Tyre

• Ptolemais

Caesarea •

PALESTINE

EGYPT

Jerusalem •

R. Nile

RED SEA

realized his plan of evangelizing Spain. But the effect of his missionary activity was durable, and in his letters he has bequeathed to posterity a treasure beyond price.

Paul's missionary addresses

Two outstanding missionary addresses are ascribed to Paul in Acts. One was delivered in the synagogue of Pisidian Antioch to a congregation addressed as "Men of Israel, and [you] who worship God" (Acts 13:16). "You who worship God" are those Gentiles who had joined the Jewish congregation in worship. They could all be credited with some knowledge of the Old Testament. So Paul reminded them of the history of Israel from Moses to David and then told how the promises made to David regarding a descendant of his have been realized in Jesus. Jesus, put to death by His enemies, had been raised up by the power of God; through Him salvation was assured to all believers.

The other address was delivered in Athens, where Paul was invited to expound his teaching before the court of the Areopagus. The members of this court were pagans – highly cultured pagans, but nevertheless pagans. Paul began his exposition not by referring to Hebrew history (of which they knew nothing) but by mentioning an altar dedication he had seen in the city: "To the unknown God." You acknowledge that He is unknown, said Paul; I have come to make Him known. So he spoke of God in creation, providence, and judgment, concluding with the announcement that the man through whom God's judgment will be administered has already been marked out for this role by His resurrection from the dead.

Not many were impressed by Paul's argument. The Athenians were too sophisticated to believe that anyone could be raised from the dead. Yet Paul's words are still remembered in Athens: they are inscribed on a bronze tablet at the foot of the

The Roman agora, Philippi, Macedonia.

ascent to the Areopagus (Mars' Hill).

If it is doubted that Paul could have spoken like this, it may be said in reply that, if the author of Romans 1-3 were taken to Athens and invited to expound the teaching of these three chapters in terms intelligible to educated pagans, it is difficult to imagine how he would have begun to do so otherwise than along the lines of Acts 17:22-31.

Paul was the most versatile of men, in his missionary tactics as in other ways. His basic message remained the same "Jesus, crucified and risen, is the Son of God" – but his presentation of it varied with the audience. He knew the importance of establishing an initial point of contact with his hearers, not pre-supposing on their part a knowledge they did not possess. "I [have become] all things to all men," he said, "so that I might by all means possible save some"(1 Corinthians 9:22).

Paul's missionary policy

Paul was a pioneer missionary. His policy was to preach the gospel where it had never been heard before. His time was limited; there was no point in duplicating the efforts of others or in building, as he put it, "on someone else's foundation" (Romans 15:20). He did not always appreciate it when others invaded his mission field and tried to build on the foundation he had laid. He stayed in any one place only for as long as it took to preach the gospel there and build up a strong believing community that would itself be a center of witness in that area. He concentrated on the most important cities, standing on the main Roman roads; if the gospel took root in them, local believers could use those ready lines of communication to spread their faith more widely.

Sometimes he entrusted further pastoral ministry among his converts to his colleagues, but this was not always possible. But he had a living faith in the power of the Spirit of Christ in the lives of converts from pagan idolatry and immorality; although some of his friends thought him unrealistically optimistic, he

was convinced that his way was the way of Christ.

By putting this policy into effect, Paul was able to accomplish a great deal in a short time. In A.D. 47 (approximately) there were no Christians that we know of in the important provinces of Galatia, Asia, Macedonia, and Achaia. Ten years later these four provinces had been so thoroughly evangelized that Paul could speak of his work in that part of the world as finished. He looked west and planned to repeat in Spain the same kind of program as he had completed in the eastern Mediterranean (Romans 15:23-24).

The catalog of hardships and sufferings that he had to endure in the course of this activity (2 Corinthians 11:23-27) makes one reflect. It does indeed suggest that he was a man of constitutional toughness and staying power, though that is not how he would have expressed it. To him all this was a part of the life of faith. The hardships that attended his ministry were not to be endured reluctantly but embraced joyfully as a token of acceptance with God, a strengthening of Christian hope, a participation in the sufferings of Christ. As the hardships wore down the physical frame, they were at the same time used by God for the renewal of the inner being and the increase of the prospective heritage of glory.

Paul in Christian history

Paul has been misunderstood and ignored over long stretches of Christian history and in many areas of the church. This should not surprise us if we consider how largely he was misunderstood and ignored in his own day. In later life he had to contemplate a sad falling away from the standards he had set in the province of Asia, the scene of his most intensive missionary service: "You know," he said to Timothy, "that every one in [the province of] Asia has deserted me" (2 Timothy, 1:15). He was under restraint in Rome, unable to visit believers there, and others took advantage of his enforced absence to introduce teaching at variance with his.

Happily, healthier influences came to

The Forum, Rome.

Wesley in 1738 felt his heart "strangely warmed" and experienced the change that sparked off his own apostolic labors, with the world as his parish.

Paul's legacy

Paul, more than any other, recognized the universal implications of the ministry, death, and exaltation of Christ. He drew them out in his own teaching and translated them into practice in his work. He has thus bequeathed to succeeding generations a rich legacy, certain elements of which require to be emphasized because they are so readily forgotten:

1. True religion is not a matter of rules and regulations. God does not deal with people like an accountant; He accepts them freely as they respond to His grace and implants the Spirit of Christ in their hearts so that they may manifest His love to others.

2. In Christ the children of God have come of age, as the new humanity created by His death and risen life. God treats His children as His responsible grown-up sons and daughters.

3. People matter more than things, more than principles, more than causes. The loftiest principles and the noblest causes exist for the sake of people; to sacrifice people to them is a perversion of the divine order.

4. Discrimination against people on such grounds as race, class, or sex is an offense against God and humanity alike.

Those who appreciate these lessons should bear in grateful remembrance the one who taught them so plainly.

the churches of Asia and restored them to their true allegiance. Similarly, in the history of Christianity there have repeatedly been great movements of the Spirit in which the first principles of gospel liberty have been recovered, to the immense revitalizing and enrichment of the church. And, almost invariably, these movements can be traced to the influence of Paul and his teaching on certain individuals, chosen instruments for the work of God as Paul himself was. It was while reading words from Paul's letter to the Romans that Augustine found his soul flooded with heavenly light in A.D. 386. It was in the same letter that Martin Luther learned what "the righteousness of God" really meant – not the righteousness by which God punishes the unrighteous but the righteousness through which he justifies them by faith. "Thereupon," he said "I felt myself to be reborn and to have gone through open doors into Paradise." And it was while listening to someone reading Luther's preface to that letter that John

John

John is usually held to have lived to a great age and to have been the last survivor of the original apostolic band. This makes him a very important figure, as being the connection between Jesus and His first followers on the one hand and the earliest church that lacked contact with Jesus but enthusiastically carried Christianity through the great cities of the Roman Empire on the other. It is not known whether John engaged in systematic traveling as was the case with Paul; if so, nothing is known about such journeys. Tradition says that John settled in Ephesus and that he had a wide influence from that base.

John's writings

Be that as it may, his principal influence on the Christian church came through his writings. The fourth gospel is anonymous, and, despite the titles we give them, so are the three epistles of John. The author of Revelation calls himself John, though without specifying whether he was the apostle or some other John. But the early church saw good reason for seeing all these writings as coming from John the apostle, and they explain the tremendous influence this man had on the development of the Christian church. To this day these writings remain among the most influential books ever written.

**Above right: John was probably banished to the island of Patmos, Greece
Below right: John the Evangelist; eleventh-century mosaic from Greece.**

John

and the End of the Apostolic Age

Leon Morris

Who was John?

John is a surprisingly shadowy figure for a man who has had such an influence on Christian living and thinking. Peter and Paul come before us as great and forceful characters, but John says and does little in the pages of the New Testament, and when he does appear it is usually in the company of someone else, who often takes the lead.

We know that his father was named Zebedee and that he ran a fishing business prosperous enough to have hired workmen (Mark 1:19-20), so the family appears to have been reasonably well off. John had a brother named James (Matthew 4:21), and when the two are mentioned together James usually comes first, so he was probably the older of the two brothers.

John appears to have been a cousin of Jesus, but this depends on our identification of the women who were present at the crucifixion. The fourth gospel says that the mother of Jesus was there, and it agrees with Matthew and Mark that Mary Magdalene was there and also another Mary (whom Matthew and Mark say was the mother of James and Joseph; John says that she was the wife of Cleophas). Matthew adds "the mother of Zebedee's children," Mark says "Salome," and John speaks of Jesus' "mother's sister." If these are three ways of referring to the same woman, then Zebedee's wife was Salome, sister of the virgin Mary. The identification is far from certain, but she is not unlikely.

John was one of the first disciples of Jesus (Mark 1:19-20) and, along with Peter and James, was specifically close to Jesus. These three were with Him on great occasions like the transfiguration (Mark 9:2), the raising of Jairus's daughter (Luke 8:51), and the experience in the Garden of Gethsemane (Matthew 26:37). The one mention of John outside the gospels and Acts links him with these men as "those reputed to be pillars" (Galatians 2:9). These three together with Andrew came to ask Jesus when the end would come (Mark 13:3). And Jesus sent John, along with Peter, to prepare the Passover on the last evening of His earthly life (Luke 22:8). Luke mentions John's astonishment (as well as that of others) at the miraculous catch of fish (Luke 5:9-10), which would be important as John's expertise lay in the area of fishing.

James and John

Such passages show that John was a significant figure in the apostolic band. But at first he was a long way from understanding Jesus' message. Along with his brother James he bore the nickname Boanerges, which Mark expains as "Sons of Thunder" (Mark 3:17). This seems to point to a certain hardness and bluster of the kind we see when John found a man casting out demons in Jesus' name and told him to stop because he did not belong to the group (Mark 9:38). Incidentally this is the only saying of John's in all the gospels. In every other place he is with someone else who is the spokesman. We see the same spirit in the request of James and John, spoken through their mother, that they should have the principal places in Jesus' kingdom (Matthew 20:20-23).

In the same incident these brothers

said that they were ready to drink of Jesus' "cup," evidently a metaphor for suffering, and Jesus said that they would. There is devotion in their words but also a complete failure to understand that the follower of Jesus must engage in humble service. There is a similar failure in their wanting to call down fire from heaven on Samaritan villagers who refused to receive them (Luke 9:54). Clearly they were zealous, and we cannot but be impressed by their conviction that God would send fire if Jesus allowed them to call for it. But the incident also shows that they could manifest a spirit of lovelessness.

In Acts, apart from the two passages that do no more than mention his name (Acts 1:13; 12:2), John is always in the company of Peter, as when the lame man was healed (Acts 3) or when they were arrested for preaching the Christian message (Acts 4:1-3). When they stood before the council they were regarded as unducated, ordinary men (Acts 4:13), but they refused to stop speaking about the wonderful things Jesus had said and done (Acts 4:19-20). John was involved with Peter in the mission to the Samaritans, the first group of non-Jews to be evangelized (Acts 8).

The disciple whom Jesus loved

In the fourth gospel there are references to "the disciple whom Jesus loved" (John 13:23; 19:26; 20:2; 21:7,20). He is never named, but the evidence shows that John is meant. The beloved disciple was in the group that went fishing (John 21:7), and it is not easy to identify him with anyone except John among those mentioned in John 21:2. He could not have been Peter, for Peter is mentioned as being with the beloved disciple. Nor could he have been James, for he died early (Acts 12:2). No good reason has been found for seeing him as Thomas or Nathaniel or one of the unnamed pair. The frequent mention of the beloved disciple along with Peter favors John, as does the fact that John is not named throughout the fourth gospel.

John's father, Zebedee, ran a fishing business on the Sea of Galilee.

This is inexplicable unless he wrote it himself, as we are told the beloved disciple did (John 21:20,24).

The designation does not mean that Jesus did not love the other disciples. Of course He loved them all. But it shows that this man was specially close to Him, a truth illustrated by the fact that he leaned on Jesus' breast at the Last Supper (John 13:23). It was to John that Jesus committed Mary as He hung on the cross (John 19:26-27). That He chose him before one of the immediate family shows something of the close relationship between them.

It is probably this close relationship that makes John so important. As we have seen, there is little in the gospel narratives to indicate that he was a leader. But clearly he was very close to Jesus, and the fourth gospel shows us something of what that meant. The man who wrote that gospel was obviously a man with great spiritual insight. We may well be right in seeing John as a thinker and a spiritual giant rather than a man of action and a natural leader.

John on Patmos
From Revelation we learn that he came to be on the island of Patmos because of "the word of God and the testimony of Jesus" (Revelation 1:9). This probably means banishment on account of his activities in forwarding the Christian movement. Revelation shows that he was a visionary, and this book records a number of visions that God gave him. It is interesting that in such a situation John produced a book full of exultation at the triumph of God. At the beginning of 2 John and 3 John he calls himself "the elder," which may point to his advancing years or to ecclesiastical office.

There is little we can add from nonbiblical sources. There is a tradition that John lived to a great age at Ephesus, a tradition that can be neither proved nor disproved. That might account for some of his influence. In Revelation, as we have seen, John was on the island of Patmos (Revelation 1:9), an exile on account of his

Christian life and work. This would likely mean that he would have finished his life there. Eusebius, however, says that he returned from Patmos to Ephesus and lived there until the time of Emperor Trajan. There is a story that he raised a dead man there and another that he was the means of bringing a robber to conversion. He is also said to have opposed the heretic Cerinthus. These and other stories are not without interest, but we have no way of knowing how much truth is in them.

John's writings
But it is clear that John's great importance for the Christian church arises from his writings. His gospel has been a source of blessing for every generation of believers, as have his epistles. Revelation is a mysterious book, and some have argued that the John who wrote it is not the apostle. The case cannot be proved either way, but there is good reason for seeing this book, too, as coming from the son of Zebedee.

Together these writings form a considerable part of our New Testament, and they give us teaching that we find nowhere else. John has put all subsequent generations of Christians heavily in his debt by what he has preserved of the teaching of Jesus and by what he has contributed from his own understanding of the Christian way. Small wonder that Christians have always felt that in his old age John had tremendous influence. These days scholars often draw attention to indications of what they call "the Johannine circle," people who gathered round John and delighted in his teaching.

John is the transitional figure between the days of Jesus, followed as they were by the exciting time of the first proclamation of the gospel, and the days of the early church. These were people who lacked personal contact with Jesus and with leaders like Peter and Paul. John smoothed the way for them to see themselves as authentic followers of the Crucified One.

Ignatius of Antioch

Ignatius was the third bishop of Antioch in Syria. The seven letters that he wrote on his way to martyrdom in Rome in the reign of Trajan (A.D. 98-117) are among the most important of the so-called apostolic Fathers, the earliest church writings from the late first and early second centuries. They have been called "one of the most beautiful treasures bequeathed by the second-century church."

It is significant that Ignatius wrote to two of the cities (Ephesus, Rome) addressed by Paul and to three of the cities (Ephesus, Philadelphia, Smyrna) among the seven cities of Revelation 2-3.

We know few details of his life, except for those revealed incidentally in his letters. We are not sure why he was arrested by the Romans. He was taken by ten Roman soldiers across Asia Minor to Smyrna, where he was welcomed by Bishop Polycarp and greeted by Christians from Ephesus, Magnesia, and Tralles.

Ignatius then proceeded north to Troas and crossed by boat to Neapolis. He passed through Philippi and then proceeded on the Egnatian Way across Macedonia to board a ship for Rome. There Ignatius's passionate desire to be "wheat" ground by the teeth of beasts for the sake of Christ was fulfilled.

Ignatius was an important link between the New Testament and the developing "catholic" church. He admired and quoted Paul. Like Paul, Ignatius fought the Docetists' view of Christ; that is, those who denied that the Son of God was truly incarnate (see 1 John). To unite the church Ignatius laid great stress upon the role of the bishop, who was to receive the obedience of all Christians.

Ignatius devoured by wild beasts in Rome; a Dutch engraving.

Ignatius of Antioch

Edwin M. Yamauchi

Ignatius's arrest

Antioch in Syria was the third largest city in the Roman Empire. The gospel was preached both to the Jews and the Gentiles by Peter, Paul, and other disciples (Acts 11:19-20; 15:22-26; Galatians 2:11 ff.). It was at cosmopolitan Antioch that believers in Jesus as the Messiah were first nicknamed *Christianoi*, "Christians" (Acts 11:26). Ignatius was the first to use the word *Christianismos*, "Christianity" (Ign. Rom. 3:3; Magn. 10:3).

According to Eusebius (*Eccles Hist.* 3.36.2) Ignatius was the third bishop of Antioch. We know that he was arrested in the reign of the emperor Trajan (A.D. 98-117), a time when Christianity was spreading rapidly among all classes, according to the letters of Pliny the Younger to the emperor. But we do not know why Ignatius was arrested.

Ignatius was taken into the custody of ten soldiers, "leopards," who responded to kindness with greater severity (Ign. Rom. 5:1). The company probably sailed to Tarsus, Paul's birthplace in Cilicia, and then traveled inland through southern Turkey, following a route taken by Paul. They passed through Philadelphia, eighty-five miles from the coast, and reached the port city of Smyrna (modern Izmir) in August. There Ignatius received visitors from the churches of Ephesus, Magnesia, and Tralles. Ephesus was thirty-five miles north on the coast, Magnesia was about fifteen miles inland, and Tralles fifteen miles farther.

Ignatius's letters

From Smyrna he wrote his letters to these churches (abbreviated: Ign. Eph., Magn., Tral.) and also to the Romans (Ign. Rom.), begging them not to intervene on his be-half because he was determined to be a *martyr* (literally "witness") for Christ.

Traveling north, the party stopped at Troas, where Ignatius, with the help of the Ephesian deacon Burrhus, wrote his letters to the Philadelphians, Smyrna-eans, and to Bishop Polycarp of Smyrna (Philad., Smyr., Poly.). Like Paul and his companions, Ignatius probably sailed to Neapolis and then traversed the Egnatian Way, passing through Philippi and Thessalonica on his way to the Adriatic coast. Polycarp later wrote to the Philippians (Poly. Phil. 9:1), admonishing them to follow the example of "the blessed Ignatius."

In his letters Ignatius makes rather sparing use of quotations from the Old Testament. He cites Proverbs 3:34 (Ign. Eph. 5:3) and Proverbs 18:17 (Magn. 12) and possibly alludes to the Old Testament in about ten passages. Some scholars believe that Ignatius's thoughts on martyrdom have been influenced by 4 Maccabees, a book which praises Jewish martyrs.

Ignatius seems to have known the gospel of Matthew, and some of his phrases bear strong resemblance to the gospel of John. But it is above all the Pauline writings that inspired him. He was especially fond of 1 Corinthians, from which he cites 1:20 in Ign. Eph. 18:1, 4:4 in Ign. Rom. 5:1, and 6:9-10 in Ign. Eph. 16:1. His own letter to the Ephesians has many parallels to Paul's letter to them.

Ignatius and Paul

He speaks of Paul in words of highest praise: "Paul, who was sanctified, who gained a good report, who was right blessed, in whose footsteps may I be found when I shall attain to God" (Ign.

Eph. 12:2). He does not put himself in the same class as the apostles: "I do not order you as did Peter and Paul; they were Apostles, I am a convict" (Ign. Rom. 4:3; see also Eph. 3:1; Tral. 3:3). Indeed, in words which repeat Paul's own expression of humility (see 1 Corinthians 15:8-9) Ignatius, in speaking of the Syrian Christians, says of himself: "for I am the least of them, and born out of time" (Ign. Rom. 9:2; see also Ign. Eph. 21:2; Magn. 14; Tral. 13:1).

Ignatius was greatly concerned about false teachers – "wild beasts," "mad dogs," "specious wolves" – who were endangering the churches to which he wrote. Scholars disagree as to whether he was confronted with two different heresies – Judaistic and Docetic; or with a single hybrid heresy – Judeo-Docetic. The attempts to view Ignatius as attacking a fully-developed Gnosticism and being influenced by it have not been convincing.

A Judaistic emphasis was attacked only in Ignatius's letters to the Magnesians and Philadelphians. According to Philad. 6:1 those who preached this message were evidently not themselves circumcised Jews. To the Magnesians (8:1) he writes: "For if we are living until now according to Judaism, we confess that we have not received grace."

Ignatius and Docetism

On the other hand, the more dangerous emphasis or heresy was that of Docetism, a word derived from the Greek word "to appear." Already in the New Testament era there were some who were denying the incarnation of Jesus Christ and contending that the Son of God only "appeared" human and only "seemed" to suffer (1 John 4:1-3; 2 John 7). Such a view arose from the assumption of Greek philosophers that the material world, including the body, was innately evil.

Ignatius urgently warned the Trallians (9:11-2): "Be deaf therefore when anyone speaks to you apart from Jesus Christ, who was of the family of David, and of Mary, who was truly born, both ate and drank, was truly persecuted under Pontius Pilate, and was truly crucified and died in the sight of those in heaven and on earth, and under the earth; who also was truly raised from the dead." Furthermore he vehemently protested: "But if ... his suffering was only a semblance ... why am I a prisoner, and why do I even long to fight with the beasts? In that case I am dying in vain" (10:1; see also Smyr. 1-3).

Ignatius's references to Pilate and also

Ancient portrait of Ignatius of Antioch.

to the tetrarch (Smyr. 1:2; Magn. 11) stressed the historicity of Christ's suffering, an emphasis that was later incorporated into the historic creeds.

According to Ignatius, the refusal of the Docetics to take seriously the humanity of Christ made them inhumane to others: "They have no concern for love, none for the widow, none for the orphan, none for the distressed, none for the afflicted, none for the prisoner, or the one released from prison, none for the hungry or thirsty" (Smyr. 6:2; see also 1 John 3:17).

Ignatius himself stresses the obligation for Christians to love (the word occurs sixty-four times) as Christ loved. He advises Polycarp (Poly. 4) to care for widows and not to be haughty to slaves. But slaves themselves were not to be puffed up or freed at the church's expense.

Bishops

In the New Testament era the *episcopos* (literally "overseer") or bishop was just another name for *presbyter* ("elder"), as even Jerome was to acknowledge later. By the end of the first Christian century, churches in Egypt, Rome, and Greece were still ruled by groups of bishops or presbyters. It was Ignatius who first stressed the concept of "monepiscopacy" (or monarchical episcopacy), that is, a single bishop in a given city presiding over a threefold ministry: (1) bishop, (2) presbyters, (3) deacons.

The all-important role of the bishop was developed by Ignatius not on the basis of "apostolic succession" following Peter, but on a mystical theology that holds that the bishop presides in the place of God (Magn. 6:1; Tral. 3:1). Submission to the bishop is necessary to achieve *henosis* ("unity," Ign. Eph. 5:1). Even when a bishop is youthful as at Magnesia (Magn. 3:1) or is silent as at Ephesus (Ign. Eph. 6:1) or at Philadelphia (Philad. 1:1), they are not to be despised, for silence is a characteristic of God Himself.

Ignatius describes himself as "set on unity" (Philad. 8:1) and urges the Philadelphians (7:2) to "love unity, flee from division." He urges Polycarp (1:2) "care

for unity your concern for there is nothing better." Ignatius was the first to use the word *katholikos* ("universal") of the church (Smyr. 8:2).

The Eucharist

A key to unity was the celebration of the Communion or, as Ignatius first called it, the Eucharist. The Eucharist emphasized the incarnation of Christ against the Docetics who abstained from it (Smyr. 7:1). Ignatius was also the first to maintain that either the bishop or his authorized representative has to be present for a Eucharist to be valid (Smyr. 8:1). He called the gathering of Christians to celebrate it the *pharmakon athanasias*, "the medicine of immortality" (Eph. 20:2). He also began the association of the Eucharist with the concept of a sacrificial altar, *thusiasterion* (Magn. 17:2; Philad. 4:1).

It was Ignatius's consuming passion to "attain" (*epituchein*, used twenty times) to God and Christ through his martyrdom. Unlike Paul (Phil. 1:23) Ignatius had no doubt as to whether it was better for him to live or to die. He begged the Romans not to prevent his martyrdom (Ign. Rom. 1:2, 2:1). He proclaimed: "Suffer me to be eaten by the beasts, through whom I can attain to God. I am God's wheat, and I am ground by the teeth of wild beasts that I may be found pure bread of Christ" (Ign. Rom. 4:1).

We are informed of his martyrdom in Rome in the reign of Trajan (c. A.D. 108) by Polycarp, Irenaeus, Eusebius, and Jerome. Later legendary accounts from the fourth and fifth centuries (the Martyrium Colbertinum and Antiochenum) relate that his bones were collected and brought back to Antioch. These relics were later brought back to Rome in the sixth or seventh century.

Justin Martyr
c. 100-*c.* 165

Justin Martyr was one of the earliest, and probably the most important, of the Apologists, spokesmen who offered an *apologia* (see Acts 22:1; 1 Peter 3:15), that is, a reasoned defense of Christianity, in the second and third centuries. Born of Gentile parents in Neapolis in Samaria, Justin pursued truth through a variety of philosophies before

Justin, apologist and martyr.

finding the truth in Christ.

Of Justin's numerous works, we have preserved two apologies and a remarkable dialogue with a Jew named Trypho (Dial). In his lengthy *First Apology* (*1 Apol.*), Justin first defends Christianity against various pagan calumnies and misunderstandings. He argues that Christianity is not a novelty, but that it is the fulfillment of the Old Testament prophecies that were older than the Greek philosophies. Justin's doctrine of the logos enabled him to acknowledge that there were partial revelations of truth in such thinkers as Socrates before the coming of Christ, the entire logos. However, pagan myths and mystery religions that resembled Christianity were demonic falsifications.

Trypho was a Jew who had recently escaped the Bar Kochba War in Palestine (A.D. 132-135). He encountered Justin, who was still wearing a philosopher's garb, in Ephesus and interrogated him about Christianity. Justin attempted to convert Trypho by expounding not only Old Testament prophecies but by citing numerous foreshadowings of the cross in natural objects. Trypho listened with interest but had too many objections. The discussion was heated but still remarkably amicable.

Justin's shorter *Second Apology* (*2 Apol.*) protests a particular case of injustice against Christians in Rome, where he taught from 150. Along with six other believers, Justin went bravely to his death *c.* 165, earning the epithet "Martyr." His impassioned defense of Christian truth and denunciation of error greatly influenced many other church Fathers.

The Life of
Justin Martyr

c. 100	Birth.
c. 133	Important encounter with elderly Christian.
c. 150-155	*First Apology* dedicated.
c. 160	*Second Apology; Dialogue with Trypho.*
c. 165	Martyrdom.

Justin Martyr

Defender of the Faith

Edwin M. Yamauchi

Justin's conversion

Justin was born about A.D. 100 in Neapolis (modern Nablus) in Samaria. His grandfather's name, Bacchius, is Greek; his father's name, Priscus, and his own name are Latin. Justin was an uncircumcised Gentile rather than a Samaritan.

He followed various Greek philosophies in a pursuit of truth (*Dial. 2*) but found each failed to satisfy. The Stoics were not concerned with whether God cared for men. A Peripatetic teacher (follower of Aristotle) seemed more interested in profit than truth. A Pythagorean teacher required Justin first to learn music, arithmetic, and geometry. Finally, the example of Socrates and the teachings of Plato caused Justin to contemplate invisible realities.

Then about the year 133 Justin encountered an elderly Christian who undermined some of his Platonic ideas and pointed him to Christ. Another factor that convinced him of the truth of Christianity was the courage demonstrated by Christian martyrs: "For I myself, too, when I was delighting in the doctrines of Plato, and heard the Christians slandered, and saw them fearless of death ... perceived that it was impossible that they could be living in wickedness and pleasure" (*2 Apol.* 12).

Justin the teacher

Justin was one of the first highly educated Gentiles to use his learning to defend Christianity even before the emperor himself. His writings use citations from Euripides, Xenophon, and above all Plato to strengthen his case for Christianity. Numerous allusions have been traced to Plato's *Apology, Republic,* and *Tim-*

aeus. Justin seems to reflect the closest affinities to what is called Middle Platonism.

Justin spent some time at Ephesus, where he encountered Trypho, and then came to Rome, where he taught at the house of Martinus located perhaps on the Via Tiburtina. One of his famous students was Tatian from Assyria, who later compiled a *Diatessaron* or harmony of the gospels and then became a heretic. A rival teacher at Rome was Marcion. Whereas Marcion taught that the New Testament contradicted the Old Testament, Justin held that the New Testament fulfilled the Old Testament.

Justin quotes from the synoptic gospels, perhaps from a harmonized edition. He found Matthew's emphasis on the fulfillment of Old Testament prophecies particularly useful for his dialogue with Trypho. His one possible reference to John (3:3, 5) appears in a baptismal context (*1 Apol.* 61). He has no certain quotations, but numerous allusions to most of the New Testament, except for the pastoral epistles.

Justin cites two agrapha, that is, non-canonical sayings of Jesus: "In whatsoever I find you, in this will I also judge you"; and "There shall be schisms and heresies." He also records the tradition that Jesus was born in a cave in Bethlehem, and that the Magi came from Arabia.

Justin's Apologies

Justin's *First Apology* was dedicated between A.D. 150 and 155 to Emperor Antonius Pius (138-161) and his adopted sons, Marcus Aurelius and Lucius Verus. To support his plea for toleration for Christians, Justin appended a letter from the previous emperor, Hadrian.

The *First Apology* is a rather lengthy exposition of sixty-eight chapters. After an introduction, chapters 4-13 refute some of the charges against Christianity. Justin contrasts the moral power of Christ's teaching (chapters 14-20) with the irrational fables of paganism (chapters 21-22).

It is Christ who is the only Son of God, the fullness of the divine logos, as demonstrated by the fulfillment of Old Testament prophecies (chapters 30-53). Even before the coming of Christ, the logos was manifested partially in such Greek philosophers as Socrates and Heraclitus, and in such Hebrews as Abraham, Ananias, Azarias, Misael (Daniel's three companions), and Elijah. Myths that anticipated aspects of Christ's life were inspired by demons (chapters 54-58). Plato's truth was dependent on Moses (chapters 59-60).

Chapters 61-67 contain an invaluable account of Christian rituals, including baptism and the Eucharist. These passages are indeed the fullest accounts to come down to us from the second century. It is noteworthy that Justin does not refer to bishops or presbyters.

The *Second Apology*, a shorter work of fifteen chapters, has been regarded by some scholars as an appendix to the first, but should be considered a later independent work dated *c.* 160. It is a passionate protest against the unjust execution of Ptolemy by Urbicus, the prefect of Rome. The pagan husband of a Christian woman had denounced her teacher, Ptolemy, to the authorities.

Justin responds to pagan jibes as to why Christians did not kill themselves if they believed in martyrdom (chapter 4).

Dialogue with Trypho

The *Dialogue with Trypho*, written about 160, was dedicated to a certain Marcus Pompeius. Some scholars believe that it was written to Gentiles sympathetic to Judaism to show Christianity's superiority. According to the introduction, Trypho, a Jew schooled in philosophy at Corinth, along with his companions encounters Justin in his philosopher's garb in the colonnades at Ephesus. Trypho had recently escaped from the Bar Kochba War (132-135) in Palestine. The suggestion that Trypho was actually the anti-Christian rabbi Tarphon has now been abandoned.

Trypho was acquainted with the gospel, though the Jewish leaders had warned him not to have any contact with Christians (*Dial.* 38). In fact, Jews were cursing Christians in the synagogue services (16.4; 47.4). Justin complains that such leaders had been spreading false information about Christians, such as the accusation also found in the Talmud that Jesus was a magician (69.7). Despite such hostility, Justin maintains that Christians do not hate Jews but rather that they pray for them (108.3).

Justin argues that the law (11-12), fasting (15), circumcision (16), dietary injunctions (20), Sabbath (21), and sacrifices (22) were given to the Jews because of their rebellious nature.

Using the Septuagint, or Greek translation of the Old Testament, Justin cites numerous prophecies to prove that Jesus was the promised Messiah, or Christ, and that Christianity had now superseded Judaism. (The Christian appropriation of the Septuagint inspired the Jews to authorize more literal translations into Greek of the Old Testament.)

Justin and the Old Testament

Justin cites Psalm 22 twenty-six times to show how Jesus' crucifixion was foretold, Psalm 45 five times to show that Christ is the king who is fairer than the sons of men, and Psalm 72 nine times to show that Jesus is the Messiah who judges His people in righteousness. He accuses the Jews of excising the phrase "from the tree" from their version of Psalm 96:10; the phrase, however, turns out to be a Christian interpolation. His favorite passage is Isaiah 52:13-53:12, which he cites some twenty-nine times to prove that Jesus was the "suffering servant." On the basis of Isaiah 53:2 he even declares that Jesus was not of a comely appearance.

Justin uses the concept of typology in finding Christ prefigured in many other Old Testament passages. The wood of Noah's ark prefigures the wood of the cross. Leah represents the synagogue, but Rachel the church. Joshua anticipates Jesus because his name is the same as Jesus's. The cross is anticipated not only in Moses' uplifted hands, but in nautical masts, military standards, and even the horn of the unicorn. His free and sometimes erroneous citation of Scriptures may have been based on anthologies of the Old Testament, known as testimonia, such as were found at Qumran.

Trypho does not believe that Jesus is the Messiah, or Christ, because Elijah has not yet come (49). He questions the concept of the pre-existence of Christ (38.1; 87.1), His incarnation (68.1), and His virgin birth (43.7; 63.1). He objects to the use of Isaiah 7:14 in the Septuagint to prove the latter (67.1-2). The Messiah must be a man (49.1); Justin's concept of a "second God" is blasphemous (55.1; 65.1). He can accept a "suffering" Messiah but a "crucified" Messiah is unthinkable (89.2; 90.1), according to Deuteronomy 21:23.

Trypho maintains that Jews are of Abraham's seed (44:1) and urges Justin to be circumcised and keep the Torah to obtain mercy from God. It is noteworthy that Trypho was not merely a "straw man" but a well-informed Jew, who resisted Justin's arguments to the end.

Justin's theology

Though Justin on the whole appealed to the Scripture, he was also influenced by his philosophical background. The seed of God's logos (*logos spermatikos*) was disseminated to all men in their God-given capacity to respond to truth. This enabled Justin to claim: "Whatever things were rightly said among all men are the property of us Christians" (*2 Apol.* 13.4), and also to hold that there were Christians before Christ, such as Socrates and Heraclitus (*1 Apol.* 46.3). L. W. Barnard comments: "The boldness, scope and vigour of his conception of the logos command admiration even if, from a later

vantage point, we see that he allowed his philosophical presuppositions to modify the biblical basis of his Christianity to too great an extent."

His Middle Platonic concept of the transcendence of God the Father caused Justin to attribute all theophanies (manifestations of God) in the Old Testament to God the Son, "For the ineffable Father and Lord of all neither comes to any place... but remains in His own place..." (*Dial.* 127:2).

Justin failed to develop the Pauline emphasis on the solidarity of the human race with Adam's sin, or to speak about the believer's life in Christ. But he succeeded in refuting the charges of atheism, immorality, and cannibalism against Christians, and in showing the moral superiority of Christianity over paganism. In contrast to Marcion and the Gnostics he stressed the continuity between the Old Testament and the New Testament. In his view the Greeks had some partial truths and the Jews a revelation of temporary validity, but the fullness of truth came only in the incarnate Logos, Jesus Christ.

Martyrdom

According to an accurate account compiled in the third century, Justin was brought to trial with six other believers *c.* 165. He answered his interrogator simply and went courageously to his death. As he had declared earlier to the emperor, "And you, you can kill us, but not hurt us" (*1 Apol.* 2.4).

Justin's writings, including a lost *Syntagma* against the heresies, had a profound impact, especially upon Irenaeus and Tertullian. Modern scholars have been impressed by Justin's modesty, honesty, and courage. According to Barnard he was "the first thinker after St. Paul to grasp the universalistic element in Christianity and to sum up in one bold stroke the whole history of civilization as finding its consummation in Christ."

Irenaeus
*c.*130-*c.*200

Irenaeus holds a significant place in the history of Christianity because of his important role in the Gnostic controversy of the second century. Gnosticism was a syncretistic religious movement in which different teachers shaped different systems out of elements from Judaism, Greek philosophy, pagan religion, and Christianity. There was enough of a common viewpoint in these systems to make Gnosticism the major theological threat to the Christian church in the second century. Irenaeus met the threat by making a thorough study of Gnosticism and writing the most extensive response to it produced up to his time.

Irenaeus's refutation of Gnosticism involved the fullest synthesis from the second century of Christian doctrine as a whole. He expounded the fundamental Christian doctrines of God, Christ, man, and redemption. This exposition was set within a theology of history, which took seriously God's historical plan of salvation. Irenaeus was the first Christian author whose works survive to use the Bible as a whole, reflecting a canon of the New Testament on the same level as the Old Testament.

Irenaeus aimed to be a biblical theologian; he knew the Bible's contents well and had a good grasp of its basic doctrines and perspectives. His work, however, marks the change from the sub-apostolic church of the early second century to the old catholic church that emerged from the Gnostic controversy. As a transitional figure whose work points both backward to the apostles and forward to the Roman Catholic church, he deserves careful attention.

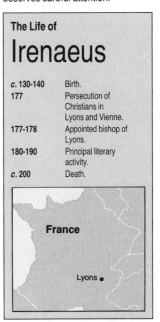

The Life of

Irenaeus

c. 130-140	Birth.
177	Persecution of Christians in Lyons and Vienne.
177-178	Appointed bishop of Lyons.
180-190	Principal literary activity.
c. 200	Death.

France

Lyons ●

The Roman theater, Lyons. Irenaeus became Bishop of Lyons in A.D. **177/178.**

Irenaeus

Adversary of the Gnostics

Everett Ferguson

Irenaeus at Lyons

Irenaeus was born in the Roman province of Asia around A.D.130 to 140. As a youth he listened to the teaching of Polycarp, bishop of Smyrna (died *c.* 155), who in turn had heard the teaching of John. Irenaeus went to Gaul, where he became a presbyter in the church at Lyons. After the persecution under Marcus Aurelius claimed the life of Bishop Pothinus and approximately fifty other Christians in Lyons and Vienne in 177, Irenaeus succeeded Pothinus. A man of the church, Irenaeus was a devoted pastor of souls, giving his attention to spreading the gospel in Gaul

and to defending his flock from heresy. Maintaining close relations with the church at Rome, he united the teaching traditions of Asia Minor and Rome. Late sources say he was martyred in 202.

The literary remains of Irenaeus show his polemical and pastoral concerns. His major work, known as *Against Heresies* was dedicated to the fight against Gnosticism. He described its contents as "The Unmasking and Overthrow of the Knowledge [Gnosis] Falsely So-called." Although written in Greek and with parts extant in several languages, it survives complete only in an early and literal Latin translation. The five books may be summarized as follows:

1 – Exposition of Gnosticism; 2 – Refutation by means of reason; 3-5 – Refutation from Scripture, based on the prophets, words of the Lord, and the apostles.

A shorter work is the *Demonstration* (or *Proof*) *of the Apostolic Preaching*. Also written in Greek, it survives only in an Armenian version. It is a work for the

Remains of Byzantine church, Sardis.

Irenaeus, bishop of Lyons.

guidance of those who instructed new converts in the faith. It follows biblical history, giving the main lines of the biblical message and proving the nature of Christ from Old Testament prophecy. Excerpts from two letters by Irenaeus are cited by Eusebius in his *Ecclesiastical History*: a letter to Florinus on Gnosticism and a letter to Victor, bishop of Rome, pleading for peace in the dispute between Rome and Ephesus on the date of Easter. His efforts to mediate in the Easter controversy, and earlier in the Montanist controversy, earned for him from Eusebius the recognition that he lived up to his name, irenic.

Enemy of the Gnostics

Irenaeus's theology formulated traditional Christian teaching in opposition to Gnostic heresies. Against the Gnostic dualism Irenaeus emphasized the oneness of God, of Christ, and of the plan of salvation. "One and the same God" was both Creator and Father of Jesus Christ. He created the world out of nothing. As the God of both the law and the gospel, He presided over the history of salvation, revealing Himself in progressive covenants with Adam, Noah, Moses, and Christ.

There is one Christ, in whom is united the Son of God and the Son of Man. He was pre-existent, had been prophesied in the Old Testament, and became incarnate for human salvation. The reality of His human flesh, born of the virgin Mary, and the reality of the bodily resurrection are stressed over against the Gnostic depreciation of what is fleshly.

The one saving plan of God unites creation and redemption, the Old and New Testaments. Christians are no longer under the law of Moses; but the gospel of Christ is in continuity with it and not in contradiction to it. God was preparing the human race for the coming of Jesus Christ. The unity of the divine plan is shown by the way in which Christ recapitulated the story of Adam by reversing the latter's disobedience and its consequences. Sin had come through free will, but God led the human race from infancy to maturity, progressively educating it to accept freely the grace at work in Christ. Human free will in responding to God's grace is important for Irenaeus in contrast to Gnostic determinism.

Special attention focuses on Irenaeus's views about man and redemption and about the church and Scripture.

Flesh and spirit

The salvation of the flesh is an important theme in Irenaeus. For the Gnostics, the nature of that which is truly man is spiritual, and the essential principle in the saved person is the spiritual seed or nature planted in him. For Irenaeus, that which truly defines human nature is its being made by God as a composite of flesh and soul. Adam was made in the image and likeness of God; the image remained after sin, but the likeness was lost. For Irenaeus, the situation is not that the soul sins with the aid of the body, but that the body sins with the aid of the soul. The redeemed person receives a third element, the Holy Spirit, who works to effect the salvation of the flesh by preparing and accustoming the flesh for fellowship with God.

The incarnation is another central concept for Irenaeus. Christ took on Himself the whole human condition, including existence in the flesh, in order to bring salvation. Created flesh is the object of salvation, and Christ's fleshly body is the means of accomplishing it. The resurrected Christ restores the likeness of God to believers. The human ideal and goal is the glorified flesh of Jesus.

What was lost in Adam is recovered in Christ. Irenaeus describes salvation in itself as communion with God; the vision of God, salvation in us, as possession of the Holy Spirit; and salvation in its effects as immortality, adoption, and realization of the image and likeness of God.

The flesh is raised at the resurrection. The disobedient receive eternal punishment, but the righteous enjoy eternal life. The book of Revelation was an important book to Irenaeus, and from it he adopted a chiliastic eschatology. The millennial kingdom will prepare the flesh for a heavenly home. The literal resurrection was important to him in arguing against the Gnostic dualism of body and soul in which the salvation of the soul alone was important.

The church is one and universal, and it confesses one and the same faith throughout the world. The tradition preserved in the churches of apostolic foundation is witness to this one faith. The common faith is confessed at baptism, at which one act the believer receives forgiveness of sins and the Holy Spirit.

The apostolic succession
The argument between the church and the Gnostics came down to a question of what was apostolic. Both claimed that their teaching came from the Lord through the apostles. Whose interpretation was right? Irenaeus took his stand on the apostolic Scriptures as preserving the genuine teaching of the apostles. The Scriptures are inspired and authoritative. The apostolic tradition (teaching) was

A Christian sarcophagus from the catacombs, Rome.

found in the Scriptures and was preserved in the churches. The Gnostics claimed a secret tradition preserved privately by favorite disciples of individual apostles.

Irenaeus argued that if the apostles had any secrets to impart they would have delivered those to the same persons in whom they had enough confidence to entrust the leadership of the churches. Their teaching had been passed down from one teacher in the church to the next. The stability of this teaching was assured by its publicity: any deviation could be detected. Its correctness was assured by its uniformity: what was taught at one place could be checked against what was taught at other places. These arguments involved what is termed *apostolic succession*. It should be noted that, for Irenaeus, apostolic succession was not an article of faith but an argument, and an effective argument against the Gnostic teachers, who were outside the succession of leadership in the churches and differed much among themselves. Moreover, it was not a succession passed from ordainer to ordained, as in later formulations, but from one teacher to the next in the church. In Irenaeus's terminology, the succession included presbyters as well as bishops.

The New Testament canon

Irenaeus's arguments from and use of Scripture presuppose a New Testament canon already in existence for some time. The exact contours of that canon cannot be determined with perfect exactitude, but the way Irenaeus combines passages and uses one book to interpret another shows that he was dealing with an established and recognized collection of books. He was thoroughly acquainted with biblical vocabulary, but his knowledge of the Old Testament was not as intimate as was his knowledge of the New. The Old Testament was for him a Christian book because of its witness to Christ. He gives a Christological, often non-literal, interpretation to the Old Testament, yet he maintains the distinction between before and after Christ. His arguments for there being only four gospels, neither more nor less, is typical; these were books received in the church. Irenaeus's illustrations of the appropriateness of the number four are an argument after the fact, not an argument for something new.

When Irenaeus appealed to tradition in the churches, it was to determine the correct understanding of the apostolic teaching. His phrase "canon of truth" referred to what others called the "rule of faith." It meant the content of the apostolic preaching in summary form, and it served as a norm for interpreting Scripture and determining the apostolic faith.

Later developments in Catholicism carried Irenaeus's thought well beyond what he himself had said. Irenaeus took Rome as the representative church in his argument from apostolic succession. His affirmation that the apostolic faith was preserved there, and consequently the necessity of agreeing with this church, has been subject to many different interpretations. The reality of the physical presence of Christ in the Eucharist was affirmed by Irenaeus against the Gnostic depreciation of material elements. Mary, in reversing the disobedience of Eve, found a place in Irenaeus's doctrine of recapitulation.

The biblical emphasis in Irenaeus's argumentation and his defense of the central biblical doctrines of creation, redemption, and resurrection have made Irenaeus important to all branches of Christianity.

Timechart 0-300

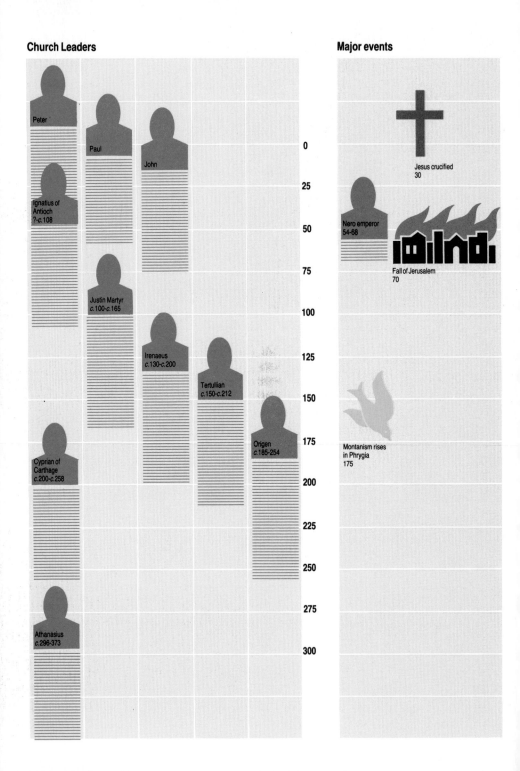

Church Leaders

Peter

Paul

John

Ignatius of
Antioch
?-c.108

Justin Martyr
c.100-c.165

Irenaeus
c.130-c.200

Tertullian
c.150-c.212

Origen
c.185-254

Cyprian of
Carthage
c.200-c.258

Athanasius
c.296-373

0
25
50
75
100
125
150
175
200
225
250
275
300

Major events

Jesus crucified
30

Nero emperor
54-68

Fall of Jerusalem
70

Montanism rises
in Phrygia
175

Tertullian
c. 150-*c.*212

Tertullian wrote an enormous amount, about thirty books totaling more than 1,500 pages in the space of little more than fifteen years (*c.* A.D. 196-*c.* 212). The range of his interests was greater than that of any other Christian writer in ancient times. For that reason, his works are a valuable source of information about church life, as well as about doctrinal and controversial matters. His style is vivid and unconventional, which makes his Latin difficult to translate. His writings were so important to the Latin church that, although he went into schism, his books were preserved and studied by all the great Western Fathers. They were not, in fact, condemned until 496, and even then some of them survived intact.

Tertullian of Carthage; bottom: Roman Coliseum, El Djem, Tunisia.

The Life of
Tertullian

c. 150	Birth.
c. 196-212	Extensive writing output.
c. 212	Death.

Africa

Carthage

Tunisia

Tertullian

and Western Theology
Gerald L. Bray

Tertullian and Carthage

Quintus Septimius Florens Tertullianus was born in Carthage, near modern Tunis in North Africa, sometime after A.D. 150. He probably came from a middle-class family and received a sound literary, legal, and philosophical education that included a good knowledge of Greek. Nothing is known of his private life or occupation, apart from the fact that he was married. Some scholars believe that his wife died young, because in Tertullian's later works there is no mention of her, and it seems that his attitude toward women and marriage became more and more negative as time went on. That is possible, but too much should not be made of an argument from silence.

There are many puzzling features about his writings that defy solution in our present state of knowledge. For example, we do not know how he was able to write so freely at a time when the church was suffering persecution, nor is it at all clear what his relationship to his local church at Carthage was. Many of his works were directed at different heresies that he was trying to refute, but we do not know how serious a threat any of them actually was. An ancient tradition, recorded by Jerome, says that he seceded from the main church at Carthage about halfway through his career. Jerome puts the blame on the elders of the church, who were supposed to have been jealous of him, but most modern scholars believe that he was attracted into Montanism.

Montanism

The Montanists were a chiliastic sect from Asia Minor who, under the leadership of the prophet Montanus, had predicted the descent of the New Jerusalem and the end of the world. That event was supposed to have occurred in the year 177, but its failure to arrive provoked reprisals against the sect, and it disappeared soon afterwards. The puzzling thing is that Tertullian was drawn to Montanist teaching about thirty years afterwards, when the falsity of the so-called New Prophecy must have been obvious to everyone. He was also noticeably selective in his use of their writings, saying nothing about the end of the world, but concentrating to a considerable extent on their holiness teachings. It seems probable, therefore, that Tertullian saw Montanism as a movement that advocated some of his own teachings. He was therefore inclined to rate it highly, though it is most improbable that he ever became a Montanist in the strict sense.

Nothing is known about his death, though it is probable that he passed away at Carthage sometime after 212.

Tertullian's apologetics

Great efforts have been made to divide Tertullian's writings into pre-Montanist and Montanist works, the main criteria for the latter being quotations from Montanus and his associates, the use of characteristically Montanist words like *Paracletus* (the Holy Spirit) and *psychicus* (carnal Christian), and his willingness to attack the leaders of the main church. However, attempts to demonstrate that the books that show evidence of Montanist influence have a doctrinal character markedly different or stricter than the others have not been entirely successful. It has not been particularly helpful to divide his works according to the subjects they treat.

The first major category of writings is *apologetic*. Tertullian continued the tradition of second-century Greek Christians who had written defenses of their faith and addressed them to pagans or Jews. His most famous work is called simply the *Apology*, a long treatise in which he dissects pagan religion in order to point out its irrationality and in which

Site of Roman villas, Carthage, Tunisia.

he strongly criticizes the Romans for their negative attitude toward the Christians in their midst. In another work, *The Testimony of the Soul*, he takes up the theme first propounded by Justin Martyr, that the human soul is naturally inclined toward Christianity, from which sin has deflected it. Although Tertullian has traditionally been portrayed as a strongly anti-philosophical writer, the evidence of this and other treatises shows that, in fact, he was deeply sympathetic to many elements of the pagan philosophical tradition.

Polemics

The second major category of writings is *polemical*. Here pride of place naturally belongs to the five books against Marcion, which remain our chief source of information about his teachings. Tertullian used the portions of the New Testament that Marcion considered to be genuine revelation to demonstrate that the heretic's anti-Semitism could not be based even on the most "Gentile" parts of Scripture. Tertullian also wrote against the Gnostic heretics Hermogenes and Valentinus in great enough detail for us to be able to reconstruct the substance of their teachings from his refutation of them. He also wrote a general work against heresies, in which he maintained that the Scriptures could only properly be used by those who were spiritually attuned to their message. Heretics by definition were not, and so they perverted the Word of God with their own human ideas. One more polemical work must be mentioned, the famous treatise against Praxeas. In that book Tertullian outlines the substance of his teaching about the Holy Trinity, which was to remain a classical source of doctrinal discussion until the time of Augustine.

Doctrine

The third major category of writings is *doctrinal*. Tertullian wrote an important book about baptism, in which he upholds an extreme view of baptismal cleansing and regeneration. So strong was his insistence on the power of baptism that he refused to allow any remedy for post-baptismal sin except martyrdom (the baptism of fire). Tertullian also opposed infant baptism, because he feared that a child might sin unwittingly afterwards and lose his salvation through ignorance. Other important works in this category are his long discourse on *The Soul*, in which he shows himself to be pro-Stoic and anti-Platonist in his general philosophical outlook, and two treatises about the flesh, one concerned with the incarnation of Christ, the other with the resurrection of the dead. Both these latter works are noted for their theological maturity: Tertullian reached a point of development that the Eastern church would not get to until the Council of Chalcedon in 451.

Pastoral writings

The fourth major category is *pastoral*, but these fall into at least four different subgroups, according to subject matter. First come the exhortations to the martyrs to stand fast in the face of persecution. That was a constant theme of Tertullian's life, and it is remarkable how often he appealed to the examples of heroism set by the ancient Romans, rather than to figures from the Bible, with whom his readers would probably have been less familiar. Next come the treatises that deal with matters of personal spirituality. Tertullian wrote with great sensitivity about suffering, prayer, and repentance, though his ascetic streak is apparent in his work on fasting.

Better known than those writings is the series of short works devoted to women and their place in the church. There are two books addressed to his wife, two that deal with female dress, and three that handle the delicate question of chastity. Tertullian had an opinion of women that was generally favorable, certainly by comparison with some of the things many of his Eastern contemporaries were saying. He was strongly against any form of sexual license, and prescribed behavior that today would be called "Puritan" for Christian women. He was not against matrimony, which he recognized as a gift from God, but he believed that married couples should abstain from sexual intercourse and devote themselves to fasting and prayer. His main reason was that, as the end of the world was nigh and the likelihood of martyrdom was great, there was no point in having children.

Finally, there are a number of writings that attack pagan practices in which Christians were often involved. These included public sports, which in ancient times had a religious significance, military service, idolatry of various kinds, and the wearing of the *pallium*, a type of cloak associated with pagan philosophy. This latter work is usually classed as a satire, the first to have been written by a Christian, and one of the few to have survived from antiquity.

Tertullian's theology

Tertullian's theology is largely typical of his time and cannot be said to have suffered serious distortion as a result of Montanist influences. It is remarkably well-rounded, and the large number of his writings enables us to reconstruct a doctrinal system that was to remain of fundamental importance in Western thought.

Tertullian rejected the philosophical schools of his time, and in particular the Platonism that was enjoying a modest revival. He regarded Platonism as anti-Christian because it was antimaterialist, believing that only the soul, and not the flesh, could be saved. Tertullian was much closer in that respect to Stoicism, which held that both soul and flesh were material substances, though he was careful to avoid the cruder sort of materialism that is so prevalent today. His main purpose in inclining toward the Stoics was to insist that Christianity preached a resurrection of both the soul and the flesh and denied that the latter was evil, as Plato had taught. For Tertullian, the credibility of the incarnation of the Son of God depended on the belief that matter was good, and he emphasized that belief at every opportunity.

Unlike his contemporaries in the Greek-speaking world, Tertullian was not particularly inclined to philosophical terms in the expression of his theology. It is true that he borrowed a large part of his vocabulary from Greek sources, but he recast that in the framework of Roman law. He may have been a lawyer himself, but that cannot be demonstrated from his writings. Rather it seems that he used the fairly general concepts of Roman law familiar to most educated people and applied them to the Bible, not forgetting that the Old Testament was itself called the law of God. Tertullian's legalism could be oppressive and fantastic, particularly in moral matters, but the wider implications of his thought have remained formative in the mind of the Western church, both Catholic and Protestant, to this day. Reliance on legal terminology gave him both the precision of philosophy and the practical application that most philosophers lacked. Of particular importance was his borrowing of the word *persona* to describe the Father, Son, and Holy Spirit.

Tertullian did not regard the divine Persons as absolute in the sense in which they were to be so regarded in later orthodox theology, but that was a failure of imagination rather than of will. He said, in fact, that the difference between the Persons is not one of *status* but one of *gradus* (rank), an important advance that undercut the general belief of the time, that the Father was somehow God

Remains of the Roman amphitheater, Carthage, Tunisia.

in a way that the other Persons were not. Tertullian placed the Father first in the order of *gradus* but did not accord Him a kind of divinity that the Son and the Holy Spirit cannot share.

Christology

His fundamental orthodoxy is even more apparent in his Christology, where he stressed that the incarnation was an assumption of human nature by the Person of the Son, the Word of God. At a time when it was widely believed that Jesus was inferior to the Father, and some were even saying that He was no more than a man whom God had adopted as His Son, Tertullian had the clarity of vision to advocate a fully divine and at the same time fully human Christ, the two natures being united in a single Person. That doctrine later formed the substance of the so-called *Tome* of Leo (449), which was incorporated into the dogmatic definition of orthodox Christology made two years later at Chalcedon.

Tertullian is known for his high doctrine of Scripture, and he quoted from all but two of the books of the New Testament, putting them on a par with the Old Testament Scriptures. He is also known for his many references to what he called the *"regula fidei"*, or rule of faith. It appears by this term he meant some kind of doctrinal statement, which from quotations in his writings appears to have been remarkably similar to what we now call the Apostles' Creed. As is to be expected, the term *regula* comes from Roman law, where it was used to refer to a summary of statute law that could be cited in court as an authoritative résumé of what the statute in question actually said. In Tertullian's case, the statute law was the Bible, and the *regula* was simply a handy way of referring to its teaching on the vital matters of faith.

In eschatological matters, Tertullian was a firm "dispensationalist" who believed that history could be divided into three ages, according to the Persons of the Trinity. Thus the Old Testament was the age of the Father, the Incarnation was the age of the Son, and the time since Pentecost was the final age of the Holy Spirit, in which the promises of the earlier ages would at last be fulfilled. That outlook made him favor asceticism, which he saw as a preparation for spiritual warfare both in this life and against the forces of Satan that would be unleashed in fury just before the end. It was also, of course, a mortification of the flesh that testified to the Christian belief that he was a sojourner on earth whose true abode was the kingdom of heaven. Many of those ideas were subsequently modified, but a number of them were later incorporated into the monastic traditions of the medieval church, and some still exert a powerful influence today.

Origen

c. 185-254

The best scholar in the Christian church in the first half of the third century was born about A.D.185 and died in 254. During the six decades of his life he defended the faith against heretics and the Roman authorities, he was active as a Christian educator, he was a witness to the Jewish community, and he was a spiritual guide in the church. He was respected but controversial, disliked by some and suspected by others of holding unorthodox beliefs. But through it all he remained intellectually dynamic and creative, patient, persevering. He eventually faced the possibility of martyrdom. His place in the history of the church is based upon his biblical scholarship, including his use of the original languages of the Bible and his method of exegesis, his pioneering of key theological concepts and organizing those concepts into the first systematic theology, and his asceticism, which became the seed-bed for monasticism. His writings can still inspire Christians today.

Who was this scholar and ascetic? Origenes Adamantius, better known as Origen.

Origen of Alexandria, scholar and ascetic.

The Life of

Origen

c. 185	Birth in Alexandria, Egypt.
c. 202	His father, Leonides, is martyred.
215-220	Begins to write and publish.
250	Imprisoned and tortured.
254	Death in Tyre.

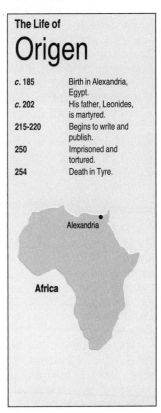

Alexandria

Africa

Origen

Scholar and Ascetic

Robert V. Schnucker

Origen of Alexandria

Origen was born in Alexandria, Egypt, about A.D.185 and died in Tyre about 254. From early childhood on, it seemed that God had chosen him to be a leader in the church. His father, Leonides, recognized in his son a precocity for grasping the Christian faith. He thus provided Origen with a superb education, which included a detailed knowledge of the Bible. It is possible that Clement of Alexandria was one of his teachers. During the Servian persecution of 202, Leonides was martyred by decapitation. While he was in jail, young Origen wrote him a letter encouraging him to remain true to the faith and indicated that he was not unwilling to share with his father the martyr's crown. Tradition claims Origen was spared that crown because his mother hid his clothes so that he could not appear in public.

Due to his remarkable intellectual skills and unusual piety, Origen was soon named by Bishop Demetrius to head the catechumens' school in Alexandria. As he instructed new Christians in the faith, he came to realize he had to counter arguments of heretics within the faith as well as attacks from without the faith from the Jewish and pagan communities. Thus he came to study with Ammonius Saccas, the father of Neo-Platonism, and began the task of mastering Hebrew. Between 215 and 220, with the financial help of a recent convert, Ambrose, Origen began to write and publish.

His fame spread, and he was invited to travel to various places in Europe and the Near East to serve as an expert in disputes between Christians and as an apologist to the unbelieving world. In 230, during one of his journeys, he was ordained to the priesthood by bishops Theoctistus of Caesarea and Alexander of Jerusalem. This caused a rupture between Origen and his bishop, Demetrius. It prompted Origen's exile from Alexandria and his career's shifting to Caesarea, where he spent the rest of his life writing, teaching, preaching, and following an existence of rare rigorous asceticism. During the Decian persecution of 250 he was imprisoned and cruelly tortured. He did not abandon his faith, although the ordeal did weaken him physically. He was released from jail and lived for another three years, dying in Tyre some time in 254.

Origen the ascetic

Origen's asceticism was famous in the early church and is still remembered today. One event demonstrating how rigorous was his dedication to the exercise of faith in daily life concerns his supposed self-castration as the result of taking Matthew 19:12 literally. He wanted to remove from the pagan world's imagination any hint of scandal as he taught the young women in his school. Eusebius wrote that Origen put away youthful lusts; he was serious during the day and stayed up most of the night studying Scripture and praying. When he did sleep, it was on the floor. He fasted frequently, ate meager meals, walked about barefoot, and almost destroyed his health. While a teacher at Alexandria and later in Caesarea, he took only the smallest wages for his work.

In his *On Prayer*, probably written in honor of his Alexandrian patron, Ambrose, who was about to be martyred, Origen wrote that one cannot make a comparison between earthly riches and "a healthy mind and robust soul and a balanced reason" (XVII/1). Origen went on to argue that the sufferings of the body in persecution are as something less than a scratch to the body in the light of the truth of the Christian faith.

Along with his zealous asceticism, mysticism was also an integral part of his religious life. This can be seen in some of

Sculpture of a shepherd from Caesarea.

human being's fallen state. When one can control the body, it is an evidence of the rejection of sin and the desire for a higher life. Consequently, there must be an ascetic-mystical component of the Christian's life that will directly affect the life of action and vice versa.

That life of Christian action for Origen was observable in his teaching, preaching, disputations, and above all in his writings, which numbered, according to some, more than 6,000. They established his reputation in the church as one of the earliest, most productive, and seminal scholars. He was a pioneer in systematic theology, one of the great biblical exegetes of the church, and in his *Contra Celsus* he provided a model for the apologists of the future. A pagan critic, Celsus, had unleashed a torrent of criticisms against the faith. Origen painstakingly answered every charge one by one, unless he deemed the charge simply silly.

While teaching in Alexandria he wrote his *Peri Archon – First Principles –* usually considered to be the first systematic theology of the church. Included in this work were sections on the doctrine of God, creation, the Fall, man, ethics, the role of Scripture and the rules for interpreting it, free will, and the resurrection. Not all of the sections have survived into the modern world.

his writings. In his commentary on the Song of Songs, the soul of the Christian was portrayed as the spouse of Christ. Closely related to this was Origen's idea that if the incarnation was to have a positive impact on a person, Jesus must be born in the person through baptism. Then Jesus grows within and will lead the Christian to a virtuous life.

Origen also thought that a total rational explanation of the faith was impossible. Thus he urged Christians to make progress in their spiritual lives by meditating upon the Scriptures. Such spiritual contemplation should give the soul a vision that would enable the believer to live a Christian life. The Christian life in turn tended to purify the soul and that in turn aids in the contemplation of God.

Christian activist

In a word, there was a dynamic dialectic and tension between the ascetic-mystical approach of Origen and his life of Christian witness and activity. In his *Peri Archon* (chapter 3, no. 15, Book Two) Origen argued that the body is a sign of a

Origen and Scripture

It was in Book Four of *Peri Archon* that Origen set forth his exegetical method, one of his important contributions to the church's life. The proper interpretation of Scripture was a driving force in his life and partly explains his work on the *Hexapla*. It suggests why most of his works – commentaries, homilies, and *scholia* – were exegetical in nature. He used all the technical tools of his day in establishing the proper biblical text and was knowledgeable in the exegetical techniques used by Jewish rabbis as well as the allegorical methods used in interpreting Homer and Hesiod.

Origen believed that God dwells in Scripture just as in the Body of Christ.

There could be no worthless word in Scripture. Every word had a meaning, and to find that meaning, Origen engaged in word studies, using the original languages, numerology, and allegory. When he found inconsistencies or difficult problems in Scripture, he left the literal grammatical sense and sought a deeper spiritual meaning (often allegorical) that was Christocentric.

For Origen, Christ was the center of history and the key to understanding the Old Testament. Christ had superseded the laws and ceremonies of the Old Testament, and the literal approach to its meaning had to be changed. Old Testament events, people, rules were really images or reflections of Christ or the Body of Christ, and the allegorical method revealed this truth. The spiritual meaning of Scripture in turn provided the principles and rules that should govern the believer between Christ's appearance in the New Testament and the second coming. Later Origen would be criticized by Methodius and others for his use of the allegorical approach. It is important to note that even in his practical theological works, such as *On Prayer* and *An Exhortation for Martyrdom*, Origen's biblical studies and exegetical method provided the basis for his advice and counsel to the Christian community.

Origen's contact with the Jewish community in Alexandria and later throughout the Near East prompted him to create one of the great monuments of scholarship in the early church, the *Hexapla*, a work twenty-eight years in the making. The *Hexapla* was to provide a valid text of the Old Testament for Christians as they dealt with Jews and heretics. The book consisted of six columns, containing the Hebrew text, the Hebrew text in Greek, the Septuagint, the Greek versions of Aquila, Symmachus, Theodotion, and sometimes three other translations. Only parts of the *Hexapla* have survived into our own day.

Origen did more than try to create a reliable text; he wrote commentaries on John, Matthew, Song of Songs, Romans, Genesis, Psalms, the major and minor prophets, and the Pauline epistles. He wrote hundreds of homilies, some of which were taken down by stenographers as he delivered them. His technical studies of passages of Scripture, the *Scholia*, were available to Jerome in his Bible translation work.

Origen the apologist

At various times in his life Origen had opportunity to defend the faith against the Marcionites, the Valentinians, the Modalists, the Adoptionists, the Docetists, various Chiliasts, and the Gnostics. In these disputes he affirmed free will, the goodness of God, the agreement of the Old Testament with the New Testament, as well as the worthiness of the Old Testament; he defended the personness of the Logos, the eternal generation of the Logos, the true humanity of Christ as necessary for redemption, and the spirituality of God. Yet he was accused of subordinating the Son to the Father, of affirming the preexistence of the soul and the ultimate redemption of all including the devil, and other heresies.

Perhaps this is made more understandable by the fact that many of Origen's works did not survive; thus it is difficult to have a complete and clear picture of what he taught. Moreover, he was one of the first to attempt to bridge the gap between the Graeco-Roman world of thought and the faith so that there could be a meaningful intellectual and personal witness to the former. It is important to remember that Origen was a pioneer blazing spiritual and scholarly trails where none seemed to exist. Those who followed were in debt to him even though they might find a better trail.

Origen is important because his ascetic-vigorous intellectual life stopped heretics, won converts from the pagan world, and provided a foundation for the great ecumenical councils to come and the budding movement of monasticism. As Gregory of Nazianzus, one of his students, aptly wrote of Origen, he is "the stone that sharpens all of us."

Cyprian of Carthage
c. 200-258

Cyprian ranks as the second most important Latin-speaking leader of the church after Tertullian. His ideas strongly influenced Augustine and, through him, all of Western Christendom.

Cyprian wrote almost entirely on practical matters and derived his theology from a mixture of Scripture, Roman law, and pragmatic pastoral decisions. Although he aimed at preserving the faith, he sowed seeds of several doctrinal innovations. He was a strong advocate of church order and discipline and had a high view of the objective power of baptism and the Eucharist. Even though he also held the post of bishop in high esteem, and venerated the historical position of Peter and Paul, he was quite ready to remain totally independent of the bishop of Rome when he believed that bishop was in error.

Cyprian's views gained added weight because he was the first martyr-bishop of the North African churches.

Cyprian (Thascius Caecilius Cyprianus), bishop of Carthage.

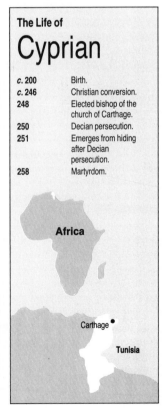

The Life of

Cyprian

c. 200	Birth.
c. 246	Christian conversion.
248	Elected bishop of the church of Carthage.
250	Decian persecution.
251	Emerges from hiding after Decian persecution.
258	Martyrdom.

Africa

Carthage •

Tunisia

Cyprian of Carthage

and the North African Church

Michael A. Smith

Bishop of Carthage

Born at Carthage in North Africa of a well-to-do pagan family about A.D. 200, Thascius Caecilius Cyprianus seems to have had considerable training in rhetoric and law. But we know little about him before his conversion in about 246 through the influence of the presbyter Caecilianus.

As a very young Christian, Cyprian was elected bishop of the church at Carthage in 248. This election was largely due to popular clamor, and Cyprian was opposed by a clique of five presbyters led by Novatus. He himself seems to have been hesitant about accepting the post, but once elected he threw himself enthusiastically into the task of pastoring a church that had become somewhat slack over a long period of peace.

Decian persecution

In 250, the emperor Decius began a systematic empire-wide persecution of Christians in an attempt to revitalize the old values of Rome. All citizens were required to sacrifice to the Roman gods and to hold certificates verifying that they had complied.

The churches in many areas were thrown into confusion. In Carthage, numbers of Christians immediately gave way and went to sacrifice, even before they were threatened. Cyprian himself went into hiding, and during the troubles tried to pastor the church by letters. For this he was censured by some, and they drew damaging comparisons between him and the bishop of Rome, Fabian, who was martyred at the time.

The persecution ended in 251 when Emperor Decius was killed fighting the Goths. Cyprian emerged from hiding to try to reestablish the church in Carthage. Many of those who had denied Christ during the persecution now clamored to be readmitted to the church. Led by Novatus, they demanded a general amnesty. Some of those who had been imprisoned for their faith (the confessors) started to issue letters of pardon to huge numbers of people. Unscrupulous individuals also issued letters of pardon in the name of dead martyrs.

It was with great difficulty that Cyprian restored order. Eventually it was agreed that those who had actually sacrificed to the pagan gods should be readmitted to communion only when dying. Those who had obtained a certificate ("libellus") indicating that they had sacrificed when in fact they had not done so, were to be readmitted after penance. No mercy was to be shown those who evidenced no sign of sorrow for their desertion.

The Novatianists

About this time Cyprian became friendly with the new bishop of Rome, Cornelius (d. 251). He backed Cornelius in his dispute with Novatian over who should be bishop of Rome. Cornelius, like Cyprian, took a middle course with regard to what should be done to those who had lapsed. Cyprian's old enemy Novatus went to Rome and joined forces with Novatian, who had adopted a rigorist position, denying restoration to any who had lapsed. For a time both the lax party and the Novatianists set up rival bishops in Carthage, but their influence was small.

Cyprian gained considerable acclaim when he mobilized the church in 252 to help victims of a plague in Carthage. In the next few years he showed himself to be an able administrator and conscientious pastor.

Problems arising from the Decian persecution still troubled other churches. Cyprian wrote to Stephen, a new bishop of Rome, to enlist his help to depose Marcian of Arles, who had sided with Novatian. At the same time, Cyprian supported the congregations at Leon and Merida in Spain, who had deposed their bishops for denying Christ during the persecutions. The deposed bishops had appealed to Stephen for reinstatement. Cyprian wrote to Stephen to warn him that he had been deceived by them.

Cyprian and Stephen of Rome
Shortly after this, Cyprian clashed with Stephen of Rome. The point at issue was what to do about people who left heretical sects and wanted to become members of the mainstream churches. At Rome, such people were received into membership by having the bishop lay hands on them. In North Africa, and in quite a number of the Eastern churches, there were those who insisted that such people needed to be baptized. Obviously cases could vary. Some individuals were coming out of Gnostic sects that practiced weird baptismal ceremonies, whereas others, like Novatianists, were theologically orthodox and differed from the mainstream churches only on matters of discipline.

Stephen of Rome demanded that Cyprian and the North African churches give up their practice of baptizing heretics who wanted to join the orthodox churches and threatened to break off communion with them. Cyprian retaliated by summoning several councils of North African bishops, who unanimously upheld the North African practice. Cyprian also gained support from other areas. A letter of Firmilian of Caesarea in Cappadocia survives that is highly critical of Stephen and censures him for unnecessarily dividing the unity of the church leaders.

The controversy was left unresolved and fell away on the death of Stephen (257). Cyprian seems to have resumed

The Roman amphitheater, Carthage, Tunisia.

friendly relations with his successor. Many years later a compromise arrangement was reached whereby baptisms were accepted if they were Trinitarian, but otherwise those coming from sects had to be baptized properly.

Cyprian's theology
Cyprian based his theology upon a legalistic reading of the Bible. He was also much influenced by Tertullian. To a certain degree he was charismatic, in that he gave considerable weight to revelations and dreams. A charismatic influence was quite pervasive in North Africa.

Cyprian held a high view of the church, based no doubt on his reading of the Old Testament and his equation of Israel with the church. He taught there was no salvation outside the church: "He cannot have God for his father who has not the Church for his mother." The bishop occupied the position of high priest, and the sacrifice of the new Israel was the Eucharist. Here Cyprian's legal training comes into clear view. He insisted that "everything must be done as Christ did," when he was writing against the practice of using water instead of wine at Communion.

Because of his high view of the church, Cyprian held that there could be no sacraments outside the official churches. He could not imagine a position where there could be several separate but orthodox churches. While believing that Christ's commands to Peter ensured the unity of the church, he also saw this unity taking place in practice through mutual love and acceptance between church leaders.

There are two versions of a crucial passage drawn from his treatise "On the Unity of the Church." In the most widely circulated one, he mentioned, but played down, the position of Peter as the leader of the apostles. In another version he made much more of Peter's primacy. Some scholars have proposed that the second version was a forgery. Others have argued that it was the original version and that Cyprian himself altered it to the more usual version as a result of his dispute with Stephen.

Infant baptism
Cyprian was perhaps the first writer of the Western church to advocate infant baptism. However, he expressly repudiated the idea that baptism is analogous to circumcision and so should be performed on the eighth day after birth. Instead, following Tertullian, he held that infants inherit actual guilt from their parents and in consequence need to be baptized as soon as possible after birth.

Cyprian greatly admired martyrs, confessors, and those who voluntarily accepted celibacy. But he maintained that they should be subject to their local bishops and that their virtues did not give them special powers over against the official leaders of the churches.

In Cyprian's day worship was only slowly beginning to become fixed. He quoted the call "Lift up your Hearts" with its response as being used at worship during his time. People also believed that Christ was actually present in the Communion elements in a quasi-magical way. However, Cyprian's main concern was always that of a lawyer: the "sacrifice" should be performed in the correct way, by a proper minister, within the orbit of a legal church.

Cyprian's views were influential in future generations because of his prestige as a martyr bishop. Both Augustine of Hippo and his Donatist opponents looked upon him as their spiritual father.

Most of his written works were practical (listed in F.L. Cross, *Early Christian Fathers*). He made a collection of Bible texts for refuting Jews and for teaching Christian doctrine and practice (this is an important witness to the North African text of the Bible). His letters were collected soon after his death. There is also a "Life" written by one of his clergy (deacon Pontius) and a contemporary account of his martyrdom.

Athanasius
c. 296-373

In his own lifetime (*c.* 296-373), Athanasius became a legend. His name was synonymous with Nicene orthodoxy, the faith that was to triumph eight years after his death at the first Council of Constantinople (381). Later generations came to regard him as the archetypal representative of the Alexandrian school of theology, even though he himself had done little to develop a distinctive theological outlook.

Athanasius's anti-Arian discourses and related works form the bulk of his literary output. His treatise on the Incarnation, though faulty in places, has remained a classic work on the subject to this day. Moreover, his *Life of St. Antony* is now universally regarded as a classic of the solitary life. In a word, Athanasius left an enduring imprint on the life and thought of the Christian churches.

Athanasius, bishop of Alexandria.

The Life of
Athanasius

c. 296	Birth.
319	Ordained a deacon.
325	Attends Council of Nicea.
328	Elected bishop of Alexandria.
335	Deposed from office.
337	Returns to Alexandria.
339-346	Deposed; lives in Rome.
355	Exiled.
362	Exiled again.
373	Death.

Alexandria

Africa

Athanasius

A Pillar of Orthodoxy

Gerald L. Bray

Bishop of Alexandria

Athanasius was born at Alexandria about A.D.296. As a young man, he was strongly attracted to the hermits of the Egyptian desert, and in later life he did much to popularize their beliefs and way of life. In return, the hermits (or monks, as they came to be called) provided him with a solid base of support in the controversies that dominated his career. Though he was a child of Christian parents, he received the normal classical education of a gentleman. He was ordained deacon in 319 and became the bishop's secretary, accompanying him to the Council of Nicea in the year 325.

In 328 Athanasius was himself elected bishop of Alexandria, an office he occupied until his death forty-six years later. Most of his episcopate was taken up with the struggle to defend the decisions of the Council of Nicea against Arius and especially against those who wanted to work out some kind of compromise with Arius. Athanasius was ordered by the emperor to admit Arians to communion, but he refused and in 335 was deposed from office. Soon afterwards, he was exiled to Trier, but when the emperor Constantine died (337), Athanasius was able to return to his see.

Adversary of Arianism

He was not there long, though, because his many enemies in the church managed to have him deposed and exiled again, and from 339 to 346 he spent most of his time in Rome. His periods of exile in the West had great political importance because he was able to use them to rally Rome and the Latin churches to his cause. In Egypt, his sufferings made him a popular hero and ensured that Arianism would never gain a firm foothold in Alexandria.

Athanasius was eventually allowed to return to his diocese, but in 355 he was exiled again, this time at the instigation of the emperor Constantius II, who, like his father, was trying to accommodate the Arians and their sympathizers. On this occasion, Athanasius went to the monks of the desert, where he had spent much of his youth, and devoted himself to writing. In 362 he returned to Alexandria, only to be exiled again almost immediately, but the following year Athanasius went back permanently and remained until his death in 373.

Athanasius the writer

Athanasius wrote a large number of works, though most of his writing was done during the various periods of exile he endured. He was particularly productive during the last of them, when the solitude of the desert and the tense spiritual and political conditions combined to provide him with an unusual degree of inspiration. His style is lucid and attractive, quite unlike the more literary compositions of his contemporaries, though he lacks their scholarly depth and range. Most of what he had to say was connected in one way or another to the battle against Arianism, in which his skills as a debater were employed to the full.

Apart from a few fragments, only one of his commentaries on the Bible has survived. That is a lengthy exposition of the Psalms, which he relates to the spiritual needs of the believer. Oddly enough, there is no evidence that Athanasius ever wrote a commentary on any part of the New Testament, although his hermeneutical ability is brought out clearly in his writings against Arius.

Against Arius

The anti-Arian discourses and related works are noted for the way in which Athanasius took the favorite proof-texts of the Arians, especially Hebrews 3:2 and

Athanasius wrote a life of Antony, one of the first hermits to settle in the Egyptian desert.

Proverbs 8:22, and demonstrated that they do not mean what the Arians claimed. Athanasius's refutations are all the more remarkable in that he was not adverse to using allegorical methods of exegesis. In particular, he was prone to regard the entire Bible as fundamentally Christological. That put him at a disadvantage in dealing with many Old Testament texts, where a modern exegete would not find any direct reference to Christ at all. But that difficulty did not worry Athanasius unduly. He treated such texts as a special challenge and often used great ingenuity to demonstrate that Arian interpretations, which were also Christological, were basically mistaken.

Another important work is the double treatise *Against the Heathen* and *On the Incarnation*. The second part of that work is often printed separately and is well-known as a classical statement of Alexandrian Christology. It is remarkable in that it is largely free of anti-Arian statements, a fact that has encouraged many scholars to assign an early date to it. The first section is less well-known, but it contains an important refutation of paganism in the traditional style. In particular, Athanasius argued that idolatry and pantheism must be wrong because God and man are distinct essences. However, he accepted the common Greek view that the human soul can have a true knowledge of God in creation, because the soul is a mirror-image of the Logos, or Word of God.

Athanasius and Antony

In addition to those major works, there are a number of sermons and letters extant, as well as the remnants of what seem to have been several treatises on virginity. That interest testifies to Athanasius's well-known ascetic leanings, which are clearly stated in his famous *Life of St. Antony*. Antony (251-356) was a hermit who lived to the remarkable age of 105. He was among the first to seek solitude in the Egyptian desert, where he warred against the spiritual forces of temptation in a way that recalls the wilderness experiences of many biblical figures, including Jesus Himself. Athanasius believed that such a form of spirituality was most to be desired for a truly serious Christian, and he wrote in order to encourage monasticism among the members of the wider church. In that effort he was outstandingly successful.

Because of Athanasius's importance as a symbol of orthodoxy, there are a large number of spurious works to which his name is attached. Most of these subsist today only in fragments, but one is exceptionally famous. This is the so-called Athanasian Creed, or *Quincunque Vult*, a statement of post-Chalcedonian orthodoxy that later generations erroneously attributed to the great bishop of Alexandria. It is a Latin text of *c.* 500, which defined the church's faith for many generations. As a theological statement, it is particularly notable for its endorsement of the double procession of the Holy Spirit, from the Father and the Son (*Filioque*), which makes it the earliest creedal document to do so. For that reason, it was always regarded as spurious in the Eastern church, and today it is no longer widely used, even in the West. The main reason for that is its uncompromising insistence that those who do not hold the orthodox faith are doomed to everlasting damnation, a sentiment that does not appeal to the liberal spirit of our age, though it undoubtedly represents the belief of Athanasius and of the vast majority of Christians in ancient times.

Athanasius's theology

Athanasius was not an original theologian, though his writings have come to be regarded as the essential statement of the Alexandrian position on the key Christological controversies of the time. That can best be understood by saying that both Athanasius and his Arian opponents were indebted to Origen (*c.* 185-254), the greatest and most original theologian of the ancient Greek church. Both sides in the controversy employed the same allegorical techniques in their exegesis of Scripture, and both regarded Origen as the privileged exponent of that method. Where they differed was that Arius emphasized certain aspects of Origen's teaching that appeared to Athanasius and the other leading Alexandrians to contradict the Scriptures and distort the true meaning of Origen's interpretations.

Arius emphasized the Origenist theme

The Roman Porta Nigra, Trier. Athanasius was exiled to Trier in 335/336.

of the unique divinity of the Father, to whom the Son was eternally subordinate. However, the Son's eternal existence was purely relative and looked toward the temporal future only. In the past, claimed Arius, there was a time when the Son had not existed. That went against Origen's teaching that the Son was eternally begotten of the Father, even though Origen had been ready to concede that the Son was in some respects the inferior of the two Persons. Origen had been able to hold that rather curious doctrine because he was fundamentally a Platonist, who believed the differences of name between the Father and Son implied a necessary difference of substance as well. That meant the Father could be God, but not the Son, since the Son had a different name.

Arius, in fact, believed that the Son was a creature, the "first-born of all creation." As a being, He was higher than the angels but lower than God Himself. Furthermore, Arius insisted that inferiority to God was necessary if the Son were to become a man and take on the human sorrows of suffering and death. All the ancients believed that God was impassible. From that Arius concluded that the suffering Savior could not be God. He also believed that only a creature could properly be identified with us, because between the being of God and the existence of man there is no common measure or point of contact.

Athanasius attacked Arianism by saying that Arius had misunderstood Origen (which was true), and that the latter had always insisted that the Son was just as eternal as the Father. To Athanasius, eternity meant equality, and he therefore repudiated the subordinationist streak in the Origenist tradition. That was strictly in line with the decree of the Council of Nicea, which had declared that the Son was consubstantial (*homoousios*) with the Father. The precise meaning of that term became a matter of heated debate when semi-Arian sympathizers like the church historian Eusebius of Caesarea tried to maintain that what Nicaea had meant was that the Son was of a similar substance *(homoiousios)* to the Father but that He was not the same, because He was numerically distinct, and God was One.

The Trinity

To that challenge Athanasius replied that the Persons of the Trinity all shared in the oneness of God, and that they could not be regarded as distinct in substance. The differences between them were expressed in their names, which were not interchangeable. Athanasius lacked the developed doctrine of the Person that would give weight to this idea later on, but his instinct for the scriptural concept of the name was sound, and it was incorporated into later systematic reflection.

In the development of his Christology, Athanasius repudiated the philosophical foundations that had underpinned so much of what both Origen and Arius had said, and moved instead to the biblical concept of redemption as the foundation for a true Christology. Redemption, argued Athanasius, could only come from God, since only God was righteous enough to satisfy the demands of His own justice. For that reason, our salvation could be guaranteed only if God Himself became man and did the impossible (by suffering and dying for us) so that we, too, might do the impossible (become like God).

To that end Athanasius developed a Christology that to a great extent is an extended commentary on John 1:14: "The Word became flesh." His Word-flesh (or in the Greek, *Logos-sarx*) Christology is what is so typical of Alexandrian theology. Its great strength is that it makes the Logos (Word) the subject of the Incarnation; Jesus Christ is God in the flesh, not a glorious or glorified creature, and therefore He can exercise all the prerogatives of divinity, as of right. Its weakness is that it has an understanding of the flesh that is inadequate.

Soul and flesh

For Athanasius, as for most philosophically-trained Greeks of his time, the flesh

Roman baths, Trier, site of Athanasius's exile.

was no more than the physical part of man. It did not include the soul, which was created in the image of the divine Logos. That, however, raised a serious problem. Did Jesus have a human soul in addition to the Logos, or was the Logos equivalent of a soul in Him? The argument is not trivial, because the soul is the seat of sin, and if the sinless Logos has taken its place, then Jesus could not have sinned (which would have made all the temptations meaningless), nor could He have become sin for us.

Athanasius did not actually say whether he believed that Jesus had a human soul or not, but it seems likely that he *did* allow for it, although because it was attached to the Logos it had no independent life of its own. That compromise was unsatisfactory, however, and led to a crisis in Alexandrian Christology shortly after his death. Apollinarius, a pupil of Athanasius, took his master's teaching to its logical conclusion and denied the existence of a human soul in Jesus. He was condemned at a number of synods between 377 and 388, but Alexandrian Christology was thenceforth branded as docetic, because it was supposed to be denying the full humanity of Christ.

In other matters Athanasius was very much a child of his time. He advocated the rebaptism of those who had been baptized by heretics, on the ground that they had been baptized with the wrong intention and in the wrong spirit. He also held a high view of Holy Communion and believed that the Holy Spirit descended into the elements at the moment of invocation (*epiclesis*). That teaching was rejected by the Western church, and especially by the Reformers, but it has been revived in modern times and forms a prominent feature of modern liturgical reforms that seek to recover the spirit of the early church.

Basil the Great
c. 330-379

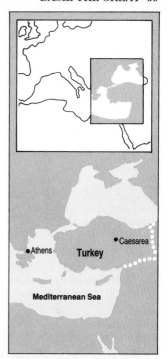

Much of what we now think of as normal monastic life was actually begun by Basil the Great (*c.* 330-379). He was strongly in favor of community life rather than solitary asceticism, pointing out that many of the commands of Christ could only be fulfilled when living with others. He also taught that monks should help each other rather than compete in "holiness." From the start Basil insisted that his communities should be under the control of the local bishop. He limited numbers to manageable proportions (about thirty) and strictly discouraged all excesses of austerity. The monastic system of seven periods of prayer in a day was Basil's invention.

But perhaps Basil's most significant contribution was his plan for his monks to care for the poor and sick. Basil considered it dishonoring to Christ if such people were neglected. In spite of the hostility of many court officials, Basil built large buildings around his church for the work. There was a hospice for strangers, a hospital, special care for lepers, a school, and programs of social help. Interestingly, he did not put in writing a definitive rule like that of Benedict. Basil's example, together with his writings, made sure that his influence on monasticism would be very great.

The Life of
Basil the Great

c. 330	Birth in Caesarea in Cappadocia.
c. 358	Founds small monastic community.
364	Ordained.
370	Becomes bishop.
379	Death.

Basil the Great; fifteenth-century mural from Cyprus by Philip Goul.

Basil the Great

and Eastern Monasticism

Michael A. Smith

Basil in Cappadocia

Basil was born in Caesarea in Cappadocia (not to be confused with the biblical Caesarea in Palestine) in eastern Asia Minor about A.D. 330. He was the first great Christian with a long Christian pedigree. His family had been notable Christians since the evangelization of that area by Gregory the Wonderworker in the middle of the third century, and several of them (grandmother, mother, sister, and two brothers) are venerated as saints in their own right.

Following in the steps of his father of the same name, Basil trained in rhetoric and literature, studying at Constantinople and Athens. While at Athens he met the future emperor Julian and became a life-long friend of Gregory of Nazianzus (330-389). Basil, Gregory of Nazianzus, and Basil's younger brother, Gregory of Nyssa (330-c. 395), are often bracketed together as the Cappadocian Fathers, and were to be very effective in the second part of the struggle against Arianism.

Highly talented, and with a high opinion of himself, the young Basil returned home intent on a career in public life, but his sister Macrina pointed out to him that worldly success was far less important than being right with God. At this point Basil himself came to a living faith. He was baptized and decided to renounce ideas of high office in favor of ascetic life. Basil traveled widely to meet various hermits and holy men of the desert in Egypt, Syria, and Mesopotamia. He was very impressed and vowed to follow their example of devotion to Christ. With his brother Gregory of Nyssa and his friend Gregory of Nazianzus, he sold most of his property and retreated to a remote place in Pontus (northeast Asia Minor) to found a small monastic commune where they could pray and meditate without distraction (c. 358). It was there that they worked out the basic monastic rule that was to become normative for all Eastern monasticism in the future.

Bishop of Caesarea

Basil was not allowed to retreat permanently from public life. The bishop of Caesarea persuaded him to come back to the city, where he became involved in pastoral work. He was ordained in 364 and eventually became bishop of Cappadocian Caesarea in 370.

At that time many of the Eastern churches were under the domination of the state-supported Arianism backed by the emperor Valens. Basil was strongly orthodox and quickly became leader of the orthodox reaction in his part of the Empire. He was on good terms with the aged Athanasius and did much to help many of the Eastern bishops to become less suspicious of the Nicene Creed. Among those who helped at this time were the two Gregories, and also Apollinarius, later to become notorious for his erroneous views concerning the humanity of Christ.

The emperor Valens made several attempts to have Basil removed from his bishopric. He tried to bribe him to tolerate heretical Arian bishops, and, when that failed, Valens sent officials with open threats. Basil felt sufficiently confident to defy the emperor, and such was his power and popularity that Valens did not dare actually to depose him. Basil's popularity was in part due to his many good works. He had organized his monastic community in Caesarea for practical social work, setting up a hospital and also a school, as well as distributing poor-relief. That was a radical departure for monks. The community was well-organized, with carefully planned buildings, for Basil was both a very spiritual man and a highly efficient administrator.

Basil spent much effort trying to heal the split in the church at Antioch. At the beginning of the Arian dispute, the orthodox Christians had formed a separate church under a presbyter, Paulinus. Later, Bishop Meletius had renounced Arianism and had been deposed by Valens, but he had taken with him a large part of the remaining congregation. Paulinus was recognized as bishop by the Western churches, Meletius by the Eastern. Basil tried for a long time to get the bishop of Rome and the other Western bishops to accept Meletius's claim and to arrange some accommodation between him and Paulinus. But in spite of Basil's best efforts, the schism was unresolved at his death. Nevertheless, Basil's efforts helped to unite Eastern and Western church leaders in the struggle against Arianism, which finally began to disintegrate on the death of the emperor Valens in 378.

Basil himself died in 379, just before this triumph of orthodoxy. His friend Gregory of Nazianzus presided at the Council of Constantinople in 381, where the orthodox faith finally triumphed and the Nicene Creed in its present form was accepted.

Hermits and monks

Prior to Basil, the ascetic and monastic life had been very individualistic. Men (and sometimes women) had retreated into the remote deserts to fast and pray, usually living as solitary hermits. In places such as Nitria and Scitis in Egypt there were large groups of hermits, but only in a loose fellowship, perhaps seeing each other only once a week. Many hermits, especially in Syria, practiced all kinds of austerity often verging on sheer masochism.

In reaction to that, Pachomius (*c.* 287-346) had founded communities for ascetics in Egypt, ruled by an abbot. But

A town of cave-dwellings in Cappadocia dating from the early Christian period.

these had often become very large groups, numbering hundreds or thousands. Also, both hermits and monks had had minimal contact with the outside world. Pachomius's monks did support themselves with work such as making and selling palm mats, but their prime aim was to seek God for themselves. Both monks and hermits were totally separate from the normal life of the church and often hostile to it. On the contrary, Basil strongly favored community life rather than solitary asceticism.

Like many of the early monastic pioneers, Basil believed that with human effort it was possible for a Christian fully to follow the law of Christ. Also, he tended to have a low view of the body and considered it as merely a prison for the soul. Both those attitudes were widespread in the Eastern churches in his time, however. Basil was only a man of his time in holding them.

Unlike some of his contemporaries, Basil saw considerable use in the pagan literature of his day. He commended studying it, both for the expertise in expression that it would give and also for the examples of virtue that it provided. Although there is no evidence that he ever considered manuscript copying as part of his monks' work, he would have been in full agreement with Cassiodorus, who introduced that into the work schedule of his monks in Vivarium in southern Italy in the early sixth century.

Basil's writings

Basil produced a considerable number of works that survive. He wrote against Arianism and also on the doctrine of the Holy Spirit (there was some dispute over the deity of the Spirit in the Nicene Creed). He wrote a work to explain how young men could make profitable use of pagan literature, and a considerable number of his sermons survive (there is doubt over the genuineness of some). His ascetic writings consist of two "rules" that are in a series of questions and answers about the duties and virtues of a monk. Basil is also credited with reforms

of the liturgy, and a "liturgy of St. Basil" is still used occasionally by the Orthodox churches of the East. However, in its present form it is much later than the time of Basil. His collected letters number more than 350.

In spite of all his learning and ability, Basil was a humble man before God. He taught that it was quite impossible to have a full knowledge of God and that we only have real knowledge of God through His working with us. God's essential being is far beyond our understanding.

Unlike many of his contemporaries, Basil was mainly concerned with practical Christian life rather than speculative theology. In that he differed greatly even from Gregory of Nazianzus and Gregory of Nyssa, who were abler theologians but very bad at the practical business of running churches. As leader of the "Cappadocian Fathers," Basil was largely instrumental in the final demise of eastern Arianism and in setting the path for the best of Eastern monasticism.

The First Monks

It was not until the late third or early fourth century that the first ascetic Christian monks began to appear. With the general acceptance of Christianity in the Roman Empire, persecution decreased, and membership of the church increased. Some men felt there was too much laxity in the church and believed they should withdraw from the world and try to reach a purer form of Christianity in solitude.

The first monks appeared in the deserts of Egypt and Syria, the most famous of them being Antony (*c.* 256-356), a Coptic peasant from Egypt. He was soon followed by many other hermits, who lived alone or in small groups on the fringes of the desert. They spent their time in prayer and meditation, often fasting for days on end. These early monks were celibate, and sometimes they went to such extremes as living on the tops of pillars or walling themselves up.

Pachomius

The first monastic community seems to date from *c.* A.D. 320 when Pachomius founded a monastery at Tabennisi, on the river Nile. He resisted extreme asceticism; his community had regular meals and worship and was self-supporting. Under his "rule," or pattern for organizing a monastery, the monks had to hand over their money to a common fund. Although his earliest communities were for men, Pachomius later founded women's communities.

It was travelers such as Jerome and Athanasius who first brought monasticism to the West. Athanasius (see p.63) spent part of his exile concealed among the Egyptian hermits and wrote a life of Antony that helped introduce the monastic ideal to Western leaders, such as Ambrose and Augustine of Hippo.

Basil the Great

Basil the Great (see p.69) was the most important figure in Eastern monasticism. After visiting many ascetic communities, he established his own monastery, with the aid of Gregory of Nazianzus. Basil bound the monks closer to the church and emphasized that the local bishop should have overall authority. He also encouraged a more outward-looking approach, with an emphasis on medical care, poor relief and education for the surrounding population. He opposed excessively individualistic piety and set down a pattern of seven set

The Monastery of St Catherine, Sinai, dates from the sixth century A.D.

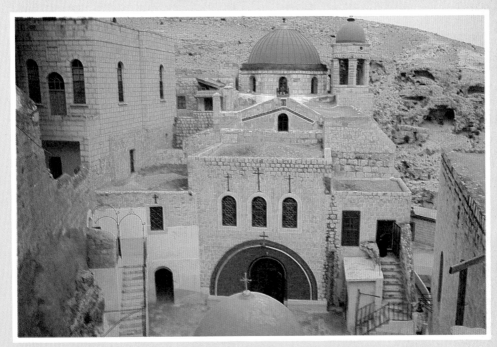

The Monastery of St Sabas (Mar Saba) in the Judean mountains, founded by Sabas in A.D. 492.

periods of prayer daily. Basil's monastic ideals were set down in the rules, which remain broadly the basis for Eastern monasticism today.

Monasticism was stimulated in the West by Martin of Tours and later by John Cassian. Martin's example of the solitary hermit's life attracted others to join him, and he eventually set up a monastery at Marmoutier as a centre from which to evangelize rural France. A life of Martin served to attract many more men to the monastic life.

Augustine

Augustine of Hippo (see p. 85) made another innovation in monastic organization when he returned to North Africa in 388. He formed a group of friends into an ascetic community that continued after he became bishop of Hippo in 395 and that became the pattern for the medieval cathedral "chapter," the bishop's "family" of subordinate clergymen and ordinands.

The great writer in the West on monasticism at that time was John Cassian, whose detailed instructions for the monastic life helped popularize the movement.

Cassiodorus (490-583), formerly a courtier to Theodoric the Great, later retired to the monastery of Vivarium in southern Italy, where he introduced a new emphasis on the copying of manuscripts and the study of ancient writings. This helped ensure the transmission of Greco-Roman culture to the Middle Ages.

The Rule of Benedict

During the fifth and sixth centuries monastic rules multiplied, but all were overshadowed by the Rule of Benedict, which first appeared c. 540. Benedict was born at Nursia in northern Italy, c. 480, and founded several monasteries before finally moving to Monte Cassino, where he died c. 547. He wrote his rule during his first years as a monk, and it was later popularized by Gregory the Great in his life of Gregory. Benedict's rule stressed two activities, work and prayer, and insisted that a monk stay in the same monastic house and obey his abbot.

Celtic monasticism

Celtic monasticism probably began in the late fifth century. It seems to have been similar in form to the Egyptian pattern, and may have been brought to Ireland by Ninian (c. 397), who had set up a monastery at Whithorn in Scotland. The Irish monks stressed extreme asceticism and scholarship, and their monasteries made a major contribution to church life in tribal Ireland, with the abbot having a superior position to the bishop. The wandering Irish monks, and particularly Columba (see p.99) and Columbanus, later helped found many great monasteries in Europe, including Luxeuil, St. Gall, and Bobbio.

Opposite: Good Friday in the old city of Jerusalem.

Timechart 300-600

Church Leaders

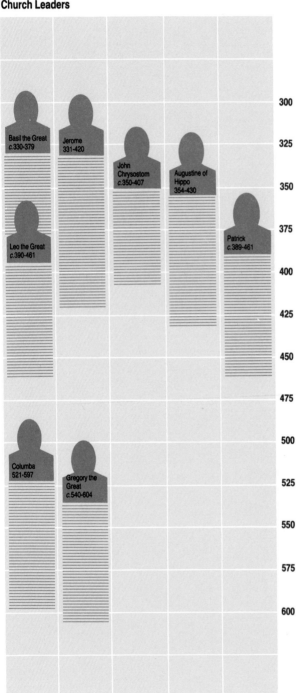

Basil the Great
c.330-379

Jerome
331-420

John Chrysostom
c.350-407

Augustine of Hippo
354-430

Leo the Great
c.390-461

Patrick
c.389-461

Columba
521-597

Gregory the Great
c.540-604

Major events

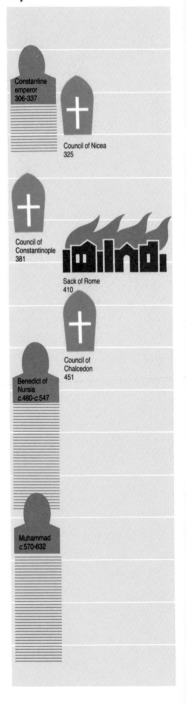

300

325

350

375

400

425

450

475

500

525

550

575

600

Constantine emperor
306-337

Council of Nicea
325

Council of Constantinople
381

Sack of Rome
410

Council of Chalcedon
451

Benedict of Nursia
c.480-c.547

Muhammad
c.570-632

Jerome
331-420

Jerome was the most learned man in the Latin-speaking church of the late fourth century. He made two major contributions to the religious history of the Christian West: the Latin translation of the Bible, known as the Vulgate, and the promotion of monasticism. There had been Latin translations of the Bible since the second century, but they were poor in style, colloquial in language, and, for the Old Testament, based on the Greek version and not the Hebrew. Jerome's wide reading and brilliant linguistic gifts equipped him to be one of the most successful Bible translators of all times.

Not disposed toward original theological thought, Jerome encouraged the popular

Catholicism that was developing in his time. Monasticism had begun in Egypt in the early fourth century but was still little accepted in most parts of the West when Jerome became an earnest advocate of asceticism. His writings and his influence on pious women spread the monastic ideal to the West and among women.

Jerome was a man of intense friendship and fierce enmities. His retentive memory extended beyond books to affronts (real and imagined). His sensitive

disposition was easily offended. This personality, plus his desire to appear orthodox, led him into a series of controversies in which he displayed his satirical and polemical skills. He defended virginity, monasticism, and the cult of the saints, and he attacked Origenism and Pelagianism.

Jerome has been recognized by the Roman Catholic church as one of its four great doctors who wrote in Latin, along with Augustine, Ambrose, and Gregory the Great.

Statue of Jerome, Church of St Catherine, Bethlehem.

The Life of
Jerome

331	Birth.
342	Begins studies in Rome.
372	Departs for Antioch.
374-377	Stays in the desert of Chalcis as a hermit.
c. 378	Ordained presbyter in Antioch.
381	Second Ecumenical Council, Constantinople.
382-385	Secretary to Bishop Damasus in Rome.
386	Settles in Bethlehem and establishes monastery.
393-410	Controversy over Origenism.
406	Completes his work on the Vulgate.
410	Sack of Rome by the Goths under Alaric.
420	Death.

Jerome

Biblical Scholar

Everett Ferguson

Jerome in Antioch

Jerome was born in A.D. 331 at Stridon, a town in northeast Italy. His well-to-do parents sent him to Rome to study grammar and rhetoric. During his advanced student days in Rome he was baptized. He read widely from the Latin classics and began collecting an excellent library. After a stay at Trier in Germany, during which he added Christian theological books to his reading, Jerome felt the call to the asceticism that was coming to be considered the highest form of the Christian life. He became part of an ascetic group at Aquileia in Italy; but his sharp tongue, lack of tact, and passionate temperament made him difficult to get along with for extended periods of time, and the group soon broke up.

Jerome set out for Palestine in late 372, but reached no farther than Antioch. There he improved his knowledge of Greek but began to feel the profound tension between his intellectual interests and his ascetic aspirations. In a dream, the Lord told him, "You are a Ciceronian, not a Christian" (*Epistle* 22:30). He resolved not to study pagan literature (a promise kept for a decade) and went into the Syrian desert near Chalcis to become a hermit. Sensual desires continued to preoccupy him, and in spite of severe disciplines he dreamed about the dancing girls in Rome (*Epistle* 22:7). With the aid of a Jewish convert, Jerome began the study of Hebrew, of which he would eventually gain a mastery unequalled among Christians of his time. Jerome was never accepted too well by the other hermits in the area, so he returned to Antioch, where he was ordained a presbyter.

Following a stay in Constantinople, Jerome was back in Rome from 382 to 385.

The bishop of Rome, Damasus, set him to work preparing a new Latin translation of the gospels and Psalms. Jerome had found the life's work that was to be his chief service to Western civilization. Working off and on for the next twenty-two years on the Bible translation, he was eventually to complete the entire Old Testament as well.

While in Rome Jerome became the spiritual guide and Bible teacher to groups of wealthy, aristocratic widows, led by Marcella, Paula, and the latter's daughter Eustochium. But Jerome's advocacy of asceticism, his influence with prominent women, and sharp criticisms of a worldly church led the clergy of Rome to request him to leave.

After visiting the Holy Places of Palestine, Jerome and Paula settled in Bethlehem in 386 and established separate monasteries for men and women. This began a fruitful period of study and writing, interrupted by frequent illness and a series of personal and literary controversies. Jerome finally fashioned a form of ascetic life that combined his ideals of withdrawal with his needs for companionship and intellectual activity.

The Vulgate

During his Bethlehem years, Jerome became settled in his conviction that translations of the Old Testament must be based on the Hebrew and not the Greek. Not completed until 405/406, his Latin version of the Bible was to be his crowning achievement. By the end of the sixth century, his version was being used equally with the old Latin, and in the eighth and ninth centuries it came fully into its own. Since the thirteenth century it has been known as the Vulgate, that is, the common version. The fourteenth-century English translation by John Wyclif and the sixteenth-century Douay Version were made from the Vulgate.

The acceptance of the Hebrew as the standard text meant also the recognition of the Hebrew canon of the Old Testament. As a result Jerome rejected the apocryphal books that were being circulated in manuscripts of the Greek and Latin versions. In general Jerome had a low opinion of books in the Apocrypha. He did eventually translate Tobit, Judith, and the additions to Daniel and Esther, but rapidly and without much care. The interest in the Hebrew text and contact with Jewish scholars prompted Jerome to take an interest also in Jewish exegetical traditions, and some information from Jewish sources was incorporated into his biblical commentaries.

Jerome produced other translations of works from Greek into Latin. His theory of translation was to render sense for sense and not word for word (*Epistle* 57:5, 10). He professed to be more literal in dealing with Scripture, but in practice was not especially literal even there. In support of paraphrase he appealed to the apostles' use of the Old Testament and the practices of the Greek translators of the Old Testament.

Jerome the writer

Jerome is remembered as a literary man. He hoped to be a Christian Cicero, a teacher and model of a comprehensive Christian culture; but at the same time a holy ascetic. The tension between these ideals reached to the root of his being, drove him to relentless work, and perhaps accounted for some of the contradictions in his character.

The 150 letters in his collected correspondence provide much of the available information on his life and also rich data for the social history of the time. The letters range in content from personal affairs to doctrinal topics, often amounting to treatises. Jerome's *Lives of Illustrious Men* was the first history of Christian literature. It was written to show pagans that Christians had produced distinguished literature. It discusses 135 authors from Peter to himself. Jerome's most polished productions were his lives

The basilica, Aquileia, Italy. For a time Jerome belonged to an ascetic group here.

of monks, written to promote the ascetic ideal–the *Life of Paul the Hermit* (the historical core of which may be nothing more than the name of the hero), *Life of Malchus* (a brilliant example of his flair for story-telling), and *Life of Hilarion.*

Commentaries and controversies

Jerome's commentaries were the least original of his works, for he borrowed wholesale, often without acknowledgment, from earlier Greek commentators, especially Origen. His early commentaries show a predominance of allegorical interpretation, but the later commentaries contain more historical and philological exposition. His faults were working too rapidly and relying too much on his memory.

Jerome was drawn into a series of controversies, and many of his surviving works are polemical. An early controversy with Helvidius concerned the perpetual virginity of Mary. Although Helvidius had the best of the argument exegetically, Jerome's defense of the virginity of Mary after the birth of Jesus shaped the Mariology of the Latin church and Western Christian sexual ethics until the Renaissance. Jerome's attitude so exalted virginity that he considered the benefit of marriage to be that it brings virgins into the world (*Epistle* 22:20).

Similar themes recur in the treatise *Against Jovinian*, an ascetic who had given up extreme practices and wrote against the monastic life. This is Jerome's most exaggerated but most skillful polemical work. Jerome's characteristic claim was that "eating meat, drinking wine, having a well-fed stomach – there you have the seed-bed of lust" (*Against Jovinian* 2:7). Jerome's own sarcastic reply to the charge that he was against wedlock was, "I should like every one to take a wife who, because of the terrors of the night, is afraid to sleep alone" (*Epistle* 50:5). When Vigilantius attacked the cult of the martyrs, Jerome outdid himself in heaping abuse on the critics in his *Against Vigilantius.*

Jerome and Origen

The longest running and most bitterly personal controversy was with Rufinus, friend of his youth, on the orthodoxy of Origen. Jerome, like others, had made considerable use of Origen in his commentaries and other works. The late fourth century saw a long, smouldering antagonism in the church toward Origen burst into a fire of criticism, kindled by Epiphanius, bishop of Salamis on Cyprus, and fanned by Theophilus, bishop of Alexandria.

Jerome had restricted his admiration for Origen to his exegesis and not to his theological speculations. Always jealous of his reputation for orthodoxy, but with a literary man's distaste for theological thought, Jerome quickly joined in the condemnation of Origen. Rufinus refused to denounce one to whom he was so indebted and appealed to Jerome's principles of translation in order to justify his own free rendering of Origen's *On First Principles*, which was aimed at making Origen's theology more consistent with fourth-century standards. Jerome reacted furiously (*Apology Against Rufinus*). He was always impatient with those who did what Rufinus did: plagiarizing, exaggerating, and adapting the story to suit his position.

The arrival of Pelagius in Palestine led Jerome in 415 to write *Dialogue Against the Pelagians*, the last controversy to occupy his pen. Jerome particularly objected to Pelagius's claim that Christians can live without sin and to his limited definition of grace. Augustine had converted Jerome to the doctrine of original sin.

Jerome's brilliant satires and fierce polemics leave his personal failings for all to see: partiality, pettiness, unfairness, vanity, and a carelessness that impaired his erudition. His vitriolic personality has been overlooked in deference to his literary virtuosity. Even with his considerable personal failings, he made incalculable contributions to Western Christendom with his Bible translations, commentaries, and other scholarly works.

John Chrysostom
*c.*350-407

The golden age of the church Fathers in the fourth and fifth centuries witnessed many fine preachers, but none so gifted as John, who was a priest at Antioch and bishop at Constantinople. His eloquence later earned him the title "Chrysostomos," "golden-mouthed." He counts among the greatest preachers in the whole history of the church.

For twelve years (386-397) John occupied the leading pulpit in Antioch. His sermons were marked by directness and vigorous simplicity. He excelled in moral and spiritual teaching rather than doctrinal exposition, and he followed the Antiochene tradition of interpreting the Scriptures in their natural meaning rather than allegorically.

He preached right through many of the books of the Bible.

His episcopate at Constantinople exposed the sordidness of ecclesiastical politics in the later Roman Empire, when Christian emperors and empresses reigned. Corruption flourished on all sides. John's reforming zeal and uncompromising tongue fell foul of churchmen and court alike, and he ended his life a persecuted exile in the northeast of modern Turkey.

John Chrysostom; fifteenth-century mural from Cyprus by Philip Goul.

The Life of
Chrysostom

c. 350	Birth at Antioch.
c. 365	Studies rhetoric under Libanius.
c. 367	Baptized.
c. 368-370	Attached to Bishop Meletius; studies in ascetic school under Diodore.
370s	Lives as monk and hermit in mountains.
381	Ordained deacon by Meletius.
386	Ordained priest by Bishop Flavian.
386-397	Preaches in main church of Antioch.
387	Affair of "the statues."
398	Consecrated bishop (patriarch) of Constantinople.
403	Deposed by Synod of the Oak; exiled but soon recalled.
404	Exiled to Armenia.
407	Banished to remote Black Sea, but dies on route at Comana in Pontus (September 14).
438	Remains returned for burial in Constantinople.

John Chrysostom

Master Preacher

David F. Wright

John of Antioch

Antioch in Syria was one of the earliest centers of Christianity. It was there that John Chrysostom was born, sometime between A.D. 344 and 354. (All the dates in his life prior to 381 are uncertain.) His father died when he was an infant, but his mother, Anthusa, was both godly and strongminded, and she resolutely devoted herself to his spiritual nurture and general education. (A prominent pagan was provoked to comment: "Good heavens! What women these Christians have!") He studied philosophy under Andragathius, but far more important was his instruction in rhetoric from the world-famous teacher Libanius – who remained a decided pagan. It was intended that John become a lawyer. He rapidly made his mark as an effective public speaker.

When he was about eighteen, John was baptized by Meletius, bishop of Antioch (361-381). The ascetic life attracted him, and from then on he gave himself to the service of Christ and His church. Meletius soon made him a reader (lector), and he studied for a few years in a kind of monastic school under Diodore, an influential teacher and later bishop of Tarsus (378-*c.* 390). A fellow-student was Theodore, later to become an outstanding biblical commentator and bishop of Mopsuestia (392-428). From Diodore they learned the distinctive Antiochene respect for the literal interpretation of the Bible, that is, for the grammatical or historical sense intended by the biblical writers, not the subtle allegorical or spiritualizing meanings favored by Alexandrian interpreters.

The death of his mother had by then, it seems, set John free to pursue the path of monastic solitude, like so many Christians in the East. For much of the 370s he lived as a hermit in the hills outside Antioch, at first apprenticed to a senior abba (master or father) of the ascetic way, and then totally alone. He wrote treatises about monasticism, carried on studying the Scriptures, and inflicted permanent damage on his health.

Bishop of Antioch

On his enforced return to Antioch, Meletius ordained him deacon (381), and five years later Flavian, his successor as bishop (381-404), made him priest. Probably written soon after 386 were his little book on the Christian nurture of the young and his work *The Priesthood*, which is perhaps his best-known writing. Both are marked by profound wisdom, and the latter set the highest standards for the ministry he had recently begun.

John was a supreme preacher. For twelve years in Antioch's principal church he taught and applied the Scriptures. During that period, he delivered long series of expositions on books of the Bible – Genesis (67 homilies), Matthew (90), John (88), Romans (32), 1 and 2 Corinthians (74), as well as shorter series on other books and on more topical issues.

The preacher's power to master the volatile people of Antioch was dramatically demonstrated during Lent in 387. A new imperial tax had provoked rioting, bloodshed, and the desecration of statues of the emperor Theodosius I and his family. Order was soon restored, executions began, and the city awaited with dread the emperor's vengeance. While Bishop Flavian was sent to intercede, John preached some twenty sermons *On the*

Statues. He had to comfort and inspire, if only with a contempt for death, a populace that was partly panicking, partly despairing, and above all paralyzed with fear. "Though such a crowd had come together, the silence was as deep as though not a single person had been present."

John the preacher
Yet they could not be spared the salutary correction of well-deserved rebuke, and Chrysostom's preaching, fulfilling almost the role of the media in the tense situation, moved easily between the fearsome trials in the city and "that other dreadful judgment-seat." When, by Easter, Flavian's persuasiveness and the irresistible sanctity of a band of hermits from the hills had wrung an amnesty from the emperor, John urged the people to light not only torches of celebration but "the true light of good works as the adornment of your soul." It was a remarkable tour-de-force of prophetic preaching.

Bishop of Constantinople
Such was Antioch's veneration for Chrysostom that when he was chosen to be bishop of Constantinople, he had to be virtually hijacked from the city. The capital was a very different world. John was the choice of Eutropius, the agent of Emperor Arcadius. The previous bishop had been an ineffective establishment figure, and John found a crying need for reform among clergy, monks and nuns, and prominent laity alike. His rejection of the lifestyle of a court-bishop made him popular with the Christian rank and file, but his disciplinary zeal and his denunciation of extravagance and vice in high places made him numerous enemies, including Empress Eudoxia. He was in part his own worst enemy; he lacked the conciliatory touch and quickly became obstinate.

He spearheaded a forceful mission to the increasing Gothic population in the city, without tolerating their Arianism. His absence in Ephesus in early 401 (to restore order in the church under a new bishop) allowed his opponents to gain

The old quarter of Antioch, eastern Turkey.

ground, headed by an unholy episcopal trio Severian of Gabala, Antiochus of Ptolemais, and Acacius of Berea. Bishop Theophilus of Alexandria (385-412) joined in. The two sees were old rivals, and Theophilus had consecrated John in 398 with some embarrassment. Some monks who had fled from his rough justice in Alexandria received, in his view, outrageous consideration from John in the capital. So when Theophilus was summoned to Constantinople in 403 to answer their charges, he came with a phalanx of Egyptian bishops in support. Teaming up with the other malcontents in the city, they staged their own synod at the Oak, near Chalcedon across the Bosphorus, and deposed Chrysostom (who refused to attend, despite an imperial order). Most of his alleged offenses reflected grudges against his austere life-style and disciplinary harshness. In the face of popular protest, Arcadius exiled him to Praenetum on the other side of the Bosphorus.

Within days, however, the wheel came round full circle. Fears of a mass uprising and alarm caused by an earthquake induced even Eudoxia to plead for Chrysostom's recall. He returned in triumph, Theophilus fled with his tail between his legs, and the Synod of the Oak was annulled.

Second exile

Agitation against Chrysostom soon resumed. He was supposed to have likened Eudoxia to Herodias, who had demanded the head of another John. At first he defied the emperor's order of deposition. At the Easter baptisms in 404, imperial troops burst in and stained the waters with blood. The "Joannites," as his supporters were called, began to be victimized, and even John himself was sent packing to a settlement named Cucusus in the Taurus mountains in Armenia.

All his extant letters, more than 230, come from his final exile. Dogged by ill-health, pursued by his enemies, imperiled by marauding robber-bands, he nevertheless had some consolations. "His place of exile became a veritable place of pilgrimage," especially for Christians from Antioch. He was, therefore, ordered to Pityus, on the remote northeast coast of the Black Sea. But on the way, in the heat of the summer of 407, still cruelly treated, he died at Comana in Pontus. The date was September 14, and his death was virtually a martyrdom.

Posthumous vindication came in due course. Pope Innocent I of Rome (402-417) had taken up his cause, even breaking off communion with the bishops of Constantinople, Antioch, and Alexandria. Over a period of years they relented one by one and inserted Chrysostom's name into the diptychs, or the lists of Christians remembered in the prayer liturgy. Finally, in 438, his remains were fetched from Comana and reburied in the Church of the Apostles in Constantinople. Theodosius II, the son of Arcadius and Eudoxia, paid his respects and pled for mercy for his guilty parents.

Chrysostom's strength did not lie in theological controversy, but he backed the orthodox faith of Nicaea against Arianism. Like a true Antiochene he affirmed the two perfect natures of divinity and humanity in the incarnate Christ. (He never called Mary *theotokos*, "Godbearer," and Thomas Aquinas found his low view of Mary offensive.) He had a weak notion of original sin, like many Eastern churchmen, and his teaching on the Eucharist reflected the increasing prominence of sacrificial ideas.

John's sermons

His fame rests securely on his preaching ministry. More than 600 sermons and homilies survive, in a total corpus of works larger than any other Greek Father's. Many of them can still be read as sermons today. Most would have lasted an hour or more, as he worked his way, not very systematically, through a biblical passage. He taught chiefly about the Christian life, like a pastor of souls. His rhetorical skills were normally well under control, and his preaching engaged closely with his hearers, sometimes almost in dialogue with them. Occasionally they broke out into spontaneous applause. He combined the purity of Attic Greek with an abundant vocabulary and drew with easy familiarity on the broad expanse of the Scriptures. He could be intemperate, as in his violent invectives against the Jews, but in the main he instructed the Christian populace about their daily concerns. "I treat of so many things in each of my sermons and make them so varied because I want everybody to find something special in it and not go home empty-handed." He reserved some of his sharpest criticisms for the careless and greedy rich. The inequalities of wealth and poverty in Antioch offended his social conscience: "The world is meant to be like a household, wherein all the servants receive equal allowances, for all men are equal, since they are brothers."

For all his gifts and popularity, Chrysostom held no conceit about his preaching ministry. "My work is like that of a man who is trying to clean a piece of ground into which a muddy stream is constantly flowing." The realism and simplicity of this comment well reveal the man.

Augustine of Hippo
354-430

For Protestants, Augustine (354-430) is the dominant figure in the history of Christian thought between the close of the New Testament canon and the Reformation. For Roman Catholics, Augustine's influence during this period is rivaled only by that of Thomas Aquinas (1225-1274). Augustine is only slightly less important in the history of philosophy, where he is easily the major philosopher between Plotinus (third century) and Aquinas.

Augustine was the last major thinker of the ancient world and the first philosopher and theologian of the Middle Ages. His work is still a model for those Christian thinkers who would use Platonism as a framework for their Christian world and life view. Many ideas that received emphasis in the work of the Protestant Reformers were anticipated by Augustine. But his views of the church and the sacraments played a role in the development of doctrines that are distinctly Roman Catholic. Among the areas of Christian thought where Augustine's ideas are still much studied are the relationship between faith and reason, the problem of evil, divine grace and predestination, the doctrine of the Trinity, and philosophy of history.

The Life of
Augustine

354	Birth in North Africa.
371	Makes his first visit to Carthage.
372	Takes a mistress.
373	Augustine's son, Adeodatus, is born; Augustine begins a nine-year attachment to Manichaeaism (or Manichaeanism).
383	Crosses the sea to Rome with his mistress and son.
384	Assumes the post of public orator at Milan. Separates from his mistress.
386	Converted. Writes the first of his extant books, including *Against the Skeptics* and *Soliloquies*.
387	Baptized in Milan.
388	Returns to North Africa.
391	Ordained as a priest.
395	Consecrated as bishop of Hippo Regius.
400	Completes his *Confessions*.
410	Rome is sacked.
413	Begins writing *The City of God*.
430	Dies during the Vandals' siege of Hippo Regius.

Augustine of Hippo, from a medieval manuscript.

Augustine of Hippo

Philosopher and Theologian

Ronald H. Nash

Opposite: Augustine of Hippo; fourteenth-century Italian painting by Pacino di Buonaguida.

Augustine's youth

Augustine's life is an important key to understanding his thought. He was born in A.D.354 in what is now Algeria. Centuries before, Augustine's homeland had been a part of the great Carthaginian Empire that almost conquered Rome. After Carthage was itself defeated by Rome, it became romanized in culture and language. Augustine's father, Patricius, was not a Christian and had relatively little influence on him. But his mother, Monica, was a devout Christian and played an important role in his life, even during the years when he rejected her Christianity.

From the time of his first visit to the great city of Carthage, when he was about sixteen, Augustine seldom lost an opportunity to pursue one sin or another; or so he tells us in his *Confessions*. He took a mistress (the polite term is concubine) when he was seventeen or eighteen and fathered an illegitimate son before he was twenty. About that same time, he began a relationship with a religious and philosophical system known as Manichaeism, which claimed that two principles, Light and Dark, God and Matter, are eternal. Manichaeism appealed to Augustine intellectually because it appeared to offer a superior answer to the problem of evil than he could find in his mother's Christianity. Augustine was also drawn to Manichaeism because it made fewer moral demands than Christianity. He could be a good Manichaean and continue to live as he pleased.

During his late twenties, Augustine began to have serious doubts about Manichaeism. He was especially disappointed by the inability of Manichaean leaders to answer his questions. In 383 Augustine crossed the Mediterranean to Rome with his mistress and son where he planned to teach rhetoric. But because his students were often delinquent in paying his fees, he left Rome for Milan in 384 for the more secure position of public orator. There Augustine became friendly with Ambrose, the bishop of Milan, who helped him to see that many of his objections to Christianity were based on misconceptions of the faith.

Augustine the skeptic

By that time Augustine had rejected Manichaeism for a brief fling as a skeptic. His experiment with skepticism was followed by another brief period in which he studied the writings of certain "Platonists," including perhaps some books by the great Neo-Platonist Plotinus. Augustine's study of that late version of Platonism helped remove many of the remaining intellectual obstacles to his becoming a Christian. For one thing, the Platonists taught him how evil could exist in a world that depended for its existence on one good God. One by one, Augustine found that his assorted intellectual, moral, and spiritual objections to Christianity had been stripped away. In 386, in a villa outside of Rome, he underwent one of the more dramatic conversions in the history of the Christian church (recorded in *Confessions*, book 8). After hearing a voice say, "Take up and read; Take up and read," Augustine recounts he picked up "the volume of the Apostle":

"I seized it and opened it, and in silence I read the first passage on which my eyes

Remains of Roman Ostia, where Augustine had a remarkable vision.

fell. 'No orgies or drunkenness, no immorality or indecency, no fighting or jealousy. Take up the weapons of the Lord Jesus Christ; and stop giving attention to your sinful nature, to satisfy its desires.' I had no wish to read more and no need to do so. For in an instant, as I came to the end of the sentence, it was as though the light of faith flooded into my heart and all the darkness of doubt was dispelled."

By this time Augustine had separated from his mistress, who had returned to North Africa leaving their son, Adeodatus, with him. After being baptized in 387, Augustine determined to return to North Africa with his son and Monica, who had joined him. Augustine and Monica shared a remarkable vision in Ostia, the seaport to Rome, shortly before Monica died at the age of fifty-six. Augustine and Adeodatus continued their journey back to North Africa, where Adeodatus, his promising and much-loved son, died.

In the years that followed his conversion, Augustine studied philosophy, theology, and the Scriptures and wrote a number of short books including *Against the Skeptics, On the Happy Life*, and *Soliloquies*. His growing commitment to a religious vocation led to his ordination in 391. Four years later he was consecrated bishop of Hippo Regius.

The Confessions

Augustine completed what many regard as his greatest book, *The Confessions*, in 400. In spite of the details that the book provides about his life prior to 387, it would be a mistake to view it as an autobiography. Augustine was less interested that readers knew the specifics of his life than that they understood the moral, intellectual, and spiritual struggles he went through in his search for the truth about God and himself. Augustine used the word *confession* in two senses: to acknowledge his many sins but, more important, to glorify the God who had delivered him from his sins.

The immediate occasion that led Augustine to begin writing *The City of God* (written between 413 and 427) was the sack of Rome by Alaric, king of the Visigoths, in 410. Non-Christians throughout the Roman Empire blamed Rome's disaster on its turning from its pagan deities to Christianity. Augustine began *The City of God* for the express purpose of answering such charges. Before he was finished, however, he found himself involved in discussions of numerous other topics, including what amounted to a Christian philosophy of history. The first ten books of *The City of God* contain Augustine's answers to the pagan accusations as well as much important information about the late Roman Empire. The most interesting passages occur in the last half of the work (books 11 through 22), where he turns to the major theme of his study, the existence within the world of two cities or societies – the City of God and the City of Man. The two cities will coexist throughout human history. Only at the final judgment and the end of human history will the two cities finally be separated so that they may share their appropriate destinies – heaven and hell.

Versus the Manichaeans

Augustine's many other writings included a long and influential study of the Trinity, as well as numerous works against the Manichaeans, the Donatists, and the Pelagians. Augustine's personal acquaintance with Manichaeaism led him to reflect on two great problems: the relationship between faith and reason and the problem of evil. The Manichaeans had ridiculed faith as an activity unworthy of any cultured and educated person. Never take anything on faith, they taught; trust only what you know by reason. Augustine defended the faith against this kind of attack. For him, faith is not inferior to reason; true faith never conflicts with reason. In fact, faith is an indispensable step in any act of knowledge, a point Augustine expressed in the now famous phrase *Credo ut intelligam*: I believe in order that I may know. All knowledge begins in faith. Faith is not unique to religion. Rather, it is an indispensable element in every act of knowing.

The Manichaean "solution" to the problem of evil prompted many, including the young Augustine, to regard their view as superior to Christianity. Christianity teaches that all reality is created by one true God. If this is so, and God is both good and all-powerful, as Christians claimed, why does evil exist? Manichaeaism explained the existence of good and evil as the unavoidable product of a never-ending struggle between two coequal and coeternal deities, one good and the other evil. Evil exists because the good god (Light) is powerless to defeat the evil god (Darkness). Eventually, Augustine came to see that this kind of dualism was unnecessary to explain the existence of evil. There was only one God, and He was both good and all-powerful. Everything God created was good. But the creation contained degrees of goodness. One feature of God's good creation was his endowment of certain creatures (the angels and humans) with free will. Evil came into being when these creatures misused their free will to turn from a higher good to a lower good.

Augustine and the Donatists

Donatism arose in North Africa about 312, approximately eighty years before Augustine was to become personally involved in controversies surrounding it. Donatism developed in protest against the fact that some Christian leaders had surrendered copies of the Holy Scriptures to save their lives, during the Diocletian persecution (303-305). In the eyes of some North African Christians (Donatists), this disqualified the traitors from any further service as priests and bishops. The Donatists caused a split that led eventually to the development of two parallel and competing churches in North Africa.

Augustine became involved because Hippo Regius, the city in which he was the Catholic bishop, was largely Donatist. After his first attempts to bring about a reasonable settlement failed, Augustine became active in the political and ecclesiastical battles that contributed finally to the condemnation of Donatism and its eventual demise.

Augustine's disagreement with Donatism led him to develop theories about the nature of the church and its sacraments that have become central in disputes between Roman Catholics and Protestants. For example, Augustine argued that sacraments performed by those who are not duly ordained representatives of the Catholic church have no validity. It is important to recognize, however, that Augustine's use of the word *catholic* was not synonymous with *Roman Catholic.*

Augustine and Pelagianism

Pelagianism is the name given to the views (or the implications of views) of a British monk named Pelagius who was a contemporary of Augustine. Pelagius first moved to Rome and then began traveling throughout the Mediterranean world. As the implications of Pelagius's theories were drawn out, it became clear that the system denied original sin. Pelagius believed that Adam's sin affected only himself; it had no effect on the rest of humanity. Hence, according to Pelagius, human infants are not born with a predisposition to sin; they are born innocent, without sin. This means that humans have the ability to live lives that will please God. Augustine countered this heresy with the biblical doctrine that all humans are born with a bent to sin; their sinful human nature predisposes them to commit acts of sin. No human life can possibly satisfy the demands made by God's holy law.

Pelagianism also denied that human salvation was an act of divine grace, a gift of God. It taught that human beings can, in effect, either save themselves or at least cooperate with God in effecting their salvation. For Augustine, both the origin and growth of faith are gifts of God. Augustine distinguished three major stages in the effect of sin upon the human will that he summarized in three Latin phrases: *Posse non peccare* described Adam's condition before the Fall, he was able not to sin; *Non posse non peccare*

describes the condition of all humans after the Fall, they are not able not to sin, *Non posse peccare* will describe the condition of the redeemed in heaven, they will not be able to sin.

Augustine the apologist

Augustine's discussions of many other subjects are still worth consulting. For example, his arguments against skepticism still constitute the proper starting point for any refutation of this error. For Augustine, the skeptic contradicts himself. While he claims that no one can know anything, he himself claims to know that no one can know anything. Moreover, even the most radical skeptic had to know that he himself existed. *Dubito ergo sum*, Augustine wrote. If I doubt, then I am. If the skeptic didn't exist, he couldn't doubt. And if I know that I exist, then skepticism (the view that no one can know anything) must be false.

Augustine's Christian Platonism remains a viable resource for thinkers who believe that the philosophy of Plato can serve as a foundation for the development of a Christian world and Christian lifeview. In his theory of knowledge, Augustine was a rationalist, which is to say that he believed the human mind knows things that it does not receive through the senses. He believed that the physical world that we know through our senses is an imperfect copy of a more ideal world that we can only know through our minds. In the perfect world of forms exist eternal, unchanging essences. But; unlike Plato, Augustine refused to allow the forms an existence independent of God. The eternal forms subsist in God's mind as eternal thoughts of God.

It is clear that any Christian who hopes to understand the development of Christian thought must be familiar with the work of Augustine of Hippo. Many would go further and insist that any attempt to grapple with the great intellectual problems confronted by the contemporary Christian church must begin with Augustine's own efforts to deal with these difficulties.

Leo the Great
*c.*390-461

Two situations dominated Christian history in the mid-fifth century: the Christological controversies over the relation of the divine and human in Christ and the barbarian invasions of the Roman Empire. Leo I, bishop of Rome, played a key role in both. His teachings on the nature of Christ were adopted as the orthodox doctrine at the ecumenical council of Chalcedon in 451, and he negotiated with

Attila, the leader of the Huns, for their withdrawal from Italy in 452.

Leo had major importance in two areas of church history: doctrinal and organizational. His clear teaching of the two natures (true God and true man) united in one person, repeating the traditional Latin doctrine, has remained the standard formulation of the doctrine of Christ in most branches of Christianity. His statement of the

place of the bishop of Rome as holding the same position in the church as Peter held among the apostles established the doctrinal basis for the papacy. Both in his claims to authority and in the influence he exercised, Leo has the right to be called the first pope who fulfilled the meaning that the term has since come to have.

Leo is the first one of only two or three popes (along with Gregory I and sometimes Nicholas I) to be called "Great." His firmness, adherence to principle, and diplomatic skill in a time of political and ecclesiastical confusion well earned him this designation. The powers and prerogatives of the future papacy are outlined in his methods, policy, and ideals.

Leo the Great; from a stained glass window in Wells Cathedral, England.

The Life of
Leo the Great

c. 390-400	Birth.
422-432	Celestine bishop of Rome and Leo archdeacon.
431	Council of Ephesus (Third Ecumenical).
432-440	Sixtus III bishop of Rome and Leo archdeacon.
440	September 29, is consecrated bishop of Rome.
449	Second Council of Ephesus (Robber Synod).
451	Council of Chalcedon (Fourth Ecumenical).
452	Attila and the Huns withdraw from Italy.
455	Vandals pillage Rome.
461	Death.

Leo the Great

Pioneer Pope
Everett Ferguson

Bishop of Rome

Almost nothing is known about Leo's early life; even the date of his birth is a matter of conjecture. Under the bishops Celestine and Sixtus III in the 420s and 430s he was the leading deacon in the church of Rome, exercising considerable influence in the affairs of the church. During his twenty-one years as bishop of Rome (A.D. 440-461) Leo was concerned with establishing Rome's primacy in relation to the other Western churches, upholding canon law in relation to the Eastern churches, defending the traditional Christology of the Roman church in the controversies that originated in the East, and with administering the Roman church in the face of barbarian threats.

As primary sources for his episcopate and for his own thought there survive 96 genuine sermons and 173 letters (30 addressed to Leo and 20 spurious). The sermons are brief exhortations based on the liturgical year. In simple language aimed at popular edification, Leo gave instruction in what to believe and do. The so-called *Leonine Sacramentary* may contain some prayers going back to Leo, but it is a compilation of the late sixth century. Leo's Latin is clear and forceful, as sturdy as the man himself.

Leo's correspondence

Leo's letters to the churches of the West dealt with such heresies as Manichaeism, Priscillianism, and Pelagianism, and such disciplinary and practical questions as qualifications of bishops, rebaptism, and problems caused by the barbarian invasions. The primacy of the church of Rome was generally recognized in the West. Leo used his influence to maintain the rights of metropolitan bishops in relation to other bishops and to preserve canon law, but he was ready to make allowance for ignorance or exceptional circumstances.

Through the bishop of Thessalonica, who was recognized as the papal vicar for the churches in Illyricum, Leo gave guidance to the churches in that region, but his authority was not always acknowledged. Farther east, although there was great respect for the Apostolic See of the West, the churches lagged far behind the Western churches in accepting Rome's own view of its position in the universal church. Much of Leo's correspondence with churches and individuals in the East grew out of the Christological controversies.

The Council of Ephesus in 431 (the Third Ecumenical Council) had resulted in the exile of Nestorius (bishop of Constantinople) and the rejection of his teaching, which was believed not to give adequate place to the personal union of the divine and human in Jesus but to leave two persons in only a moral union. The Christology of Cyril of Alexandria, built on John 1:14 and emphasizing the one personality of the Word who altered His circumstances to dwell in flesh, prevailed.

Leo's Tome

Cyril's successor as bishop of Alexandria, Dioscorus, sought to advance further the authority of the Alexandrian church over the churches of the East. He had an ally in Constantinople in the influential monastic leader Eutyches, who carried Cyril's doctrine to the extreme of not giving adequate place to the human nature of

A Roman temple now occupied by a church.

Christ (the position that came to be known as Monophysitism). A second council at Ephesus, held in 449 and presided over by Dioscorus, condemned as Nestorian the bishop of Constantinople, Flavian, and other leaders who championed the reality of the human nature of Christ and so spoke of two natures. Dioscorus refused to allow the reading of a statement of Leo's position contained in his *Epistle* 28 (the *Tome*) to Flavian in 449. The tyrannical proceedings at Ephesus, during which the monks resorted to violence to enforce their will, led Leo to give to the council the name Robber Synod (Ep. 95.2), by which it is still known.

Leo's Christology, as set forth in his *Tome* and elsewhere, avoided the extremes of Nestorius and Eutyches and taught that Christ was fully human and fully divine, two natures united in one person. Mary conceived and gave birth to Him without the loss of her virginity. "The Lord assumed his mother's nature without her faultiness" (*Ep.* 28.4). By "remaining what he was and assuming what he was not" (*Serm.* 21.2) Christ provided in His earthly life an example of virtue and secured through His death and resurrection redemption for humanity. "Both natures retained their own proper character without loss" (*Ep.* 28.3). Although "he partook of man's weaknesses, he did not share our faults" (ibid.).

The Council of Chalcedon

The Eastern emperor, Theodosius II, died in 450 and was succeeded by his sister Pulcheria and the general Marcian, whom she married. This brought about a change in government policy, for Pulcheria had long been in sympathy with Leo and the two-nature Christology. Another council was called, and 520 bishops convened at Chalcedon in A.D. 451. Leo, relying on the precedent that bishops of Rome had not attended prior Eastern councils, did not attend; but he was represented by legates, who had seats of honor and took a leading role in the proceedings.

When Leo's *Tome* was read, the *Acta* of the council record that the members acclaimed: "That is the faith of the fathers, the faith of the apostles. We all believe thus, the orthodox believe so! Anathema to him who believes otherwise! Peter has thus spoken through Leo! The apostles taught so!" Although Leo thought the earlier definitions of faith were sufficient and all that was required was to undo what had been done at Ephesus in 449, the council, at the urging of the government commissioners, went further and approved a new definition of faith. It adhered to Leo's doctrine, declaring that Christ was in "two natures, without confusion, without change, without division or separation . . . one Person and one Hypostasis."

The doctrinal triumph for Rome at Chalcedon was offset by a disappointment in the canons approved at the council. The twenty-eighth canon declared that New Rome (Constantinople) should have the same privileges as Old Rome and rank second after it in ecclesiastical affairs. This decision was based on the principle that the rank and jurisdiction of episcopal sees should follow the civil importance of the cities. This principle became normative in the East, but it was repudiated by Rome, which favored the ranking of churches according to apostolic foundation. Leo argued that canon twenty-eight contradicted the canons approved at Nicea in 325, and that it damaged the prestige of Antioch and Alexandria.

The Church of Rome

Equalling Leo's importance in the history of the doctrine of the incarnation is his contribution to the history of the constitution of the church. Using materials from his predecessors, he elaborated the Petrine claims of the Roman church to shape a consistent and authoritative doctrine of primacy. His *Sermons* preached on the anniversary of his ordination use the texts of Matthew 16:16-19; Luke 22:31f.; and John 21:15-17 to claim that Peter had authority over the bishops. Peter became bishop of Rome and transmitted his authority to subsequent bishops of Rome, so there is a perpetual authority of Peter in the church. Through the blessed Peter, prince of the apostles, the most holy Roman church possesses sovereignty over all churches of the whole world (*Ep.* 65.2). Leo all but identified himself with Peter: "He is speaking whose representative we are, so the bishop of Rome is primate of all bishops" (*Serm.* 3.4).

Leo's conception of the pope in relation to Peter was developed in terms of the Roman law of inheritance. The doctrine of the episcopacy in the third century had treated all bishops as essentially equal, but Leo made their authority in some sense dependent on him. Other bishops might share in the pastoral care of the churches, but not in the "plenitude of the power" of the Roman bishop (*Ep.* 14.2). The word *pope* (from the Greek *papas*, father) had been in use for bishops of major churches since the third century

and for the bishop of Rome since the fourth century. With Leo it began to gather special connotations.

In his political theory there was an analogy between the two natures of Christ and the two parts of the Empire, the church and the state. In his *Sermon* 82 he draws a comparison between Rome and the church. Peter and Paul as founders of the church of Rome were like Romulus and Remus, the twin founders of the city of Rome. Elsewhere Leo neglects Paul, because the Petrine texts offer more support for a primacy for Rome.

Leo joined two senators in an embassy from Emperor Valentian III and the Senate to Attila in 452. As a consequence the Huns withdrew across the Danube. Leo was not so successful in negotiating with Gaiseric and the Vandals in 455. They plundered Rome but agreed not to burn, massacre, or torture. Political authority continued to disintegrate in the western provinces, but Leo left a church with the doctrinal clarity and institutional strength to survive the shocks and be able to take the lead in building a new order.

Patrick

c. 389-?461

Many of the Irish legends concerning Patrick the missionary (*c.* 389-?461) are clearly false but charming relics of the veneration in which he has been held. And yet, if we reject all the legends, Patrick remains. His integrity and sweetness of character have rarely been duplicated in Christian history.

The Christianity of the historical Patrick belongs to a very ancient British church, whose origins date from the second century of the Roman occupation of Britain. Recent archaeological evidence has shown that the faith was widespread among the Britons and that a sophisticated Romano-British culture existed before the fourth century, when British bishops first appeared at church councils.

The barbarian invasion of Europe in the fifth century convinced the Britons to secede from Rome because the Empire could no longer provide the law and order that the romanized British upper classes had so enjoyed. For a time they were spared wholesale barbarian (German) occupation, and the withdrawal of Roman authority saw a revival of Celtic culture. Coins ceased to be minted, the economy collapsed, Latin education declined, and the old system of warring tribal chiefs revived. Patrick was born into this fragmented but energetic society.

Patrick, missionary to Ireland.

The Life of

Patrick

c. 389	Birth in Roman Britain.
405-411	Captivity as a slave in Ireland.
431	Palladius's mission to Ireland.
432	Patrick's mission to Ireland.
?461	Death in Ireland.

Armagh ●

Ireland

Patrick

Missionary to the Irish
Caroline T. Marshall

Adventurous youth

In his own words, Patrick was born of a Christian family in Britain, probably in western Britain, although there is no way to identify Bonavem Taberniae, the Romano-British town that the missionary says was his home. When he was sixteen, Patrick was taken captive by pirates and sold into slavery in Ireland. Six years later he escaped from his master and returned home. He says that his education was interrupted by his captivity, and when he left Ireland he resumed it. He studied in Britain and probably in Europe. He may have visited Auxerre and Lérins.

In a dream Patrick heard the Irish pleading with him to return to them: "Holy boy, we are asking you to come home and walk among us again." He was, in his own words, "struck to the heart," and immediately made plans to go again to the land of his hated captivity. The suffering induced by his slavery had led Patrick from the nominal Christianity of his upbringing to a profound faith and to the belief that it was his mission in life to convert the Irish.

By tradition, Patrick was appointed a bishop and apostle to the Irish. Palladius had been appointed by Pope Celestine I but quickly disappeared from the medieval records. His fate is not known. The Irish records agree that Patrick arrived in Ireland in A.D. 432, one year after the mysterious Palladius.

Patrick's Ireland

Although many places in Ireland lay claim to close links with the missionary, Patrick's greatest efforts seem to have been in the west and the north of the island. By tradition his episcopal seat was Armagh. The people whom he evangelized were Celts untouched by the Roman culture that had helped to mold the British society into which Patrick was born. The Irish had no towns; their primary social order was the tribe, or extended family. They raised cattle, lived in wattle-and-turf houses, and repaired to forts, mostly wooden, during raids and wars. Their lives were full of superstition and magic presided over by Druid priests who were Christianity's chief Irish opponents.

Patrick established a decentralized church, in sympathy with the realities of Irish life. The heart of this church was a semi-reclusive monastic system, with power in the hands of the abbots. The bishops were selected by the monastic clergy on whom they were dependent. This religious order prevailed in Ireland and Great Britain until the triumph of the Roman episcopal order more than two centuries later.

Patrick traveled extensively in Ireland, preaching the gospel. He turned to local kings and sub-kings for protection. Frequently the sons of the Irish aristocracy accompanied him; he made many converts from all levels of society.

Patrick's writings

The character of Patrick is revealed in his writings in a singular and touching fashion. He frequently notes that his education was interrupted by the years of Irish captivity and laments that his rhetoric was thus limited and crude. The absence of great learning and the simplicity of the Latin in which he wrote haunted Patrick. He makes frequent reference to

Remains of the Franciscan friary of Armagh. By tradition Patrick was bishop of Armagh.

this throughout his *Confessions*: "I had long had it in mind to write, but up to now I have hesitated. I was afraid lest I should fall under the judgment of men's tongues because I am not as well read as others" (*Confessions*: 10). Even in a long and dramatic letter in which he excommunicated the British chieftain Coroticus, Patrick humbly introduces himself as "I Patrick, a sinner, very badly educated" (*Coroticus:* 1).

What Patrick did not realize was that the very absence of refined rhetoric, which he so regretted, made his writing honest and direct. The impact on the reader of his language is considerable. It is simple and very moving and reveals a person of great courage and humility.

Patrick was fundamentally a missionary. Though he did not understand why he should be chosen, he nevertheless believed that God, acting through him, would overcome all deficiencies. His personality was evangelical; his writing is alive with thanksgiving and faith.

Beyond the *Letter* and the *Confessions*, there is great controversy concerning the writing of Patrick. Of three short works entitled simply *The Writings of Patrick*, only one is certainly by him. There are two reports of Irish synods that mention Patrick. One may be genuine. However, many scholars doubt that Patrick had any episcopal peers in Ireland. If this is correct, there would have been no need of episcopal synods. None of the several poems and hymns attributed to Patrick appears to be authentic. Even the beloved hymn the "Breastplate of St. Patrick" is written in Irish of a much later date than the language of the *Confessions*.

Lives of Patrick

There are several medieval biographies of Patrick. Two of these, found in the *Book of Armagh*, seem authentic. The *Book of Armagh* dates from the early ninth century. One narration is by a writer known as Muirchu who provides details concerning Patrick's life and his mission. Armagh is identified as Patrick's see. In the other reputable *Life of Patrick*, the narrator, a man named

"St Patrick's grave", Downpatrick, Northern Ireland.

Tisechan, devotes much time to identifying Patrick with the church of Rome.

Patrick's life and mission are also reported in the Irish *Annals*, the medieval records of Ireland's greatest monastic establishments. All of these narrations agree that he arrived in Ireland in 432, the year after Palladius's mission to Ireland. They provide details of his birth, family, captivity, and mission. They disagree about the date of his death and a few of them speak of a second Patrick, an "ancient" Patrick. Some modern scholars have tried to identify this other Patrick with Palladius.

Columba
521-597

Columba (521-597), the great missionary to the people living in what is today Scotland and northern England, grew up in a tumultuous society characterized by quarrelling and fighting. It was peopled by rugged individualists fond of song and music, talented, and capable of higher learning. He spent his first forty-two years in Ireland, mostly in the service of the church. He became a priest/monk and later a founder of new monasteries throughout the island.

Then, in 563, after a two-year period of controversy and violence concerning a book he had obtained by surreptitious means, Columba entered a self-imposed exile.

After he had settled on the small island of Iona off the western coast of Scotland, Columba set up a missionary outpost from which he and his companions could evangelize the pagan Scots and Picts. Iona became a hive of missionary activity – a place where, under Columba's direction, missionary monks were trained and from which they were sent out eastward and northward to preach the gospel. By the time of his death in 597, Columba had established himself as a respected Christian leader and had made an immeasurable impact on Scotland and the entire Celtic Christian world.

A stained glass portrait of Columba ("Columcille"), from Iona.

The Life of
Columba

521	December; birth in County Donegal, Ireland.
545	Founding of first monastery.
561	Quarrel over a disputed book and the Battle of Culdrevney.
563	April; departure from Ireland.
563	May; establishment of missionary community on Iona.
564	Conversion to Christianity of King Brude of the Northern Picts.
575	National convention at Brumceatt, near Derry, Ireland.
597	June; death.

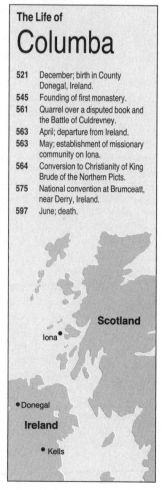

Columba

Missionary to the Scots

Robert D. Linder

The "dove"

Columba was born in December A.D. 521 near Lough Gartan in County Donegal in that part of Ireland known as Ulster. He was christened "Colum," from the Latin word for dove. Himself a Celt (the ancient race that inhabited western Europe before the coming of the Germanic tribes, among the descendants of whom are today's Irish, Welsh, and Scots), Columba's grandfather Conall had been baptized by none other than Patrick himself. Columba's parents were both Christians: his father, Phelim MacFergus, was a member of the royal O'Neill family, from which the high king of the Irish at Tara was chosen; his mother, Ethne, a descendant of a king of the Irish province of Leinster.

All accounts refer to Columba as a robust child, full of mischief and energy, and somewhat combative. Tall and strong, he was soon recognized for his first-rate mind and zeal for learning. These factors, combined with a powerful and pleasing voice and a well-developed sense of humor, made him a winsome individual.

Since fostering was a common practice among the Irish nobility of the age, the decisive influence in Columba's early life would not be his parents but a foster father named Cruithnechan, a priest who baptized, reared, and taught the youngster. It was during his early years that the boy's apparent religiosity earned him the nickname of "Columcille," "Colum of the Church," affectionately bestowed upon him by his young companions, who used to watch daily for his emergence from the little church where it was his habit to read the Psalms.

Even though, as a close relative of the current high king, he might have been chosen someday to reign at Tara, Columba's obvious inclination toward the religious life led his foster father to arrange for the boy to study under Finnian of Moville. It was Finnian, a leading scholar/abbot of the day, who introduced Columba to a meaningful commitment to Christ, the systematic study of the Scripture, and the monastic life.

Columba and mission

Around 556, when he was in his mid-thirties, Columba left Finnian of Moville to join another eminent Finnian at Clonard in order to increase his scholarly and spiritual skills. As the reputation of Clonard grew, hundreds of young men flocked there to study at the feet of this second Finnian. Almost immediately a favorite of his new mentor, Columba was eventually ordained to the priesthood and began to take an interest in missions. Before long, Columba and several other

Interior of the Abbey Church, Iona.

Iona Abbey, Scotland.

young monks from Clonard began to establish monasteries throughout Ireland in order to advance spiritual life in that country. Columba himself planted a number of monasteries during this period – legend says a hundred – first at Derry and later at Durrow in Offaly, Kells in Meath, and elsewhere. As he did this, his reputation as a godly and scholarly Christian also increased.

However, around 561 an incident occurred that was to change the course of Columba's life forever. Eager for scriptural knowledge and for the best Bible texts, he copied without permission a manuscript of Jerome's version of the Psalter and gospels that Finnian of Moville had brought from Rome. Upon learning of this, Finnian of Clonard was angry and demanded the copy of the rare text. When Columba refused, Finnian sought judgment against him from Columba's own kinsman, the high king at Tara, who rendered a verdict against Columba. Still, he refused to surrender his precious book.

Even though a reconciliation between Finnian and Columba was eventually achieved, the rift between Columba and his cousin, the high king, widened. Civil war finally erupted, with Columba arousing the clansmen of the north country to attack the forces of the high king. Columba and his allies were victorious at the bloody battle of Culdrevney near Sligo, in which more than 3,000 men were killed. Although the exact details of the events that followed are shrouded in mystery, Columba upon reflection apparently felt such remorse over the carnage he had caused that, as an act of rededication, he decided to leave his native Ireland and become a missionary. Thus, he became what he called "an exile for Christ." Determined to win to Christ at least as many souls as had been lost at Culdrevney, he was eventually to convert many times that number during the last thirty-four years of his life.

The voyage to Scotland

Selecting twelve companions from among his old and trusted friends at Clonard, and in imitation of the early disciples,

Columba set out for the pagan lands to the northeast. They sought an island out of the sight of Ireland, yet close enough to the coast of Scotland to have easy contact with the non-Christian people there. After a rugged voyage of several weeks, during which time the little band visited two or three potential places of refuge, Columba and his companions finally landed on the small island of Iona, about half a mile off the Scottish mainland, on the borderland between the Picts and Scots.

Intensely beautiful, Iona consisted of about 2,000 acres, of which about one-fourth was under the plow. Columba moved quickly to build his monastery, which, according to the Celtic manner, was not an enormous edifice but a simple structure that could serve as a missionary base-camp. Each monk had his own hut, part of an irregular circle surrounding the larger hut of the abbot (Columba). The large hut was situated prominently at the top of a knoll. Other necessary buildings were soon erected: a refectory, a library, a guesthouse, a smithy, a kiln, a mill, two barns, and a small church.

Columba himself lived in the greatest austerity, sleeping on a bare rock with a stone pillow. Monastic life on the island was carefully organized into three groups: the seniors (who led worship services and transcribed manuscripts), the workers (who taught and engaged in manual labor), and the juniors (who performed miscellaneous tasks). As abbot, Columba was the unquestioned master of the monastery, which he ruled with strictness seasoned by affection, as both participant and director. Under his leadership, the Iona community was a place of constant activity, with monks engaged in work, prayer, and study – all in preparation for missionary preaching in nearby Scotland.

Iona

During the period 563-597 Iona became the center for the evangelization of Scotland and northern England. Like other missionaries of the time, Columba and his sea-roving evangelists made use of contacts with political personages who could aid in the conversion of their subjects. By his royal lineage and his superior personal gifts, Columba was well qualified for the political aspects of his role. Moreover, his Christian devotion contributed to the generally pacifying effect that he seemed to have over the warlike Picts and Scots. For these reasons, Columba and his monks soon brought the gospel, and with it greater orderliness and peace, to Scotland.

In 575 Columba revisited Ireland to attend a national convention of the Irish tribes, at Drumceatt, near Derry. His influence at this assembly was dominant, illustrating the great respect in which his person was held by his countrymen. Among other matters, he intervened to settle a dispute between the Irish bards and the high king concerning the essential position of the bards in Irish society. After Columba eloquently and convincingly defended the singing poets, 1,200 bards entered the meeting and lauded in song the embarrassed abbot of Iona, who covered his face with his cowl.

Until the final days of his life, Columba exercised his enormous prestige and unusual gifts to secure the success of his epochal mission. At the age of seventy-five, after a day spent transcribing a psalter, he arose from his hard bed to join his brethren at their traditional midnight service. Arriving ahead of them and weakened from years of labor, he knelt before the altar and collapsed. Columba revived briefly, gave his beloved monks a farewell blessing, and died peacefully in the early hours of Sunday, June 9, 597.

Columba's influence

Columba, by his example, left an indelible impression on Irish and Scottish Christianity. In particular he bequeathed to his beloved monks – and through them to their converts – a love for books, especially the Bible. Out of this devotion to the Bible grew Columba's emphasis on bold missions. He correctly understood the evangelistic impulse in Christianity and promoted it in any and every way he could.

The shore, Iona. The Abbey Church can be seen in the background.

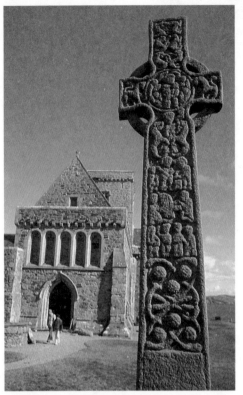

St Martin's Cross and the Abbey Church, Iona. There are several similar crosses on the island.

Columba also contributed certain ideas and ideals to later British Christianity. For example, to Columba the ideal Christian life consisted of "work, prayer, and reading." This became the heart of his monastic code and, in turn, central for his converts. Moreover, Columba's emphasis was biblical. As it was said of Patrick that he "lived with the Bible," so it could be said of Columba. The preaching of Columba and his monks was direct, simple, biblical, and based on an appeal to accept Christ as Savior and live a life of devotion to him.

Further, Columba's life served as a model of devotion for future generations of Christian believers, especially among the Irish and Scots. His personal piety inspired untold numbers of Christians to live a more godly life. Columba's example of self-denial and pious living was reinforced by an abundance of reported miracles performed by Columba during his lifetime – miracles of power, prophecy, and healing.

A passion for mission

But most of all, there was the example of Columba's passion for missions. He preached missions, lived missions, and practiced missions. In fact, one of the first journeys Columba undertook after establishing his community on Iona was a missionary journey in 564 to the fortress of Brude, king of the Northern Picts, located on the banks of Loch Ness.

Upon his death, Columba was remembered as a practical, kind-hearted, and deeply committed Christian, one who had devoted his extraordinary gifts and energy to a mission of epochal importance. Iona remained for centuries an active center for the propagation of the gospel and an outpost of the Irish church. It was also the most influential member of a widening circle of monastic communities owing allegiance to Columba, communities that sprang up among both the Celts of Ireland and Scotland and the Angles and Saxons of northern England.

He also understood the peacemaking role of the Christian leader and sought to settle disputes and to minimize violence wherever he could. This desire to establish peace no doubt also received impetus from the hard lessons he had learned from his own personal experiences as a young hothead in Ireland before his life-changing departure from his native land in 563.

In addition, Columba was a man of cultural and literary achievement. He wrote poetry and dearly loved the poetic books of the Bible, especially the Psalms. He instilled this love of poetry and music into his own monks. On one occasion, in a contest with the Druids, the pagan priests tried to outshout Columba's singing monks, but the ancient record reveals that the monks simply drowned the Druids' din by chanting Psalm 145 "like a peal of thunder."

Gregory the Great
c. 540-604

Gregory the Great (*c.* 540-604) is often called the first of the medieval popes and is ranked with Ambrose, Jerome, and Augustine as one of the four great leaders of the Latin church. During his reign there was a change in papal relations with the secular powers. A new wave of barbarian invaders caused the pope to become more involved in government because the emperor at Constantinople could not subdue the intruders and the Western Roman power had collapsed. The only effective leadership was provided by the papacy because it had resources and power that the civil authorities lacked.

Many individuals had willed their land to the church in return for the intercession of the religious authorities for the forgiveness of sins. The pope managed the properties so given and used the income for functions that previously had been provided by the government. Gregory supplied food and services for the poor, ransomed individuals who were captured by the barbarians, and made treaties to avoid the destruction of Rome. He also engaged in diplomatic relations with the emperor at Constantinople and with the barbarian kingdoms in France, Spain, and England.

Gregory was the first pope to send missionaries to England. His interest in that project was aroused by a visit to the market place in Rome where he saw some English slaves for sale. He asked who they were and was told that they were Angles, to which he is said to have replied, "They are not Angles, but Angels!" Gregory's response was to send several monks, led by Augustine of Canterbury, to evangelize the English. Thus the papacy became involved in the conversion to Christ of the western pagan Germanic tribes.

In addition to the administrative and missionary roles that he pioneered for the medieval church, Gregory also simplified and clarified Christian doctrine, thereby enabling it to survive among the less cultured barbarian peoples of the early Middle Ages. Despite his numerous contributions and exceptional abilities, there was a humility and Christian meekness about the man that is summed up in the title he preferred as church leader, "the Servant of the Servants of God."

The Church of St Gregory the Great, Rome.

The Life of

Gregory the Great

c. 540	Birth.
c. 70	Made prefect of the city of Rome.
575	Becomes a monk.
579	Ordained a deacon and sent to Constantinople as papal representative.
586	Recalled to Rome to serve as advisor to Pope Pelagius II.
590	Elected pope.
597	Sends Augustine of Canterbury to evangelize the Anglo-Saxons.
604	Death.

Gregory the Great

and the Medieval Church

Robert G. Clouse

Gregory the Great, depicted on a
fourteenth-century tapestry.

Administrator and monk

Gregory was born in Rome to a pious and aristocratic family that had given two of its members, Felix III (A.D. 483-492) and Agapetus (A.D. 535-536), to serve as pope. He was reared in a setting that encouraged not only religious commitment but also scholarship. His achievements in the study of law led to his appointment as prefect of Rome in 570. This position involved presiding over the Roman Senate and administering the charity efforts and defense of the city. The experience gained during this appointment gave him a thorough knowledge of business and administrative practices that would influence his later conduct as pope. After the death of his father, he resigned from his worldly duties and endowed seven monasteries, one of which he dedicated to St. Andrew. He became a monk in that foundation in 575.

Gregory did not enjoy the contemplative life for long, however, because he was called to serve the church as a deacon in 579 and was sent to Constantinople as the papal representative to the Byzantine court. His experience in the East convinced him that the papacy needed to pursue a policy independent of the Eastern emperor, because there was little prospect of help from Constantinople for the Western provinces. On his return to Rome in 579, he became Abbot of St. Andrews and advisor to the pope. In 590 he was elected pope by popular acclaim, despite his own reluctance to leave the monastery.

Pope Gregory

Gregory's activities set important precedents for later popes and for the medieval church. He became heavily involved in secular affairs and assumed the role in Italy previously exercised by the Eastern emperor and the Imperial representative, the Exarch of Ravenna. He was forced to do that because of the inability of the Empire to deal with a new group of barbarians, the Lombards. They had invaded Italy in 569 and occupied territories situated between Rome and Ravenna.

The emperor would not send troops to defeat them, but neither would he make a truce with them for fear that this would legalize their presence. Consequently Gregory sent his own forces against them and made a temporary peace with their king in 592. Later he paid tribute to the Lombards in order to save the city of Rome from being sacked. He used the revenues from papal landholdings in southern Italy, Corsica, Sicily, Gaul, and North Africa to finance those activities. This income was also spent in caring for the poor, to ransom captives from the Lombards, and to provide government services for the city. Because it was the pope rather than the civil authorities who undertook those duties, the papacy ended up ruling central Italy.

The Empire divides

Gregory strengthened the position of the papacy through his handling of ecclesiastical affairs in both the eastern and western portions of the Roman world. By the sixth century, those two sections of the Empire had drifted apart. In the East there was still an emperor, but he was a Greek who had difficulty relating to the Latin-speaking West. Meanwhile, the Western provinces were occupied by a series of barbarian states that were increasingly independent of the Empire.

Gregory dealt with both of those worlds. In the East he was careful to recognize the rights of the other major church leaders – the patriarchs of Constantinople, Antioch, Alexandria, and Jerusalem – but at the same time he maintained that the papacy had been entrusted with the care of the entire church and therefore had jurisdiction everywhere. His position was revealed in two controversies with the patriarch of Constantinople. In the first of these Gregory reversed a decision by the Eastern church leader involving two priests, whereas the second arose over an argument concerning the use of the term *ecumenical* or *universal bishop* by the patriarch. To assume such a title, Gregory believed, was a sin of pride that indicated that the spirit of Antichrist was in the world. His objection was not made in order to claim the description for himself. In fact, when the bishop of Alexandria referred to Gregory as "Universal Pope," he refused the title, claiming it would inflate vanity and damage Christian love.

In his role as leader of the church, Gregory was especially concerned with affairs in the western regions of the Empire. He tried to select competent individuals to serve as bishops for the area and ensured that they were elected by canonical procedures. He also attempted to heal the division in the church caused by the Donatists. He established a link with the independent Frankish church by sending a vicar to represent papal opinion and by introducing a reform program that attempted to modify the Frankish tradition of lay control. He encouraged the conversion of the Visigoths from Arianism to orthodoxy and was able to make his friend, Leander, bishop of Seville. Gregory also led the way in missionary activities among the pagan barbarian tribes of the West by sending Augustine of Canterbury and forty monks to preach to the Anglo-Saxons in England in 597.

Gregory's writings

Gregory was not only an able administrator, a devout monk, a competent diplomat, and a sound moral leader, but he was a capable writer who communicated Christian truth in a concrete way to the barbarian people of early medieval times. His thought, although not original, was well expressed for his own and succeeding generations, so that he is remembered as an important link between the wisdom and piety of the ancient church and medieval Christianity. He is considered one of the four great teachers of moral theology in the Roman Catholic tradition. Gregory blended popular Catholicism and Augustinianism in a form that dominated early medieval thought. He established the teaching of purgatory by elevating it from an opinion to a dogma. He believed that souls in purgatory could be freed by the sacrifice of the mass. He also encouraged the veneration of relics and the use of images. These ideas are developed in a series of works including letters, dialogues, an exposition of the book of Job, sermons on Ezekiel and the gospels, and a guide for bishops called the *Pastoral Rule*.

Many of Gregory's letters have been preserved and give readers a rich source of information about the times in which he lived. They deal with missionary, administrative, and social aspects of the church and its relationship with the Empire, the Germanic kingdom of western Europe and the emerging monastic movement. They illustrate his wide-ranging abilities in dealing with the problems of his age and furnish the best evidence for the validity of the judgment of history that he be called "the Great."

The Dialogues

The Four Books of Dialogues on the Life of Miracles of the Saints and on the Immortality of Souls were written by Gregory in 594 and consist of a series of conversations between the author and the Roman archdeacon Peter. The first three describe the holiness and the miraculous aspects of the lives of several sixth-century religious leaders. Among them is Benedict of Nursia, who Gregory maintained was the leading example of dedi-

The ruins of St Augustine's Abbey, Canterbury. Gregory sent Augustine to England in A.D. 597.

cation to God. In these accounts he states that miracles were not limited to biblical times but were still being performed in response to the prayers and faith of God's people. The last book presents his views on eschatology and is the chief source of the teaching of purgatory for the medieval church. In a series of vivid portrayals of heaven and hell, Gregory tries to comfort his readers who were suffering persecution at the hands of the barbarian invaders. Those who are faithful, he teaches, enter heaven immediately after death, but for others who are not prepared to be with God there is purgatory. He explains this doctrine carefully and lays out the necessity of the sacrifice of the mass in helping those individuals pass through purgatory more quickly.

Many Roman Catholic writers contend that the dialogues are simply a literary form that Gregory used to communicate Christian truth to the simple and un-educated. Those believers would not have been able to follow detailed, abstract doctrinal discussions but would have been fascinated by the legends of miracles and of the experiences of saints. Thus the stories merely state that God is still with His people, despite the hardships of the age in which they live. However, Protestants have not been as charitable, most of them agreeing with Philip Schaff that "it is strange that a man of his intelligence and good name should believe such grotesque and childish marvels."

Exposition of Job

Another of Gregory's major writings is an exposition of Job, which he began to write when he was the papal representative to Constantinople. He labored over this for many years. It contains thirty-five books and deals with Job from three aspects: the historical or literal meaning, the allegorical significance, and the moral implication of the work. The historical treatment would not be considered adequate by modern standards, because Gregory did not know either Hebrew or Greek and showed little acquaintance with Eastern history or culture even though he lived in Constantinople for several years. The allegorical section is of more value because it contains a whole system of theology that he read between the lines of the

Old Testament books. The names of persons, places, and things are filled with Christian meanings. "Job represents Christ; his wife the carnal nature; his seven sons (seven being the number of perfection) represent the apostles, and hence the clergy; his three daughters the three classes of the faithful laity who are to worship the Trinity; his friends the heretics; the seven thousand sheep the perfect Christians; the three thousand camels the heathen and Samaritans; the five hundred yoke of oxen and five hundred she-asses again the heathen, because the prophet Isaiah says: 'The ox knoweth his owner, and the ass his master's crib; but Israel doth not know, my people doth not consider.'" Gregory closes his exposition with an extended discussion on the moral significance of the book that gives his readers a summary of Christian ethics.

The twenty-two sermons or homilies on Ezekiel are based on chapters 1-4 and chapter 40 of the prophet's writings. The homilies illustrate again how Gregory read into the Old Testament themes such as the life of Christ, the church, and Christian ethics. In addition to doctrinal matters they contain words of comfort for the people of Rome as they faced the Lombard threat.

The forty sermons on the gospels illustrate the importance of preaching in the sixth century. They are made more graphic by the use of vivid illustrations. Many of his exhortations demonstrate a belief that the end of the world was near. Everywhere he looked he saw signs of the end, such as plagues, barbarian invasions, and the physical decay of the old Roman world. He felt an urgency to warn his listeners of death and to explain to them the danger of hell and the bliss of heaven, thus preparing them for the day of judgment.

Gregory's Rule

His most important book was a guide for bishops or pastoral rule that became a standard manual for practical theology during the Midde Ages. It is divided into four sections, describing the sort of person who should be a church leader, his conduct, his attitudes toward teaching, and finally warning of the temptations involved in leadership. He demands celibacy of clergy and insists that a pastoral leader must be a capable speaker. He urges his readers to teach by example and precept, as he states: "Every preacher should give forth a sound more by his deeds than by his words. He should, by his good life, imprint footsteps for men to follow rather than, by speaking, merely show them the way to walk in" (*Pastoral Rule* 3:40). Insisting that a spiritual leader combine compassion with meditation he counsels: "The leader should be a near neighbor to everyone in sympathy, and yet exalted above all in contemplation... The same eye of the heart, which in his elevation he lifts to the invisible, he bends in his compassion upon the secrets of those who are subject to infirmity" (*Pastoral Rule* 2:5). Much of his advice speaks to Christians across the ages, as he warns: "The leader should understand how often vices pass themselves off as virtues. Stinginess often excuses itself under the name of frugality while, on the other hand, extravagance hides itself under the name of generosity. Often inordinate laxity is mistaken for lovingkindness, while unbridled wrath is seen as the virtue of spiritual zeal" (*Pastoral Rule* 2:9).

Opinions of Gregory have shifted with the times, but there is no doubt that he is one of the great leaders of the church. He left his mark on medieval faith through his encouragement of monasticism, his elevation of the status of the papacy, his homiletic advice, his missionary zeal, and his exegetical interpretation. As a recent biographer states: "He did his duty as a Christian, a gentleman and a Roman. No one could have asked for more. Well did he deserve the title his epitaph bestowed – 'The Consul of God.'"

Bede
*c.*672-735

Bede (*c.* 672-735) was the most important Christian scholar, teacher, and writer between the age of the church Fathers and the Carolingian revival of learning. So significant were his contributions that the period 600-800 is often called the Age of Bede.

Bede's writing became the basis for vocational religious education in the West. In addition to his works on time, history, and the Scriptures were his hymnology, geography, and studies of natural phenomena. The scope of Bede's scholarship defies imagination. His teaching literature dominated monastic education in the West until the rise of the universities. His writing style has influenced generations of Christian historians.

Bede spent almost his entire life in the monasteries of Wearmouth and Jarrow in the north of England, where, by his time, a lively Anglo-Saxon culture was flourishing. From the ninth century Bede was generally known as 'Venerable,' for the saintliness of his life. He is most famous today for his *Ecclesiastical History of the English People,* which remains a major source of information on life in early England.

Bede, a modern stained glass portrait from Norwich Cathedral, England.

The Life of
Bede

663/664	Synod of Whitby.
674	Monastery founded at Wearmouth.
669	Benedict Biscop goes to Rome and collects manuscripts.
672/673	Birth of Bede in Northumbria.
681/682	Monastery of Jarrow established.
c. 700	Becomes an oblate.
c. 712	Ordained a priest.
731	*Ecclesiastical History of the English Nation* completed.
735	Death at Jarrow.

England

Jarrow ●

The Venerable Bede

Caroline T. Marshall

Bede and Jarrow

Born about A.D. 672 in what is today the far north of England (Northumbria), Bede was given by his parents at age seven to be an oblate in the twin monastic houses of Wearmouth and Jarrow. At nineteen he was a deacon, and he was a priest at thirty. All his life was spent in Northumbria. Though he visited other monasteries in the area, Jarrow was his home and the scene of his considerable spiritual and literary labors.

Bede was heir to two major Christian traditions, the Celtic and the Latin. Established by Patrick in the fifth century, Celtic Christianity was emotional and evangelical. In its organization, the monastic ideal triumphed. Abbots appointed bishops and were, in general, more powerful than the secular clergy. The soldiers of this church were the peripatetic monks who carried the faith into Britain by way of the great monastic foundations of Iona and Lindisfarne.

In the sixth century the last of the Latin patriarchs, Pope Gregory I (the Great), dispatched a mission to Britain under Augustine of Canterbury. Their purpose was to convert the heathen Angles, Saxons, and Jutes and to advance the centralization of the church under the Latin papacy. Quarrels arose between the two churches over organization, the date of Easter, the use of the tonsure, and other matters. However, the Latin church, with its disciplined secular clergy, won.

St Paul's Church, Jarrow, part of Bede's monastery of St Peter and St Paul.

Bede's Chair, St Paul's Church, Jarrow.

Bede the scholar

During his long life at Jarrow, Bede concentrated upon scholarship and upon didactic and ethical writing. His researches included exegesis, biography, hagiography, studies of time, poetry and rhyme, music and history. Research, writing, and teaching, however, did not seduce him away from the *opus dei*, the praise of God, chanted at Jarrow and throughout the Christian world. He said that he feared the angels would visit the chair and find him missing from the labor that he and all monks believed to be the most important function of the Christian. Bede also admired the simple domestic work of the monks, although he cannot have been much involved with such activities.

Bede was a Saxon and decidedly proRoman in the struggle between Celtic and Latin Christianity. In his *Ecclesiastical History of the English Nation* he gives the Irish monks and their converts full credit. After the Roman missions, however, he seems almost callous in descriptions of the subjugation of the old church. He took the side of order rather than that of spontaneity and revelation.

However, in spite of this, Bede's education included gems from both systems. The democratic charity of Bede reflects the Celtic past; his vast scholarship reflects the wealth and efficiency that the new order provided.

Bede's abbot, Benedict Biscop, the founder of the Wearmouth-Jarrow monastery, was a friend of the Greek-educated archbishop of Canterbury, Theodore of Tarsus. Benedict and the archbishop visited Rome and the European continent, where they collected a huge treasury of manuscripts for Wearmouth-Jarrow and Canterbury, making those libraries the best in Britain. Therefore, Bede had at his disposal many of the works of the Fathers of the church, the Vulgate (Latin) version of the Bible, and much classical pagan literature as well.

Bede's History

Certainly Bede knew Latin and Greek, and perhaps some Hebrew. Of his writing, *Ecclesiastical History of the English Nation* is the best-known work. Composed toward the end of his life, it is an intimate description of the formation of the English nation from its earliest British-Roman experiences to the death of Archbishop Bertwald of Canterbury in 731. Bede's *History* is distinguished by the care with which its sources are treated. Not only did he outline these at the beginning of the book, but he was always careful to check materials where he could. He sent to other churchmen in other monasteries for clarification and advice on his work. Unquestionably, Bede's devotion to truth and to accuracy set an unprecedented standard for the writing of history.

Bede emphasizes the evangelical and civilizing mission of the church. He sees one English nation, rather than a multiplication of warring tribes. However, the

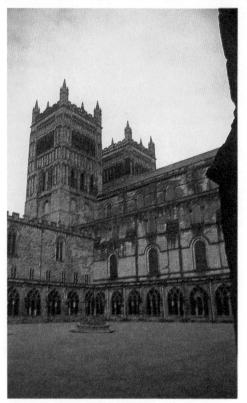

The cloisters, Durham Cathedral.

uniquely his own. They express his democratic vision of the faith and his poetical turn of mind: "We never think that the door of the Kingdom of Heaven lies open, not to those who only know in their learned minds the mysteries of faith and the commandments of their Creator, but to those who have progressed far enough to live by them."

Bede the monk

Above all, Bede was a monk. He engaged in lengthy researches concerning the seasons of the church year, the cycle of saintly feasts, and, by extension, the question of time and chronology. He loved the revolution of the monastic year. In 703 he wrote *On Times* and twenty years later, *On the Reckoning of Times*. In this literature Bede speculates on the symbolic use of numbers and describes the transformation of the seasons from their old pagan designation and significance to something uniquely Christian in meaning. He spends a lot of effort on the order and listing of Christian holy days because of the debate between Celtic and Roman Christians on the date of Easter.

The various streams of medieval life that flowed together in Bede helped make him unique: the eccentricity of the Christian Celts, the wildness of the heathen Saxons, and the pragmatic orderliness of the Catholic church. He died in 735. Later his body was stolen from Jarrow by agents of the prince-bishop of Durham and his bones were interred at Durham Cathedral. His tomb was desecrated during the Protestant Reformation. In 1899 the Roman Catholic church declared Bede a "divine doctor," and in 1935 he was sainted. He has continued to be studied and admired by English-speaking people for his scholarship and for the splendid example of his Christian life.

most unforgettable elements of the *History* probably lie in the poetry of his description of the Christian mission in Britain.

His work also demonstrates the Judeo-Christian theory of linear history, in which there is a particular beginning and a specific end to creation. In between the beginning and the end the events of men and nations have moral meaning. Thus periodization and chronology are important. Individualism is also emphasized, which helps to account for detailed and tender portraits of Celtic and English personalities.

In addition, Bede wrote biblical exegesis. At least half his writing, twenty-four titles, falls into this category. He relied on the Fathers for his interpretations and was especially dependent on Augustine of Hippo and Jerome of Bethlehem. He copied the Alexandrian style of allegory, but his digressions are interesting and

Opposite: The interior of Durham Cathedral, England. Bede's body was moved here in the eleventh century.

Timechart 600-1000

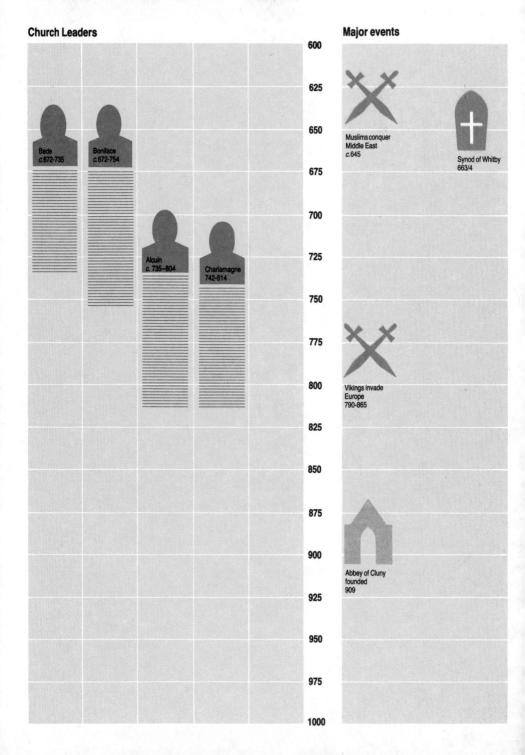

Church Leaders

Bede
c.672-735

Boniface
c.672-754

Alcuin
c. 735–804

Charlemagne
742-814

Major events

Muslims conquer
Middle East
c.645

Synod of Whitby
663/4

Vikings invade
Europe
790-865

Abbey of Cluny
founded
909

600

625

650

675

700

725

750

775

800

825

850

875

900

925

950

975

1000

Boniface

c.672-754

Winfrith, or Boniface (early 670s-754), as he chose to be called in later life, was the most famous in a series of missionaries who came to the European continent from the British Isles in the seventh and eighth centuries. Although he was only one of a number of effective evangelists, reformers, and reorganizers of the church in the Germanic lands of northern Europe, Boniface is known as "the Apostle to the Germans." His goals were spiritual: to reform corrupt churches where they already existed in the Germanic lands and to win to Christ the remaining unconverted Germanic tribes.

Nevertheless, Boniface sparked two developments that he could neither have foreseen nor intended: first, a kind of rebirth of the old Roman Empire in a new, Christian dress in northern Europe (the "Holy Roman Empire of the German Nation"); second, the reorientation of the papacy away from the old Christian lands of the East and from Constantinople, the "New Rome" (where there was still an "Emperor of the Romans,") toward the Germanic lands of the West. Those lands were to become France and Germany. In a way, Boniface stood as sponsor at the baptism of Christian Europe, of medieval Christian civilization. One historian aptly calls him "the founder of the West, before Charlemagne, for whom he paved the way."

Statue of Boniface, "Apostle to the Germans," at Fulda.

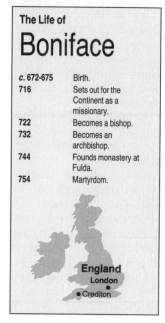

The Life of

Boniface

c. 672-675	Birth.
716	Sets out for the Continent as a missionary.
722	Becomes a bishop.
732	Becomes an archbishop.
744	Founds monastery at Fulda.
754	Martyrdom.

England
London
• Crediton

Boniface

Apostle to the Germans

Harold O. J. Brown

Winfrith of Crediton

At the end of the seventh century, as the number of Celtic, Irish, and Scottish missionaries declined, many of the English Saxons whom they had led to Christ felt called to follow their example and take the gospel to the still-pagan Germans on the European continent. The first to do so was a Northumbrian, Willibrord (A.D. 658-739), who evangelized among the Frisians in what is now the Netherlands and became the first bishop of Utrecht. The most famous of them, however, was the Saxon Winfrith.

The man known to history as Boniface was born Winfrith at Crediton, near Exeter, in the little Saxon kingdom of Wessex, sometime between 672 and 675. The first forty years of his life were spent as a teacher, poet, and grammarian in a Saxon monastery. He knew of Willibrord's work on the Continent. In 716 Winfrith learned that the pagan Frisian king, Radbod, had wiped out Willibrord's work in Frisia. Winfrith set out alone for the continent, in the manner of the earlier Irish monks, but his initial efforts met with no success.

Believing that he needed official backing for his mission, he secured the endorsement of the Carolingian "Mayor of the Palace," Pepin (the real ruler of the Franks under the declining Merovingian royal family) and then went to Rome to seek the pope's endorsement. Faced with devastating losses to Islam in the whole Mediterranean region, the pope was only too happy to give his blessing to Winfrith. It proved a wise move because Winfrith, who symbolized his new Roman connection by taking the patrician name of Boniface, brought more to Rome in Ger-

many than it had lost to the Muslims in Spain.

The Oak of Donar

For the next few years, Boniface worked with Willibrord in Frisia. Radbod's death made their task easier and freed Boniface to go farther south, to the pagans of what is now the German state of Hesse. In 722 the pope made Boniface a bishop, and he began work in earnest. In a dramatic confrontation with the pagans of Hesse, Boniface hacked down the sacred Oak of Donar in Geismar and took its wood to build a church dedicated to the apostle Peter in nearby Fritzlar. The triumph of Christianity in Germany thus began with the building of a church of St. Peter.

Successful in Hesse, Boniface pushed eastward to Thuringia (now in East Germany), where he reorganized the rem-

Fulda Cathedral, site of Boniface's tomb.

Interior of Fulda Cathedral, West Germany.

nants of an existing church. In addition to evangelism, Boniface and other Anglo-Saxon missionaries took the lead in removing corruption in existing churches, an action that caused friction with the native Frankish clergy, especially with its more vigorous members who wanted to carry out the task themselves. Pope Gregory III consecrated Boniface archbishop in 732 and gave him authority to appoint subordinate bishops of the Rhine. Frankish opposition prevented him from establishing the seat of his archdiocese in Cologne, the most logical place. Most of the Frankish clergy resisted his efforts to enlist them in his work of reform and evangelism, and he had continually to call on Christians from England for help.

The abbey of Fulda
Much of his work consisted in founding monasteries, which became centers of learning as well as of piety: Amöneburg and Fritzlar in Hesse; and in 744, the most famous of all, the abbey of Fulda. Fulda was to become the great spiritual center of Roman Catholicism in Germany.

Meanwhile another Pepin (c. 714-768) had succeeded Charles Martel as the Frankish "Mayor of the Palace," in other words, as the real ruler. Pepin at first favored the native Frankish clergy over the "foreigner" Boniface, but was won over to Boniface's side by a noble Frankish priest, Fulrad of St. Denis, who had worked with Boniface and who promised that Pepin could benefit from Boniface's ties to the pope. Boniface then helped Pepin to secure the pope's recognition as King of the Franks. This was the beginning of the Carolingian royal line and of the long and intimate relationship between the papacy and French kings and German emperors who would be derived from Pepin's son Charlemagne.

Boniface is alleged to have anointed Pepin king, but more probably this was done by Pope Stephen II himself, who came to St. Denis in 754. Anointing the Carolingian "Mayor of the Palace" as king

The tomb of Boniface, Fulda Cathedral.

768) as bishop in Mainz and set in order affairs at his great abbey in Fulda. Afterwards he once again went north, where the tribes were still largely pagan. Already an old man, Boniface took not only his books but a burial shroud, perhaps anticipating that his career would end in martyrdom.

Martyrdom

On Wednesday of Pentecost week 754, Boniface summoned a host of newly-converted Frisians to Dokkum to be confirmed. There they were surprised and massacred by a horde of unconverted barbarians. By suffering martyrdom at the end of his long life, Boniface sealed his work in a unique way. He left a legacy of dedication, hard work, and heroism in defense of the faith that would live long after him and that would give German Catholicism a distinctively militant character, one later reflected in the Christian chivalry and military orders of the Middle Ages. By his death, Boniface fulfilled words he had spoken years earlier: "Let us die for the holy laws of our fathers. Let us not be dumb dogs, silent spectators, hirelings who flee from the wolf, but faithful shepherds, watchful for the flock of Christ. Let us preach the whole counsel of God to the high and to the low, to the rich and to the poor, to every rank and age, whether in season or out of season, as far as God gives us strength."

created a parallel with the anointing of David by the prophet Samuel (although many subsequent monarchs were to be more like King Saul than like David). For a thousand years Frankish (later French) kings would claim, explicitly or implicitly, a special divine authority. The papacy gained, too, for by crowning kings (and even emperors after the coronation of Charlemagne as Holy Roman emperor in 800) the pope implicitly appeared to have authority over them, something the church could never claim in the East, where the emperors reigned as successors to Augustus Caesar and felt no need for the church to endorse their authority as monarchs.

In the year that Pope Stephen II came to St. Denis, Boniface himself wound up his own work of church organization in Hesse in preparation for his last great labor, a new missionary campaign. Boniface left his Saxon friend Lul (710-

Boniface was only one of the host of Irish, Scottish, and Anglo-Saxon missionaries who brought the light of the gospel back to a Europe darkened by barbarism. More than any other man since the Emperor Constantine, Boniface did not merely convert individuals, but led an entire nation into the church. By bringing the papacy in Rome into association with Frankish kings and German emperors, he became a key figure in the creation of medieval Christian Europe, with all its glory and contradictions. Thus he merits the title "the founder of the West."

Alcuin

*c.*735-804

It would be hard to find a parallel friendship in all of Christian history to that of Alcuin (*c.*735-804) and Charlemagne (742-814). They were both extraordinary in their gifts and accomplishments. In the course of his reign, Charlemagne succeeded in uniting under his governance the western sector of the old Roman Empire, and with the help of Alcuin established a base for the recovery of classical learning. They began public education and

fostered the common use of Latin as the language of educated discourse.

Alcuin was an accomplished poet, biographer, biblical commentator, and theologian. In addition, he published textbooks on grammar, rhetoric, and dialectics. At a time when spiritual anarchy and churchly decadence prevailed, Alcuin made notable contributions to the defense and promulgation of the faith. He played a role in liturgical reform and in providing a structure for theological education. He was an ardent correspondent. More than three hundred of his letters survive, and they form a rich treasury of insight into his mind and that of his time.

Charlemagne was an

impressive man; seven feet tall, with a strong, vigorous body and a cheerful demeanor. There was nothing artificial about his piety. He professed Christ as his Saviour and lived with a conscious sense of reliance upon God's will. Yet he was a lusty man of his period. He had four wives and numerous mistresses (five of whom are on record as having borne him children). He carried himself with dignity, and it appears seemly that he was declared "Patrician of the Romans."

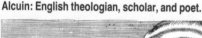
Alcuin: English theologian, scholar, and poet.

The Life of
Alcuin

c. 735	Birth of Alcuin.
742	Birth of Charles the Great (Charlemagne).
766	Alcuin appointed headmaster of York Minster School.
771	Charles becomes sole ruler of the Franks.
775	Charles undertakes long-term effort to subdue and Christianize the Saxons.
780	Charles meets Alcuin in Parma.
781-790	Charles launches revival of learning under Alcuin's direction.
794	Alcuin defends orthodoxy against Adoptianism at the Council of Frankfurt.
796	Alcuin becomes Abbot of St. Martin of Tours.
800	Pope Leo III crowns Charlemagne and declares him emperor.
804	Death of Alcuin.
813	Charlemagne crowns Louis of Aquitaine co-emperor and his successor.
814	Death of Charlemagne.

York • England

Alcuin

and the Emperor Charlemagne
James H. Pain

Alcuin at York

Alcuin was probably orphaned as a child, for he tells us nothing of his life prior to his school days at York Minster, and he speaks of his masters there as having cared for him from infancy "with a mother's affection." In his biography of Willibrord he appears to claim blood relation with Willibrord's father, Wilgils. If this is a correct reading of the text, it indicates that Alcuin came from a noble family of literate Christians. It is likely that he was born near York about A.D. 735, though no record of his birth or baptism seems to have survived. In any event, Alcuin was a precocious youngster, who distinguished himself in the eyes of the York headmaster, Aelbertus.

In the eighth century, York Cathedral had one of the finest libraries in the Christian world (rivalled, but not excelled, by Jarrow and Canterbury.) There Alcuin had access to works of Ambrose, Aristotle, Augustine, Bede, Boethius, Cassiodorus, Cicero, Gregory the Great, Lactantius, Lucan, Orosius, Pliny, Statius, Virgil, and many others. Much of the material in the British libraries had been brought from abroad after 675, and the search for manuscripts was a lively one in Alcuin's day. It was on such a quest that, as a young man, he accompanied Aelbertus to Rome. Their journey served to confirm the headmaster's growing admiration for, and confidence in, Alcuin.

When Aelbertus was made archbishop of York in 766, he saw to it that Alcuin was his successor in the Cathedral school. For fifteen years Alcuin served with great distinction. Then in 780 the papacy awarded archbishop Eanbald the pallium, and Eanbald sent Alcuin to Rome to claim it for him. (The object itself is a yoke-like garment worn over the shoulders, and indicates that the wearer has a share in the pontifical office. In more recent times, all archbishops petition for and receive it as a condition of office, but in Eanbald's day it was a distinction of honour. Alcuin's errand was thus one of high privilege.) It was on this trip that he met Charles the Great (Charlemagne) at Parma.

Charlemagne

Tradition has it that Charles was born on April 2, 742. He was a grandson of Charles Martel and the eldest son of Pepin III, "Mayor of the Palace" of the Merovingians. In 751 Pepin assumed the title "King of the Franks", and three years later Pope Stephen II anointed him and his young sons Charles and Carloman for kingship.

When Pepin died in 768, his domains were divided between his sons. Charles came to rule Austrasia, Neustria, and Western Aquitaine. But upon the death of Carloman in 771, Charles claimed all his father's territory, thereby reunifying the Frankish monarchy.

He soon launched a series of campaigns designed to Christianize and subdue the Saxons, a project that occupied his attention sporadically until 804.

In 778 Charlemagne entered Spain, intending to take Zaragoza. His troops captured Pamplona, but while approaching Zaragoza they were called back because of a Saxon revolt. In their retreat across the Pyrenees they were ambushed by Basques at a narrow pass near Roncevaux. Charles's rear-guard was cut off from the rest of his troops and annihilated. Hroudland or "Roland" legends, such as the *Chanson de Roland*, perpetuate fanciful accounts of the defeat. Hroudland is presented as a nephew of Charles who served on his baronial council. In the narration he is betrayed by a spiteful stepfather (Ganelon). At the Battle of Roncevaux, all of the rear guard perish save Hroudland, who, with his faithful sword Durandel, stands alone sounding his mournful horn when Charlemagne and

York Minster, northern England. Alcuin spent his schooldays here.

his troops finally arrive.

In spite of his failure in Spain, Charles did succeed in putting down the Saxon uprising. In 788 he brought all of Bavaria into his domain, thus bringing political unity to the Germans for the first time.

During the eighth century the church in western Europe made a number of attempts to combat aspects of pagan practice that had seriously compromised Christianity in what are called the Dark Ages. On 21 April 742 a German council passed a decree condemning pagan rites that "foolish men perform in the churches" – such as the sacrifice of animals, sacrifices to the dead, incantations, and divination. The people of God were ordered to perform no pagan rites, but to reject and cast out all the foulness of the Gentiles, including phylacteries and auguries.

The Carolingian Renaissance

Charles undertook to support the battle against sacrilegious idolatry. He understood that as long as great numbers of the clergy and the people were uneducated it would be impossible to root out paganism or to realize Augustine's vision of Christianization.

This led him to Alcuin, with a commission to introduce Latin education into the Frankish court. Charles's dream was to revive ancient learning, to educate the court and clergy, and to establish parish schools. Parochial, public, and theological educators in the modern era all have common ancestors in Charles and Alcuin.

From 781-790 Alcuin devoted his whole attention to the implementing of Charles's scheme. His first pupils were the royal family, members of the court, young priests, and clergy of the palace chapel. An indication of his teaching method survives in the charming *Dialogue of Pepin and Alcuin* (Pepin was one of Charles's sons).

Apart from actual teaching, Alcuin's chief task was the building of a court library. His catalogue included writings of the church Fathers and other "ancient authors." It also reflected Charles's interest in history, mathematics, and astronomy.

To begin with, the efforts at educating the public were basic enough: all Christians must know the Lord's Prayer. Alcuin and Charles later added the Ten Commandments. This was to be the starting-point for a revival of popular justice and morality.

Alcuin understood that the content of the gospel would be subject to distortion if the form and language in which it was conveyed were inappropriate to it. By form he implied both rhetoric and philosophical structure. He held that, though in essence the gospel was simple enough for a child to grasp, maturity of faith demanded understanding. And understanding was in turn a function of the reason. But human reason itself is the tool of heresy as well as of orthodoxy. His concern for propriety of form and orthodox content is the subject of *Epistola de litteris colendis*, written in 784-785. He insists that orthodoxy (right faith) must be clothed in a form consistent with sound doctrine and conveyed in language that is universally understood.

Alcuin the theologian

In 790 Alcuin returned to York. His responsibility to Charles continued, though, and is reflected in his involvement in two theological disputes.

The first of those is recorded in the *Libri Carolini* of 791. In these writings Charles and Alcuin address issues of the iconoclastic controversy. They attack both the position of the Seventh Ecumenical Council (Nicea II, which met in 787) and that of the Iconoclastic Council of 754. Sadly, Alcuin was working from a very poor Latin translation of the *Acts* of Nicea II, which had been provided by Hadrian I. As a result, his efforts contributed more to confusion of the issues than to anything else.

He was on firmer ground in attacking a resurgence of adoptianism in Spain. In 794 Charles called a council at Frankfurt-am-Main at which Alcuin defended orthodox doctrine concerning the eternal

York Minster at dusk.
Inset: The twin towers of York Minster.

sonship of Christ and its Trinitarian implications. The council condemned two
Spanish bishops: Felix of Urgel and El-
ipandus of Toledo. Both had been accused
of heresy at the Council of Ratisbon in
792, but the outcome was unclear. Alcuin
pursued the matter at Frankfurt and
again at Aachen in 798 until Felix not only
recanted but professed to be persuaded to
the truth by his opponent.

Abbot of St. Martin of Tours

In 796 Alcuin accepted Charles's invitation to become abbot of the great abbey of
St. Martin of Tours, and there he spent
the last years of his life. He was in no
sense retired, for he undertook to reorganize the abbey school into a large
enterprise, renowned for its superior standards. He instituted a new curriculum that
was centered on the study of Augustine
and Boethius. He stressed the importance
of grammatical structure in the study of

Frankfurt-am-Main, Germany.

had also written textbooks, educational manuals, theological treatises (the best known of which is *De Fide Trinitatis*), biblical commentaries, a revision of the Gallic Lectionary, and an edition of Charlemagne's *Sacramentary*.

Alcuin did more than any other single person to establish the Carolingian Renaissance. He brought an Anglo-Saxon influence into a court previously Italian in orientation, and he gave new life to the liberal arts, with theology at their center.

Charlemagne crowned emperor

Charles did not have the benefit of Alcuin's company when in 800 he journeyed to Rome seeking to consolidate the papal domain. There in St. Peter's, after the first mass of Christmas Day, Charlemagne was acclaimed emperor and crowned by Pope Leo III, who declared that the ancient Roman dignity was restored. Charlemagne could claim succession from Caesar Augustus. The fact that the pope had no constitutional right to do any of this was no obstacle. It mattered little that Byzantium claimed a dignity dating from July 25, 306, when, in Alcuin's beloved York, Constantine the Great was acclaimed Caesar Augustus.

From his palace in the spa of Aachen, Charlemagne now reigned over Rome and the entire western segment of the old Roman Empire. But in the providence of God the time for the restoration of that empire was not yet. Charlemagne lacked the ability of ancient Rome to regularize the military, economic, and civil aspects of its vast domain. The Normans were at the ready, and his empire survived by only one generation his death at Aachen on July 28, 814.

Charlemagne had been successful in uniting Europe, and he was properly called *Rex pater Europae*. But his lasting contribution was intellectual, and much of that he owed to his faithful friend Alcuin. The antipope Paschal III sainted Charlemagne in 1165.

Scripture and began programs for training monks and spiritual directors in scriptural literacy.

In this period Alcuin had as students the controversial liturgist Amalarius of Metz (730-850) and the German evangelist Rabanus Maurus (784-856), who was later to become the archbishop of Mainz.

Alcuin did not neglect his skill as a librarian; he launched a project for the copying of great manuscripts, which was to be the source of splendid illuminations. In his last years he kept up a substantial correspondence, including many letters to Charles. Much of this survives and is an invaluable source of historical and spiritual insight.

When he died unexpectedly on 19 May 804, Alcuin left a considerable literary legacy. His longest effort as a poet is a verse history of the church at York. He

Anselm of Canterbury
*c.*1033-1109

Anselm (*c.* 1033-1109) was one of the most prolific and profound writers of the Middle Ages. In all, twelve treatises, nineteen prayers, three meditations, and about four hundred letters have survived as a reflection of his immense literary production.

Of enduring importance for philosophical theology are Anselm's *Monologium* and *Proslogium*, produced at Bec. His *Cur Deus Homo*? (Why God Became Man), written while at Canterbury, is the first serious attempt to give rationale to the atonement. The same principle of *credo, ut intelligam* – of faith "seeking understanding" – underlies his philosophical-theological and theological-philosophical works. Anselm insisted that Christian faith and dogma should be subject to rational reflection. This procedure does not rob either of the residue of mystery.

According to that dictum, Anselm sought to justify his faith in God's existence and triunity and the impossibility of salvation apart from Christ by adducing for them "necessary reasons." The results of his reflections have challenged the faith and unbelief of succeeding generations. Eadmer recounts the amazement caused in his own day by Anselm's endeavor "to unravel the darkest, and before his time, the unsolved and unusual questions concerning the Divine Nature and our faith, which lay hid, covered by much darkness in the Divine Scriptures."

Archbishop Anselm of Canterbury.

The Life of
Anselm

c. 1033	Birth in Aosta, Italy.
1060	Enters abbey of Bec as monk.
1078-1092	Prior of Bec, Normandy.
1092	Begins to organize the monastery of St. Werburg's at Chester, England.
1093	Inaugurated as archbishop of Canterbury.
1103-1107	Exile.
1109	Death.

Anselm of Canterbury

Pastor and Thinker

H. Dermot McDonald

Prior of Bec

Anselm was born at Aosta, northern Italy, about the year 1033. One story only is preserved by his contemporary biographer, Eadmer, of the influence the exquisite scenery of Anselm's Alpine surroundings exerted upon him. His mother taught him that "there is one God in heaven". But in his childish thought God was conceived as dwelling in a mountain-top palace. He dreamed he visited the place and protested the reason of his coming was to seek truth. There refreshed "by the bread of heaven", he returned vowing to declare the knowledge he had gained.

When "not yet fifteen" Anselm sought how best "to shape his life according to God." Thereupon he decided to become a monk. The times were such that a man who would be active had little choice but to be a soldier; and a man who would serve God, free from worldly entanglements, had few options but to be a monk. After several altercations with his father, Anselm entered the Dominican monastery of Bec in Normandy. There, under the influence of its founder, Herwin, and the learned Lanfranc, its prior, he developed as a philosophical-religious thinker of extraordinary originality. On the elevation of Lanfranc to the see of Canterbury, Anselm was chosen prior of Bec, where he remained for the next fourteen years, from 1078 until 1092.

Archbishop of Canterbury

Anselm's monastic career overlapped with that of William, Duke of Normandy, who became conqueror of Britain in 1066. In William's reign "was the great minster of Canterbury built," only to have its possessions plundered and its revenues looted by his son.

In 1092, after repeated refusals, Anselm acceded to the invitation to come to England to organize the monastery of St. Werburg's at Chester. On his arrival, however, in response to popular and ecclesiastical clamor, he was appointed archbishop of Canterbury on the death of its first occupant, his former teacher and religious superior, Lanfranc.

Anselm's inaugural ceremony took place on December 4, 1093. For the next sixteen years he served in a distinguished episcopate that was, unfortunately, interrupted by periods of conflict with the secular and regal authorities over their interference in the affairs of the church. And then, as one commentator wrote, "He passed away, as morning was breaking in the year of our Lord's Incarnation 1109."

Devotional writings

Anselm's earliest writings, the prayers and meditations, are characterized by a deep devotion to Christ, Mary, and the saints and thus presuppose the monastic setting in which his contemplative life developed. His letters of advice, compliments, consolation, reproof, and on ecclesiastical and theological subjects are all models of pastoral affection and understanding. They are, besides, full of sound spiritual and practical sense. To his "very dear brother Odo, monk and cellarer," for example, he writes to encourage perseverance: "Of evil works we ought to repent, and forsake them before we die: lest the day find us in them. But of good works we ought to persevere till the end, that in them our soul may be taken out of life."

He would have his brother Rodolf (Dominicum Rodulfum) "be one perpetual act of thanksgiving." To his (spiritual) "brother and son, Maurice," he counsels diligent study "to the best of your power, and especially about Virgil, and the other authors which you did not read with me."

Although Anselm did not work out a theological system as such, he did advance ideas that were taken up in later systematics. *On the Virginal Conception and Original Sin* he developed the thesis later designated the "voluntary appropriation of depravity." Acknowledging with Augustine that human nature was corrupted by the Fall, Anselm maintains nevertheless that the individual person is not guilty for his original sinfulness. Although everyone at birth has a sinful nature derived from his parents, none is accounted guilty as a sinner unless and until he wills to act according to the bias of his nature. Anselm distinguishes between "nature" and "person." In Adam, the person made nature sinful; in his posterity, nature makes the person sinful. The treatise *Concerning the Agreement of Foreknowledge, Predestination and the Grace of God, with Free Will*, written during the last two years of his life, attempts a harmony between divine sovereignty and human autonomy.

Faith and reason

Anselm believed that man's mind, as created by God, is equipped to probe the essential rationality of the Christian revelation. It is the possession of reason that sets off man as superior to other animals. It is his distinctive as made in the image of God. Faith indeed precedes reason. But we cannot believe at all unless we have rational minds. In common with Augustine, Anselm affirmed it to be remiss of Christians not to attempt to make credible to the mind the items of their essential faith.

His first writing, initially entitled an *Example of Meditating on the Rationale of Faith*, was later renamed the *Monologium* (Soliloquy) *on the Rationale of the Faith*. Here Anselm seeks to secure his basic premise of God as perfect being. Beginning with the observation of degrees of perfection in the world, such as greatness, goodness, and the like, he declares that these of necessity point to a final perfection with which they contrast and in which they have their ultimate fulfillment. Likewise is it with being. Degrees of existing beings must indicate the one self-existing ultimate being, and "this must be the best and highest of all that is." Anselm then proceeds to give reasons for the triune nature of this one supreme being, arguments for which are conducted solely within the area of natural religion and philosophical thinking.

The ontological argument

In the *Proslogium* (Colloquy), first called *Faith Seeking and Understanding*, Anselm develops what is known as the ontological argument for the existence of God. Response to a request from the monks of

Interior, St Martin's Church, Canterbury.

Bec led him to consider the possibility of setting forth a proof which would be sufficient of itself to assure that all he had declared about the Divine Substance in the *Monologium* referred to an actual existent. In the style of an address to God he begins with the affirmation of His being as "that than which no greater can be thought." He thereupon argues that to exist in mind only is less perfect than to exist both in mind and in reality. He concludes, consequently, that the most perfect conceivable being, namely God, must then exist in reality as well as in mind.

Anselm's "proof" has had varied acceptance throughout history. Rejected by Aquinas, it was reaffirmed by Descartes; denied by Kant, it was rehabilitated by Hegel. The main criticism of it is that it is not proper to move from an idea in the mind to an actuality in the outside world. Nor is it proper to regard existence as if it were a quality that a thing may or may not possess. On the other hand, it is hard for the mind to have the notion of God as non-existing. The *idea* of God does appear to hold in it the idea of His existence. Thus, to affirm that God as the self-existent One exists, yet He may not exist, must look like an unbearable contradiction in terms.

The atonement

Anselm brought the same combination of logical analysis and grammatical definition to the idea of the atonement. His *Cur Deus Homo?*, written in the form of a dialogue between himself and Boso, a supposed disciple, first refutes the medieval notion of the devil's "rights" over fallen humanity. It then goes on to elaborate the idea of atonement as a "satisfaction" made to God and by God. Such a satisfaction Anselm declares necessary because of man's sin. Sin is itself conceived as the robbing of God of the honor due Him. Were angel or man always to render to God what is owing, neither would have sinned. "Everyone who sins ought to render back to God the honor he has taken away, and this is the *satisfaction* which every sinner ought to make to God."

God could not forgive sin without atonement, for otherwise His righteous magisterial authority would be compromised. Yet the sure fact is that no man can make good the deficiency of honor due. But man must do that if he is to avoid the punishment of eternal condemnation. For it "must needs be that satisfaction or punishment follow every sin." Man's case appears consequently hopeless. For, on the one hand, his debt is infinite and can only be paid by an infinite being. On the other hand, it is man who owes it, and by him it must be paid. Since, therefore, no one *can* make satisfaction but one who is God; and no one *ought* to make it but man, "it is necessary that One who is God-man should make it."

Anselm then goes on to discuss how the God-man makes such satisfaction. As man the incarnate One rendered throughout His life full honor to God. But in His death He went beyond what was due. He was under no obligation to die because He was not a sinner. For this excess of obedience of utmost self-sacrifice he deserved a reward. "To whom could he [God] assign the fruit and recompense of his death more suitably than to those for whose salvation (as truthful reason has taught us) he made himself man, and to whom (as we said) by his death he gave an example of dying on behalf of righteousness. For in vain will they be imitators of him if they be not partakers of his reward." In sum, then, for Anselm the essence of the atonement lies in God's acceptance of Christ's sacrifice as an offering to satisfy the divine honor.

Many defects and merits have been found in Anselm's theory of the atonement throughout subsequent history. But it has continued to hold its place and shape the thinking of large numbers of both Roman Catholic and Protestant writers on redemption theology down to modern times.

Opposite: St Martin's Church, Canterbury.

The Crusades

The First Crusade set out in 1095, after Pope Urban II had called on Christians to help the Eastern church defend itself against the Turks, who had taken Jerusalem and were threatening Constantinople. The Crusaders marched overland to the Holy Land and eventually succeeded in recapturing Jerusalem from the Turks in 1099, setting up four Crusader states.

The Crusades brought together two characteristic strands in eleventh-century Europe — the holy war and the pilgrimage to a holy place, and many of the Crusaders were undoubtedly motivated by religious ideals. However, the later Crusades were much less successful than the first, although the papacy continued to encourage men to go on crusade, promising tax immunity, indulgences, and financial support.

Historians have listed seven or eight distinct Crusades, but it is important to see in them a new and continuous surge of European expansion after centuries of defensive strategy. From 1150 onward there was a steady stream of soldiers, traders, and religious pilgrims to the Middle East.

The Second and Third Crusades

In 1144 Edessa, one of the Crusader states, fell back into Muslim hands, and in 1150 Islam was reunited under a single dynasty, threatening the Crusader hold on the Holy Places. The Second Crusade, organized by Bernard of Clairvaux, was defeated at Damascus, and in 1187 Saladin, the Islamic leader, beat the Crusaders at Hittim and recaptured Jerusalem. Although the Third Crusade, led by Richard the Lionheart of England and the rulers of France and Germany, succeeded in recovering some of the lost lands, Jerusalem itself remained in Muslim hands.

Richard the Lionheart, Crusader king of England.

The Crusades continued into the thirteenth century, but only that of Frederick II of Germany, which regained Jerusalem by negotiation, achieved any success. Jerusalem was lost again in 1244, and Acre, the Crusaders' last stronghold in the Holy Land, fell in 1291, effectively ending Crusader rule in Syria.

The Crusades ultimately failed. The Crusaders were never strong enough numerically to retain their captures in the Holy Land. Those Crusaders who settled in the East tended to adopt Eastern customs and forfeited the sympathy of later Christian Crusaders. The Crusades to the East were superseded by the popes' crusades against European heretics such as the Albigensians, and in the thirteenth century men such as Raymond Lull began to question the efficacy of military expeditions against Islam; peaceful missions were now advocated in their place.

Bernard of Clairvaux

1090-1153

Bernard of Clairvaux (1090-1153) is one of the noblest figures of the Catholic Middle Ages. He not only represents much of what is best in the Catholic tradition but also reveals many of its paradoxes and shortcomings. As the son of a knight who fought in the First Crusade, and as the man who engineered the Second, Bernard was acquainted with worldly weaponry, but he fought his own combats with spiritual weapons – for the church, for the purification of the monastic movement, and for traditional Trinitarian orthodoxy.

The author of deeply devotional hymns that both Protestants and Catholics love, including "Jesus, Thou Joy of Loving Hearts" and "Jesus, King Most Wonderful," Bernard is nevertheless not a hero to many modern Christians, conservative or liberal. Yet Bernard is not an aberration, but rather one of the most impressive characters that medieval Christian piety could produce. We cannot reject him without repudiating the Christianity of the Middle Ages, and that would cut us off from our roots in the apostolic age.

Statue of Bernard of Clairvaux.

The Life of

Bernard

1090	Birth in Burgundy.
1112	Joins the Cistercian house at Cîteaux.
1115	Founds monastery at Clairvaux.
1128	*Book of Praise of the New Chivalry.*
1140	Struggles against Abelard, who is condemned at the Council of Sens.
1153	Death.

Bernard of Clairvaux

Medieval Saint

Harold O. J. Brown

Bernard's youth

Bernard was born in 1090 at the castle of Fontaines-les-Dijon in Burgundy. His family belonged to the lesser nobility and combined an unpretentious life-style with old-fashioned Catholic piety. Bernard's father, Tescelin, left for the First Crusade when Bernard was six. Tescelin appears to have been among the Crusaders who objected to the excesses (such as the attacks on German Jews) that marred what turned out to be the only successful Crusade.

Bernard was destined at first for a worldly career and received the usual training of a young nobleman. Instead, like so many young men of his era, he chose to become a monk. Although he never sought high office, from his monastery he advised kings and popes and was virtually the uncrowned ruler of Europe. The fact that a monk who seldom left his monastery could exercise such an influence testifies to the tremendous respect in which spiritual leaders were held. The ability of one man without political office or power to change history solely by his teaching and example is without parallel until the sixteenth century, when Martin Luther would once again transform Europe from his pulpit and professor's chair in a small town in Saxony.

Although a towering figure in his own century, Bernard is not well-known among Protestants today. They look on his greatest accomplishments with suspicion: he reformed monasticism and gave it a new and firmer structure, and he sent the military elite of Europe on the Second Crusade. Modern Roman Catholics are hardly more enthusiastic about this monk, though he represents the finest example of medieval religion, precisely because he was a friend of kings and popes and had no qualms about the use of the sword to support the proclamation of the Word. Bernard stands for the triumphalism that modern Catholicism rejects. He not only sent soldiers to Palestine to battle infidels, but he himself fought hard for orthodoxy as he understood it. A number of preachers and teachers, such as Peter Abelard, Gilbert de la Porrée, Peter de Bruys, Henry of Lausanne, and Arnold of Brescia, felt his wrath, and subsequent generations look on Bernard as a kind of forerunner of the Inquisition.

Bernard's calling

As a youth, Bernard was "converted" from the world, or "called to religion" in the medieval sense. In other words, he "received a vocation" to enter the monastic life, which was held to be the only really consistent way to live as a Christian. In later years, Bernard would teach that it is the only way to be really *human*: disciplined obedience and devotion are the foundation of all spiritual life, and unless we are spiritually alive, we are little better than mere animals. Bernard spent his life trying to fulfill his own high standards. In the process he made the Christian life seem so exacting that ordinary people came to the conclusion that it was beyond them. Not until Luther would the ordinary Christian be told that the real meaning of "vocation" is to be "called" to faith in Christ, not to monasticism, and that every Christian has a "vocation" to serve and honor God in daily living.

Bernard did not simply become a monk;

he took three of his brothers and more than two dozen friends with him, making a total of thirty young men who presented themselves with him at the recently founded monastery of Cîteaux (in Latin, *Cistercium*). Cîteaux was established in 1098 by a reforming Benedictine abbot, Robert of Molesme, when his own monastery proved unreceptive to his call for stricter discipline and less worldliness. In founding Cîteaux, Robert broke with the Benedictine tradition that a monk was "married" to his monastery and should remain faithful to it for life. Cîteaux became something new – a "mother house" from which scores of daughter monasteries were formed, contrasting with the older pattern, in which each monastery was independent under its own abbot. Cîteaux became the mother house of the first true order, the Cistercians, setting a pattern for several other new orders.

Clairvaux, France.

Bernard enters Cîteaux

Although he was not the founder of the Cistercian order, having entered Cîteaux fourteen years after its establishment. Bernard became the most famous member of the new order. After him, not only monks in his daughter houses, but Cistercians in general, were frequently called "Bernardines." When Bernard and his thirty noble young friends joined Cîteaux in 1112, this fresh blood sparked a runaway growth of the order. Cîteaux's strict asceticism and Bernard's own selfimposed rigors permanently weakened his health; his accomplishments over the next forty years were the triumph of a strong spirit over a weak body.

In 1115 Bernard, only twenty-five, was sent to found a new monastery at Clairvaux. Clairvaux became the center of his life work; from it he directed not only the expansion of the Cistercians but the fate of kings and nations. By the time of his death in 1153, Bernard had directly founded seventy monasteries and had an additional ninety under his authority. In addition, he profoundly influenced several new orders, such as the Carthusians and the Premonstratensians – and even the Benedictines themselves through a personal friendship with Suger, abbot of the great Benedictine monastery of St. Denis.

The military orders

Bernard not only revitalized existing monasticism; he also vitally influenced a development for which modern Christendom has scant appreciation: the establishment of the monastic military orders. These were communities of knights and men-at-arms living under monastic discipline, committed to the defense of the faith, of the church, and of Christians, first of all in the Holy Land but then elsewhere as well. They were not founded by Bernard, but their development is unthinkable without his influence and example. He wrote the rule for one of the two most famous military orders, the Knights Templar. (This celebrated order was to enjoy almost two centuries of prominence before being exterminated by an autocratic French king; its memory is preserved in romance and legend as well as in the symbolism of Freemasonry.)

In addition to the international Templars, Bernard's ideas inspired the purely German military orders as well, the Brethren of the Sword and the Knights of the Cross. After being pushed out of the Holy Land, the German orders would follow a strategy at least partly inspired by Bernard and devote themselves to the forcible Christianization of the Baltic region of northeastern Europe. Eventually these "crusades" of the two German orders (combined as the Teutonic Knights, or *Deutschritterorden*) were to be stopped by the opposition of other Christians, Lithuanians, and Poles. The Teutonic Knights founded Prussia, which later would make militarism synonymous with morality. The symbolism of the crusading orders lingers on into the present not only in the military insignia of Germany but also in the crosses awarded for military valor by Great Britain and the United States. In his *Book of Praise of the New Chivalry* (1128), Bernard endorsed a kind of militant Christianity that seems a far cry from the days of the apostles and martyrs and that meets with very little understanding among Christians today.

Medieval monasticism

Bernard's impact on his own age shows how central monasticism was to medieval Christendom. The monks represented the only "full time" Christians, rather like foreign missionaries in the eyes of many evangelical Protestants today. Ordinary people supported the monks to do what they themselves were unable or unwilling to attempt. The rise of modern independent missionary societies, with their *esprit de corps* and their loyal, lifelong supporters, offers a modern parallel to the proliferation of new monastic orders in the Middle Ages.

Neither monks nor the Templars could protect the hierarchy from itself. The pope symbolized the unity of the Latin church, but suddenly there were two

popes at once. When Pope Honorius II died in February 1130, two reformist parties each elected its own pope: Innocent II and Anaclete II (the Schism of Anaclete). Bernard supported Innocent, who stood for the more radical reform movement. He left the seclusion of Clairvaux and traveled through the south of France and Italy pleading Innocent's claim. This papal schism led many to think that the return of Christ was at hand and to look for a final world ruler, the "Emperor of the Last Days." Bernard resisted such apocalyptic speculation at the time, although later he was to become more interested in this matter.

The schism ended with the death of Anaclete II in 1138, but in the meantime the subtle scholastic theologian Peter Abelard was causing turmoil of another kind by approaching basic doctrines in a critical spirit. Bernard threw his tremendous prestige into the scales against Abelard at the Council of Sens in 1140. Abelard's writings were condemned, and Abelard himself recanted.

Shortly thereafter, in Burgundy and in the south of France, two charismatic preachers, Peter de Bruys and Henry of Lausanne, began propagating a radical, other-worldly Christianity that foreshadowed the Albigensian heresy. In 1145 Bernard traveled extensively, preaching against them. Wherever he appeared, heresy calmed down, though only for a time.

The Second Crusade

While campaigning against this heresy, Bernard learned of a military disaster in the Near East. The county of Edessa, one of the Crusader states, had been reconquered by the Muslims, the first in a protracted series of military reverses that were eventually to wipe out the Christian position there. Bernard saw the danger to the Christian kingdom of Jerusalem and called for a fresh crusade. This required papal endorsement. Eugene III (ruled 1145-1153), the first Cistercian to become pope, was Bernard's former pupil and readily authorized him to preach a new crusade in France and Germany. Bernard believed that a great Christian victory in the Holy Land would convert countless pagans and prepare the way for the return of Christ. King Conrad III, who had a shaky hold on the German crown, was at first unwilling to join the crusade, but Bernard won him over in a show of Christian unity. Bernard called it a "miracle of miracles," but his joy was brief.

Like the successful First Crusade, Bernard's Second Crusade began badly, before even leaving Germany. A monk named Radulf urged the Crusaders to kill the defenseless "infidels" and "God-killers" – that is, Jews – in Germany before facing the well-armed Muslims in the East. Although Bernard was critical of the Jews – his is the first recorded voice to call usury a "Jewish" practice – such atrocities horrified him. His prompt personal intervention put a stop to the pogroms. Perhaps Bernard's defense of the Jews of Germany is still responsible for the subsequent popularity of Bernard as a boy's name among them.

While the troops he had recruited were fighting infidels in the Holy Land, Bernard once again had to fight heresy in the form of the novel Trinitarian ideas of Gilbert de la Porrée, whom he charged with teaching that an essence of God exists alongside the three Persons. Bernard successfully confronted Gilbert at the Council of Reims in 1148 but not without harming his own reputation by his intemperate zeal.

It was at Reims that Bernard heard his Crusade had ended in disaster. Blamed for the débacle, he commented: "It is better that they blame me than God." Even before the Crusade, he had warned the Germans that God would not bless their arms if they allowed people to fall away from the faith in Christian lands. This led to a "crusade" against the Slavic Wends east of the Elbe River, a foretaste of the later crusades of the Teutonic Knights against the Balts and Slavs of Lithuania and Courland. Thus Bernard bears some blame for turning the Crusades from their original goal in the Holy

Part of the Crusader city, Caesarea.

Land into plain wars of aggression.

Bernard saw the world as a battlefield between God and Satan. He fought the devil in his own life by a rigorous asceticism, and he fought him within monasticism by far-reaching reforms and the establishment of new monasteries. In theology, he fought heresy with arguments and, where that failed, with force. He fought the devil in the Holy Land by starting a crusade and by fostering the military orders. To us it seems that all his labor was in vain. The Crusades fizzled out, monasticism has waned, and hardly anyone considers heresy a mortal danger. Few twentieth-century Christians think that Muslims and heretics should be fought with military force or that monasticism is the only truly human life-style.

Nevertheless Bernard of Clairvaux towers above his contemporaries as one who really lived what he believed. Like the martyrs of the early church and the missionaries closer to our own day, Bernard offers an example of obedience that must be respected even if we are not persuaded to imitate him.

Timechart 1000-1400

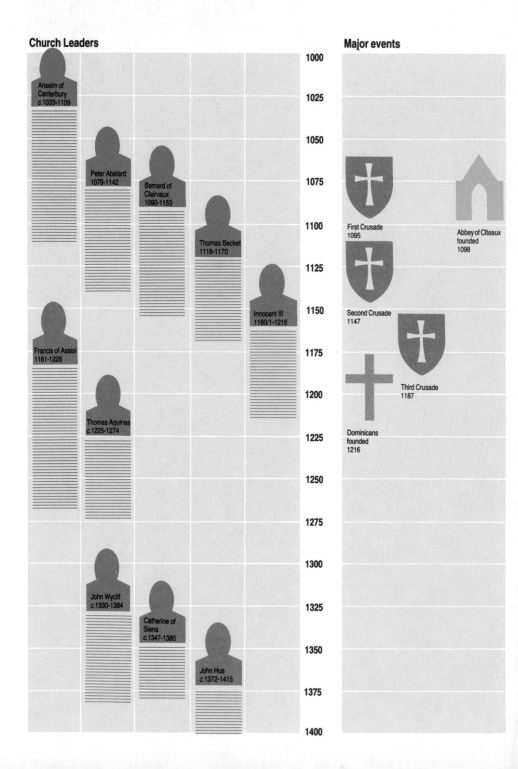

Church Leaders

Anselm of
Canterbury
c.1033-1109

Peter Abelard
1079-1142

Bernard of
Clairvaux
1090-1153

Thomas Becket
1118-1170

Innocent III
1160/1-1216

Francis of Assisi
1181-1228

Thomas Aquinas
c.1225-1274

John Wyclif
c.1330-1384

Catherine of
Siena
c.1347-1380

John Hus
c.1372-1415

Major events

First Crusade
1095

Abbey of Cîteaux
founded
1098

Second Crusade
1147

Third Crusade
1187

Dominicans
founded
1216

1000
1025
1050
1075
1100
1125
1150
1175
1200
1225
1250
1275
1300
1325
1350
1375
1400

Peter Abelard

1079-1142

Peter Abelard (1079-1142) was a controversial teacher of Breton descent. He gave up the possibility of glory in the First Crusade and renounced his inheritance in order to pursue a career in philosophy and theology. His life was never free from controversy. On the one hand, he rejected the nominalism of Roscellinus of Compiègne, and on the other he refuted the radical realism taught by William of Champeaux. He affirmed the inerrancy of the Scriptures, attributing any perceived errors to copyists; and he denied that the Dominical commission to remit or bind sins (Matthew 16:19; 18:18) applied to any but the original disciples, thus disputing the church's claim to sacramental power of absolution.

Abelard's career as a teacher was marred by a disastrous affair with a teenaged pupil of his named Héloïse, and though they subsequently produced a correspondence of remarkable spiritual sensitivity, their alliance was held in derision.

Twice in his life Abelard was tried for heresy concerning the Trinity, and, though on both occasions he was found guilty, the charges were not established in fact.

Peter Abelard, controversial theologian and teacher.

The Life of

Abelard

1079	Birth near Nantes, France.
1102	Begins to lecture at Melun, and later at Corbeil.
1108	Returns to Paris and establishes school on Mont Ste. Geneviève.
1115	Elected canon of Notre Dame Cathedral.
1118	Takes up residence with Canon Fulbert, becomes tutor to Héloïse. Calamitous love affair.
1119	Retires to the Abbey of St. Denis.
1120	Reopens school at Maisoncelle. Publishes *Theologia Summi Boni*.
1121	Condemned by Council at Soissons.
1122	Decides to become a hermit. Founds a small school at Aube.
1123-24	Publishes *Theologia Christiana*.
1125	Elected abbot of St. Gildas de Rhuys, Brittany.
1132	His monks turn against him and he flees. Publishes *Historia Calamitatum*.
1136	Returns to teach in Paris.
1139	In public dispute with Bernard of Clairvaux.
1141	Synod of Sens condemns him; appeals to Rome.
1142	Death in the Cluniac Priory of St. Marcel.

Peter Abelard

Teacher and Theologian

James H. Pain

Peter's childhood

Born in Le Pallet, a small village about ten miles southeast of Nantes, France, Peter was the eldest of several brothers and at least one sister. His devout parents, Berengarius and Lucia, sought to bring him up to be both learned and pious. When he went to school he was simply known as Pierre du Pallet, but his friends soon gave him the nickname "Bajolardus". Just what they intended is not clear, but the title probably derived from *bajolare* which means "to carry" in the sense of being heavy laden. In the Latin of Abelard's day *bajolus* was a term for porter, from *baiardos* ("bay horse"). Whatever the sense, Abelard accepted it and bore it for the rest of his life, albeit with spellings unlike the original. In addition to the present form it appears as Abaelard, Abailard, Abeillard, and even on occasions as Esbaillart.

On November 26, 1095, when Abelard was sixteen years old, Pope Urban II preached a sermon at Clermont that was instrumental in launching the First Crusade. A French pope on French soil calling for holy war stirred many to knightly pursuit, Berengarius among them. But Abelard writes that he "inwardly withdrew from the court of Mars to learn at the feet of Minerva." His father went crusading without him. When Jerusalem was liberated, Abelard was twenty.

He went to Paris to study dialectics and there he attached himself for a while to the rising star of the new nominalism, Roscellinus of Compiègne (d. 1125.). Abelard soon discerned that, however clever his teacher might be as a philosopher, he was wrong theologically. As a result, he became embroiled in arguments against nominalism. If, he charged, there is no more than mere breath to the concept of God, if there is no reality to the Godhead, and the Trinity is only a name invented by Tertullian, then there can be no consubstantial unity of the Father, Son, and Holy Spirit. Under such a view we are left with three persons or particular substances with equal power. In other words, we worship not one God but three gods. (Roscellinus had been accused of teaching Tritheism by a church council in 1092, but he had denied the charge.)

Nominalism and realism

Departing from the nominalists, Abelard sought out the opposing camp. He enthusiastically attended lectures by William of Champeaux (1070-1121), only to discover that, while eager to refute nominalism, William was arguing for an heretically extreme form of realism. Once again Abelard charged that the dogma of the Trinity was being subverted. If genus and species alone are real and indistinguishable, then all being in a given case is present in the particular, and individuation is only accidental. This would imply that Godhead alone is real and that the Persons of the Trinity are fully the same as regards their essence and differ only in accidental properties. Abelard saw that this was clearly contrary to the Athanasian Creed. He also thought that it was logically absurd, as if one were to argue that all of Plato was in Socrates, and all of Socrates in Plato.

Thus it was that at age twenty-one, having argued against both nominalists and realists, Abelard set up his own school. First at Mélun, later upriver closer to Paris at Castle Corbeil, and finally in Paris, he lectured on dialectics to large audiences.

He taught that universals are not *voces*, but *sermones*. That is, not mere words but discourses or conceptual predicates. Universals are not things. The verb is the part of speech appropriate to them. They declare or proclaim particular things that are real in themselves. Truth is in the thing *(Est in re veritas jam non in schemate).* As the apostle has written, the truth is *in* Jesus (Ephesians 4:21), of whom the gospel speaks as that holy thing that shall be called the Son of God (Luke 1:35).

In 1105 Abelard's health failed and he had to return to Le Pallet, where his mother nursed him through two years of serious illness.

After his recovery, Abelard returned to Paris in 1108, where he continued his arguments with William and established his school on Mont Ste. Geneviève. In 1113 his father determined to renounce the world. Having helped him to settle his estate, and having seen both of his parents established in monasteries, Abelard went to study with Anselm of Laon (*c.* 1040-1117). He argued with some of Anselm's students that one might interpret the Scriptures without having been taught a formal system. They challenged him to do so and to use as his text the book of Ezekiel. In this way he came to produce his first biblical commentary (The Book of Ezekiel). His approach is not novel, though he gives priority to the literal sense of the text in contrast to the common preference for allegorizing which prevailed in his day.

Abelard and Héloïse

In 1116 Abelard was invited to join the Cathedral School of Notre Dame in Paris as a canon, a post he accepted with alacrity. It was here that he met Canon Fulbert. While being entertained at Fulbert's table, Abelard met and fell in love with the canon's niece Héloïse, then a seventeen-year-old schoolgirl. He was thirty-seven. Not long thereafter he talked his way into becoming a boarder in Fulbert's house and, in time, tutor to Héloïse.

Fulbert appears to have loved his niece dearly and to have sought the best education for her, but he neglected her. So

Notre Dame Cathedral, Paris; Abelard became a canon of Notre Dame in 1116.

it was that Abelard came to take responsibility for her general welfare as well as for her lessons. And, in this, he confesses that he betrayed Fulbert's trust and seduced Héloïse. Eventually, they were caught in flagrante delicto. Fulbert was devastated and drove Abelard from the house. Héloïse subsequently discovered that she was pregnant and eloped with Abelard to Brittany.

He proposed marriage to her, but she would have none of it, arguing that it would ruin his career and that on the advice of Paul and Jerome it was better not to marry. She bore a son and named him Astrolabe, little knowing what an effect his birth would have on the charting of her life and that of Abelard.

Abelard and Héloïse were finally married with Fulbert's knowledge. Initially he agreed to keep the matter secret but then came to distrust Abelard. Fulbert conspired with members of his family and others to seek vengeance. A servant betrayed Abelard and admitted a party of men to come upon him in his sleep to castrate and mutilate him. (That servant and another member of the party were apprehended and punished by being deprived of their eyes and their genitalia.)

Abelard remarks that he suffered far more from remorse than he did from physical pain. He was deeply moved to contrition and repentance. Astrolabe was sent to his sister at Le Pallet. Héloïse entered a nunnery at Argenteuil, and Abelard himself sought refuge in the monastery of St. Denis. His career in Paris was at an end.

The abbot and the monks at St. Denis proved to be too worldly and superstitious for Abelard. He was critical of their behaviour and sought to expose to ridicule the legends surrounding their patron saint.

Abelard condemned

As he was attacking the Denis legends, others throughout France were attacking Abelard. In 1121 a council was convened at Soissons to hear charges that he taught Sabellianism. The council itself followed irregular practices, but in the end it did not make a case against his Trinitarian teaching. However, it condemned him for publishing a theological work without securing the requisite *imprimatur*. He was required to burn the book publicly and to read aloud the Athanasian Creed. Thereafter he was confined for a year in the monastery of St. Médard.

After all those events Abelard decided to become a hermit and retired to a "desert place" – open country between Romilly and Nogent-sur-Seine. There he built a thatched cabin for himself and a small hut for prayer, which he dedicated to the Holy Trinity. However, his students (among whom was Peter Lombard) would not leave him in peace and soon a community was established and an oratory and school founded in the name of the Paraclete. It was there in 1123-1124 that Abelard wrote his *Theologia Christiana*. During that period also he came to a knowledge of the forgiveness of his sins. Abelard wrote to Héloïse that God had forgiven him that which he had been unable to forgive in himself.

In 1125 he was appointed as abbot to the troubled monastery of St. Gildas-de-Rhuys on the shore of Lower Brittany. There, under appalling conditions, he wrote his *Historia Calamitatum*, a work that has proved to be one of the most original and significant of all medieval autobiographies.

After seven trying years during which his monks were continually seeking to do him harm (once even tipping poison into his altar chalice), Abelard was forced to flee in the face of attack. He returned to Mont Ste. Genevieve where he lectured again. Arnold of Brescia and John of Salisbury were among his students at this point.

Bernard and Abelard

Alerted to his return, Bernard of Clairvaux intensified a long-standing argument against Abelard, denouncing him to the bishops of France. In 1139 the two men had open disputation.

Bernard argued that, as a result of

"Abelard lecturing," by A. Steinheil.

human sin, Satan held just dominion over the human race, and that the sufferings and death of Christ had been in payment of a ransom to Satan in order to break that dominion. Anselm of Canterbury had argued that the payment was not made to Satan, but to God in recompense for mans failure to give Him due honor. Abelard contended that both positions were unscriptural and immoral. He taught that Satan had been allowed by God to be instrumental in punishing sinners, and that the wages of sin is death. Christ bore the full penalty and consequences of sin on the cross, thereby showing forth God's perfect love and justice – which, said Abelard, are one. For His love and justice are not things particular in themselves. Rather, they are predicates of His being, revealing to us the unity of His purpose.

In 1140-1141 the Council of Sens reviewed Abelard's doctrine, condemned nineteen of his propositions, and ordered that his works be burned. Bernard secured approval of the condemnation by Pope Innocent II and demanded that Abelard be excommunicated. Abelard refused to defend his teaching before the council and appealed to Rome. While journeying there he became ill and sought the hospitality of Cluny, where he was welcomed by Peter the Venerable.

On the morning of April 21, 1142, he died in the Cluniac Priory of St. Marcel (near Chalon-sur-Saône), where he was buried. Héloïse died in 1164. In 1817 their remains were reinterred together in Père Lachaise, Paris.

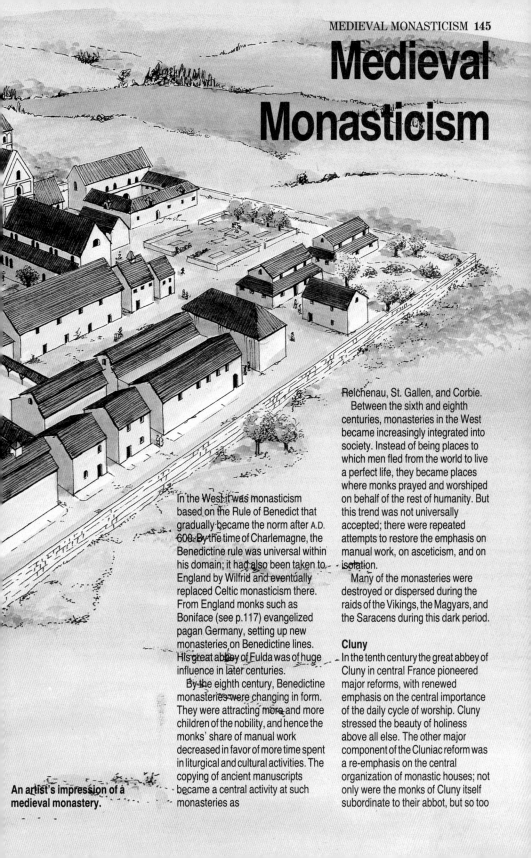

Medieval Monasticism

An artist's impression of a medieval monastery.

In the West it was monasticism based on the Rule of Benedict that gradually became the norm after A.D. 600. By the time of Charlemagne, the Benedictine rule was universal within his domain; it had also been taken to England by Wilfrid and eventually replaced Celtic monasticism there. From England monks such as Boniface (see p.117) evangelized pagan Germany, setting up new monasteries on Benedictine lines. His great abbey of Fulda was of huge influence in later centuries.

By the eighth century, Benedictine monasteries were changing in form. They were attracting more and more children of the nobility, and hence the monks' share of manual work decreased in favor of more time spent in liturgical and cultural activities. The copying of ancient manuscripts became a central activity at such monasteries as Reichenau, St. Gallen, and Corbie.

Between the sixth and eighth centuries, monasteries in the West became increasingly integrated into society. Instead of being places to which men fled from the world to live a perfect life, they became places where monks prayed and worshiped on behalf of the rest of humanity. But this trend was not universally accepted; there were repeated attempts to restore the emphasis on manual work, on asceticism, and on isolation.

Many of the monasteries were destroyed or dispersed during the raids of the Vikings, the Magyars, and the Saracens during this dark period.

Cluny

In the tenth century the great abbey of Cluny in central France pioneered major reforms, with renewed emphasis on the central importance of the daily cycle of worship. Cluny stressed the beauty of holiness above all else. The other major component of the Cluniac reform was a re-emphasis on the central organization of monastic houses; not only were the monks of Cluny itself subordinate to their abbot, but so too were all the monks at Cluny's dependent houses. This gained them a new independence from the local bishop or landlord.

Cluny's reforms were widely emulated. In England, Archbishop Dunstan (c.909-988) founded or re-established more than fifty monasteries. Similar reforms occurred elsewhere. In Germany, the abbey of Gorze brought about rather less rigorous reforms; in Italy the hermit type of monasticism was revived, with the founding of the Camaldoli by Romuald and the Vallombrosa by John Gualbert. Bruno of Cologne, who founded La Grande Chartreuse in southern France in 1084, and with it the Carthusian order, also favored the hermit form of monastery, with its greater rigor.

The Cistercians

Of the new orders attempting to revive the original Benedictine principles, the most successful was the Cistercian order, founded in 1098 by Robert of Molesme at Cîteaux in France. The Cistercians tried to break with the Cluniac tradition; their monasteries were simple and undecorated, and situated in remote, desolate places. They stressed silence, austerity, and manual work and had an elaborate system of organization. By 1300 there were more than 600 Cistercian houses.

Ironically the Cistercians' success in surviving during difficult conditions eventually brought them the material wealth that bore with it the seeds of their downfall.

Monastic decline

By 1200 monasticism had passed its peak of popularity. The number of monks began to fall, and monastic standards gradually declined. By the late Middle Ages, though there had been renewed attempts at monastic reform, such as those by the Celestinians (thirteenth century) and Olivetans (1319), monks had become integrated into society. However, they had lost the special respect earned in earlier centuries.

The Friars

At the beginning of the thirteenth century new groups of preaching monks, the friars, sometimes known as the begging "mendicant" orders, arose. They were very ascetic and concentrated their efforts in the towns and cities, preaching in the open air and taking a major role in the newly developing universities.

The Franciscans developed from the teaching of Francis of Assisi (p.160), who taught complete poverty. Their order, the Minor Friars, was approved by the pope in 1209. The other great order of friars, the Dominicans, was founded by Dominic de Guzman and recognized in 1220. He stressed the importance of teaching and preaching, and the Dominicans, with their white habit and black cloak, became known popularly as the Black Friars. It was the Dominicans, with their stress on learning, who contributed so much to medieval theology and education.

The friars achieved much in social, pastoral, educational, and missionary enterprises, Francis himself providing a pattern by serving the sick and those with leprosy. The friars' popular preaching methods were widely recognized. They also founded schools and set up houses at the great new university towns.

The abbey of Cluny, France.

Thomas Becket
1118-1170

Thomas Becket was a twelfth-century saint and martyr whose life and career illustrate the medieval struggle between church and state. Born in London of Norman parents, he was a tall, handsome, vigorous, intelligent man who, after receiving a legal education, entered the service of the archbishop of Canterbury. He attracted the attention of King Henry II and was appointed to the position of royal chancellor. He performed his duties very capably and became the king's trusted servant and friend. Later, Becket was made archbishop of Canterbury because Henry believed that he would serve the state as well as the church.

However, upon his election to the episcopal office Becket changed his allegiance and his life-style. Abandoning his worldly, materialistic ways, he became a saintly soul living a disciplined, pious, and austere life. He steadfastly resisted all efforts to impose the royal will on the church. Discord developed between the church and state over the punishment of clerics convicted of crimes.

As a result of that quarrel, Thomas was forced into exile in France from 1164 to 1170. When he returned to England in 1170 he was murdered in Canterbury Cathedral by a group of knights who believed they were doing Henry a service. Becket was sainted in 1173, and his shrine became the most popular destination for pilgrims in medieval England.

Thomas Becket, from a twelfth-century window, Canterbury Cathedral.

The Life of
Becket

1118	Birth in London.
1143	Joins the staff of Archbishop Theobald.
1154	Made archdeacon of Canterbury.
1154	Appointed chancellor to King Henry II.
1162	Elected archbishop of Canterbury.
1164	Forced into exile in France because of church-state quarrel.
1170	Returns to England.
1170	Murdered at Canterbury Cathedral.
1173	Sainted by the medieval church.

England

London

Canterbury

Thomas Becket

Church and State in Conflict

Robert G. Clouse

The king's friend

Thomas Becket (*c.* 1118-1170) was one of the most famous leaders of the medieval English church. Born into an upper-class Norman family in London, he spent most of his adult career at the court of Archbishop Theobald of Canterbury. After receiving a legal education in the university, he was for a time archdeacon of Canterbury and then became chancellor to King Henry II. Becket served the crown in an effective manner by providing military leadership for the English in several campaigns against the French in 1156 and 1158. He also arranged for the marriage of Margaret of France, daughter of Louis VII, to Henry II (1158). In addition he was itinerant justice, supervisor of taxation for England, chief of diplomatic correspondence, and dispenser of royal patronage. His impressive service to the crown led him to become the king's right-hand man. Thomas and Henry also became good friends, spending their time not only in serious governmental work but also in drinking, hunting, and in carousing.

When Theobald died in 1162, Becket was made archbishop of Canterbury by Henry. The king had assumed that

Canterbury Cathedral, Kent, England.

The font, St Martin's Church, Canterbury.

Thomas would continue to look after the interests of the state as well as those of the church, but in this he made a great mistake. As the leader of clerical interests in England, Becket was transformed from a strong supporter of royal policy to a staunch defender of the rights of the church.

Church and state

To understand the intensity of the struggle that followed between Becket and the king it is necessary to know something about the background of church-state relations in medieval Europe. The likelihood of tension between God and king was inherent in the very nature of Christianity. Christians were commanded to be separate from those around them while still being in the world. To carry this out, the church had developed its own governmental structure, with a law code that in many respects contradicted the codes of secular governments. Believers were exhorted to

obey God rather than man.

With the conversion of Constantine (A.D. 312) church-state relations became even more confused. Imperial support changed the position of the church from that of a persecuted minority to that of a dominant majority. By the fifth century, Christianity had become the official religion of the Roman Empire. The church in the Eastern Empire came to accept imperial control, but in the West a tradition of rivalry developed between the church and the state. This was reflected in the medieval struggle between secular rulers and leading churchmen, such as Becket. Although at times, as in other church struggles, personalities were heavily involved, it was more than a matter of personal ambition. The basis of tension centered on the attempt to reconcile the claims of the temporal with those of the spiritual. In other words: How should the doctrine of creation relate to that of redemption?

Many arguments were put forth to support clerical domination. Most of them relied on the thought of the leading church Father, Augustine of Hippo, who believed that government was essentially negative. In his view, secular power was established to maintain order by restraining evil and by punishing those who do wrong. Because sin had made it necessary to establish states, it followed that secular power was inferior to the church, which was the source of God's forgiveness on earth. Church spokesmen also pointed out that God wanted a separation of powers into civil and religious. Other theologians, not as generous to the secular authorities, insisted that God had established a hierarchical pattern on earth, with the pope at the top and secular rulers on a lower level. It was God's will that the higher power should be obeyed, so that chaos would be avoided.

The powers that be

Just as church leaders had their arguments, so those who supported royal power made their case. Among the reasons given for secular rule having the higher authority were the precedents of Old Testament rulers, such as David and Solomon. It was claimed that those kings ruled by divine right. Statements made by the apostle Paul, including those in Romans 13 that "the powers that be are ordained of God," served to support the royal position. Kings were compared to Christ, and many rulers in medieval times believed they had miracle-working powers that were demonstrated by healing the sick. Supporters of the royal position also cited the two natures of Christ to support their view. As they explained, Christ was both king and priest, but as king, He was higher than priest in His religious functions.

For several centuries during early medieval times, the church was not forced to contend with a strong state. But with the establishment of the empire of Charlemagne in the eighth century, the situation changed. Charlemagne believed he should regulate the religious as well as the secular aspects of life. To establish this control he called church councils, defined Christian doctrine, supervised the election of major church officers, initiated liturgical reform, selected special clothing for the clergy, and designed church buildings. His support of clerical education set the pattern for later medieval scholarship. Following his death, however, his empire declined, and the church was left to fend for itself.

By the eleventh century, new dynasties began that were once again able to assert royal power. In 1046 King Henry III of Germany, who also claimed to control Italy, called a church council that deposed an ineffective, immoral pope and elected the first of a line of capable individuals to the papal office. This imperial reform was very helpful to the papacy, because it took control of the institution away from decadent, rival Roman factions and placed individuals of high moral character in the leadership role of the church. But the new situation proved to be a mixed blessing, because papal independence was lost even in spiritual matters. Royal control extended to the selection of bishops, who were appointed by the crown and usually took their secular duties more seriously than the spiritual functions of their positions.

The Gregorian Reformers

In 1056, with the ascent of the infant Henry IV to the German throne, a group of reformers challenged the control of the secular authorities over the church. Those individuals, often called the Gregorian Reformers, had been members of the court of Pope Leo IX (1049-1054), and included such capable leaders as Humbert of Moyenmoutier, Peter Damien, and Hildebrand. In 1059 they encouraged Nicholas II to issue a decree declaring that popes should be elected by the college of cardinals rather than by the emperor.

By the time Hildebrand became pope, as Gregory VII (1073-1085), the struggle between church and state reached its greatest intensity. Often called the Investiture Controversy, after the ceremony by which a vassal swore loyalty to his lord, this contest involved both physical and intellectual forces. Before it was over, the papacy claimed the right to depose emperors, and the kings were appointing rival popes who supported royal power. The struggle eventually led to a compromise at the Concordat of Worms (1122) in which Emperor Henry V agreed that bishops should be elected by the church and given their spiritual investment by the archbishop. However, the king was to be present at the election and could invest the bishop with the secular power of the office.

The Investiture Controversy

In a sense the events in England were a sideshow to the main act of the Investiture Controversy in Germany and Italy. From the time of the conversion of the Anglo-Saxons under Augustine of Canterbury, there had always been a close relationship between church and state in England. Rulers such as Alfred of Wessex (871-899) were involved in church activities, such as reforming clerical abuses and converting heathen Norsemen. In 1066, when William of Normandy ("The Conqueror") wished to invade England, he received the support of the papal reformers. After his successful campaign, he instituted certain limited ecclesiastical reforms in the land. He separated the civil from the church courts but decreed that no pope could be recognized in England without royal approval. He also declared that his vassals could not be excommunicated without royal permission.

King William II (1087-1100), who succeeded his father to the throne, completely ignored the rights of the church. He looked on clerical property as something to be looted and refused to recognize any pope for several years. A serious illness led him to appoint the reformer Anselm as archbishop of Canterbury (1093). Later a quarrel developed between them and Anselm was forced into exile in France. Under the next ruler, King Henry I (1100-1135), a compromise was negotiated in 1107. The king gave up

the practice of investing bishops with a ring and a staff, the symbols of their spiritual office, but he received the right to their subservience for the lands they held. This agreement had Europe-wide importance because it set the precedent for the later imperial settlement at the Concordat of Worms.

During the period from 1135 to 1154, England was racked by civil war and the church gained a great deal of independence. With the coronation of King Henry II (1154-1189) the period of anarchy drew to a close, and the new ruler was determined to reestablish a greater measure of royal control over his realm. Henry was the first of the Angevin kings to govern England, and he proved to be one of the greatest rulers in British history. Through inheritance and marriage he controlled a vast region that stretched from Ireland to the Pyrenees. For the next two centuries the English monarchs ruled half the territory of France in addition to their holdings in the British Isles.

Ruins of St Augustine's Abbey, Canterbury.

Archbishop Thomas Becket

The controversy during Henry's reign came to involve his relationship with the man he appointed archbishop of Canterbury, Thomas Becket. The main reason for the bitter dispute between the king and his church leader was a clash of jurisdiction involving royal and ecclesiastical courts. In medieval England, the church courts had complete control over many types of cases, including the trial and punishment of clerics accused of criminal offenses. This exemption from the secular law was called "benefit of clergy" and extended not only to priests and monks but also to students and many types of professional men. Such privilege was important because the penalties given by church courts were much more lenient than those decreed by the royal system of justice. An example of the differences in these systems that upset the king was a case involving a cleric who murdered a knight and was cleared of the crime simply by taking an oath in the church court.

In 1164 Henry attempted to remedy the situation by the Constitutions of Clarendon. This code contained a series of articles defining the relationships between church and state. The more important of its numerous provisions were those limiting the right of Englishmen to communicate with the papacy without the king's permission, asserting royal rights over episcopal vacancies, and repealing the benefit of clergy. According to the last provision, a cleric accused of a crime had to be brought first to a secular court to plead guilty or not guilty. After that he was to be tried in a church court, and then, if found guilty, he was to be unfrocked and turned over to the state system of justice to receive the punishment for his crime.

Becket's stand against such judicial reform meant that thousands of individuals would be exempted from royal control. Henry believed that it was necessary for all Englishmen to be subject to the same law so that justice would be more equally administered in the land. Despite the logic of that position, it appeared to the arch-

bishop that the state was taking away the power of the church. Caesar was once again claiming that which was to be rendered only to God.

Becket in exile

Months of struggle followed the attempt to enforce the Constitutions of Clarendon. Finally Becket was forced to leave England and go into exile in France. He appealed to Pope Alexander III for support, but the pontiff hesitated, hoping to achieve a compromise between the royal and ecclesiastical positions. Such accommodation proved impossible, and Becket became more extreme and stubborn in his defiance of the king. He stayed in exile for six years, until 1170, resisting all efforts to mediate the dispute and condemning any clergyman who cooperated with Henry.

In 1170 the king wanted to have his son crowned to ensure an orderly succession. Because Becket was not present in England to conduct the ceremony, Henry had Archbishop Roger of York and other churchmen perform the coronation. That infuriated Becket, who was determined to carry the campaign against the king back to England. Therefore he accepted a compromise with Henry and returned to his episcopal duties. With papal support he excommunicated and suspended those who had participated in the coronation. He also secured papal condemnations of most of the Constitutions of Clarendon.

Murder in the cathedral

Those who were punished by Becket went to Normandy where the king was staying at the time and told him of Becket's resumption of hostilities to the royal cause. The king reacted angrily, and voiced his famous wish that someone would rid him of the traitor. Four knights took the king too literally and, without his knowledge or consent, hurried to Canterbury, where they carried out the royal desire. The murder of the archbishop in his cathedral is one of the most dramatic scenes in church history. The incident is best understood in the following dialogue

The gatehouse, Canterbury Cathedral.

from a medieval chronicler:

"'Are you then come to slay me?' Becket asked of the knights. 'I have committed my cause to the great Judge of all mankind; wherefore I am not moved by threats, nor are your swords more ready to strike than is my soul for martyrdom.' Finally after a bitter exchange of insults they murdered him leaving his body, bespattered with blood and brains, as though in an attitude of prayer . . . prone on the pavement, while his soul rested in Abraham's bosom."

The immediate result of the murder of Becket was such an outpouring of public rage that Henry was forced to do penance and to acknowledge church control over those activities upon which Becket had insisted. Another medieval chronicle has left a description of the way the king "barefoot and clad in woolen garments, walked to the tomb of the blessed martyr ...his tender feet being cut by the hard stones, a great quantity of blood flowed from them to the ground. When he arrived at the tomb it was a holy thing to see the affliction which he suffered with sobs and tears, and the discipline to which he submitted from the hands of the bishops and a great number of priests and monks."

The king's sorrow may have resulted from more reasons than the contemporary writer realized, because Henry surely understood that the murder had seriously damaged his power in an age when people took their faith seriously. To share the horror with which most medieval people would have reacted to the incident it is necessary to keep in mind that churches in those times were looked upon as sanctuaries, where even those accused of crime were safe from royal justice. On this occasion, however, even the highest ranking churchman in England was not safe in his own cathedral. The result for church-state relations was a standoff in the struggle over royal and ecclesiastical courts. The king was forced to withdraw some of the terms of the Constitutions of Clarendon and, although they were gradually brought under the control of secular courts, members of the clergy continued for many years to get lighter punishments.

Historians, theologians, and creative writers have debated whether Thomas Becket was a saint, a traitor, a shrewd politician, or a demented fanatic. The Becket made famous by T.S. Eliot abandons himself to the will of God after resisting temptations that included spiritual pride and good works.

Thomas Becket was sainted in 1173. He became the most popular saint in English history, and people from all parts of the land flocked to his place of martyrdom. One of the most enduring pieces of English literature, *The Canterbury Tales* by Chaucer, describes a group of pilgrims on their way to worship at his shrine.

The Cathedral Builders

Between about 1200 and 1400 nearly two hundred Gothic style cathedrals sprang up in western Europe. They remain the most familiar and striking image of medieval faith. With their soaring spires, delicate flying buttresses, astounding stained glass windows, and ornate stonework they represent a huge investment of money, effort and faith.

Soaring faith
The age of cathedrals was particularly marked in England and France. Old St Paul's Cathedral, in London, was 585 feet long; Winchester Cathedral marginally shorter, at 526 feet. The cathedrals of France were yet larger. Notre Dame in Paris was 110 feet in height; Chartres Cathedral 114 feet; Rheims Cathedral 125 feet; and Beauvais 154 feet to the top of its spire.

The cathedral buildings themselves convey much about medieval Christianity. These towering structures were invariably sited in the highest part of the city, totally overawing the ordinary dwellings below. They are undoubtedly a reflection of an age of faith and vision; but also of the vast riches of the church of that period, in stark contrast with the squalid poverty of the mass of the population.

Distinctive design
The architecture itself sheds further light on the medieval church. The flying buttresses, pointed arches, and upward-pointing spires all tell of a reaching up towards heaven. Inside the cathedrals, the decoration told another story; one of mystery, brilliance, and illumination. The stained-glass windows, sometimes amounting to whole walls of glass, served as picture sermons to the illiterate worshippers; the stonework was similarly covered in carvings, sculptures and paintings, all

Cologne Cathedral, West Germany.

reflecting some aspect of faith.

It has sometimes romantically been suggested that the cathedrals represent the result of spontaneous voluntary labour by a town's faithful and pious citizens. This is far from the truth. In fact the cathedrals were built by professional masons, and construction was tightly organized and proficiently financed. The work was normally supervised by a master-mason, who was architect, builder and manager in one. The various specialist jobs – woodwork, sculpture, stained glass, and so forth – were all carried out by craftsmen from specialist guilds.

Raising the finance
Financing such major enterprises was clearly a huge endeavor. It was normally the bishop's responsibility

to raise the cash, by such means as begging missions, selling spiritual privileges, and employing professional fund-raisers, much like modern charities. Popular shrines, such as that of Thomas Becket at Canterbury Cathedral, could earn valuable money by charging entry fees to visiting pilgrims.

The cathedrals came in for a wide range of uses. They were often pilgrim centers, but also provided the setting for the daily worship of the resident monks or canons. There were normally no services in the cathedral for local Christians; in fact the nave was often used for business by merchants and as a meeting place. Sometimes strangers were permitted to sleep in the nave, and at special holidays plays were staged around the building.

Innocent III
1160/61-1216

Innocent III is universally recognized as one of the greatest and most important of all the popes, ancient, medieval, and modern. His significance rests upon the quantity of work he accomplished, his power inside and outside the church, his administrative vitality and capabilities, his legal and theological contributions, and his sense of the spiritual missions of the church at a critical moment in her history.

Pope Innocent was a careful and frequent correspondent who wrote more than 5,000 letters to bishops, abbots, kings, and others. On one occasion he wrote to the Muslim king of Morocco seeking to gain the conversion to Christianity of the infidel. The pope, a man of sincere evangelistic interests, was involved in missions, crusades, efforts to turn back heresy, and the education of the faithful.

Innocent's work brought him to a position where nearly every crowned head of Europe (most notably John of England and Phillip II of France) was brought into submission to him. He considered himself God's representative to bring the divine kingdom to fulfillment on this earth, regarding himself as somewhat more than an ordinary human being but less than God.

The twelfth and thirteenth centuries are often looked upon as the zenith of medieval civilization. The church crowned the Middle Ages with her religious perspectives. It was Pope Innocent III who presided over the church during some of its greatest moments, but who also contributed to the forces that were to weaken seriously both the civilization and the church of the Middle Ages.

Giovanni Lotario de Conti, Pope Innocent III.

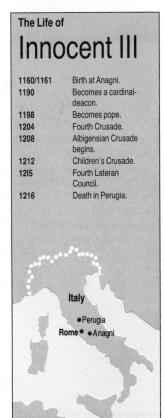

The Life of

Innocent III

1160/1161	Birth at Anagni.
1190	Becomes a cardinal-deacon.
1198	Becomes pope.
1204	Fourth Crusade.
1208	Albigensian Crusade begins.
1212	Children's Crusade.
1215	Fourth Lateran Council.
1216	Death in Perugia.

Italy

●Perugia

Rome ● ●Anagni

Pope Innocent III

and Papal Power

Thomas Kay

Lotario de Conti

The future Pope Innocent III was born in 1160 or 1161 as Giovanni Lotario de Conti. Following his early education in the area around Rome, he enrolled in the university at Paris where he studied theology. He also studied law at Bologna. Both of those schools were very highly regarded at that time. The young Lotario took advantage of these excellent opportunities and was highly respected as a student. He had taken up the clerical vocation early in his life, as had other members of his family. It was his uncle, Pope Clement III (1187-1191), who raised Lotario to be a cardinal with the rank of deacon in 1190.

He served his church well during these early years and gave evidence of his administrative talents. When his uncle died in 1191, Lotario went into seclusion because a member of the rival aristocratic Colonna family had been elected Pope Celestine III (1191-1198). During those years Lotario was involved with minor responsibilities and did some writing, none of which has been of lasting significance.

When Celestine III died, Lotario was

The city of Rome from the Forum.

elected pope the same day and consecrated a few weeks later, on February 22. At that time he received the papal crown and took the name Innocent, possibly because of his regard for the life and work of Pope Innocent II (1130-1143). He immediately set out on a determined course of action designed to provide moral authority and leadership in both temporal and ecclesiastical affairs. He was hard-working, gave great attention to detail, had a clear set of goals, and was deeply committed to the task of being the head of Christendom.

Pope Innocent III

Contemporaries describe the young pope as having a profile of conviction, a small mouth, and large eyes. These features seemed to characterize his determination, his visionary ideals, and his effectiveness with words. He was a prolific correspondent. He wrote to kings and princes, bishops and abbots, universities and dignitaries. The registers listing that correspondence are nearly all intact and support his wide-ranging efforts to influence the course of events in Europe and with neighboring leaders. He spent most of his time at Rome and traveled outside the city only occasionally. His most immediate concerns had to do with organizing a crusade to the Holy Land, combating heresy that seemed to be prevalent in some sections of Europe, dealing with lay rulers whose public sins created problems, and presenting himself to everyone as a symbol of the unity of Christendom.

The setting in which Pope Innocent found himself was one of the most creative and progressive eras of European history. A veritable explosion of culture had taken place. There were giants of arts and letters whose work is superior to any other. The common denominator in all things was the concept of Christian civilization.

Society experienced many changes during those decades. Increased wealth, opening of new lands, growing populations, crowded cities, and changes in the location of political authority all stimulated unrest and even social revolution. For Innocent that was a challenge to order and a challenge for orthodoxy, because such social unrest was often the seedbed of heresy. Kings and princes were seeking to gather as much authority as possible into their hands.

The church was tending to state Christian truth in more specific terms. This dogmatization of theology made it easier to identify heresy. There was also concern regarding the secular and material interests of the clergy. Christian ideals of apostolic poverty and Christian devotion were not always obvious to those onlookers who more easily saw the wealth of the church.

Papal reform

Many scholars regard ideas as the primary motivation of Innocent. The ideas are best understood in terms of some of his activities. Even before his consecration, Innocent set out to rectify the ills of the city government of Rome. Those civic ills had been a frequent problem throughout the history of the papacy, and Innocent's actions made clear that the pope was in charge. He also cleaned out most of the dead wood and ill-advised appointments from the papal government.

His next project took him out into the papal states, those lands of central Italy that the popes had sought to control. Innocent initiated a program of recovery to re-establish strong papal authority throughout the region. For the effectiveness of his efforts he has been styled the second founder of the papal states. In carrying out those programs, the pope made clear that he was God's vicar for all of Christendom, not just the church.

That concept was to be a source of tension very early in Innocent's reign. In 1198 Henry VI, Holy Roman Emperor, died. These emperors, elected by the German nobility and consecrated by papal anointing, were generally regarded as equal or second in rank to the pope. The pope's involvement in the disputed election of 1198, in the conflicts that followed, and in the nomination and acceptance in 1212 of Frederick II demonstrate Innocent's idea of the superiority of pope to emperor.

A similar pattern is seen with other rulers of the day. King Philip II of France took back his first wife on the pope's command. King John of England was brought to his knees and forced to accept the pope's nominee as archbishop of Canterbury. He also agreed to pay tribute to the papacy, much to the shame of the English people. Most of the other princes of Europe found themselves submissive to Pope Innocent in one way or another. Although he was not technically superior to kings, for they were responsible to God, the pope argued that he was in effect their spiritual leader and advisor, and had a responsibility to deal with the sins of rulers. In his writings, Innocent used figures such as sun and moon, or soul and body, to illustrate relationships between pope and monarch.

From the beginning of the Crusades in 1095 most popes envisioned their role to include the continuation of those efforts to regain the Holy Land from Islam and maintain it in Christian hands. Following the limited success of the Third Crusade in 1189, which did not regain control of Jerusalem, Pope Innocent believed he should initiate a major effort of conquest. The crusade was called, but response was limited. The Crusaders, mostly from France, bargained with the Venetians for travel by sea to the east.

The Venetians had other commercial and military objectives in mind and used the army of Crusaders to fight two small battles on the eastern Adriatic coast. The Crusaders were then carried on to Constantinople and readily attacked that Christian city. Rape, pillage, and all other sorts of violence ensued. This attack resulted in the establishment of the Western church in the areas of Constantinople that had been formally separated from Rome since 1054. Although Innocent did not achieve the stated goals of the Crusades, the reunion with the East was nearly as important to him. Unfortunately for Rome, the reunion was only superficial, and no lasting establishment of the Roman hierarchy in the East succeeded.

The Albigensian Crusade

The crusading concept was readily transferred by the pope to the eradication of heresy in southern France. There the Cathari or Albigensians had developed a large and popular following, with strong support from political and nominally orthodox church officials. Innocent had a deep commitment to theological orthodoxy. He found laymen who had political interests in this region willing to take the sword against heretics. The Albigensian Crusade began in 1208 following the assassination of the pope's envoy. Over the next twenty years southern France was devastated in the name of the church and the political power of the French king. This crusading mentality was also excuse for the king of France, Philip II, to prepare war against King John of England, with whom Innocent had a quarrel and whose lands were under interdict at the time.

Innocent's concerns for war on heresy were not limited to violent or extreme tactics. He acknowledged the popularity of the message and personality of the itinerant preachers whose teachings were suspect. He encouraged clergy true to the faith to develop similar styles and to meet and debate with the perceived false teachers in the market places. Many were to take up this challenge. Of note is the success of Dominic and Francis, who, with their followers, soon came to be recognized as effective preachers and ministers of the gospel. Innocent encouraged both groups and provided the initial authorizations that eventually led to their establishment as approved orders within the church.

Fourth Lateran Council

The highpoint of Innocent III's career was the great assembly of the Fourth Lateran Council held at Rome in 1215. More than 1,200 persons from all over Europe gathered to hear the pope and to affirm his leadership of the church and of all Christendom. There were 70 patriarchs and archbishops, 400 bishops, and 800 priests, abbots, and laymen. The council set forth seventy decrees. Some of the canons were addressed to the suppression of heresy, the tithing of ecclesiastical revenues, the active role of the church in providing for secular justice, support for a new Crusade, and the requirement for Christians to confess to a priest once a year and to attend the Easter mass.

The matter of greatest theological significance was the definition of transubstantiation as the only way of understanding the Eucharist. These ideas had been current for many centuries, but it was only in 1215 that they became a matter of essential Christian dogma necessary for all believers. The doctrine of transubstantiation maintains that the eucharistic elements of bread and wine do indeed miraculously become the actual body and blood of Christ at the time of the consecration and elevation of the elements. Although the elements retain the characteristics of bread and wine, they possess the actual substance of the body and blood of Christ. This doctrine was one of the major concerns for the Protestant Reformers three hundred years later.

The Fourth Lateran Council has been described as a rubber stamp of the will of an autocratic pope. The Council also reflected the unity and universality of Christendom at its peak in the Middle Ages. Whether or not one agrees with the conclusions reached by the Council, it certainly marked a major phase in the history of the church and highlighted the papacy of Innocent III.

Pope Innocent died in 1216 having served his church with vigor, enthusiasm, sincerity, and deep commitment for eighteen years. His successors were to try to maintain the norms established by their illustrious predecessor. This they did with mixed effectiveness.

Innocent and medieval Christendom

Innocent was a man governed by ideas – ideas that would serve to mold institutions, which would in turn shape the lives of people. Herein was his chief strength and his greatest weakness. The commitment to ideas provided Innocent with a set of goals his legal mind could develop, including the implications those goals involved. This gave him confidence in his ability to structure Christendom on the models of Holy Scripture and the history of the church. At the same time such a commitment to ideas often removed the pope's goals from reality and practicality. He became rigid, unyielding, and unwilling to recognize the need for changes in his program at critical times.

Although Pope Innocent enjoyed great popularity, the cracks in the papal armor were becoming apparent – opposition by the bishops, the crusading disaster, secularization of political interests. The designs of the young emperor Frederick II on Italy were to be a constant irritant to Innocent's successors. But certainly without the able and forceful administration of Pope Innocent, the medieval church would have collapsed sooner than it did.

Was Innocent III playing the game of secular power politics? Or was he a child – a most outstanding one – of his times? Innocent was a person of his age and, yes, he played the power game. But not because it was to his personal advantage or that of a small group of ecclesiastical administrators. He was a man born to the church, who sought to promote its good and the cause of Christ as he understood it and as it had been exercised in the preceding centuries.

Francis of Assisi
1181-1228

Opposite: Portrait of Francis of Assisi by Cimabue, *c.* 1280, from the Lower Basilica, Assisi.

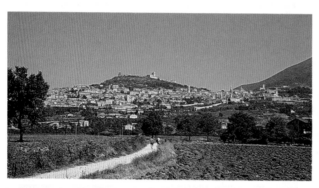

The hill-town of Assisi, Italy.

The legends began the day Francis died. He was sainted (1228) by the medieval church; artists and poets added to this beatification by granting to Francis an almost unparalleled place in the history of Christianity. The painter Giotto depicted him as the one who most suffered the wounds of Christ. Dante placed him above the doctors and founders of medieval orders in his *Divine Comedy* (*c.* 1305). Francis was so celebrated as the perfect imitator of Christ that the Protestant Reformers believed memory of him had usurped the place of Christ in popular piety. The Enlightenment followed that criticism by citing Francis as the supreme example of medieval rationality gone to seed.

All those factors aside, Francis continues to attract us. Since the nineteenth century, Roman Catholics and Protestants have increasingly seen spiritual sanity in his worldly irrationality. Indeed, when one thinks of the thousand years between the fall of Rome and advent of the

Reformation or onset of modernity, his is one of the few names likely to be recalled. Francis is frequently referred to as either the peculiar saint among the rosebushes or as the conscience of Western civilization, or both. As such, he is remembered not only as the one who sought to rebuild a church engulfed by spiritual callousness, but for his consciousness of the divine unity and interdependence of the creation.

Although he is frequently pictured as taming wolves or preaching to birds, Francis's work began with the reconstruction of a broken-down chapel and soon took him to the courts of Rome and to the sultan's tents in Egypt in an effort to share his simple faith in Christ. Our difficulty in understanding Francis derives from his own sensitivity and apparent guilelessness and from the reactions of opposition he elicited from his contemporaries and successors.

The Life of
Francis

1181	Birth.
1202	Enlists in the army and is taken prisoner.
1205	Moved by the beggars at St. Peter's, Rome.
1208	Draws up a rule for himself and associates, the *Regula Primitiva*
1209	Secures approval for the brotherhood from Innocent III.
1211-1212?	Mission to the East.
1219	Preaching tour to Eastern Europe, the Holy Land, and Egypt.
1220	Returns to Italy.
1223	Possibly abdicates leadership of Franciscans.
1224	Spends remaining years in solitude and prayer.
1226	October 3, death at the Chapel of the Portiuncula.
1228	July 16, sainted by Pope Gregory IX.

Italy

• Assisi

• Rome

Francis of Assisi

and the Franciscan Ideal

Rodney L. Petersen

Francis's calling

Born in Assisi (1181) to the wealthy textile merchant Pietro de Barnadone and his wife, Pica, Francis (baptized Giovanni, but later renamed Francesco) received the usual education and privileges of a child in the aspiring merchant class. When war broke out with the rival commercial city of Perugia, Francis enlisted and sought to defend Assisi's interests and advance his own. After he was captured, in 1202, and ransomed a year later as ill, he sought

The Piazza del Comune, Assisi.

to fight again but was prevented from doing so following a disturbing nocturnal vision.

Overwhelmed by self-doubt and conscious of the vanity of his past, Francis entered a protracted period of introspection. In 1205 he went on a pilgrimage to Rome. There he exchanged clothes with a beggar in order to experience the reality of destitution. Later, while praying in the church of San Damian, Francis heard Christ telling him to rebuild the wasted church. Uncertain of the message's meaning, Francis began by reconstructing the church of San Damian and ministering to society's outcasts. He sold his horse and some of his father's textiles to raise money toward this end, in the meantime incurring his father's wrath. The former extravagant and now (in his father's eyes) shiftless son was hauled before the local bishop and told to return to his father all that he owed him. To this Francis replied by stripping himself naked, returning clothing and property to Pietro, and calling God alone as his father.

Francis spent the following years nursing victims of leprosy in Gubbio, later returning to Assisi as a hermit to continue to repair the church of San Damian and two others. It is said that a spirit of joy and freedom characterized his efforts, contrasting sharply with prevailing religious attitudes. If Francis's conversion was now complete, his specific call was still to come. In the winter of 1208, while worshiping in the church of Portiuncula ("the little portion"), he listened to the first commissioning of the disciples of Christ (Matthew 10:7-19). Francis heard that call as his own, exchanged his

The Basilica of St Francis, Assisi.

hermit's habit for that of a barefoot preacher, and went out without money or knapsack to proclaim the kingdom of God.

The little brothers

Others soon joined. The little band grew, taking the name *friars minor* ("little brothers") as it sought to identify with the poor and oppressed. Francis gave the group a set of basic rules (*Regula Primitiva*), probably derived from the gospels. This was submitted to Pope Innocent III when Francis and his troop sought and received official sanction in 1209. Such recognition was either a stroke of genius from a consummate church politician or, quite simply, an example of the surprising work of the Spirit. Francis's ideas not only attracted the attention of the church, but soon a second order for women was founded by Clare Schifi, an heiress of Assisi. Invested by Francis in 1212, these "Poor Clares" would in many ways remain truer to the Franciscan ideal in a period of future conflict than the first men's order. Sometime between 1209 and 1221 a third order, the Franciscan Tertiaries, was founded as a lay community of penitents. Its members, married or single, continued in their vocations, living as nearly as possible in the spirit of the gospels and being forbidden to bear arms.

Francis's early rule is now lost to us. However, his ideas and life inspired a renewal according to the counsels of evangelical perfection. His aim was simply to follow the Lord. His effort was not an attempt simply to reach back to the first Christian community (as was the practice in monasticism), but rather to the Lord and His Disciples. The counsels of perfection (Matthew 19) called one to live in terms of obedience, poverty, and chastity. Franciscans sought obedience to God through a sense of spiritual immediacy. There was no distinction between clergy and laity in the brotherhood. We read that Francis simply "went about ... announcing the kingdom of God ... with the learning and power of the Spirit.... It seemed at that time... that a new light had been sent from heaven."

Franciscan poverty

The central character of the movement lay in its attitude toward poverty. Francis wanted nothing of his own and encouraged this spirit among his brethren. The story is told of a friar who picked up money left as alms on an altar and placed it upon a window ledge. Hearing of this, Francis ordered him to take the money in his mouth from the ledge and to place it on a dung heap. It is said that the early followers of Francis "thenceforward despised money as ass' dung."

Possessions became symbolic of all that might come between the individual and God. Poverty took on an almost mystical personification: "He had become a lover of her beauty.... He rejoiced to exchange a perishable treasure for the hundredfold." Life took on a single-mindedness that carried into sexual affairs. If possessions could serve as an impediment to service of God, so could the distractions of sexuality and marriage. Francis's commitment to Christ elicited the following from Bonaventure: "No human tongue could describe the passionate love with which Francis burned for Christ, his Spouse; he seemed to be completely absorbed by the fire of divine love like a glowing coal."

Francis's message was extended through a series of missions beyond Italy. In 1215 he went to Spain, but he was prevented by illness from reaching North Africa, his primary goal. In 1219 Francis and eleven companions did reach the Holy Lands of Egypt, preaching before the sultan, Melek el-Khamil.

When Francis returned to Italy (1220), things were not the same in the movement he had left. The first change he noticed was that a monastery had been built that some of his brothers regarded as their property, despite the consequent dissension. Furthermore, decrees had been issued that appeared to betray this divisiveness. Earlier, Francis had condoned a yearly meeting of the order at Pentecost, although fearful that supervisory offices would eliminate the movement's immediacy before God. Further structuring was now apparent, and to

The Basilica of St Francis seen from below the town of Assisi.

some the order was being transformed from a brotherhood into an order of priests.

The First Rule

Francis was encouraged to issue a new rule for the order in 1221 (First Rule, or *Regula Prima*). The friars were "to live in obedience, in chastity and without property, following the teaching and footsteps of our Lord Jesus Christ...." (*Rule of 1221*, 1). There was to be no test for admission. Brothers were to serve the despised and rejected with a spirit of joy and trust in the power of Christ. A third rule soon followed (1223), written with more precise terminology. Regarded as definitive, it betrays a growing divisiveness in its pointed exhortation not to despise or judge those "wearing soft or gaudy clothes and enjoying the luxuries of food and drink," but to pardon the weaknesses of others and rather despise one's self (*Rule of 1223*, 2).

Rather than trying to regain control of the movement, ill health, a perception of the choices others would have to make, and Francis's own desire to plumb the depths of Christ led him to relinquish the order's direction to Peter Catanii and Elias of Cortona. Francis spent the remaining years of his life in solitude and prayer at a hermitage on Mount Alverno. There, by tradition, he received the stigmata, while overwhelmed with a sense of failure. There he wrote and gave us two of his richest gifts: the *Testament*, calling for no gloss upon the gospels, and the *Canticle of the Sun*, his hymn to the Creator as alone deserving of praise. With respect to the latter, Francis Thompson noted that although Francis was sworn to poverty, he did not forswear beauty.

The Franciscans

The first period of the Franciscan movement ended with Francis's death in 1226. The next one hundred years would see bitter debate within the order between his strict followers, the Spirituals, tinged with the fanaticism of acute Joachite apocalypticism, and the Conventuals, who appeared to soft-pedal Francis's ideals.

Francis of Assisi.

The Spirituals trailed off into sectarian division as they faced a church that appeared to them to define spirituality in terms of compromise with the world. Pope John XXII (1316-1334) even declared their ideals heretical. The history of the Franciscan movement provided the twentieth-century theologian and sociologist Ernst Troeltsch with a paradigm for his discussion of church-type and sectarian Christianity.

A third Franciscan era began with the emergence of a new spiritual party, the Observants (1368). By the middle of the sixteenth century the Observants had grown sufficiently lax in the opinion of some to call forth another reforming order, the Capuchins (1529). A fourth period can be marked from 1897, when Pope Leo XIII united the different factions under a uniform constitution. Today, Roman Catholic, Anglican (Episcopal) and Lutheran Franciscan orders exist. In addition to these, many others are inspired by Francis, servant of Christ, patron of peace and creaturely dependence under the Creator.

Thomas Aquinas

c.1225-1274

Opposite: Thomas Aquinas in stained glass, from Florence.

In common with the great scholastics, Thomas Aquinas (1225-1274) was a voluminous writer. His shorter works, *De Ente et Essentia, De veritate,* and *De Unitate Intellectus,* are marked by the same powerful and penetrating genius as his more extended ones. His three larger works, in particular the *Commentary on the Sentences* (1253-1257), the *Summa Contra Gentiles,* (1261-1264) and the *Summa Theologica,* I and II (1266-1271) and III (1272, unfinished at his death), provide the Roman church with reasoned statements of its interpretation of the Christian faith.

Recognized as the greatest thinker and theologian of his age, Aquinas found no adequate biographer. The few personal details tradition has preserved about him are that he was corpulent and in attitude almost stoical. His habit of silence won for him the title of "dumb ox." His writings are marked by the cold language of reason; although, if the hymn *"Adore Te"* is his, it shows him not without the warmth of passion and devotion. Although he gave pride of place to the mind in the apprehension of truth, he recognized a wisdom from above that some possess in an eminent manner. A passage in his *Commentary on the Sentences* (D. 35, q. 2, art. 1) best sums up Aquinas's epistemology, of which divine knowledge is the summit:

"Wisdom by its very name implies an eminent abundance of knowledge, which enables a man to judge of all things, for everyone can judge well what he fully knows. Some have this abundance of knowledge as a result of learning and study, added to a native quickness of intelligence; and this is the wisdom Aristotle counts among the intellectual virtues. But others have wisdom as a result of the kinship which they have with the things of God; it is of such the Apostle says, 'The spiritual man judges all things.' The Gift of Wisdom gives a man this eminent knowledge as a result of his union with God, and this union can only be his by love, for 'he who cleaveth to God is one spirit with Him.' And therefore the Gift of Wisdom leads to a godlike and explicit gaze at revealed truth, which mere faith holds in a manner as it were disguised."

The Life of

Aquinas

c. 1225	Birth near Cassino, Italy.
1224	Becomes a Dominican.
1252-1255	Teaches in Paris.
1259-1263	Teaches in Italy.
1261-1264	Writes *Summa contra Gentiles*.
1266-1272	Writes *Summa Theologica*.
1274	March 7, death at Fossanuova.

Italy

●Rome

●Cassino

Medieval plaque from Cologne Cathedral, Germany.

S^{VS} THOMAS DE AQVINO

Thomas Aquinas

Master Theologian

H. Dermot McDonald

Student and teaching career

Details of the personal life of Thomas Aquinas are sparse. If he wrote letters, none have been preserved. And there is no specific allusion to himself in his many writings. Yet of his more public life the broad outline can be traced.

The younger son of the large family of the Count of Aquino, he was christened Thomas. He was born in the castle of Roccasecca near Cassino, Italy, in the year 1225 or 1226. Through his mother he was related to the Roman emperor Frederick (1194-1250). As a child Thomas was dedicated to the monastic life at the cloister of Monte Cassino. He became a student in the University of Naples, taking the Dominican habit in 1244. He was destined for Paris, only to be kidnapped by his brothers and held captive for a year.

On his release, he went first to Paris and thence to Cologne. At the latter place he became a pupil and friend of Albertus Magnus and lodged with him there in the Stolkstrasse. From 1252-1255 Aquinas taught as bachelor in Paris. In 1257, in company with Bonaventura, he completed his licentiate. Back in Italy, from 1259 to 1263 he taught at various papal centers. Returning to Paris in 1269 he became embroiled in various philosophical and theological controversies. He died on March 7, 1274 at the age of 48/49, at the Cistercian abbey of Fossanuova on his way to the Council of Lyons.

Aquinas's methodology

Aquinas's *Summa Theologica* has been likened to a lake into which many streams have flowed and from which many have drawn; but it is not a spring. Nevertheless, it is a masterpiece of logical thought that touches on almost every question of theology and morality. The modern reader, however, may be repelled somewhat by its frustrating methodology; as he may by its equally detailed treatment of apparently trivial things and those that are vital. Such extrabiblical notions as the worship of Mary, penance and purgatory, and the like, are stated as if assent to them were of the essentials of the Christian faith and message.

Basic to Aquinas's whole construction is his sharp dichotomy between reason and revelation. Rejecting the theory of double truth, he credits to each its own distinctive method. Reason is supreme in its own sphere, being limited to the external world, according to the dictum, *nihil est intellectum, nisi prius fuerit in sensu* ("nothing in the mind, which is not first in the senses"). This was the thesis Aquinas learned from Aristotle. It was consequently his whole endeavor to present scholasticism in Aristotelian terms.

The being of God as such – *what* God is in Himself – is beyond the range of reason to discover. Such particulars of the faith as the Trinity and Incarnation are known only in revelation as these are conveyed to the faithful on the authority of the church. But *what* God is as the self-existing One reason can know of a certainty by the contemplation of His works. The universe of things is a ladder whereby man can ascend to God. From analogy with sense phenomena, man is assured of the existence of that which is supernatural and eternal. Analogy points beyond itself to that which is outside the limits of reason and which is inexpressible by the human mind.

Aquinas's doctrine of analogy depends

upon his distinction between essence and existence. He followed Aristotle in regarding every human being as a composite of actuality and potentiality, essence and existence. But in God there is no such distinction. In Him essence and existence are one. He alone *is* Being. Every other thing *has* being. God is the only necessary Being. It cannot therefore be that God does not, and cannot, exist. He is the "I-Am" of Exodus 3:14; the only self-subsisting actuality, unique and transcendent. It follows that such qualities exhibited in His creatures, as goodness, truth, and such like, are in God in virtue of His being and also in a communicable and super-eminent manner. The quality of goodness, for example, cannot be stated of God and ourselves univocably, that is, in the same degree. Nor yet can it be stated of God equivocally, that is, having a different meaning in His case from that of ours. It is used analogically. Thus to affirm God is "good," its finite *mode* has to be negated and its *meaning* declared of Him in an absolute way. Put otherwise, goodness in God is like in some respects to such goodness in man, but unlike it in other important and essential respects. God exists as good *par excellence*, beyond all that can be described.

Aquinas's Five Ways

Aquinas's "Five Ways," his quintet of proofs for the existence of God, are all built on the principle of analogy with the things of sense in the space-time world. They are thus empirical and *a posteriori*. As based on God's effects in His created order, it is open to all men to be convinced that God is. The Five Ways appear in the *Summa Theologica* as a rational preamble to Aquinas's theology of revelation. The cogency of the principle of analogy is, however, much in debate in the contemporary discussion of the significance of religious language. No less debatable are questions of the meaningfulness and validity of the Five Ways themselves. As an Aristotelian empiricist, Aquinas rejected the Platonic doctrine of innate ideas and consequently the ontological argument of Anselm. But it must seem that he had already some idea of God in his mind before setting out proofs for His existence.

In the body of the *Summa Theologica*, the theology of revelation is subjected to rigorous philosophical analysis, with a view to elucidating its propositions as revealed truths. As a mosaic of systematization, it exhibits the substance and method of Aquinas's teaching. Much of what he declared appeared novel to his contemporaries. Guglielmo de Tocco, who lived with Aquinas during his last years at Naples, speaks of his "new theses," "new manner of proof," "new reasons," and "new doctrines," which, to him, were the result of "new inspiration" surely given Aquinas "to teach and write new things."

Others, however, equally convinced of the novelty, such as Franciscan John Peckham, archbishop of Canterbury, were less inclined to admit its divine source. Indeed, in Aquinas's own time, and for decades following, dissatisfaction with his work was widespread. In fact some of his teachings were condemned as error after his death, although this was reversed later. Duns Scotus (1266-1305), among others, offered a sustained criticism of Aquinas and brought into opposition the two rival schools backed up respectively by the hostility between the Dominicans and Franciscans. In modern times, however, there has been a revival of "Thomism," mainly the result of Pope Leo XIII's commendation of his study in Leo's papal encyclical *Aeterni Patris* of 1879.

Faith as assent

A notable feature of the *Summa* is its stress on knowledge. Sustained throughout is the idea of faith as assent to Catholic doctrine, in contradistinction to faith as *fiducia* (personal trust) of the Reformers. Aquinas distinguished between faith, opinion, and knowledge. *Faith* is stronger than opinion, in that it involves a firm assent to its object. But in the end it is almost equated with credence. *Faith* is, however, less than knowledge because it is lacking in comprehension and vision. Present in Aquinas is the usual scholastic distinction between *fides informis* ("unformed" faith, bare orthodoxy) and *fides caritate formata* (faith formed and informed by love). Both sorts of faith are, however, worthy of merit. The former as merely *congruent*, by rendering the divine reward fitting, though not obligatory. The latter has a *condign* distinction, in which the divine reward is due as a matter of justice.

When considering some of the specifics of the *Summa Theologica*, it is noted that Aquinas had a strong doctrine of creation. The existence of the world is the result of God's action *ex nihilo* – "out of nothing." It is not however an act of God *in* time. Like Augustine, Aquinas argues that with the creation of the world was the creation *of* time. When there was no world, there was no time. He is not disposed, however, to accept the idea of eternal creation, although he is ready to admit it as logically possible. There is no logical reason that an eternal cause should not be causing eternally. Aquinas is emphatic that there was when the world was not; and it is here altogether by the fiat of God.

Man

On the important interrelated theological subjects of man, sin, and grace, there is much of worth to be learned from Thomas Aquinas, with some things' less acceptable.

Aquinas conceived of the first man as a creature of dignity, whose specific goal as a rational being, in contrast with animals, was to know God. The knowledge of God open to man was nevertheless limited to a knowing about Him. To have known God in His essence would have been to love Him, and that would have assured man's remaining without sin. The knowledge possessed by the unfallen man was, however, more perfect than ours in a sin-marred state, because it was not derived from the things of sense. Still, the man unfallen had need of God's supernatural gift of grace to maintain his original state

of righteousness. Thus, from the beginning, in Aquinas's doctrine, divine grace was made to depend on human merit.

Aquinas adopted the creationist view of the origin of the soul. In fact, he declared any other view unacceptable and heretical. He regarded every soul as created immediately by God *de novo* ("anew") and united at, or before, birth to the body produced by human parents. While he stressed the unity of the body and soul in the individual, he at the same time carefully specified the distinctiveness of each. He rejected the "double-aspect" theory, which regards soul and body as the one person seen from two different perspectives.

The question of the soul's immortality for Aquinas belonged to the realm of natural theology. He advanced consequently a number of arguments designed to prove its after-death continuity. He contended, for example, that the intellectual element in man's constitution, which he virtually equated with the soul, shows by its independence of matter that it is nonmaterial. Being thus spiritual, it does not partake of corruptibility, which is the nature of all that is material. And being spiritual the soul is consequently "simple," that is, not composite. It is only the composite that can disintegrate and perish.

Sin

Somewhat after the fashion of Augustine, Aquinas regarded sin as resulting from an upsurge of pride in the first man. It expressed itself in our first parents as an inordinate outburst of self-love. Aquinas circumvented the problem of how the soul newly-created by God and joined to the body becomes corrupt. He was convinced, however, that human nature that existed seminally in Adam, and corrupted in him, is passed on from one generation to another. He did not, however, concur with Augustine that man is guilty and condemnable for original sin. He would have sin related, in the last analysis, to individual free-will.

The freedom of the will, like that of God's existence and the immortality of

Notre Dame Cathedral, Paris. Thomas Aquinas spent many years studying in Paris.

the soul, is open to absolute rational proof, according to Aquinas. He placed the will somewhere between the reason and action, and as vitally related to each. The reason, as specifically the divine element in man, is intrinsically true and good. In this respect it is given impetus by the will. On the other hand, the will has an ambiguous relation to man's lower desires. It would control them; yet it finds itself induced to yield to them. The will is free in the sense of being self-determined. It is not under the dominion of chance; nor yet is it, or need it be, directed by the strongest motive. Aquinas's stress upon the priority of reason and the freedom of the will follows from his at best semi-Pelagian view of man.

Grace

Aquinas made a strenuous effort to reconcile the tendencies that came prominently to the fore in medieval theology, and which appear in his work. There is, on the one side, ample recognition of human merit, and, on the other, the requirement of divine grace. In the section in his *Summa Theologica*, "Of the Necessity of Grace," he sees for it a double requirement. He argues if the first man before his fall needed a superadded help of God to live righteously, how much more must man the sinner. And, besides, without God's action in grace, the human free-will could not be directed Godward. It is of God's grace alone that a man is moved to meritorious goodness.

One of Aquinas's distinctive ideas is that of "habitual grace," which he distinguishes from "actual grace." He conceives of habitual grace as effecting man's natural and spiritual life. The gentlemanly catalogue of virtues of the natural man in Aristotle's *Ethics* is the result of habitual grace, as are the "theological" virtues of faith, hope, and charity. With habitual grace Aquinas associates "actual grace." This he specifies as a transient and recurring gift of God that leads the soul to undertake special activities.

"To live righteously," he declares, "man needs a twofold help of God. First a habitual gift, whereby corrupted nature may be healed, and, after being healed, is lifted up so as to work deeds meritorious of everlasting life which exceed the capacity

Cologne Cathedral, Germany.

of nature. Second, he needs the help of grace in order to be moved by God to act." Aquinas, however, for all his fourfold analysis of grace as "sanctifying," "gratuitous," "operating," and "co-operating," in the end leaves unresolved the antithesis between human merit and divine grace. He would give both a place in the scheme of salvation. But in the New Testament they stand in a relationship of exclusion.

Salvation

In his observations on the atonement, Aquinas leaves us with the thought that man's salvation is in part his own work. He does not, like Anselm, regard the cross as an absolute necessity for man's redemption: "It was possible for God to deliver mankind otherwise than by the Passion of Christ" (*Summa Theol.* 111.46.2). He, however, sees Christ's work both as "satisfaction," and "merit." It was a satisfaction in that the demands of justice were met, and it was a merit because Christ's death was a work of supererogation. Man

merited salvation because he was actuated throughout his life by no imposed necessity. Aquinas does pronounce Christ's death "efficient." But in final reading it remains somewhat inefficient. For there is a certain "configuration" to Christ by baptism and penance required on the part of the believer to fill up that which is lacking in the satisfaction of Christ. Aquinas thus affirms: "Christ's Passion works its effect in them to whom it is applied, through faith and charity and the sacraments of the faith" (*Summa Theol.* 11.49.3).

Aquinas's ethical teaching has been well described as the rational naturalism of Aristotle seen through a stained glass window. Man as a rational being possessing free-will is consequently a moral being. As such he is naturally inclined toward the good. But he cannot truly will the good, or do it, without divine aid. "God moves man's will .... to the universal object of his will, which is the good. And without this universal motion, man cannot will anything. But man determines himself by reason to will this or that, which is a true or apparent good" (*Summa Theol.* 11.9.5).

The four cardinal virtues of prudence, justice, temperance, and fortitude are possessed by all men. And as man's moral goal, they are attainable by all. Aquinas gives prudence the highest place in the catalogue of moral virtues. By wise moral choices, man can attain the ethical standard of moral well-being (*eudaimonia*). Whether, however, for the fulfillment of the natural law of the moral life, or of the "new law" of the spiritual life, man needs the reinforcing help of God. In this way Aquinas justifies the scholastic dictum *"Gratia non tollit sed perficit naturam"* ("Grace does not destroy nature; it perfects her") (*Summa Theol.* 1.8.2, and elsewhere). But that dictum, when the terms *grace* and *nature* are biblically understood, has no biblical warrant.

John Wyclif
c.1330-1384

John Wyclif (c. 1330-1384) is sometimes known as the *Morning Star of the Reformation*. He lived during the fourteenth century, a time when the Roman Catholic church was suffering from increasing corruption. Wyclif was one of the great thinkers of his age and wrote many important works in the areas of philosophy and theology. But he did not confine himself to the academic life.

In his forties Wyclif became involved in politics, siding with the government in its disputes with the papacy. During that time his views became increasingly radical, as he questioned a number of accepted Catholic beliefs. Just when Wyclif's ideas became most radical, the political situation changed, and his government no longer required his services. Wyclif's views were condemned, and he had to retire to a country parish. There he continued to write and encourage those seeking reform. His followers translated the Bible into English and went out to preach. Those so-called Lollards were fiercely persecuted, and the movement was driven underground. But Wyclif's ideas spread to Bohemia where they could be held more openly. In England they paved the way for the Protestant Reformation, which came some 150 years after Wyclif's death.

John Wyclif, "Morning Star of the Reformation".

The Life of
Wyclif

c. 1330	Birth.
1360	Master of Balliol College, Oxford.
1361	Master of Arts degree; ordained.
1369	Bachelor of Divinity degree.
1372	Doctor of Divinity degree.
1374	Enters service of the crown.
1377	Trial at St. Paul's Cathedral; condemned in papal bulls.
1378	Attempted trial at Lambeth.
1381	Peasant's Revolt; moves to Lutterworth.
1382	Condemnation of his ideas; first stroke.
1384	Second stroke; death.

John Wyclif

"Morning Star of the Reformation"

A. N. S. Lane

Oxford's leading theologian

John Wyclif was born into a propertied English family in about 1330. He went to Oxford University to study and by 1360 had become master of Balliol College. This was not as prestigious then as it would be now – Wyclif was still working for his M. A. degree. The following year he had earned the degree and was ordained. He thereupon relinquished the mastership in favor of the more advantageous position of rectorship of a Lincolnshire church. Wyclif thus became, and remained for most of his life, an absentee parson. This was considered acceptable in those days, especially as a way of financing academic studies. It was the responsibility of the absentee rector to provide a substitute to perform his duties. It is not known how conscientious Wyclif was in this regard.

By 1370 Wyclif had become Oxford's leading philosopher and theologian. He had also come to hold radical ideas on lordship, which he wrote up in his book *Civil Dominion*. Here he maintains, on the one hand, that the ungodly have no right to rule; on the other hand, that the godly man possesses all the wealth of the universe. The first point is simple to prove. All lordship is granted by God. But He does not grant it to those who are in rebellion against him. Again, those who rule unjustly are in breach of the terms under which God delegates authority, and so have forfeited all right to rule. The second point follows from the fact that the godly man is God's son, and so shares His lordship. These claims plainly have the most radical social implications. On the one hand, they justify the rejection of unjust rulers and the confiscation of their goods. On the other hand, the universal lordship of the godly has important implications. This lordship must be shared with the rest of the godly, which leads to a form of biblical communism.

In practice, Wyclif's ideas were not nearly so radical. He recognized that we cannot here and now judge who is elect and distinguish with certainty between the elect and the reprobate. But, on the other hand, he maintained that those who lead blatantly sinful lives do forfeit their rights in this world. In particular, he applied this theory to the clergy of his time. They were so corrupt that the secular authorities had the right to confiscate church properties. This teaching was of obvious interest to the state.

Wyclif and John of Gaunt

During Wyclif's time the church was immensely wealthy, owning about one-third of all land in England, and yet it claimed exemption from taxation. Wyclif's doctrines were a suitable threat to be used to extract taxes out of a reluctant clergy, at a time when the king had to finance an expensive war with France. They could also be used in negotiations with the papacy over the pope's alleged right to tax the English clergy (to finance his own wars). Wyclif was included in a delegation sent to Bruges in 1374 to negotiate with the papal authorities. During the 1370s Wyclif enjoyed the favor and support of the government, especially of John of Gaunt, who was the Duke of Lancaster and one of the most powerful people in England. But Wyclif's doctrines also came to the ears of the pope, who in 1377 condemned eighteen of Wyclif's statements in a series of bulls. That year the English

Wyclif became Master of Balliol College, Oxford, in 1360.

bishops tried to put Wyclif on trial, at St. Paul's Cathedral, but John of Gaunt intervened on his behalf.

The following year everything changed for Wyclif. That year saw the election of a rival pope and the beginning of the forty-year Great Schism, with two or more popes confronting one another throughout the period. That drastically weakened the power of the papacy, with important implications for Wyclif. On the one hand, the government no longer needed his dangerously radical ideas in order to subdue the clergy. But on the other hand, the papacy was preoccupied with other issues and so left Wyclif to his own devices. This was very convenient for Wyclif, as about this time he began to develop more radical ideas, which at any other time in the Middle Ages would have spelled his doom. These ideas led to a loss of favor with the government, but his former patrons continued to exert enough pressure on his behalf to protect him from the attacks of the English clergy. Another trial, at Lambeth in 1378, was thwarted by the queen mother's support for Wyclif.

Wyclif condemned

In 1378 Wyclif retired from public life to continue his studies and writing at Oxford. The bishops put increasing pressure on the university to act against his radical ideas, but such pressure was at first resisted. In 1381, however, there was a peasants' revolt, and one of its leaders, John Ball, was reported to be a disciple of Wyclif. Wyclif disowned the revolt, but the damage was done. Furthermore, the rebels had killed the archbishop of Canterbury and his place was taken by William Courtenay, a longstanding opponent of Wyclif.

The following year Courtenay called a council that condemned twenty-four of Wyclif's statements. During the council there was an earthquake. Wyclif interpreted it as a sign of divine displeasure with the outcome, while Courtenay claimed that the land was breaking wind of Wyclif's foul heresies! Shortly after the Peasants' Revolt, Wyclif withdrew to Lutterworth in Leicestershire, where he had been the absentee rector since 1374. There he devoted himself to writing for

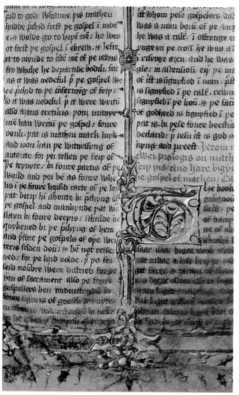

A page from the Wyclif Bible.

teaching to be supplied by church tradition, the pope, or any other source. Scripture contains all that is necessary for salvation. Furthermore, all other authorities, such as tradition, canon law, councils, and even popes, must be tested by the Scriptures. The Bible is the ultimate norm by which all other teaching must be tested. Here Wyclif clearly anticipates the position of the Protestant Reformers. Finally, the Bible is to be available to *all* Christians, the laity as well as the clergy.

If the Bible is to be available to all, it clearly follows that it must be translated into the vernacular, the common language of the people. Wyclif states as much in his other works. And so it was that Wyclif's disciples translated the Bible into English. But what Wyclif's own role was in the production of the *Wyclif Bible* no one knows for sure. It is certain that it was produced by his disciples, under his influence. It is quite likely, but not certain, that he played *some* supervisory role in the translation. The tradition that he actually took part in the translation is possible, but far from certain.

Wyclif and the papacy

As well as exalting the role of the Bible, Wyclif also downgraded the papacy. At that time Europe was confronted with the unedifying spectacle of rival popes anathematizing one another. The time was ripe for a re-examination of the role of the pope. In 1379 Wyclif wrote *The Power of the Papacy*, in which he argues that the papacy is an office instituted by man, not by God. Furthermore, the pope's authority is confined to the church and does not extend to secular government. More important, the pope's authority is not automatic, but depends on his having the moral character of Peter. In Wyclif's time, such a statement implied the rejection of nearly all recent popes. A pope who does not follow Jesus Christ is the Antichrist, claimed Wyclif. Later Wyclif went one step further, branding not just bad popes, but the institution of the papacy itself, as Antichrist.

Where Wyclif shocked his contempor-

his few remaining years. In 1382 he suffered a stroke. In December 1384 he suffered a second stroke and died a few days after on New Year's Eve.

Why did Wyclif's ideas cause so much controversy? He was by no means the first person in the Middle Ages to protest against the corrupt practices of the church. Where he broke new ground was in attacking the *doctrines* that underlay the practices. This was already true of his theories of lordship. But from 1378 he went on to attack some of the key doctrines of the contemporary church.

Wyclif and Scripture

In 1378 Wyclif wrote *The Truth of Holy Scripture*. Here he maintains, in accord with church teaching, that the Scriptures are true, that is, free from error or contradiction. But more than this, he claims that the Bible contains the whole of God's revelation. There is no need for any further aries the most was in his rejection of the doctrine of transubstantiation. Wyclif did not deny that in some sense Christ's body and blood are present in the Eucharist. Transubstantiation is one particular way in which Christ's presence is explained. It is the belief that the substance of the bread is changed into the substance of Christ's body, while the *accidents* of bread (their physical characteristics) remain. Wyclif rejected this doctrine on a number of grounds. It was a recent innovation, having been promulgated first in the thirteenth century. It was philosophically incoherent. It was contrary to Scripture. From 1379 Wyclif repeatedly attacked transubstantiation. He notes in a sermon that honest citizens do not let friars into their wine cellars for fear they might bless the wine and turn every barrel into mere accidents!

Wyclif believed that the bread and wine remain after their consecration. They become the sacraments of Christ's body and blood. Christ's body is present in the bread in the same way that my soul is present in my body. In some sense Christ's body is present everywhere in the bread. It is not altogether clear what Wyclif meant at this point, and his support has been claimed for both the Lutheran and the Calvinistic doctrines.

The Lollards

Wyclif's disciples were called Lollards, an abusive term meaning "mumblers." Wyclif himself was left unhindered, but after his death action was taken against his followers. At first he had disciples among the nobility and the scholars, but persecution largely eliminated these. In 1414 there was an abortive Lollard rebellion, which led to further repression. After this Lollardy became an underground lower-class movement. Studies have shown that there was a real continuity between Lollardy and the rise of Protestantism in the sixteenth century. The Lollards helped to pave the way for the English Reformation in the sixteenth century by spreading the English Bible and by fueling discontent with the Roman church.

Wyclif's ideas were also influential elsewhere in Europe. Some of his pupils at Oxford came from Bohemia (modern-day Czechoslovakia) and took copies of his works home with them. Wyclif's teaching influenced the rise of dissent in Bohemia, associated especially with the name of John Hus. Hus was burnt at the Council of Constance in 1415. The council also condemned forty-five "errors" of Wyclif. In 1428 his bones were dug up and burnt. A later chronicler commented, "They burnt his bones to ashes and cast them into the Swift, a neighboring brook running hard by. Thus the brook conveyed his ashes into the Avon, the Avon into the Severn, the Severn into the narrow seas and they into the main ocean. And so the ashes of Wyclif are symbolic of his doctrine, which is now spread throughout the world."

Lutterworth parish church, Leicestershire.

Catherine of Siena
c.1347-1380

Opposite:
"St Catherine and the
Doctors of Alexandria," from a
fifteenth-century breviary of
Cardinal Grimani.

Catherine of Siena (1347?-1380) was one of the most remarkable spiritual mystics of the late Middle Ages. The times in which Catherine lived were exciting but difficult. The medieval world was giving way to profound changes in society, economics, art, and faith. Her homeland, Italy, was at the cutting-edge where medieval tradition met the spirit of the Renaissance. In this period of transition there was a good deal of spiritual restlessness.

Unlike Bridget of Sweden (d. 1373), with whom she is often compared, Catherine's visions and inspiration came directly from Jesus rather than from Mary His mother. Following Christ's instruction, Catherine believed it was her duty to reform the church, to evangelize, to comfort the sick, the poor, and the condemned. She was an activist in an age when a woman's religious vocation was supposed to be confined and apart from the world.

The richly decorated facade of Siena Cathedral, Italy.

The Life of
Catherine

c. 1347	Birth in Siena.
c. 1354	Sees vision of Jesus with Peter, Paul, and John. Vows religious life.
1363	Becomes member of the Sisters of Penitence.
1367	Sees vision of her celestial marriage. Begins her ministry.
1370	Begins her Letters.
1374	Tried for heresy by the Dominicans in Florence. Receives Raymond of Capua as spiritual guide.
1376	Travels to Avignon; persuades Pope Gregory XI to return with Curia to Rome.
1378-1380	Fails in attempt to heal Great Schism.
1380	April 29, death in Rome.

Catherine of Siena

Spiritual Mystic
Caroline T. Marshall

Catherine Benincasa

About the year 1347, Catherine Benincasa was born into the violent and colorful world of fourteenth-century Italy. Her father, Jacobo, was a dyer; her mother, Lupa, a housewife. Catherine was one of twenty-four children and a twin. The Benincasa family was artisan in class, not rich, but well able to participate in the wealth of its city.

Catherine was baptized into a church in serious disarray. The pope lived in Avignon in elegant exile. The so-called Babylonian Captivity of the papacy had already lasted for decades (since 1309). It constituted a deep and painful scandal for Christendom. The separation of the bishops of Rome from the seat of their spiritual power did not help instill confidence in the faithful.

Ordinary people were searching for religious expression outside the ordinary and accepted channels of the church. The fourteenth century witnessed a great revival of lay interest in the faith. In fact the mendicant orders, such as the Dominicans, Franciscans, Carmelites and Augustinians, had established so-called Third Orders for lay men and women, in which they might attempt more spiritual lives without the confinement of monastery or ordination.

Catherine was a child of that era and one of its lasting contributions to the expression of Christian faith. Devout from childhood, she saw a vision of Jesus with Peter, Paul, and John the evangelist when she was about seven. From that moment on she was determined to enter the religious life. Her parents objected, apparently in the belief that she was engaged in an elaborate prank. Finally, her father was reconciled, and a part of the house was set aside for her prayer, meditation, trances, and ecstacies. Most alarming to those who loved her was her practice of an extreme asceticism, in which she entered long fasts, refused to sleep, and used harsh discipline (a whip or chain).

Ministry to the world

Catherine's early years were spent at home in Siena. Her first ministry followed her entry into the Sisters of Penitences, a Dominican Third Order, in 1368. From that year until 1374 she was busy establishing a following, engaging in good works, writing the first series of her famous *Letters*, and entering the arena of public service.

Catherine does not seem to have thought of joining a convent. This would, of course, have confined her movement, and her work in the world was too demanding for confinement. She gathered about her a large group of followers, both men and women, her *famiglia* (family). It included widows and virgins, an aging anchorite, priests, noblemen, Dominicans, laity and clerics, old and young. However, laymen predominated, and most were probably older than she was.

In Siena, Catherine began her ministry to the world. She performed the most distressing nursing chores among those incurably ill of cancer and leprosy. Her patients were in pain and often abusive. She believed that these experiences helped her to share in the suffering of the crucified Christ and were, therefore, a great help along her path to the mystical union with God, which was her ultimate goal.

In addition to nursing, Catherine became interested in prisoners. She evangelized among the condemned and remained with them throughout the ordeal of execution. She also preached informally, gave advice, and grew very popular among the people of Siena. In reaction, her critics within the church became more vocal. In 1370 Catherine began her *Letters*, vehicles through which presumably she could give spiritual advice to her followers without fear.

Accusations of heresy

Like many medieval people, Catherine saw no distinction between the ecclesiastical and public orders. She was determined to go on a crusade to Palestine in order to convert the infidel Turks. In this her ambitions were neither military nor expansionist, but rather evangelical. Soon she became an object of serious criticism by conservative church leaders and was subsequently brought before a Dominican tribunal on charges of heresy.

The details of her heresy experience are not known. Often, prior to the accusation, she had been labeled a fraud. The trances and ecstacies into which she regularly fell while at Communion or in prayer were systematically denounced by the local clergy. What is known is that the General Chapter of the Dominican Order meeting in Florence in 1374 cleared her of all charges and assigned her a formal spiritual advisor, Brother Raymond of Capua, who became her secretary, one of her best friends, and her hagiographer.

Following her formal vindication before the Dominicans, Catherine became even more active in public affairs. She once again pressed for the crusade to convert the Turks and intervened in the war that Florence and other Italian city states were waging against Pope Gregory XI. Catherine quickly became attached to the pope and acted as his partisan in Italy. Most of all, she demanded that he return from "exile" in Avignon and re-establish the papacy in Rome. Clearly Catherine believed that the reform of the church would be certain if only the pope were restored to Rome.

In the summer of 1376 Catherine visited

The scallop-shaped Piazza del Campo, Siena.

the pope in Avignon. There she brought Florence's proposals for peace between Tuscany and the papacy. Peace followed between Florence and the church, and the pope brought the Curia back to Rome after more than a century of self-inflicted exile. It must be recalled that Gregory XI was rather sympathetic to mysticism and was also interested in the millenarian prophecies that were current at the time. The current apocalyptic view emphasized the reign of a benevolent pope, the conversion of infidels, and the coming of the Antichrist as signs of the end times. Although Catherine did not entertain such theories, some of her followers did. She certainly had a great effect on the pope.

A year after the great triumph of the papacy's restoration to Rome, however, came the death of Gregory XI. A Roman mob demanded an Italian pope, and Urban VI was elected. He was arrogant and tactless, and his failure to accommodate his rivals helped to create the infamous Great Schism, in which two popes claimed Christendom's confused loyalties.

The Great Schism

Catherine felt personally responsible for the Great Schism. She spent much of the last two years of her life, 1378-1380, in Rome in a vain effort to heal the breach in the church. During that period she wrote her great treatise on mysticism, the *Dialogue*, in which she describes her brilliant Christocentric faith.

When she was a young woman in Siena, Catherine while in a trance had a vision of herself becoming the "bride" or "spouse" of Christ. The language of late medieval Europe was highly romantic. Often it sounds excessive or inappropriate to modern people. However, the chaste nun as the bride of Christ was a favourite medieval ideal, and it is not strange that Catherine should think of herself in this way. However, Catherine had no idea of entering a nunnery.

Celestial marriage

Catherine's celestial marriage is the spiritual union with the deity for which all mystics yearn. Like Bernard of Clairvaux, she wanted to know God by loving Him. She came to believe that in this early union, which she later reinforced through constant prayer and ecstacy, she had submerged her will into that of God. Yet she had emerged from the experience still an individual, still intact. In Catherine's vocabulary, the word *spouse* is used to describe this relationship. She applies it to both men and women, and she seems to be describing something of what contemporary people mean when they speak of having a personal relationship with Jesus, one which they see as warm, intimate, and loving rather than formal or institutional.

Exhausted and disappointed by papal failures, Catherine died in Rome in 1380. Her *Letters* and the *Dialogue* are among the treasures of Western Christendom. Catherine's best gift, however, was her strange and beautiful life. Pope Pius II, a Sienese, sainted her in 1461. Her feast day is April 29.

The dome of Florence Cathedral.

John Hus

c. 1372-1415

In 1360 the king of Bohemia (similar in area to modern Czechoslovakia) invited one Conrad of Waldhausen to come and preach against corruption in the church. From that time on there was a national reform movement in Bohemia. John Hus (c. 1372-1415) stood firmly within this tradition. The chief distinctive feature that turned him into the figurehead of the movement and a national hero was his martyrdom. Hus lived during the Great Schism, when Europe was divided between two or even three rival popes who were bitterly anathematizing one another. It was the Council of Constance, which brought the Schism to an end, that sent Hus to the stake.

Hus confessed himself a disciple of Wyclif, and he was undoubtedly to a limited extent influenced by him. But their common ground lay in their concern about the corruption of the church hierarchy and in their willingness to challenge its authority. Doctrinally, Hus was more conservative than Wyclif. Wyclif was a largely solitary figure with few real followers. Lollardy was a small underground movement of little importance until the Reformation. Hus, by contrast, was merely one (important) member of an ongoing movement.

Furthermore, this was to become a *national* movement of reform. In this respect the Hussite reform anticipates the Reformation of the sixteenth century, with the founding of national Reformed churches.

John Hus, the Czech reformer.

The Life of

Hus

c. 1372	Birth.
1385	Elementary school at Prachatice.
1390	Studies at University of Prague.
1393	Bachelor of Arts degree.
1396	Master of Arts degree.
1400	Ordained.
1402	Rector and preacher at Bethlehem Chapel, Prague.
1404	Bachelor of Divinity degree.
1410	Forbidden to preach; excommunicated.
1412	Exiled from Prague; writes *The Church and Simony*.
1414	Travels to Council of Constance; arrested.
1415	Death: condemned and burned at the stake.

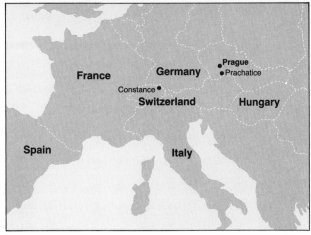

John Hus

Czech Reformer

A. N. S. Lane

Hus and Wyclif

John Hus was born in about 1372 of poor parents in Bohemia. His mother wanted him to become a priest, and so in 1385 he was sent to the elementary school at Prachatice. In 1390 he moved on to the University of Prague. There he proceeded to earn his B.A. and M.A. degrees, after which he was able to teach in the faculty of arts. In the meantime he proceeded with theology, earning his B.D. in 1404. In 1402, he was appointed as rector and preacher at the Bethlehem Chapel in Prague. This chapel had been founded in 1391 by a wealthy merchant as a center for reform preaching. Two sermons were preached each day, in Czech. Thus Hus had been appointed to a key position within the national reform movement.

There had been close links between England and Bohemia since the marriage in 1382 between King Richard II and Anne of Bohemia. Wyclif's philosophical writings were already known in Bohemia in the fourteenth century, but in 1401 Jerome of Prague brought back from England copies of several of his more radical theological works. This led to an ongoing controversy between those who wished to condemn Wyclif and his teaching and those who defended him, though without accepting all his radical doctrines.

Wyclif's attack on transubstantiation met with little favor, and Hus represented the majority of the Bohemian reformers in remaining loyal to the doctrine. But Wyclif's attacks on clerical corruption, especially simony, or the sale of spiritual privileges, met with much approval. Hus also accepted Wyclif's position at one vital point – his appeal from the institutional, hierarchical church to the invisible church of the elect. This was a crucial step because it laid the foundation for the rejection of the authority of wicked church leaders and for the appeal from the institutional church to the Bible.

The controversy over Wyclif began in 1403 with the condemnation by the University of Prague of forty-five theses from his writings. The condemnation was achieved because the Germans could outvote the Bohemians by three to one. This fact was, naturally, resented by the Bohemians. At first the archbishop of Prague, Zbynek, supported the reformers. But the question of which of the rival popes to support divided the king and the reformers from the archbishop and the Germans. The outcome was that from 1408 the archbishop opposed the reforming party. In 1409 the king eliminated the inbuilt German voting majority in the university, with the result that the Germans left *en bloc* and founded a new university at Leipzig. The Bohemians now controlled the University of Prague and chose Hus to be its rector.

Excommunication

Hus's promotion was to be short-lived. The archbishop obtained from the pope a ban on preaching in chapels, including the Bethlehem Chapel. Hus refused to obey, and so in 1410 he was excommunicated by the archbishop. In the same year the archbishop burned two hundred volumes of Wyclif's works. Hus and others responded by defending Wyclif's orthodoxy. The outcome of the controversy was that Hus was summoned to Rome. He wisely declined to go in person, but sent legal representatives instead.

In 1412 matters came to a head. Pope John XXII had launched a crusade against the king of Naples and was even offering full remission of sins to all who supported him. Hus was outraged at the use of spiritual sanctions to further the pope's own personal ends and attacked the sale of the indulgences. The result was that Hus was excommunicated by Rome and the city of Prague was placed under an interdict while he was there.

John Hus is taken to the stake; from a contemporary manuscript by Ulrich Richental.

The Old Town Square, Prague, with the John Hus memorial at its center.

This meant that no religious services, not even baptisms or funerals, could take place. In the circumstances Hus felt obliged to leave the city. He withdrew to the south of Bohemia, where he wrote two of his most important works: *The Church* and *Simony*.

Martyrdom

In 1414 a council met at Constance to heal the Great Schism. Hus was invited by the emperor Sigismund and promised safe conduct in both directions, whatever might be the outcome of the case against him. With hesitations, he decided to go. But within a month the followers of Pope John XXII had captured and imprisoned him. Hus was put on trial by the council, despite the safe conduct, and eventually found guilty of heresy. Many of the charges made against him were untrue – such as the claim that he denied transubstantiation, or that he considered the ministration of wicked priests invalid. But some of his actual teachings, especially on the church, were also tried and deemed to be heretical. Hus refused to recant so on July 6, 1415 he was condemned for heresy and taken to the outskirts of

the city to be burned. The spot is today marked by a memorial stone.

In burning Hus, the council was in fact stoking up the fire of Bohemian dissent. Immediate measures were taken against his followers, but this served only to provoke a civil war. The reform movement survived but divided into two main groups. Members of the majority were seeking only minor reforms in the Roman Catholic system. Their chief demand was that the laity should receive the cup as well as the bread in Communion. (The Roman Catholics reserved the cup for the clergy.) For this reason they were called Calixtines (from the Latin *calix*, "cup") or Utraquists (from the Latin *utraque*, meaning "both").

But there were others, called Taborites after their mountain stronghold in south Bohemia, who sought a more thorough reform. Over the coming fifteenth century they were alternately tolerated and persecuted. They entered into friendly relations with the Waldensians, another dissenting group to the west. With the rise of the Reformation they made contact with both Luther and Calvin.

Martin Luther
1483-1546

Martin Luther (1483-1546) was the father of the Protestant Reformation. He was educated as a loyal member of the medieval Roman Catholic church and became both a monk and a priest. Yet his study of the Scriptures and his own spiritual struggles led him to an evangelical breakthrough. He came to teach the basic principles of Protestant Christianity: justification by grace alone through faith alone, and the Bible as the only ultimate authority for Christian belief and practice. He led a broad movement in sixteenth-century Europe to reform theology, purify the church, and help Christians understand biblical Christianity.

Luther's achievements as pastor, scholar, theologian, and Christian were monumental and have influenced the church profoundly to this day. He was far from perfect, but Melanchthon provided a most fitting epitaph for Luther when he said in his funeral oration that God had given a violent age a violent physician.

Evangelical Christianity preserves and continues the reforming spirit of Martin Luther.

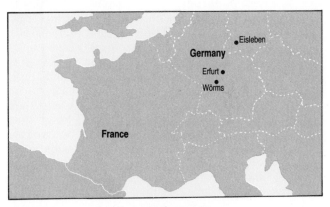

Martin Luther, the German reformer, at age 63.

The Life of
Luther

1483	Birth at Eisleben.
1501	Enters University of Erfurt.
1505	Enters Augustinian monastery.
1512	Awarded degree of Doctor of Theology.
1517	Posts Ninety-Five Theses.
1519	Leipzig Disputation.
1521	Appears before the Diet of Wörms.
1525	Marries Katherine von Bora.
1529	Marburg Colloquy.
1530	Augsburg Confession.
1534	Publication of the complete German Bible.
1546	Death at Eisleben.

Martin Luther

German Reformer

W. Robert Godfrey

Luther becomes a monk

Martin Luther was born November 10, 1483, in Eisleben, Saxony. Today Saxony is part of the German Democratic Republic (East Germany). In Luther's day, Saxony was one of more than 300 local territories that composed the Holy Roman Empire of the German nation. Luther's family were rather prosperous members of the middle class, even though Luther later said, "I am a peasant's son."

Luther received a traditional medieval early education. Some of his teachers were connected with the Brethren of the Common Life, a lay order concerned with education for devout Christian living.

Luther studied at the University of Erfurt, receiving his B.A. in 1502 and M.A. in 1505.

In May 1505 Luther began to study law, in accordance with his father's wishes. Luther himself wanted to enter a monastery to seek God, but his father believed a lawyer would be of more help to the family than a monk. But his legal studies came to an abrupt end on July 2, 1505, when Martin Luther was caught in a severe thunderstorm. Fearing for his life he cried out, "St. Anne, I will become a monk!" Now bound by a vow to his father's patron saint, Luther could follow the urgings of his conscience and become a monk.

Martin Luther's birthplace, Eisleben, Saxony.

For Luther the monastic life was the highest form of religious devotion. He had accepted the teaching of the church that those serious about religion and their salvation should become monks. His monastic vow would be a second baptism, a new beginning.

The monastic ideal

Luther gave himself to the rigorous pursuit of the monastic ideal. He joined the monastery of the Augustinian hermits in Erfurt where strict discipline was maintained. He devoted himself to study, prayer, and the use of the sacraments. He especially used the sacrament of penance, examining himself and sorrowing for his sins, confessing his sins to a priest, and fulfilling the satisfaction imposed on him. Indeed, he wearied his priest with his confessions and punished himself with prolonged periods of prayer, fasting, sleepless nights, and flagellation.

Luther's wise and godly superior, Johannes von Staupitz, encouraged Luther's studies in particular. Staupitz recognized the future Reformer's great intellectual talents and saw the value of directing him away from excessive introspection. So Luther pursued theological studies, following the nominalism of William of Ockham and Gabriel Biel. This nominalism stressed the importance of the authority of the Bible and the church in theology and minimized the usefulness of reason in building a natural theology. In time Luther also began thorough studies of the Scriptures. He learned Greek and Hebrew in the spirit of the Renaissance drive to return to, and recapture, the sources of Western civilization. Eventually he committed most of the New Testament and great portions of the Old Testament to memory.

Priest and teacher

Luther was ordained a priest in 1507, taught at the universities of Wittenberg and Erfurt (1508-1511), and in 1512 received his doctoral degree. In receiving his degree and becoming a professor, Luther took a traditional vow faithfully to teach and defend the Scriptures. This vow would later comfort him when he became a reformer. He never viewed himself as a rebel but rather as a theologian fulfilling the vow imposed upon him by the medieval church.

In 1512 he returned to the University of Wittenberg as a professor. This young university, founded in 1502, in electoral Saxony became Luther's home. There he began his lectures on the Bible: 1513-1515 on the Psalms, 1515-1516 on Romans, 1516-1517 on Galatians, and 1517-1518 on Hebrews. These books were basic in shaping the thought of the future Reformer.

Luther was a scholar but also a churchman. He undertook administrative responsibilities for his monastic order and by 1516 had become peoples' priest in Wittenberg, with regular preaching duties. It was a combination of theological and pastoral concerns for the church and the people that led Luther to take actions that made him famous.

The front of Luther's birthplace.

95 Theses

In 1517 Luther became concerned about the abuses in the sale of indulgences. Technically, indulgences removed or reduced the satisfactions required of sinners as part of the sacrament of penance. Since the late fifteenth century, popes had authorized plenary indulgences for souls in purgatory as well as for the living. Some of those who sold indulgences encouraged people to believe that they were actually buying the forgiveness of sins for themselves or for others when they bought an indulgence. As a pastor and theologian Luther strongly objected, and in response wrote his "95 Theses," which he posted on the church door in Wittenberg.

Luther's action in nailing theses to the church door was neither rebellious nor radical. It was a traditional way of inviting the academic community to discuss an issue. He dutifully sent a copy to his bishop. Yet others saw the great importance of these theses and, without Luther's permission, translated them into German and published them. Luther's concern touched a responsive chord in many who were restive with the church, either for its materialistic corruptions or for its inadequate spiritual care.

Luther's fame in disputing indulgences drew him into further disputations. An important debate occurred at Leipzig in July 1519, when Luther debated with John Eck. The Leipzig Disputation in particular helped Luther clarify his views on religious authority. There he publicly recognized that the Bible alone, not popes or councils, was invariably true and reliable.

Luther's conversion

These external events in Luther's life expressed important internal development in his thought. In his 1545 preface to his Latin writings, Luther recalled his dramatic conversion, his evangelical breakthrough, when he felt that he truly came to understand the gospel. Luther had long been troubled spiritually with the righteousness of God. God's demand for perfect righteousness oppressed him. Even with all of the grace available through the sacraments and practices of the medieval church, Luther still knew that he fell short. Try as he might he could not attain the perfection that God's standard required.

One day he was wrestling with the problem in terms of Romans 1:17. How could the revelation of the righteousness of God be gospel, or good news, Luther asked. Suddenly he saw that the gospel is the good news that, in Christ, God gives the righteousness demanded in the law. God imputes, or reckons, the perfect righteousness of Christ to sinners who receive it by faith. This insight is the essence of Luther's doctrine of justification by faith. Faith, or trust in the promises of Christ, alone justifies, because faith alone receives and rests in Christ's imputed righteousness.

Historians still debate when exactly this breakthrough took place. Luther's writings show a gradual movement away from certain elements of medieval theology as early as 1512. But Luther's own memory recalled a decisive and sudden change when many gradual changes came together. From the perspective of the 1545 preface, that decisive breakthrough occurred in 1518, after he had already become a public figure through his criticism of indulgences.

Especially in his early years as a reformer, Luther's theology did change and develop. He never wrote a systematic theology text. His writings addressed specific theological issues of the moment. His views all reflected the religious center of his thought, but he did not labor to relate them all to one another. His emblem was the rose, and his writings circled the core of this faith as petals circle the core of the rose.

Melanchthon

Luther emerged as a leader of a reforming movement. He was not alone. In addition to growing popular support, he was encouraged by colleagues at the university, especially young Philip Melanchthon and Andreas Bodenstein von

1548

Contemporary print of Martin Luther.

Karlstadt. He was also protected in his order by Staupitz and by his prince, Frederick, Elector of Saxony. Many Renaissance humanists also supported him. They saw Luther as another Renaissance critic of the antiquated ways of medieval scholasticism, and they feared that powerful obscurantists would silence Luther, as they had the Hebraist Johannes Reuchlin.

Luther's writings were a powerful source of support for him. He was a brilliant, forceful communicator, penetrating to the heart and religious core of the issues he addressed. In 1520 he produced some of his most powerful treatises. Three of his best that year were *Address to the German Nobility* (in August), *The Babylonian Captivity of the Church* (in October), and *On the Freedom of the Christian* (in November).

Luther's *Address to the German Nobility* presented his strategy for the reform of the church. Luther was convinced

The "95 Theses" church door, Wittenberg.

that the only hope for genuine reform lay in the calling of a free council to implement reforms. But he feared that the corruption of the clergy, especially the vested interests of the princes of the church, would make such a council impossible. So Luther appealed to the secular princes to call a council. He argued that God had given Christian magistrates responsibility to care for the church, and in special circumstances to act as "emergency bishops." He maintained that history confirmed his contention, as the case of the emperor Constantine calling the Council of Nicea in A.D. 325 showed.

Luther presented a list of items for such a council to consider. Basically, though, he called for restraints on the role of the papacy in directing the life of the church and a reform of serious moral abuses in the church. Luther's strategy for reform was daring. Earlier popes had declared that anyone appealing to a council against a papal ruling was excommunicated.

The sacraments

Luther's second treatise of 1520, *The Babylonian Captivity of the Church*, was more theological. It addressed the most sensitive issue for many sixteenth-century Christians: the sacraments. Luther examined the seven sacraments of the medieval church, declaring at the beginning of the treatise that he accepted as true sacraments only three, baptism, the Lord's Supper, and penance. However, by the end of the treatise he seemed to be arguing that only baptism and the Lord's Supper were true sacraments.

Luther devoted his most careful analysis to the Lord's Supper. He argued that the papacy had placed three great shackles on the sacrament. The first shackle was to allow Communion in only one kind, instead of following Christ's example of giving wine as well as bread. The second was the doctrine of transubstantiation, binding the church to believe that the substance of the bread and wine was completely replaced on the altar by the body and blood of Christ. The third

The castle of Wartburg, Luther's refuge from his enemies.

shackle, and by far the worst for Luther, was the doctrine of eucharistic sacrifice, which held that the priest offered Christ as a propitiation to the Father on the altar.

Luther not only rejected five of the sacraments of the papal church as false, but also rejected the idea of a separate priestly order in the church. Several times in this treatise he stressed the priesthood of all believers. For Luther, every true believer serves as a priest for fellow believers.

Freedom in Christ

Luther's treatise *On the Freedom of the Christian* is regarded by many as his best. Here the very heart of his message is laid out. Through Christ, man is free as he stands before God. He lives by faith in the promises of Christ and so is "the free lord of all." But in relation to his fellow man and the things of this world, the Christian follows Christ and lives by love, becoming "the bondservant of all." True, serving love does not seek to earn anything from God but arises naturally from true faith and desires to please God in all things.

Man needs the law to learn of his helplessness and to learn repentance, but the gospel is the free promise of grace in Christ, which is received by faith alone.

These treatises and others helped rally support to Luther. And he needed the support. As early as 1518 an order was issued for his arrest. Although the order was not carried out, pressure from church authorities increased. In June 1520 Pope Leo X issued a bull, *Exsurge Domine*, ordering Luther to recant under threat of excommunication. In January 1521 Luther was excommunicated and in March was summoned to appear before the emperor Charles V at the imperial diet meeting at Wörms. Luther was given a safe conduct, guaranteeing that he could travel safely to and from Wörms. But Luther remembered that the martyr John Hus had traveled to Constance with an imperial safe conduct.

Diet at Wörms

Luther appeared before the emperor and the diet in April. He was denied an opportunity to defend his teachings and was ordered to recant his errors. Luther did make a brief statement, the exact words of which are still uncertain. Even if he did not say, "Here I stand," he did declare: "My conscience is captive to the Word of God." That is where Luther stood even though the powers of the emperor and the church were united against him.

The emperor dismissed Luther and permitted him to leave the city. The elector Frederick arranged for Luther to be intercepted on the road and carried off to a secret location unknown even to Frederick. While Luther was safely at the castle of Wartburg, he was declared an outlaw. This decree meant that Luther, and anyone helping him, was subject to the loss of life and property. Still Luther survived to minister and write for twenty-five years and die of natural causes.

While Luther was at the Wartburg, he worked on translating the Bible from the original Greek and Hebrew into German. The resulting translation influenced the German language and church in a way parallel to the King James Version of the Bible did English.

Luther and Karlstadt

During his absence from Wittenberg, Luther expected Melanchthon to lead the reforming movement. But Melanchthon's timidity allowed Karlstadt to become the prime influence. Karlstadt introduced the first external changes in the worship services. He simplified the service and translated it into German. He also removed images from the churches. These changes had much popular support but were leading to some social unrest and to growing concern on the part of the elector. Luther feared that Karlstadt was placing too much emphasis on external reforms and introducing a new legalism that threatened to overshadow justification by faith and the spirituality of the gospel. In March 1522 Luther returned to Wittenberg. He slowed the pace of external reforms, arguing concern for the weaker brothers and the need for the church to act together in love.

Karlstadt left Wittenberg and became for Luther a symbol of the new legalism that Luther feared would undermine the reforming movement from within. Karlstadt was later received warmly by Zwingli in Zurich. That link between Karlstadt and Zwingli made it very difficult for Luther to evaluate Zwingli's theology objectively, and colored the debate about the Lord's Supper. Already the difficulties in maintaining Protestant unity were manifesting themselves.

The Peasants' Revolt

Another crucial year for Luther was 1525. Peasant demands for more rights led to armed conflict between peasants and nobles. The Peasants' Revolt spread to about one-third of Germany. Thomas Münzer, an Anabaptist, was one prominent leader of the revolt. He declared that the peasants were free in Christ from oppression and that God would give their struggle success. Luther was horrified. Like many medieval thinkers, Luther saw anarchy and chaos as imminent dangers to society. He believed that, as citizens, the peasants had some legitimate complaints. But if peasants sought violently to assert rights as Christians, they betrayed the gospel and its call to self-denial. They threatened peace and the social order.

Luther wrote several treatises on the revolt. One, which Luther himself called a harsh book, was entitled *Against the Robbing and Murdering Hordes*. He called on the nobility to hunt down and slaughter the insurrectionists. He wrote too strongly, but he wrote out of his great distress for the severe social disorders taking place, out of his outrage that the peasants had misunderstood the evangelical message and used it to justify their cause, and out of his fear that the opponents of the reform would blame the reform for the unrest. The revolt was brutally suppressed, and Luther's influence among the peasants may have been weakened. Many Roman Catholic authorities did blame Protestantism for fomenting sedition.

On the happier side, 1525 was the year of Luther's marriage to Katherine von Bora. Katie, as he called her, was a former nun, and the marriage was as much a testimony to Luther's view of Christian freedom as anything. Yet the marriage came to be filled with love and devotion. Luther called home life "the school of character" and frequently joked about "my lord Katie." They had six children. Luther's own experience with family life signaled a new role and importance for the family in Christianity. Family life became a crucial part of the Christian's calling.

In 1525 Luther also wrote the theological treatise that he considered his most important: *On the Bondage of the Will*. This work was a response to Desiderius Erasmus, who in 1524 had written *On the Freedom of the Will*. Erasmus was the leading Renaissance humanist and scholar of his day. He remained within the Roman Catholic church but was not eager, in spite of great pressure, to attack Luther. Finally in 1524 he did write against Luther on an area of genuine disagreement. Erasmus argued that although salvation was almost entirely of grace, there was a small but significant role that man's free will had to play.

In December 1525 Luther replied scathingly that salvation was exclusively by grace. He argued that man's will was so utterly in bondage to sin that only God's action could save. He clearly embraced an Augustinian view of predestination and declared that he much preferred that his salvation should be in God's hands, rather than his own, from beginning to end.

The exchange between Luther and Erasmus demonstrated a difference of concerns between the Renaissance and the Reformation. Many humanists ceased to support Luther. Others redirected their studies from literature to the Scriptures and became ministers.

Luther and Zwingli
In 1527 Luther began to write against Ulrich Zwingli's view of the Lord's Supper. This debate was to take a tremendous amount of time and energy. It became the most divisive issue among most Protestants in the sixteenth century.

Zwingli initially stressed that the Lord's Supper was a memorial meal in which the Christian renewed his commitment to Christ. This perspective reflected Zwingli's conviction that the doctrine of transubstantiation was Rome's worst error on Communion. The bread could not be changed into the body of Christ, because Christ's body had ascended into heaven. Rome worshiped bread and so was idolatrous. Zwingli wanted above all to avoid any such idolatry.

Luther came to the Lord's Supper from quite a different perspective. The key Roman error for Luther was the doctrine of eucharistic sacrifice. How could the church sacrifice Christ to God? Such an idea was part of the works-righteousness of medieval theology. For Luther, the Lord's Supper was not primarily what man does but what God does. Through the Supper God gives Christ and all His saving benefits. Christ is truly present in the Supper.

For Luther, Zwingli's doctrine was too bound to the self-righteousness of Rome. For Zwingli, Luther's doctrine was too bound to the idolatry of Rome. For Luther, Zwingli did not believe Jesus' words "This is my body." For Zwingli, Luther denied a basic article of the Apostles' Creed, "He ascended into heaven, and sitteth at the right hand of God the Father Almighty."

Luther offered a rebuttal to Zwingli's criticism in the doctrine of ubiquity. Luther argued that it was possible for the ascended Christ to be in the Supper because His human nature had been glorified and shared the divine attribute of omnipresence. After all, the right hand of God is everywhere.

The Marburg Colloquy
Philip of Hesse, a prince, was eager to forge a Protestant political alliance between the Lutherans and other Protestants in southern Germany and Switzerland. Luther was very skeptical about the wisdom of such a venture but insisted that if there was to be a political alliance it had to rest on religious agreement. Philip arranged a religious discussion, a

colloquy, to meet at Marburg in October 1529. Luther and Melanchthon represented one side, whereas Zwingli and Martin Bucer, the Reformer of Strasbourg, were the most important on the other side.

Some progress was made. Luther saw that Zwingli did accept justification by faith. Zwingli granted that Christ was spiritually present in the Supper. But they failed to agree on the question of a real, physical presence. After the colloquy, suspicion and disagreement overwhelmed the progress made, and Reformed and Lutherans have remained divided ever since on the Supper.

Luther went to Marburg to discuss theology, but those who arranged the colloquy were increasingly concerned about the political consequences of the Reformation. The evangelical cause had attracted many princes as well as common people. At the Diet of Speyer in 1526 the princes decided that, as a temporary solution to their religious divisions, each prince would determine the religious practice of his own territory. When the Diet met at Speyer again in 1529, there was a less conciliatory mood. The Roman Catholic majority declared that there were to be no further changes. Protestant worship would not be tolerated in Roman Catholic territories, but Roman Catholic worship had to be tolerated in Protestant territories. The evangelical princes protested these rulings, and from that protest came the label "Protestant."

The Diet of Augsburg

In 1530, Emperor Charles V returned to Germany for the first time since 1521. He called for the evangelical princes to present a confession defending and justifying their faith. Luther could not attend this Diet at Augsburg, because he was an outlaw. So Melanchthon, after consulting with Luther, drew up the Augsburg Confession. It has remained the basic confession of Lutheranism. The confession was irenic but clear in its presentation of the basics of Luther's theology.

Charles rejected the confession, and the threat of war between Roman Cath-

olics and Protestants became real. The Protestant princes organized themselves into a defensive alliance, the Schmalkaldic League. Luther dreaded the possibility of war and fretted over whether a Christian prince should ever resist a superior. But war did not actually come until 1546, a few months after Luther's death.

In spite of various illnesses, which apparently contributed to periods of depression, Luther remained very active and productive in the last fifteen years of his life. He was an advisor to princes, theologians, and pastors. He wrote on various theological topics. He continued his biblical studies, publishing major commentaries on Galatians and Genesis. He also completed his translation of the Old Testament, so that his complete German Bible was published in 1534. He continued to preach regularly and to teach at the university. He frequently entertained students at his home. The vivid, pointed character of his observations on many subjects was preserved by his students in several volumes of Luther's *Table Talk*.

Luther was a controversial figure in his day and has continued to be so in ours. His attacks on some opponents were very strong and at times very vulgar. The sharpest were against the papacy and the Jews, but lawyers and Anabaptists were also attacked. For Luther, all these groups sought salvation through the law, and so all failed to understand the gospel. They were all instruments of the devil, and one could not, Luther believed, heap too much abuse on the devil.

Luther died at Eisleben on February 18, 1546. His life demonstrated that he had trusted his heavenly Father with all earthly plans and ambitions and with his soul. As Luther the songwriter put it, this confidence was not misplaced, because our God is a Mighty Fortress.

Ulrich (Huldrych) Zwingli
1484-1531

Standing under the shadows of Martin Luther and John Calvin, Ulrich Zwingli has been called the third man of the Reformation, or even the forgotten Reformer. Like Luther, he was born at the transitional time when the medieval system was decaying and the forces of the Renaissance were preparing the ground for renewal. Born and brought up in Switzerland (apart from a brief period in Vienna), Zwingli had become a warm admirer of Erasmus when ordained to the parish ministry. He proved to be an effective preacher and pastor at Glarus even though he had not yet come to a full evangelical understanding. After a temporary chaplaincy in the papal forces, he developed a keen opposition to the mercenary system that was so important to the Swiss economy.

A period of study and reflection at Einsiedeln, coinciding with the publication of Erasmus's *Greek New Testament* brought him to a fuller apprehension of the gospel and prepared him for his reforming work. He initiated that work as people's priest at Zurich and quickly made his mark both as the pioneer of the Reformation in Switzerland and as a reformer of force and originality. As a pioneer, Zwingli not only won over Zurich itself but helped to bring reform to such cantons as Glarus, Schaffhausen, St. Gall, Basel, and Bern; and indirectly to Vaud, Neuchâtel, and the free city of Geneva.

As an original reformer, Zwingli shaped many of the Reformed distinctives. He valued expository preaching, established an educated ministry, stressed the role of the Holy Spirit, engaged in radical liturgical reform, enhanced the disciplinary role of the laity, and laid the foundations for the Reformed doctrines of predestination and the sacraments. Disputes with the Anabaptists and the Lutherans marred Zwingli's later activity, and hostile relations with the Roman Catholic cantons led to the battle of Cappel (1531) in which he met an early death.

Ulrich Zwingli, "Third man of the Reformation."

The Life of

Zwingli

1484	Birth.
1506	Ordained.
1506-1516	Stays in Glarus.
1516-1518	Stays in Einsiedeln.
1518-1523	Stays in Zurich.
1523	*Sixty-Seven Articles.*
1526	Baden Disputation.
1528	Bern Disputation.
1529	First Cappel War and Marburg Coloquy.
1530	*Fidei Ratio.*
1531	Second Cappel War and death.

Ulrich Zwingli

Third Man of the Reformation

Geoffrey W. Bromiley

People's priest

Ulrich Zwingli was born on January 1, 1484, at Wildhaus in the Toggenburg Valley. Son of the mayor, he received a varied education at Basel, Bern, Vienna, and Basel again, where the reforming Thomas Wyttenbach (1472-1526) taught him. Ordained at Glarus in 1506, he did good pastoral work but provoked opposition by condemning the mercenary system, after serving as chaplain with the Glarus contingent. Without resigning from Glarus, he withdrew to Einsiedeln in 1516. With more time for reading, he reached an evangelical understanding through work on the Greek New Testament and the Fathers. He also gained wider recognition with sermons to the many Einsiedeln pilgrims. Problems with celibacy gave added depth to his proclamation of grace, and the indulgence-peddling of a Franciscan named Samson threw the view of current evils into relief.

Zwingli's true career as a reformer began with his call as people's priest at Zurich Minster in late 1518. On January 1, 1519, he initiated a systematic, but keenly applied, exposition of the Bible, commencing with Matthew. With this series he laid the foundations for reform. Plague almost cost him his life in 1520 but added a new dimension to his work. By 1521 the city had accepted Scripture as a standard, and the time was ripe for reforming measures. Changes came with astonishing speed in the years 1522-1526: the breaking of Lent, clergy marriage, the Sixty-Seven Articles, translation of the Bible, a new baptismal order, criticisms of the mass, removal of images, severance from the papacy, dissolution of the minster chapter and monasteries, reform of the minster school, study groups for the clergy (prophesyings), the termination of music, the replacement of the mass, quarterly Communion, synodal government, and the establishment of discipline under shared lay and clerical control.

Zwingli also worked hard to extend reform beyond Zurich to cantons where he had friends, supporters, and sympathizers. He suffered a setback at the Baden Disputation (1526), but his influence spread in Glarus, Schaffhausen, Appenzell, and the city of St. Gall. The Bern Disputation (1528) reversed Baden, with its endorsement of Christ's headship, the church's birth of the Word, and church legislation only on the basis of the Word. Basel fell into line (1529), and Bern sponsored reform in Vaud, Neuchâtel, and the newly liberated city of Geneva. Even though many others contributed to this advance, Zwingli unquestionably acted as the catalyst.

Zwingli and the radicals

Controversy accompanied his outstanding success. In Zurich itself the more radical Anabaptist group contended for a gathered church, full separation of church and state, simpler government and worship, baptism on confession, and stricter discipline. Disputations favored Zwingli, and when the radicals refused submission the city replied with repressive measures: fines, imprisonment, banishment, and even execution.

Almost simultaneously, a rift came with Luther over Christ's presence in the eucharistic elements. A war of pamphlets found Zwingli arguing against a presence of Christ's humanity, while Luther demanded a literal exegesis of "This is my body." Philip of Hesse, perceiving the dangers of dissension, tried unsuccessfully to resolve the violent debate with a summit conference, the Marburg Colloquy (1529). The disagreement would henceforth separate the Lutheran and Reformed churches in spite of their basic evangelical solidarity.

Zwingli also ran into fierce opposition from Lucerne and the so-called Forest Cantons (Schwyz, Uri, Zug, and Unterwalden). After Baden, these five tried to isolate Zurich and even negotiated an Austrian alliance to check reform. A bloodless preemptive strike at Cappel (1529) offered a temporary respite for Zwingli and his supporters, but the failure of Marburg and the decisions of Augsburg (1530) revived the threat. Resort to economic sanctions provoked an attack from Zug, and Zurich suffered a defeat at Cappel (1531), Zwingli himself being killed. Prompt action by Bern, Solothurn, and Basel ended hostilities and saved Zwingli's reforming work in Zurich.

The great monastery, Einsiedeln, Switzerland.

Writings

Zwingli wrote extensively in support of his beliefs and acts. In 1523 he explained the Sixty-Seven Articles in a *Commentary* that ruthlessly set medieval teachings and practices in the light of the headship and vicarious work of Christ and the primary authority of Scripture. An accompanying study of *Divine and Human Righteousness* contrasted divine demands that drive us to Christ with civil duties that serve social ends under biblical direction. A sermon on *The Clarity and Certainty of the Word of God* stressed the efficacy of God's Word and its intrinsic clarity when read in prayer for the Spirit's illumination.

Zwingli's fullest doctrinal work, *True and False Religion*, appeared in 1525. It put Christ at the center of faith, closely related forgiveness and conversion, proclaimed mortification and renewal, offered a sacramental reconstruction, and submitted the papal system to the sharpest scrutiny. At the same time a treatise *The Pastoral Office*, supplementing the earlier *Pastor* (1524) with its modeling of the pastorate on Christ, discussed the shape of pastoral ministry within the larger priesthood of all Christian believers.

The sacramental conflicts led to *Baptism* in 1525, in which Zwingli drew the parallel with the covenant sign of circumcision, and to *The Lord's Supper* in 1526, in which he argued for the meaning "signifies" in "This is my body," in view of the present location of Christ's body in heaven. These two treatises initiated a whole series of polemical works. In 1530 Zwingli published his Marburg sermon *Providence*, advocating a strong doctrine of divine sovereignty and defending God against any charge of complicity in evil. His last two works both sought to give a brief summary of his basic convictions. He prepared his *Account of the Faith* (*Fidei ratio*, 1530) for the Augsburg Diet of 1530 and his *Exposition of the Faith* (1531) for Francis of France, whom he vainly hoped to win over to the reforming cause. Advance to a more positive sacramental understanding may be seen in these final writings.

Zwingli's achievements

Zwingli dismantled the corrupt medieval system. Like Luther, he stopped the hierarchical abuse of power and the financial racketeering associated with masses, indulgences, relics, and pilgrimages. He substituted the popular tongue for Latin and replaced the sacramentalist round by the expository preaching of a trained ministry. More radically than Luther, he simplified the liturgy, purging it of esthetic elements. He took more drastic disciplinary action, set up synodal government, brought the laity more fully into church affairs, and secured tighter biblical control.

Zwingli's work had its defects. His services involved liturgical impoverishment, especially with the odd exclusion of singing (later reversed). He tied church and state too closely together, working through the council, retaining tithes, and enforcing discipline by secular penalties. The discipline involved an unhealthy and petty legalism, and cantonal policy became subservient to religious ends, with disastrous results at Cappel.

Theologically Zwingli, like Luther, opposed the distortions linked to purgatory, merit, clericalism, sacramentalism, and tradition. He championed scriptural primacy, Christ's all-sufficient work, justification by faith, election, and calling by Word and Spirit. Distinctive emphases include the clarity and power of Scripture, the Spirit as its true exegete, the covenant, divine sovereignty in providence and predestination, and the Eucharist as a visible word by which the Spirit nourishes those who partake in faith.

Zwingli's hasty literary compositions betray many weaknesses. Elements of natural theology, used by way of introduction, jostle his theology of revelation. He lists Socrates and Cato among the elect and denies original guilt while affirming original sin. His logical development of divine sovereignty involves serious problems of theodicy. He verges on dualism with his early principle (later abandoned) that physical means cannot effect spiritual ends, and on Nestorianism with his present restriction of Christ's humanity to heaven. He so stresses the unity of Scripture as to impose Old Testament models. His writings also have a strong strain of moralism.

Nevertheless Zwingli firmly trusted in Christ alone for salvation and insisted that authentic works spring only from faith. Fundamentally, indeed, his theology was one of biblical revelation; he used philosophical concepts and arguments only in the biblical cause.

Initiator of reform

Zwingli served admirably as the initiator of reform in Switzerland. He made a definitive ecclesiastical and doctrinal break with the old order. He did an essential work of reconstruction in ministry, worship, government, and discipline. He secured a solid base in Zurich and from it pushed out into other areas, in a movement that would finally reach what was to become an international center at Geneva. He indicated the main lines of Reformed, distinct from Roman Catholic, Lutheran, and Anabaptist theology, exploring already the great themes of covenant, election, means of grace, and effectual calling by Word and Spirit. His obvious mistakes were those of a hurried and harassed pioneer. His successors, especially Bullinger in Zurich and Calvin in Geneva, would effectively correct while building on the solid foundations that he had laid.

William Tyndale
*c.*1490-1536

William Tyndale (*c.* 1490-1536) could be called the father of the English Bible. Before his time there was the *Wyclif Bible* but this had never been printed and was not altogether accurate, having been translated from the Latin Vulgate edition. Tyndale was determined to produce an accurate English version, translated from the original Hebrew and Greek, and to make it available to all of God's people. Unfortunately the church authorities were opposed to that plan. Therefore Tyndale was forced to go underground, to become "God's Outlaw," as a recent biography has been entitled.

Tyndale succeeded in translating all of the New Testament and some of the Old. But he was betrayed by an enemy agent, and so he paid for his work with his life. In the end Tyndale triumphed because his translation became the basis for almost all English translations of the Bible until very recent times.

Statue of William Tyndale, Charing Cross, London.

The Life of
Tyndale

1490s	Birth.
1512	Bachelor of Arts degree, Oxford.
1515	Master of Arts degree.
1521	Stays at Little Sodbury Manor.
1523	Interview with Bishop Tunstall.
1524	Departure for Germany.
1525	First printing of New Testament at Cologne.
1526	First complete printing of New Testament at Wörms.
1530	Pentateuch printed at Antwerp.
1535	Betrayed and arrested at Antwerp.
1536	Death: strangled and burned at Brussels.

England
Cambridge •
Little Sodbury •
London •

William Tyndale

and the English Bible

A. N. S. Lane

Student and tutor

William Tyndale was born some time in the early 1490s on the Welsh border. He went as a student to Magdalen Hall, Oxford, which was later incorporated into Hertford College. At some stage after gaining his M.A. degree in 1515, Tyndale moved to Cambridge University for a time. Cambridge was rife with Lutheran ideas around the early 1520s, and it is possible that Tyndale acquired his Protestant convictions while studying there. (At a later date he expressed his dissatisfaction with the teaching of theology at the universities: "In the universities they have ordained that no man shall look on the Scripture until he be noselled in heathen learning eight or nine years, and armed with false principles with which he is clean shut out of the understanding of the Scripture.")

In 1521 Tyndale left the university world to join the household of Sir John Walsh at Little Sodbury Manor, north of Bath. It is not certain what role Tyndale played in the household, but he may have been the chaplain (he was ordained at Oxford), or a tutor to the children, or a secretary to Sir John. Many of the local clergy came to dine at the manor. This gave Tyndale the opportunity both to be shocked by their ignorance of the Bible and to become embroiled in controversy with them. To one such cleric he declared: "If God spare my life, ere many years pass, I will cause a boy that driveth the

The High Street, Oxford.

Hertford College, Oxford.

plough shall know more of the Scriptures than thou dost." (Here Tyndale was echoing Erasmus's famous wish in the preface of the *Greek New Testament*: "I would to God that the ploughman would sing a text of the Scripture at his plough and that the weaver would hum them to the tune of his shuttle.")

Translator in exile

Tyndale had felt the call to translate the Bible into English. At that time the only English translation available was the *Wyclif Bible*, which was distributed clandestinely by the Lollards, the followers of John Wyclif. But Wyclif's translation had never been printed. Furthermore, it was inaccurate in many ways, having been translated from the Latin Vulgate edition rather than the original Greek and Hebrew. Because of the Lollard threat, the church had in 1408 banned the unauthorized translation of the Bible into English. So Tyndale left Little Sodbury Manor in search of ecclesiastical approval

for his projected translation. He went to London and obtained an interview with the bishop of London, Cuthbert Tunstall. This was a shrewd choice because Tunstall was a scholarly man and a friend of Erasmus. But Tunstall was more concerned to prevent the growth of Lutheranism than to promote the English Bible, and Tyndale received no encouragement from him. Tyndale soon perceived that "not only was there no room in my lord of London's palace to translate the New Testament, but also that there was no place to do it in all England."

Having obtained the support of some London merchants for his enterprise, Tyndale resolved to leave the country in order to pursue it. So in 1524 he sailed for Germany, never to return. In Hamburg he worked on the New Testament, which was ready for the press by the following year (1525). A suitable printer was found in Cologne and the pages began to roll off the press. But one of Tyndale's assistants spoke too freely over his wine, and news of the project came to the ears of Johannes Dobneck, alias Cochlaeus, a leading opponent of the Reformation. He arranged for a raid on the press, but Tyndale was warned in advance and fled with the pages so far printed. Only one incomplete copy of this Cologne New Testament edition survives. Tyndale moved to Worms, a more sympathetic environment, where the first complete New Testament was published the following year. Of the six thousand copies printed, only two have survived.

There is a simple reason that so few copies of Tyndale's early editions survive. They were smuggled into England, and the bishops did all they could to eradicate them. In 1526 none other than Cuthbert Tunstall preached against the translation and had copies ceremoniously burned at St. Paul's. The following year the archbishop of Canterbury had the idea of himself buying up copies of the New Testament in order to destroy them. He thereby provided the finance for a further edition! In 1530 Tyndale's translation of the Pentateuch was printed in Antwerp, where he had then settled. There were also a number of further editions of the New Testament. Tyndale continually revised the translation, in the light of suggestions received and of his own further thoughts. Some, but not all, of the editions contained marginal notes. The purpose of these was mainly to explain the meaning of the text, but at times Tyndale could not resist the temptation to apply the text against the papacy.

Tyndale's translation

Tyndale translated directly from the Greek and Hebrew, with occasional reference to Latin and German translations. His style is homely and intended for the ordinary man, in keeping with his original aim to make the Bible widely known. In the following extract from the 1526 edition (Romans 12:1-2) the original spelling has been retained:

> I beseeche you therefore brethren by the mercifulness of God, that ye make youre bodyes a quicke sacrifise, holy and acceptable unto God which is youre reasonable servynge off God.

And fassion note youre selves lyke unto this worlde. But be ye chaunged [in youre shape] by the renuynge of youre wittes that ye may fele what thynge that good, that acceptable and perfaicte will of God is.

Tyndale planned to complete the translation of the Old Testament. But in 1535 he was betrayed by a fellow Englishman, Henry Phillips. Phillips induced Tyndale to venture onto the streets of Antwerp, and he was ambushed and seized while walking down a narrow passage. He was taken to the state prison in the castle of Vilvorde, near Brussels. After nearly one and a half years of confinement, Tyndale was strangled and then burned at the stake in Brussels on October 6, 1536. His last words were reported to be: "Lord, open the king of England's eyes."

Father of the English Bible

Tyndale's translation was banned in England and destroyed when it was found. But its influence was considerable, even in the reign of Henry VIII who, despite Tyndale's prayer, continued to oppose

Tyndale joined the household of Sir John Walsh at Little Sodbury Manor, near Bath, in 1521.

Antwerp Cathedral, Belgium. Tyndale was betrayed at Antwerp in 1535.

Protestantism. In 1535 Miles Coverdale produced the first ever *complete* printed edition of the Bible in English. For diplomatic reasons, Tyndale was not named, but the translation was heavily dependent upon his. By this time there was an archbishop of Canterbury (Thomas Cranmer) and a vicar-general (Thomas Cromwell) both of whom were committed to the Protestant cause. They persuaded Henry to approve the publication of the Coverdale translation. By 1539 every parish church in England was required to make a copy of the English Bible available to all of its parishioners. All of the available translations were substantially based upon Tyndale's. Thus, while Tyndale had not been personally rehabilitated, his cause had triumphed, as had the substance of his translation.

Tyndale can justly be called "the father of the English Bible." It would not be much of an exaggeration to say that almost every English New Testament until recently was merely a revision of Tyndale's. About ninety percent of his words passed into the King James Version and about seventy-five percent into the *Revised Standard Version*.

William Tyndale is famous as a Bible translator, but this was not his only work. He also wrote a number of books, of which the most famous are his *Parable of Wicked Mammon* and *The Obedience of a Christian Man*. The theme of the former is justification by faith alone. It was heavily dependent upon Martin Luther and in places Tyndale simply translated Luther. Tyndale was one of the relatively few *Lutheran* English Reformers. Before long the Lutheran influence in England was to wane and Reformed theology would take its place. The second treatise argues the duty of man's obedience to civil authority, except where loyalty to God is concerned.

John Calvin

1509-1564

Calvin, the exiled Frenchman who became chief pastor of Geneva, was the Reformation's supreme Bible teacher. He was also, as a systematizer, its Thomas Aquinas. Many now call him a catholic doctor rather than a Protestant reformer, because of the breadth, depth, and mainstream quality of his teaching, and Calvinism in its various mutations remains a living force. Calvin's big book of doctrine and devotion, *Institutes of the Christian Religion* was and is Protestantism's classic statement, and his running commentaries on Scripture, the

first of their kind, have landmark status still.

Calvin's vision, learned from Luther and Augustine, of God sovereignly saving sinners, fired such great pastoral evangelists as Richard Baxter, John Bunyan, George Whitefield, Jonathan Edwards, Charles Haddon Spurgeon, and Martin Lloyd-Jones, along with pioneer missionaries such as William Carey. His view of the church's ministry, pastoral discipline, and proper freedom from state control created Presbyterianism, of which modern representative democracy became the secular

spin-off. His concept of the Christian's cultural calling, and of the Christian life as a militant pilgrimage leading safely home by a predestined path of service and suffering, became a world view that has never ceased to produce humble, hardworking heroes of faith.

Anchored in Geneva, Calvin was nonetheless an international figure in his own lifetime, advising and encouraging reformers in England, Scotland, France, the Low Countries, and elsewhere, while Geneva itself, adorned after 1559 with a Christian university, was a haven and inspiration to thousands of students and refugees. Calvinism shaped early America, and the modern West can hardly be understood without some knowledge of it.

Opposite: John Calvin.

Noyon Cathedral, France. Calvin was born in Noyon in 1509.

The Life of

Calvin

1509	Birth.
1521-1526 (?)	Paris University: B.A. and M.A. in Arts.
1526-1531 (?)	Orléans University: B.A. and licentiate in law.
1529-1530	Bourges University: conversion to Protestantism.
1535	Exiled from France; settles in Basel.
1536	First edition of *Institutes;* settles in Geneva.
1538-1541	Exiled from Geneva; ministers in Strasbourg.
1540	Marriage to Idelette de Bure.
1541	Returns to Geneva.
1542	*Ecclesiastical Ordinances* made law.
1549	Death of Idelette.
1553	Execution of Servetus.
1555	Libertine opponents finally leave Geneva.
1559	Last edition of *Institutes;* University of Geneva opened.
1564	Death.

I. CALVIN

John Calvin

and Reformed Europe

James I. Packer

Place in history

Calvin's signet shows a heart held by a huge hand and bears the motto *prompte et sincere in opere Dei* (with readiness and whole-heartedness in God's work). So Calvin wished to be; so in fact he was. Proud, prejudiced, and self-willed, as he afterward acknowledged, young John had originally planned a life of quiet scholarship, but a "sudden conversion" (his phrase) at or soon after age twenty led him to want God's will rather than his own and to accept God's call when it eventually came.

As a result, he spent most of his adult life exiled from his native France, serving God in Geneva, Switzerland, with maximum public exposure as preacher and teacher of the Bible, pastor, reformer, theologian, and universal Christian counselor, selflessly seeking God's honor and glory in church and community. And hereby he became the most influential man in the world in the sense that his ideas made more history than did those of anyone else alive in his day and for at least a hundred years after. The epoch from the middle of the sixteenth century to the beginning of the age of Sir Isaac Newton, toward the end of the century following, was in truth the age of Calvin. No other description covers the facts.

To see this, think of the great men and movements of those days. Think of the shaping of the churches of England and Scotland after 1550. Think of Bishop John Jewel and John Knox. Think of the Puritans in England, the heroes of the "second Reformation," and the Covenanters in Scotland, the Huguenots in France, the Pilgrim Fathers in New England, the "Beggars" in Holland. Think of the revolt of the Netherlands, the English Civil War, and the Continental wars of religion. Think of William the Silent, Gaspard de Coligny, Oliver Cromwell, John Owen, John Milton, and Richard Baxter. Think too of the great ideals for which men fought. Think of the ideal of the Christian commonwealth, in which the national church and the civil government stand independent of each other, yet recognize each other's divine authority and support each other within their own spheres. Think of the ideals of toleration, of representative democracy, of establishing the rights and liberties of subjects, of constitutionalizing monarchy. Think of the ideal, dear to all the Puritans, of a universal Christian culture, in which the secular is seen as sacred, and arts, crafts, sciences, and industries all develop freely, harmoniously, and on a moral base, to the glory of God the Creator.

The survival of Protestantism

The inspiration of these movements, men, and quests, flowed directly from Calvin. Without him, pure Protestantism might not have survived beyond the middle of the seventeenth century, for it is simple truth that the only Protestants who would stand and fight, to the last ditch if necessary, against Roman and Erastian pressures, were the Calvinists. In all the great confrontations before the Age of Reason set in, it was Calvinism – Calvin's ideas, that is, in some shape or form – that set the agendas and called the shots.

In fact, Calvin's influence extended further. If we look at more recent history and think of men like Jonathan Edwards, David Brainerd, George Whitefield, Sir Isaac Newton, William Wilberforce, Lord

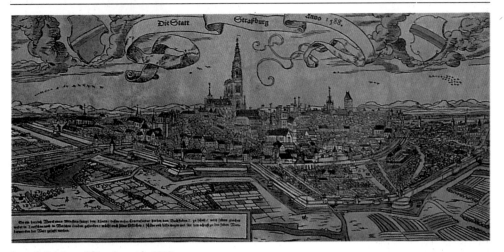

An artist's view of Strasbourg in 1588.

Shaftesbury, C. H. Spurgeon, William Carey, Robert Moffat, John Paton, James Chalmers, Robert Murray McCheyne, Abraham Kuyper, and Martin Lloyd-Jones, we see at once that the evangelical movement that began with revival in the eighteenth century and overflowed into social, political, missionary, and church-structural expression in the nineteenth could not have been what it was without John Calvin, for all those leaders, plus a host of others who stood with them, were Calvinists in their basic creed. We may fairly say, indeed, that it is not possible to understand our own religious and cultural heritage today without knowing something about Calvin, since his shadow hangs over so much of it.

Calvin the man

What kind of man was he? Not the ogre of legend! Calvin the egoistical fanatic, hard and humorless, the doctrinaire misanthrope, the cruel dictator with his arbitrary, uncaring, devilish God, is a figure of fancy, not of fact. The real Calvin was very different.

He was a sallow, sharp-featured, black-haired, slightly-built Frenchman, with big brown eyes that sparkled or glared according to his mood. To avoid attacks of migraine he ate little (one meal a day), and as he aged and his health ebbed he grew bent, gaunt, and emaciated. He was never physically strong, and by the age of thirty he had broken his health. In the closing years of his life (he died at fifty-four), he was constantly ill with indigestion, headaches, gallstones, hemorrhoids, gout, and fever, all superimposed upon chronic asthma and probably pulmonary tuberculosis. Yet John Calvin spent himself unstintingly to the last in the service of God and men.

He would not sleep more than four hours a night, and even when ill he kept four secretaries going with his French and Latin dictation, getting through an amount of work that was not far from miraculous. Daily sermons and lectures, the production of commentaries on most of the Bible, a steady flow of theological treatises, a massive correspondence, not to mention constant counseling, labor in Geneva's consistory court, and entertaining endless visitors – how did he manage it all? It is easier to ask the question than to answer it.

Though bad health made Calvin's temper increasingly short, as he himself apologetically acknowledged more than once, he was never sour. His free use of satire as a weapon in argument expressed a sense of the ugliness of untruth rather than of the worthlessness of any who embraced it. In himself he was neither malicious or morbid, and as he loved books and beauty, so he loved people. His choleric, excitable sensitivity made him ardent and intense in friendship no less than in controversy and pastoral address. His rhetoric was simultaneously passionate and rational, cool-headed and warm-hearted, and showed him resolute and steady even when he felt timid and hurt. He wrote to his former colleague Viret, when his wife died, "I subdue my grief as well as I can, but you know how tender, or rather soft, my mind is. Had not strong self-control been given me I could not have borne up so long." Such feelings were frequent in Calvin's life.

Calvin's will

Spiritually, he was honest and humble, innocent of self-pity, and with no illusions about himself. In his will, made on his deathbed, he voiced his faith as follows:

"I give thanks to God who had mercy on me.... He delivered me out of the deep darkness of idolatry in which I was plunged, that he might bring me into the light of his gospel.... I have no other defence or refuge for salvation than his free adoption, on which alone my salvation depends. With all my soul I embrace the mercy that he has exercised towards me through Jesus Christ, atoning for my sins with the merits of his death and passion, that in this way he might satisfy for all my offences and faults and blot them from his remembrance. I testify also and declare that I earnestly beg him to be pleased so to wash and purify me in the blood that my Sovereign Redeemer has shed for the sins of mankind, that under his shadow I may be able to stand at the judgment-seat....

"I also testify and declare that in all the battles and disputations in which I have been engaged with the enemies of the gospel, I have used no falsehood, no wicked and sophistical devices, but have acted straightforwardly and sincerely in defending the truth. Yet, alas, my ardour and zeal (if indeed worthy of the name) have been so slack and languid that I confess I have

failed countless times to execute my office properly, and had not he, of his boundless goodness, assisted me.... those mental powers that the Lord gave me would at his judgment-seat prove me more and more guilty of sin and sloth.

"For these reasons I testify and declare that I trust to no other security for my salvation than this alone, that as God is the Father of mercy, so he will show himself such a Father to me, who acknowledge myself to be a miserable sinner."

To Geneva's elders at the same time he said: "I have had much infirmity that you have had to bear, and the sum total of all that I have done has been worth nothing. Evil men will catch at this word, but I still say that all I have done has been worth nothing, and that I am a pitiable creature. Yet I can say that I desired your good, and that my faults have always displeased me, and the root of the fear of God was in my heart."

Plainly, the stereotype of Calvin as a haughty, scornful, ruthless, self-righteous, power-loving autocrat needs some adjusting.

Sudden conversion

Born at Noyon, Picardy, on July 10, 1509, John Calvin was religiously inclined from an early age, and his father, Gerard, a diocesan legal official, sent him to Paris University to take an arts degree in preparation for the priesthood. By John's graduation, Gerard had however changed the plan, and he directed his son to Orléans University for legal studies. Then came John's "sudden conversion" from papist prejudice to Protestant conviction, and this brought with it a spiritual quickening that made legal studies seem tame and dull by comparison with Scripture and theology. Soon Calvin was preaching, teaching, and pastoring informally among his peers, though his wish to enjoy the life of a leisured, learned, quiet-living Protestant Erasmus remained – "literary ease, with something of a free and honorable

John Calvin spent his period of banishment from Geneva in Strasbourg.

station," as he wrote later. In 1532 he produced a commentary on the *De Clementia* of Seneca, a Stoic philosopher believed at that time to have had Christian sympathies, hoping that this would establish him as a humanist scholar. But God had a different goal in view.

The year 1534 saw French Protestants posting placards in major towns attacking the mass. Official persecution then threatened, and Calvin moved to Basel, where in March 1536 the first edition of his *Institutes* appeared. In the manner of that pre-blurb age, its title page was fulsome. Translated from the Latin, it reads:

> *Basic Instruction* (Institutio) *in the Christian Religion comprising almost the whole sum of godliness and all that it is needful to know of the doctrine of salvation. A newly published work very well worth reading by all who aspire to godliness* (pietas). *The Preface is to the most Christian King of France, offering to him this book as a confession of faith by the author, Jean Calvin of Noyon.*

Calvin's preface was a fine apologia for Protestant faith, and the six catechetical chapters into which his 516 small-format pages were divided (on the Law, the Creed, the Lord's Prayer, the dominical sacraments, false sacraments, and Christian liberty) were brilliantly written. The work was an immediate success, and so it was as a distinguished young Protestant author that Calvin arrived in Geneva in August, five months later.

Called to Geneva

He was there by accident, as it seemed. He was heading for Strasbourg by a roundabout route forced on him by a local war. But someone recognized him and took him to meet Guillaume Farel, one of the Protestant pastors who had struggled there since Geneva went nominally Protestant a decade before.

Farel, a red-headed fire-eater, was on this occasion (says Beza, Calvin's first biographer) "obviously inspired with a kind of heroic spirit." He told Calvin that he must stay and help, and when Calvin pleaded other plans he threatened him with a curse. "You are following only your own wishes, and I tell you, in the name of God Almighty, that if you do not help us in this work of the Lord, the Lord will punish you for seeking your own interests rather than his."

Terrified, convicted, and ashamed, Calvin stayed and continued his Geneva ministry without a break, apart from three years of banishment between 1538 and 1541, till his death in 1564.

Calvin's goal in Geneva was a teaching, nurturing church, coterminous with the body politic, honoring God by orthodox praise and obedient holiness. There should be daily gatherings for psalm singing and expository preaching, monthly administration of the Lord's Supper (Calvin wanted this weekly but could never secure it), and an autonomous ecclesiastical court for censuring and, if necessary, excommunicating delinquent members.

Calvin was not a magistrate (he was not even a citizen until 1559), but as a preacher he told the magistrates long and often that Scripture made it their duty to back the church in all of this. He fought to a standstill their contrary craving to control the church, reinforced though this was by the anti-Calvin stance of several influential families in Geneva's high society who ominously called themselves Libertines and saw the Reformer as an upstart French whippersnapper who had grown too big for his boots.

Battle began when Calvin defied a state directive about eucharistic liturgy in 1538, an act that led to his three-year banishment, and hostilities continued after his recall until the Libertines, having gone too far by fomenting an armed riot against French immigrants, fled the city in 1555. Thereafter Calvin's church order, and with it his position as the Grand Old Man of Geneva and the Reformed world, went unchallenged.

Calvin's Geneva

Modern writers tend to depict the Genevan theocracy as a kind of gulag, or concentration camp, with the officers of the consistory court doing duty as a malevolent KGB. But it was not so. Granted, the principle of treating heresy, blasphemy, and immorality as civil crimes meant a closer confining of the liberties of the subject than is found in the modern secular state. Yet those who were prepared to respect biblical orthodoxy, observe Christian standards of public decency, and attend church regularly, found Calvin's regime admirable. The six thousand Protestant refugees who flocked there in Calvin's time from England, Scotland, and France thought Geneva exemplary – "the most perfect school of Christ since the apostles," said John Knox – and made it their model for reforming action when they went back home.

The anti-Trinitarian campaigner Servetus was burned at Geneva in 1553, and this is often seen as a blot on Calvin's reputation. But weigh these facts: 1. The belief that denial of the Incarnation should be viewed as a capital crime in a Christian state was part of Calvin's and Geneva's medieval inheritance; Calvin did not invent it. 2. Anti-Trinitarian heretics were burned in other places beside Geneva in Calvin's time, and indeed later – two in England, for instance, as late as 1612. 3. The Roman Inquisition had already set a price on Servetus's head. 4. The decision to burn Servetus as a heretic was taken not by Calvin personally but by Geneva's Little Council of twenty-five, acting on unanimous advice from the pastors of several neighboring Reformed churches whom they had consulted. 5. Calvin, whose role in Servetus's trial had been that of expert witness for the prosecution, wanted Servetus not to die but to recant, and spent hours with him during and after the trial seeking to change his views. 6. When Servetus was sentenced to be burned alive, Calvin asked for beheading as a less painful alternative, but his request was denied. 7. The chief Reformers outside Geneva, including Bucer and the gentle Melanchthon, fully approved the execution.

The burning should thus be seen as the fault of a culture and an age rather than of one particular child of that culture and age. Calvin, for the record, showed more pastoral concern for Servetus than anyone else connected with the episode. As regards the rights and wrongs of what was done, the root question concerns the propriety of political paternalism in Christianity (that is, whether the Christian state, as distinct from the Christian church, should outlaw heresy or tolerate it), and it was Calvin's insistence that God alone is Lord of the conscience that was to begin displacing the medieval by the modern mind-set on this question soon after Servetus's death.

Calvin's theology

The amount of misrepresentation to which Calvin's theology has been subjected is enough to prove his doctrine of total depravity several times over. How we hate those who squelch our pride by demolishing our self-righteousness and exalting God's sovereign grace!

Calvin is still widely regarded as a misanthrope who projected his dislike of the human race into a theology whose main point was that most people are irretrievably damned – even though the *Institutes* is in fact centrally concerned with grace, and Christ the Saviour! It is still thought that predestinarian speculation is the main mark of his teaching, though in fact he never made any assertion about predestination or anything else for which he did not offer scriptural proof. His doctrine of sin as total depravity is still taken to mean that we are all by nature as bad as we could be, despite his explicit teaching that common grace, working through conscience, law, environment, and civil government, constantly restrains the full outworking of corruption and moves even the ungodly to social and cultural enterprises of abiding worth. These are just three of the thickets of distortion through which we must hack our way if we are to reach a true estimate of Calvin as a teacher about God.

He was, in fact, the finest exegete, the greatest systematic theologian, and the profoundest religious thinker that the Reformation produced. Bible-centered in his teaching, God-centered in his living, and Christ-centered in his faith, he integrated the confessional emphases of Reformation thought – by faith *alone*, by Scripture *alone*, by grace *alone*, by Christ *alone*, for God's glory *alone* – with supreme clarity and strength. He was ruled by two convictions that are written on every regenerate heart and expressed in every act of real prayer and real worship: God is all and man is nothing; and praise is due to God for everything good. Both convictions permeated his life, right up to his final direction that his tomb be unmarked and there be no speeches at his burial, lest he become the focus of praise instead of his God. Both convictions permeate his theology too.

Calvin was a *biblical* theologian – not a speculator, but an echoer of the Word of God. The *Institutes* itself, in which the consistent teaching of the sixty-six canonical books is topically spelled out, was written, as Calvin's preface to the second edition makes plain, to be a general preparation for Bible study, orienting the reader to the divine wisdom that all Scripture, when properly exegeted, is found to set forth, and specifically paving the way to Calvin's own commentaries, which took the *Institutes* as read. Nothing is affirmed in the *Institutes* for which Scripture support is not offered.

Also, Calvin was a *systematic* theologian – not a taker of haphazard soundings, but an integrator of earlier gains. He was a second-generation Reformer, laboring to confirm and conserve what those who preceded him – Luther, Zwingli, Melanchthon, Bucer, and their colleagues – had set forth. He stood consciously on their shoulders, as he did on the shoulders of the early Fathers, and theologized as a mainstream spokesman for the true universal church (as distinct from the papal system, which for him was something else). The final (1559) version of the *Institutes*, in four books, eighty chapters, and more than a thousand pages in translation, combines in itself the qualities of catechetical handbook, theological textbook, Protestant apologia, Reformation manifesto, hammer of heresies,

The Reformation Monument, Geneva: William (Guillaume) Farel, John Calvin, Theodore Beza, John Knox.

and guide to Christian practice. It is a systematic masterpiece, one that has carved out a permanent niche for itself among the greatest Christian books. The work is worth describing in some detail.

The knowledge of God

The theme that Calvin develops to bind his material together is a biblical theme that unites in itself all Christian doctrine, experience, and behavior – namely, *knowledge of God (cognitio Dei)*. As a treatise on knowledge of God, the *Institutes* deals both with knowing God (which is religion) and with what is known about God (which is theology). Both theology and religion are to be learned and taught from God's own teaching *(doctrina)*, that is, from Holy Scripture.

To the question, What does it mean to know God? Calvin's answer is: it means acknowledging Him as He has revealed Himself in Scripture and through Christ, worshiping Him and giving Him thanks, humbling oneself before Him as a stupid sinner and learning from His Word, loving the Father and the Son for Their love in adoption and redemption, trusting the promises of pardon and glory that God has given in Christ, living in obedience to God's law, and seeking to honor God in all human relationships and all commerce with created things.

To the question, Whence comes knowledge of God, thus conceived? Calvin's answer is : from the Holy Spirit, speaking in and through the written Word and uniting us to the risen Christ for new life. To the question, On what intellectual basis does this practical knowledge of God and communion with God rest? The *Institutes* replies by expounding in its four books (1) the revealed truth about God the Creator, and our need of it; (2) the revealed truth about Christ the Mediator and our need of Him; (3) the revealed truth about the grace of Christ and the salvation it brings us through the Spirit; (4) the revealed truth about the means of grace that are given us in the church and what is involved in using them.

Topically, Calvin follows in this the sequence of the Apostles' Creed – "I believe in (1) God ... almighty, maker of heaven and earth; (2) and in Jesus Christ ..; (3) I believe in the Holy Ghost; (4) the holy catholic church ..."

Felicities of formulation occur constantly. "Oh, what a good book Calvin's *Institutes* is!" cried the Reformer's younger contemporary, the classical scholar Julius Scaliger. "Oh, what a great man!" Scaliger was right, on both counts. Reading the *Institutes* shows why Melanchthon used to refer to Calvin simply as "the theologian." Well may we concur.

Calvinism in Europe

Most of the two-thirds of Germany that embraced the Reformation, along with Scandinavia and England, followed the Lutheran ecclesiastical pattern whereby the head of state becomes head of the church. But France, Scotland, northern Switzerland, the Netherlands, Hungary, Poland, and parts of Germany (Friesland, Hesse, the Palatinate) embraced Calvin's model, which keeps civil and churchly authority-structures distinct.

Churches of the first group, apart from the Church of England, identified with the theological heritage of Luther and/or Melanchthon, highlighting justification by faith as the essential gospel, maintaining a consubstantiationist view of the Lord's Supper, and allowing, if not endorsing, the Melanchthonian drift into a synergistic doctrine of grace.

The Calvinist churches, however – "Reformed" (capital "R") as they now called themselves – upheld the teaching of the *Institutes*; they set justification in a God-centered, sanctification-oriented, covenantal frame, they detached Christ's eucharistic presence from the elements,

and they maintained an activist, crusading ethical stance, drawn from Calvin's "third use" of the law as a family code, guiding and spurring Christians in the service of their heavenly Father. They all, including the Elizabethan Church of England, went along more or less with Beza's Aristotelian recasting of Calvin's soteriology in a supralapsarian mold, and they all shared in the Synod of Dort's condemnation of Arminianism in 1619. Confessional and catechetical statements of high quality, notably the Heidelberg Catechism (1563), the Second Helvetic Confession (1566), and the Westminster Confession and Catechisms (1646-48), plus constant battles everywhere for the crown rights of Christ the royal Redeemer in His church, show to what extent the *Institutes* became an international body of homogenous theological conviction. The Pilgrim Fathers brought Calvinism to America, and today English-speaking Calvinism of the classical type (as distinct from Barth's reconstructed and arguably distorted version) has its main strength in the United States.

The bodies of four centuries of Calvinists lie moldering in the grave, but Calvinism goes marching on.

Thomas Cranmer
1489-1556

Opposite: Thomas Cranmer.

Thomas Cranmer (1489-1556), archbishop of Canterbury, is less well known than either Martin Luther or John Calvin. No denomination or form of theology is named after him. Yet his achievements as a quiet reformer in the Church of England, and as the major architect of its liturgy and theological emphases, do bear comparison with those of the men of Wittenberg and Geneva, especially when it is remembered that the liturgy he created has been the primary liturgy used for four centuries in the Episcopal churches of the Anglican communion throughout the world.

Cranmer's genius lies not in originality, but rather in taking the best from the Christian tradition of worship, theology, and ethics and using that to create forms of worship and principles of theology to guide the Church of England as it sought to reform itself in the middle of the sixteenth century. He was a Protestant in that he protested on behalf of the sacred Scriptures and the way they were interpreted in the church of the first six centuries. He did not want to introduce novel ideas but to preserve and conserve that which God had graciously given to the universal church over the

centuries, and especially before the major corruptions that began (as he believed) in the twelfth century. Thus he understood his own religious and theological quest to be for "true catholicity," and what he sought to implement in England may well be called "Reformed catholicity." It was thoroughly based upon the inspiration and authority of the Holy Scriptures and included a respect for tradition, reflected in the maintenance of a reformed and renewed liturgy, and of the threefold order of ordained ministers – deacon, priest, and bishop.

The Life of
Cranmer

1489	Birth.
1532	Appointed archbishop of Canterbury by Henry VIII.
1533	Annuls marriage of Henry VIII to Katherine of Aragon.
1549	Primary author of *Book of Common Prayer* (revised 1552).
1556	March 21, death as martyr in reign of Mary Tudor.

England

Nottingham •

Cambridge •

London •

Lambeth Church and Palace (the residence of the Archbishop of Canterbury) in about 1670.

Thomas Cranmer

and the Making of Anglicanism

Peter Toon

Cranmer the Erastian

Thomas Cranmer was born in Nottinghamshire, England, in 1489, and, after attending a local school, he went to Jesus College, Cambridge, as a student. He received a traditional education based on the Latin language and classics. He proved himself such a good scholar that he was elected a fellow of the college in 1523. For a short time he had to relinquish that position when he married; however, his young wife died in childbirth, and he was able to return to his former position. He was careful, methodical, and penetrating in his study of theology and made full use of the insights brought by the "new learning" with the emphasis upon studying the Bible in the original languages rather than in the Latin translations.

During that period of study, reflection, and meditation in Cambridge, Cranmer adopted an important principle. He rejected the claims made by popes, and by others on their behalf, that a pope had jurisdiction throughout Christendom as the vicar of Christ. He came to believe that the ruler of each country (which meant the king in England) had power to govern the church. For papal supremacy he substituted the royal supremacy and is thus known as an Erastian. Later this principle placed him in difficult moral dilemmas: for example when, as archbishop, he had to provide the legality for the acquisition and dismissal of several wives by Henry VIII; and, during the reign of Mary Tudor, who wanted to restore the old, medieval Catholicism, he eventually had to decide whether to obey her or to follow what he believed to be God's truth. He chose the latter and declared that in the last resort the truth of salvation is above the truth of the royal supremacy.

It was also in his study at Cambridge that he became acquainted with the Lutheran doctrine of justification by faith alone, and this he diligently examined and compared with the traditional medieval view that justification is a process leading to a declaration of righteousness at the Last Judgment. Later, as archbishop, he was to declare his commitment to justification by faith alone and to make valiant attempts to incorporate this biblical doctrine into the confession of faith and forms of worship of the reformed Church of England.

Archbishop Cranmer

With minimal experience of parish and diocesan duties, Cranmer was appointed archbishop of Canterbury by Henry VIII in 1532. During the previous three years he had pleased the king by advice he had offered concerning the way to dissolve the marriage with Catherine of Aragon. The offer of this important position came as a surprise both to Cranmer and those in high places. During the next twenty-four years, chiefly in the reigns of Henry VIII and his son, Edward VI, he did much to advance the cause of the reform of the Church of England. What he attempted to implement reveals that he had thought deeply about all aspects of the life and teaching of the church. His time was short and his adversaries many, but what he achieved had, as we look back, a permanent quality about it.

His most outstanding achievement was the fixing of the church's liturgical order. Out of the many books of medieval worship and prayers, he created the Book of Common Prayer in the language of the people. Instead of an assortment of Latin books containing a variety of services, he provided the church with one book containing all services for daily, Sunday, and occasional use, as well as the Book of Psalms and a lectionary for the whole year. The service of Holy Communion especially reveals the ability of Cranmer as both a theologian/liturgist and a writer of English prose. It contains, in an English style that is still most attractive today, the Reformed catholic understanding of both the Lord's Supper and justification by faith alone. This Book of Common Prayer has been of immense importance in the history of both the Church of England and the Anglican communion of churches, and it is still widely used today, despite the appearance of alternative books in recent decades.

The Forty-two Articles

Another achievement was his influential part in the fixing of the doctrinal anchors of the reformed Church of England. These are found in the Forty-two Articles of 1553

(later shortened to the Thirty-nine Articles of 1571). They anchor the church to the Scriptures, the creeds, and to Reformed catholicity; thus they reject medieval and papal errors and heresies on the one side and the excesses of the radical Reformers on the other. Though the status of these articles differs from one part of the Anglican communion to another, they are everywhere still held to be authoritative, in a major or minor way, for establishing Anglican doctrine.

Other plans and efforts of Cranmer, though admirable, did not come to fruition in those troubled times. He set in motion the work of reforming the inherited church law (Canon Law), and his commission, for which he did the major work, produced an ordered, coherent, and intelligible body of ecclesiastical law. It brought rationality into the new religious situation of the royal supremacy in the church, but was not implemented until 1604, long after his death. Further, he had all kinds of plans for the formation of an educated ministry of godly and learned

Lambeth Palace, London.

Sir Thomas More (1478–1535), Lord Chancellor of England.

men because so few of the priests of the church ever preached a sermon and the people rarely heard the exposition of the Bible in the parish churches. The plans came to nothing, but at least he did see the publication of a *Book of Homilies* in 1547, thereby providing sermons that could be read in churches. Three of the homilies were by Cranmer himself. Finally, we may note Cranmer's ecumenical spirit. He greatly desired to see much more cooperation between the new churches of the Reformation and a greater effort by their leaders to find a common way forward together; he had little success in promoting this vision.

Most of his achievements occurred in the brief reign of Edward VI, although the seed had been sown and preparations made in the reign of Henry VIII. It was in the latter's reign that Cranmer played his part in the provision of copies of the newly-translated English Bible in all the parish churches. In the reign of Mary Tudor he was accused of high treason and sentenced to death, but the queen spared his life. Then, he was tried for heresy and sentenced to death again; he died at the stake on March 21, 1556. In his final statement he affirmed his rejection of Roman Catholic doctrine contrary to the Word of God and then placed his hand – the hand by which he had earlier written to state that he accepted such doctrine – into the fire that it should burn first. He died as a martyr for the English form of Reformed, catholic Christianity.

Ignatius Loyola
1491/95-1556

From its inception in 1517 until around the middle of the sixteenth century, the Protestant Reformation seemed destined eventually to spread to all of Western civilization. By 1550 most of Germany and Scandinavia were either already Protestant or in the process of becoming Protestant; the Church of England had separated from Rome and was gradually shedding its "Roman-ness;" Protestantism had virtually overrun Switzerland and the Netherlands; and it had made serious inroads into France, Austria, Hungary, Poland, and elsewhere. There was a feeling that Italy and Spain would be next.

The Roman Catholic church had not remained inactive in the face of this threat to its very existence. Pious Catholic leaders, both lay and clerical, called for reform of abuses within the church, the dreaded Inquisition had been revived, and an ecumenical council had been called and had begun to meet at Trent in 1545 – all with the purpose of finding ways to stop the Protestant advance and, if possible, to mount a counter-offensive. As important as all of those measures were, none would be as effective in turning back the Protestant advance as would the Society of Jesus, a new religious order established in 1540 by an obscure Spanish nobleman named Ignatius Loyola (1491/1495-1556).

Loyola is one of history's most interesting characters: a crippled soldier who became a renowned warrior of God; a badly educated fortune-seeker who became an inspired religious genius; a virtually unknown member of his church until nearly the age of fifty, who became the famed leader of the most characteristic creation of the Catholic Reformation, the Society of Jesus. These zealous monks, commonly known as Jesuits, threw themselves into the gap with dramatic results. In the second half of the sixteenth century, in central and eastern Europe, the Jesuits were successful in checking the forces of Protestantism, especially in Austria, Hungary, Poland, and southern Germany. However, in accomplishing this, they gained a widespread reputation for their fanatical willingness to do almost *anything* to advance the cause of the Roman Catholic church.

Consequently, people seldom had a neutral attitude toward the Society of Jesus, and widely divergent views of Loyola and his Jesuits circulated throughout Europe. To his friends, Loyola was a "second St. Paul," whereas his enemies saw him as a kind of ruthless "Grand Inquisitor." Over the years, his followers have been characterized by admirers as "saviors of Holy Mother Church" and "sincere and gifted servants of God," whereas critics have called them "the feared and formidable storm-troopers of the Counter-Reformation" and, more recently, "the Vatican Rapid Deployment Force." Whatever the case, there is no doubt that friend and foe alike saw Loyola and the Jesuits as a key factor in reviving and strengthening the Roman church after 1550.

The Life of
Loyola

1491/1495	Birth in the Basque province of Guipúzcoa, northwest Spain.
1521	Wounded at the Battle of Pamplona, ending his military career.
1522	Conversion and dedication to a spiritual life.
1522-1523	Writes his *Spiritual Exercises*, completed later in Paris and Rome.
1523	Pilgrimage to Jerusalem.
1528-1535	Studies at the University of Paris; wins his first permanent disciples.
1540	The Society of Jesus established by papal bull.
1541	Elected first superior general of his new order.
1550	Completes the main draft of the Constitutions.
1556	Death in Rome.

Guipùzcoa

Spain

Ignatius Loyola

and the Jesuits
Robert D. Linder

Loyola's youth

Loyola was born in 1491/1495 of a noble Basque family in the province of Guipúzcoa in Spain, but little is known of his youth. The Loyolas were one of the two dozen families that made up the Basque landed gentry in that area of northwest Spain where they survived from the days when the Iberian peninsula had been overrun by the Visigoths in the fifth century. Spanish Basques were known for their fierce pride, their stoicism and determination, and for having a great many children and not much land. Ignatius Loyola was the twelfth and – youngest child – of Don Beltrán, lord of Loyola Castle. At the age of fourteen, young Loyola was attached as a page to the court of King Ferdinand II. There he was schooled in courtly manners and groomed for a military career.

Three important events during Loyola's youth helped determine his world view and set the course of his life. First, in 1492, Ferdinand and Isabella completed the conquest of Muslim Granada and expelled the last Muslims and Jews from Spain. That was the final act of the *Reconquesta*, that great drive by the Spanish Christians, beginning in the eleventh century, to "reconquer" the Iberian peninsula from the Muslims and return it to the Christian fold. In the process, it became the passion of every Spanish boy of noble birth someday to become a knight in the service of God, to aid in the reconquest. Thus developed the chivalric tradition that fused together piety and patriotism to create the religio-military temperament of which Loyola as well as the *conquistadores* of America were heirs.

Columbus and the New World

The second important event also occurred in 1492 when Christopher Columbus discovered the New World and opened the way for conquest and settlement. The riches of the New World made Spain a great world power and led to the Spanish domination of Italy and much of the western Mediterranean in the sixteenth century. (Loyola's oldest brother sailed with Columbus on his second voyage in 1493.) Thus Loyola grew up in a country that was in the process of becoming a powerful new nation-state. The third formative event began in 1517, when Martin Luther ignited the Protestant Reformation in Germany. Before long, word of Luther's movement reached Spain and rekindled religious controversy there. Although Loyola and his family were not touched personally by Protestantism, a great deal of Loyola's later life would be devoted to combating it.

While Spanish influence expanded and Luther brooded over his salvation in Germany, Loyola pursued the life of a young court dandy in Spain, frequently getting into scrapes with the law and developing a considerable reputation as a rake and brawler. He also served with the troops of his feudal overlord, the Duke of Najera, and was gravely wounded when a French army invaded northwest Spain in 1521. When defending the fortress of Pamplona on May 21, Loyola was struck by a French cannonball that smashed his right leg and wounded the left. A French doctor tried to set his leg, but it had to be broken and reset twice – all without anesthetic. Lamed for life, Loyola would never soldier again.

Opposite: Ignatius Loyola.

Conversion

During his long convalescence at the family castle, Loyola read the only books available to while away the time: Ludolf of Saxony's *Life of Christ* and a medieval *Stories of the Saints*. The books had a profound effect on him, and he began to contemplate new possibilities for heroism and fame. The exploits of the saints harmonized with his sense of chivalry. He asked himself: "What if I should do great things for God like St. Francis and St. Dominic?" During this nine-month period of convalescence, Loyola was caught up in a mystical religious experience and underwent a conversion that gave him a new vision of God. Taking the Madonna for his lady, he determined to become a "soldier of Christ."

Having recovered sufficiently to resume an active life, Loyola in 1522 set out as a pilgrim and penitent to the shrine of Our Lady at Montserrat, where he presented his mule to the abbey, gave his doublet, tunic, and Basque beret to a beggar, and left his sword and scabbard hanging in the chapel of the Madonna. Now his only possessions were a monk's cowl, a gourd that he used as a drinking cup, and a pilgrim's staff. He then withdrew for the better part of a year to the small town of Manresa, near Barcelona, where, at times on the brink of suicide, he struggled with the problem of how to deal with sin in his life and the question of how to conform to the will of God.

Manresa

At Manresa, Loyola became one of the giants of the golden age of Spanish mysticism, a movement that sought a direct, immediate encounter with God, different from ordinary sense perceptions and reasoning, with the goal of eventual union with the Almighty. In a cave near Manresa, Loyola fasted, spent seven hours a day in prayer on his knees, and scourged himself to the point of endangering his health. In this context, Loyola claimed to have many mystical experiences. Private and indescribable, those encounters often took the form of blinding, ecstatic visions.

The house of Ignatius Loyola, Rome.

The Church of Gesù, Rome.

He had hundreds of them: he saw the Trinity as a clavichord with three strings; he saw the miracle of transubstantiation as light in bread; he saw Jesus as "a big round form shining as gold;" and he saw Satan as a glistening serpent covered with bright, mysterious eyes.

Yet, in the midst of it all, Loyola kept his will fixed on his purpose: to prepare himself to serve Christ through his church. He reflected on his experiences and kept notes of his insights. These became the main outline of his *Spiritual Exercises*, the powerful and influential textbook of the Jesuits. In the *Exercises*, Loyola tries to foster in a lower key the experiences and insights that he obtained at Manresa. Finally published in its entirety in 1548, the *Spiritual Exercises* are disappointing to most readers. It is a spare volume of about 160 pages, without literary grace, and consists mostly of rules and directions calculated to lead the practitioner into a deeper spiritual life. It was written like a cookbook and intended as a guide for retreat directors. The "exercises" were designed for an elite, to help serious Christians reorient their lives into closer conformity with God's will.

The spiritual exercises

According to Loyola's formula, the person making the exercises should devote thirty days to religious experiences designed to uproot old habits and strengthen the resolve to live a life of utter dedication to God. The thirty days are split into "four weeks" or stages of growth, the actual length of which the director can adjust to individual needs. The first week is devoted to a series of meditations on the purpose of human life, sin, and hell. The second week focuses on Christ's life up to Palm Sunday, the third on Christ's agony and suffering following the Last Supper, and the fourth on Christ's resurrection and ascension. Crowning the whole work is the "Contemplation to Attain Divine Love," which draws together the progression of the four weeks so that one lives one's life for God alone in joyous service to Him.

Attached to the *Spiritual Exercises* is an appendix called the "Rules for Thinking with the Church." It embodies his view of the Roman Catholic church as the kingdom of Christ on earth and the need to conform one's thinking to its teaching. Rule 13, which emphasizes that the end of all discipline is to be the complete subjection of the individual to the church in order to serve it effectively, is that section most often criticized by outsiders. Loyola wrote: "That we may be altogether of the same mind and in conformity with the Church herself, if she shall have defined anything to be black which to our eyes appears to be white, we ought in a like manner to pronounce it to be black. For we must undoubtingly believe, that the spirit of our Lord Jesus Christ and the Spirit of the Orthodox Church His Spouse, by which Spirit we are governed and directed to salvation, is the same."

The technique of spiritual growth applied in the *Exercises* was adaptable. The exercises could be used in a full-scale retreat under a director or for an hour or two a day by an individual believer. As the guidebook of the future Society of Jesus, the *Spiritual Exercises* engendered a sense of discipline and sacrifice that kept the order mobilized for a tremendous educational, missionary, and political effort that turned back the tide of Protestantism and made the Roman Catholic church a major force in the modern world. Moreover, it faithfully reflected Loyola's emphasis on contemplation, obedience, organization, and action as a means of serving his church.

The Society of Jesus

Early in 1523, Loyola made a pilgrimage to Jerusalem and returned to acquire the education he needed to serve as a servant of Christ. He first learned Latin with a group of small boys, then studied at several universities in Spain before journeying to Paris to enroll in the greatest center of higher education in Christendom – the University of Paris. He would remain there from 1528 to 1535, eventually earning an M.A. degree. It was during this period that the Society of Jesus was born. There in Paris, his zeal attracted likeminded disciples, stalwart young men who eventually became the nucleus of his new order.

Seldom has a less promising student entered a great university. Thirty-seven years old at the time of his matriculation, he had a thin shock of graying red hair, was barely over five feet tall, and walked with a limp. He had a poor academic background and no funds. He spoke with a Basque accent. He suffered from chronic heart trouble and, in the years after 1528, experienced excruciating pains from stones in his kidneys and liver. Despite all this, Loyola possessed the attributes of a natural leader: a charismatic personality, an iron will, a sense of mission, and powerful eyes that seemed to penetrate into the very soul of those with whom he talked.

From the 4,000 students at Paris, Loyola eventually recruited six of the brightest and best: Francis Xavier, Peter Faber, Diego Laynez, Alfonso Salmerón, Simon Rodriguez, and Nicholas de Bobadilla. On August 15, 1534, in a small chapel in Montmartre, Loyola and his six companions joined in taking the vows of poverty and charity and resolved to go to Jerusalem to convert the Turks, and if that were not possible, to travel to Rome and put themselves at the service of the pope. The seven agreed to meet in Venice the next year in order to secure passage to the Holy Land. However, because war was raging in the Mediterranean they remained in and around Venice for three years, preaching, performing works of charity, and recruiting other dedicated young men to their group. Loyola was ordained there in 1537, and there the group adopted a name "the Company of Jesus," which was later Latinized to *Societas Jesu*, abbreviated S.J., and commonly called the Jesuits.

The Jesuits established

By 1538, realizing that there was little hope of reaching Jerusalem in the near future, the seven decided to journey to Rome to activate the second part of their vow by putting themselves at the pope's disposal. Once in Rome, they realized that this was easier said than done. They were virtual unknowns, had no sponsors or letters of reference, and lacked any kind of formal organization. Sizing up the situation, Loyola recommended to his young friends that, rather than continue as freelance do-gooders, they should consider devising a flexible structure that combined maximum service to the gospel with corporate union. Thus, they determined to form a religious order, elect a superior, and seek papal approval. Finally, in the summer of 1539, with the help of the godly Cardinal Gasparo Contarini, they submitted their plans of organization to Pope Paul III. On September 27, 1540, the pope issued the bull *Regimini militantis ecclesiae* establishing the order.

From the beginning, the Jesuits were an elitist corps that accepted into membership only the most intelligent, dedica-

Interior of the Gesù, mother church of the Jesuit order.

ted, physically strong and attractive men of sound character. After a two-year novitiate, they took the traditional threefold monastic vow. There followed another year of general studies and three years of philosophy, at which point they taught grammar or philosophy to younger members of the order. After four more years of theological study, they were ordained as priests. They then were expected to spend a year devoted to preaching, the study of practical theology, and an intense program of spiritual exercises, followed by a second year of "proving themselves." Only then were they permitted to take the fourth special vow of obedience to the pope and to be inducted as full members of the society. Twelve years of rigorous training produced a full-blown Jesuit.

Not surprisingly, Loyola was elected as the first superior general of the order in 1541. Directing the fast-growing society became the main task of Loyola's last fifteen years. Although the founding bull had limited the membership to sixty, a subsequent papal decree lifted this restriction four years later. By the time of Loyola's death, the society had 1,000 members distributed throughout 100 houses in twelve provinces. Most of the growth was in Italy, Spain, and Portugal. Loyola also lived to see the establishment of approximately 100 colleges and seminaries.

The Constitutions

Loyola spent his last years at his desk in the Casa Professa, the headquarters of the Jesuits in Rome, handling the order's vast correspondence and drafting the society's *Constitutions*, which he worked on in earnest from 1547 to 1550 and put into effect on an experimental basis in 1552. In its original final form, it was much longer than the rules of earlier orders. It contains 275 pages of text in the modern English edition.

The *Constitutions* reflects the Ignatian ideal. It spells out the distinctive characteristics of the Jesuits. For example, it stresses efficiency and mobility, by renouncing strict attention to certain traditional monastic offices and to a fixed monastic habit. Moreover, it stresses that all of the Society's activities must be guided by a true love of the church and an unconditional obedience to the pope. It also emphasizes the monarchical nature of the order in which the superior general is elected for life and holds absolute power in the organization. Further, the *Constitutions* faithfully reflect the tensions inherent in the Jesuit way of life – the tension between the requirements for absolute obedience to pope and church and the special concern that Loyola had for the conscience of each member; the tension between the burning desire to do whatever was necessary to win back Protestants and the temporizing influence of Loyola's emphasis on the highly personal, mystical experience as the crowning achievement of the Christian life; the tension between the Jesuit propensity to stretch – some would say circumvent – Christian ethical standards in order to serve the Roman Catholic church and more commonly accepted Christian definitions of right and wrong.

The Jesuits became known for their discipline and sacrifice, and the society reflected Loyola's military spirit and organizational talent. Loyola himself hardly slackened the pace, even on his deathbed. On July 28, 1556, the sixty-five-year-old invalid, in the throes of a painful gall-bladder attack, still managed to dictate a packet of letters. He then asked for the pope to give him a final blessing and for the last rite of extreme unction. However, before either of those wishes could be granted, Loyola, after a night of prayer, slipped quietly away early in the morning hours of July 31. He was buried in the Church of the Gesù in Rome and sainted in 1622.

Loyola and the Catholic Reformation

Many historians consider Loyola the personification of the Catholic Reformation, especially in its more anti-Protestant aspects. There is certainly a great deal of truth in this view. However, the Jesuits were more than a force determined to counter-attack the Protestants. They also were positive activists, concerned with both the threat of the Protestant defectors and the needs of the Catholic faithful, with both the personal requirements of the Christian religion and its social dimensions, with both the cultivation of personal piety and the spread of Christianity overseas. This "holy activism" set an example that almost all later religious congregations in the Roman Catholic church followed and which profoundly influenced most older orders.

In particular, Loyola made foreign missions the most esteemed form of Christian service. His Jesuits became great missionaries and won thousands to the Christian faith in the New World, in Africa, and in the Orient. By the year of Loyola's death, there were Jesuit missions in Brazil, Ethiopia, the Congo, India, Indonesia, and Japan.

Loyola also stressed quality Catholic education. As early as 1542 the Jesuits began to establish colleges for their own members. Soon there were colleges for non-Jesuit laypeople as well. During Loyola's lifetime, fifty Jesuit colleges were opened, including the Roman College in 1551 (now the Gregorian University), which was the first modern Catholic seminary and the model for succeeding ones.

Finally, the Jesuits played a decisive role in halting the spread of the Protestant Reformation. In so doing, Loyola sought to revive Catholic piety as a primary means of blunting the appeal of Protestantism. His men also won back from Protestantism many important ruling houses for the church of Rome and, by this means, many of the people of Europe too.

Holy cunning

But dealing with emperors, kings, and princes heavily involved the Jesuits in politics and intrigue. Before long, Loyola's followers went beyond the founder's own dictum, adopted from Paul, "I am made all things to all men, that I might by all means save some" (1 Corinthians 9:22). Thus, in attempts to adapt them-

Ceiling of the Church of St Ignazio, Rome.

selves to circumstances and in order to be as flexible as possible in their quest for souls, second and third generation Jesuits practiced equivocation, casuistry, and probabilism. In other words, the Jesuits came to believe that in order to attain pious ends it was sometimes necessary to proceed with "holy cunning." This, in turn, led many of their critics to accuse them of being Machiavellians – adherents of the maxim that "the end justifies the means."

Loyola himself emphatically rejected the Protestant understanding of reformation – that a fundamental alteration in the doctrine and devotional life of the late medieval church was needed. Rather, in his mind, the old devotional practices and teachings had to be revivified and applied with greater fervor and intelligence. As for the Protestants themselves, Loyola's most comprehensive statement on how to deal with them can be found in a letter to one of his Jesuit lieutenants, Peter Canisius, in Austria in 1554. There Loyola urged that the king deprive Protestants of all offices within his domains, that Protestant books be burned, that priests inclined to Protestantism should be removed, that Protestant preachers be given one month to return to Catholicism upon penalty of exile or imprisonment, and concluded with the observation that a few executions might set a good example.

Suppression

In later decades, this fanatical devotion to the Roman church led to deeper and deeper involvement in political conspiracies and assassinations in many countries. A number of rulers expelled the society from their lands in the period 1759 to 1773, and the church itself suppressed the Jesuits from 1773 to 1814 for their political activities. However, the suppression was never put fully into effect and the society was never completely extinguished. Finally, it was restored by Pope Pius VII following his release from captivity in France in 1814.

Since its restoration, membership in the society has steadily increased until it has reached a total of more than 35,000 in the twentieth century. Moreover, it has become, by common consent, the most powerful religious order in the modern Roman Catholic church, and even today it still bears the imprint of its founder, popularly conceived as the great soldier-saint of the church. In the words of Jesuit historian James Brodrick, Ignatius Loyola died "a good soldier of Jesus Christ."

Timechart 1400-1700

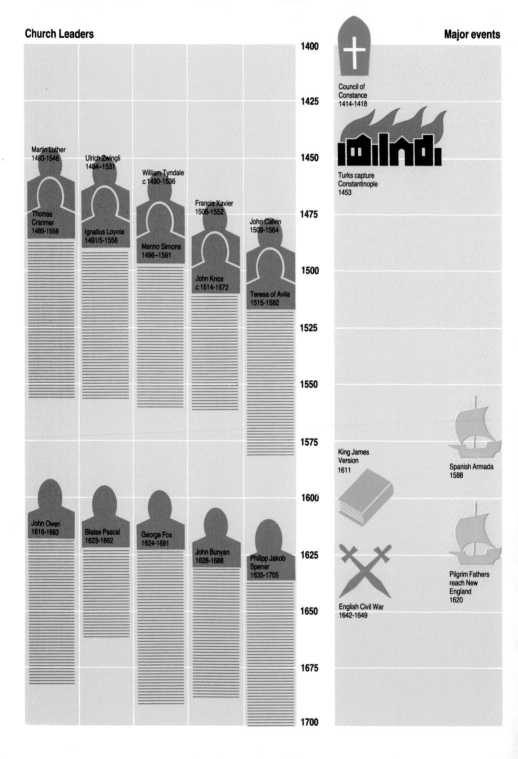

Church Leaders

Major events

1400

1425

Council of
Constance
1414-1418

1450

Turks capture
Constantinople
1453

Martin Luther
1483-1546

Ulrich Zwingli
1484–1531

William Tyndale
c.1490-1536

Francis Xavier
1506-1552

1475

Thomas
Cranmer
1489-1556

Ignatius Loyola
1491/5-1556

John Calvin
1509-1564

Menno Simons
1496–1561

1500

John Knox
c.1514-1572

Teresa of Avila
1515-1582

1525

1550

1575

King James
Version
1611

Spanish Armada
1588

1600

John Owen
1616-1683

Blaise Pascal
1623-1662

George Fox
1624-1691

John Bunyan
1628-1688

Philipp Jakob
Spener
1635-1705

1625

Pilgrim Fathers
reach New
England
1620

English Civil War
1642-1649

1650

1675

1700

Religions of
Europe in 1600

Scotland
CALVINIST
● Edinburgh

Ireland

England
ANGLICAN

Stockholm ●

Sweden

Poland

London ●
Canterbury ●

Netherlands

LUTHERAN

● Wittenberg

Germany

● Erfurt

ATLANTIC OCEAN

● Paris

Worms ●
CALVINIST

Strasbourg ●
ANABAPTIST
Basel ●
● Zurich

● Prague

● Vienna

ROMAN CATHOLIC

● Geneva

● Trent

● Venice

ROMAN CATHOLIC

Spain

● Madrid

● Manresa

● Florence

Italy

● Rome

**GREEK
ORTHODOX**

MEDITERRANEAN SEA

ISLAM

North Africa

Francis Xavier

1506-1552

Opposite: Francis Xavier
preaching in the East.

The Society of Jesus never lost sight of its original goal of world missions. Even while formal recognition of the new order was pending, in March 1540 Ignatius Loyola dispatched his trusted friend and follower Francis Xavier (1506-1552) to the Orient as a foreign missionary. During the next twelve years, Xavier would become known as "the Apostle of the Indies and Japan."

Francis Xavier was one of Loyola's first companions and the most famous Roman Catholic missionary in history. He literally burned himself out in his work, often contenting himself with only two or three hours of sleep a night. His mass conversions are legendary. In Travancore, for example, he reported baptizing more than 10,000 persons in the course of one month. Allowing for twelve-hour days, that would work out to about one baptism every two minutes for thirty consecutive days. By the same token, he took great pains to see that these new converts had priests to instruct them following their baptism. They were not left to shift for themselves, as was often the case in mass conversions of this sort. All told, the Jesuits credit Xavier with more than 700,000 conversions. Whatever the accuracy of this figure, hundreds of thousands of Asian Christians today claim spiritual lineage from this remarkable missionary.

Francis Xavier, the most famous Jesuit missionary.

The Life of

Xavier

1506	Birth in the Basque region of Spanish Navarre.
1525	Studies at the University of Paris.
1529	Meets Ignatius Loyola at Paris.
1533	Conversion and dedication to a spiritual life.
1534	Takes a special vow at Montmartre, Paris.
1537	Ordained to the priesthood at Venice.
1541	Sails for India as special missionary.
1549	Begins the evangelization of Japan.
1552	Death on the island of Shang-ch'uan, off the coast of China.

Francis Xavier

and Catholic Missions

Robert D. Linder

Xavier's youth

Born in Xavier Castle in Spanish Navarre on April 7, 1506, Francis was the fifth and youngest child of Basque aristocrats. His mother was a beautiful heiress and his father a canon lawyer and high-ranking government official in the region. After preliminary studies in his own country, Francis Xavier matriculated at the University of Paris in 1525 and took up residence at the College of Saint-Barbe, which was a stronghold of traditional medieval theology.

Apparently intended for a career in the church by his parents, Xavier soon rebelled against their wishes and became a Parisian playboy. Charming, witty, urbane, athletic, musical, good-looking, successful with women, and somewhat vain, he was a complete worldling – until one day he met a devoted Christian and fellow-Basque named Ignatius Loyola.

Loyola and Xavier

Loyola's impact on Xavier would be lifelong and far-reaching. Beginning in 1529, perhaps because of their common Spanish Basque background and connections, the two future Jesuits became college roommates. Sizing up the attractive, talented young student as the kind of man he wanted to include in his dreams of totally dedicated service to his church through world missions, Loyola began to work to recruit him to his cause. For a long time, however, Xavier wanted nothing to do with Loyola, whom he considered a bigoted fanatic. Instead, he continued his dissipated way of life. Learning came easy for Xavier, so instead of studying, he spent most of his time gambling and carousing in the numerous Paris taverns.

But the determined, iron-willed Loyola would not give up. He urged Xavier to abandon the way of the flesh and to be converted to the Christian life. He never allowed an opportunity to pass without quoting an appropriate biblical text to Xavier. In the end, Loyola used money to bring Xavier to consider more carefully the claims of Christ. Having already begged his own funds, Loyola willingly shared money with Xavier when the younger man inevitably made short work of his own income. Xavier gladly accepted the assistance offered by Ignatius, whom he esteemed so little.

However, this provided Loyola with the entrée he needed, the right to Xavier's ear. Eventually Xavier recognized the monotony, dull weariness, and disappointments of his increasingly meaningless diversions and began to take Loyola more seriously. Finally, during a late-night conversation concerning Xavier's plans for the future, following Loyola's casual mention of the words of Jesus from Matthew's gospel – "For what shall it profit a man if he shall gain the whole world, and lose his own soul?" (Matthew 16:26) – Francis Xavier yielded. The words of the Bible seared his heart, he repented of his sins, and from that day forth he became a devoted follower of Ignatius Loyola.

Xavier listened more and more attentively to Loyola's discourses on spiritual matters and soon forgot his former boon companions. He devoted himself instead to spiritual meditation, and Loyola became his model. So greatly did he come to revere Loyola, that for the remainder of his life Xavier always knelt when composing a letter to him or reading one of his replies. Eventually, on August 15, 1534,

Loyola and Xavier, along with five others, in a small chapel in Montmartre, joined in taking the vows of poverty and charity and resolved to go to Jerusalem to convert the Muslim Turks. If the Jerusalem mission proved impossible, they pledged instead to travel to Rome to place themselves at the personal service of the pope.

Subduing the soul

In the meantime, while he remained at Paris, Xavier earned the M.A. degree in 1530, taught at Beauvais College from 1530 to 1534, and studied theology from 1534 to 1536. Then, in November 1536, he left Paris with his missionary companions and made his way to Venice. Unable to proceed to the Holy Land because of international unrest, Loyola, Xavier, and their friends set about using their time in Venice to "subdue the soul" in preparation for missionary service for the church.

The companions worked in the Venetian hospitals, performing the most loathsome tasks: scrubbing the filthy floors, cleaning chamber pots, praying with the sick, putting the dead in coffins, and digging graves.

After ministering and preaching in and around Venice for many months, Xavier accompanied Loyola to Rome in 1538 in order to take part in the conferences that Loyola's followers held to prepare for the foundation of the Society of Jesus. Pope Paul III gave preliminary approval of the new order in September 1539. However, before final written authorization was secured, Francis Xavier began the journey that would take him to the other side of the world as the first Jesuit missionary in history.

At that time, Portugal was engaged in a period of colonial expansion out of all proportion to the tiny kingdom's size. In 1540 the pious king of Portugal, John III, heard of the zealous works of Loyola and his priests and desired to have some of them labor in his far-flung colonies. In view of this desire he wrote to Loyola requesting some of his followers for missionary work in Portuguese possessions in the Orient. Therefore, on March 15,

1540, six months before the final official recognition of the Society of Jesus, Francis Xavier, under orders from Loyola, slipped out of Rome to report to the Portuguese monarch at Lisbon.

Goa

Delayed at Lisbon by political complications, Xavier occupied himself by giving catechetical instructions, hearing confessions, and ministering to prisoners. After receiving appointment as papal nuncio to the Orient, he finally sailed for Portuguese India on April 7, 1541. After a journey of thirteen months, Xavier landed at Goa where he immediately busied himself with preaching, caring for the sick, learning local languages, and composing a native catechism.

Xavier's first bitter lesson came when he realized that, as in Europe, Christianity's greatest enemy in the East was nominalism. Despite its magnificent cathedral and the suggestion that it was the capital of Oriental Christendom, Portuguese Goa turned out to be full of nominal Christianity. The same was true of other areas where the native population had supposedly been evangelized by European priests. In still other places, Xavier's work among the non-Christians was plagued by the hostility of Muslim raiders and pirates.

Nevertheless, Francis Xavier set about improving the quality of Christian life, converting nominal Christians, and winning new people to the faith. His early years in Portuguese India have been described as "one jumble of journeyings." He ministered in Goa, among the Paravas of the Pearl Fishery Coast, on Ceylon (Sri Lanka), at Malacca on the Malay coast, and in the Moluccas in present-day Indonesia, a total of more than 5,000 miles traveled in the period 1545 to 1549.

For example, Xavier spent two years preaching to the Paravas along the southwestern coast of India. Christianity had been introduced there eight years previously and, because of a shortage of priests to teach the converts, had little effect. Consequently, he found an appalling mixture of Christianity and paganism being practiced by the Paravan people. Enlisting the help of the children, dressed in utter simplicity, and with a little bell in hand that he rang incessantly while he walked through their villages, Xavier won the Paravas to a more meaningful Christian experience and the eventual abandonment of their pagan rituals. They grew to love Xavier, trusted him implicitly, and saw in him the very image of the God whom he preached.

Using his great gift of languages, Xavier preached in every corner of the Portuguese empire in the East. His main themes were the power of God and the danger of eternal damnation outside of a right relationship with Jesus Christ through His church, meaning the Roman Catholic church. Mass conversions followed.

Miracle of the crab
Also during the period, many miracles began to be associated with Xavier's work. Perhaps the most famous and startling was the reported "miracle of the crab." Voyaging one day from one island to another, Xavier and his companions encountered a furious storm. In order to calm the waters, Xavier took his beloved crucifix and dangled it into the sea by its cord. However, in the roaring sea he lost the cord, and the crucifix disappeared from sight. This greatly distressed Xavier. Twenty-four hours later, when Xavier and his group had reached their destination and were standing on the beach, a crab crawled up from the sea with the crucifix held aloft in one of its pincers and halted before the Jesuit saint. Xavier dropped to his knees and joyously received the returned crucifix whereupon the "holy crab" immediately returned to the sea, leaving the little band of missionaries to go on their way rejoicing.

In July 1547, while at Malacca, Xavier met a Japanese named Anjiro. This man had committed a murder in his native land and had fled from the authorities on a Portuguese ship that lay at anchor in the bay off his hometown of Kagoshima.

For a monetary consideration, the captain brought him to Malacca. On the way, the Portuguese sailors told Anjiro about the Christian faith, especially about heaven and hell, the forgiveness of sins, and eternal salvation. The young Japanese was filled with the desire to embrace Christianity and receive forgiveness for his crime. At Malacca he met Xavier and was baptized.

Japan
As he talked with Anjiro and learned about Japan, Xavier became more and more consumed with the idea of introducing Christianity into Anjiro's native land. After returning to Goa and receiving and orienting a newly arrived detachment of Jesuit missionaries, Xavier made plans to go to Japan. Finally, after learning as much as he could of the Japanese language from Anjiro, Xavier and two other Jesuits set out for Japan in April 1549, accompanied by Anjiro.

They landed at Kagoshima in southern Japan on August 15, 1549. Xavier and his Jesuit companions spent the first year improving their knowledge of the language and translating a short catechism and an explanation of the Apostles' Creed into Japanese. Xavier, as was his habit, memorized several dozen sermons in the native language to use as he went about preaching among the people. Anjiro had warned Xavier that the Japanese would be won over only by reason. With that in mind, Xavier greatly desired to secure an audience with the ruler of Japan, in which he could persuade him by means of reasoned argumentation to embrace Christianity and thereby to win with one blow the whole island kingdom for the Christian faith.

In the meantime Xavier was welcomed by the *daimyo* (local prince), obtained official permission to preach, and began slowly to build a Christian community in Kagoshima. The Buddhist monks, however, sensing that Christianity was a powerful new rival religion, began to make trouble for Xavier and his friends. Therefore, leaving behind a congregation of about 100 converts, Xavier decied to penetrate to the center of Japan in order to spread the faith elsewhere and eventually locate the supreme ruler of the island through whom he hoped to effect the conversion of the entire population.

Preaching at Hirado, Hakata, Yamaguchi, and Sakai, he finally arrived at Kyoto, the imperial capital in January 1551. There, he was disappointed to learn that real political power at that time rested not with the *mikado* (emperor) or with the *shogun* (military leader) but with the various regional *daimyos*. Frustrated in his plan for a mass conversion of the Japanese by this turn of events, Xavier returned to Kagoshima. There, he altered his method of approach to the Japanese. Realizing that they had little regard for humility but understood only pride and arrogance, and that they would not abandon their old religions unless "reasoned into the kingdom of God," Xavier changed his tactics. Abandoning the appearance of apostolic poverty, he now put on better clothing and engaged in public debates with the Buddhist monks, eventually winning more than 2,000 Japanese to the Christian faith. Leaving the other Jesuit priest in charge of the mission, Xavier returned to Malacca after twenty-seven months in Japan.

Xavier left Japan with one overpowering impression. In his debates with the Buddhist monks, they often presented an argument that perplexed the Jesuit missionary. They declared that the Christian God could not possibly be the true God of the universe because the Chinese knew nothing of it. This line of reasoning seldom failed in its effect on the Japanese audience. As he reflected on this, Xavier realized that the Japanese were deeply influenced in all of their opinions and judgments by the example of China. After all, Japan had in fact taken over its religion, its writing, and almost all its spiritual culture from China. Xavier soon came to believe that the key to Japan was China; that if the Chinese could be won, the Japanese would follow. Therefore, as he withdrew from Japan, he made plans for a China mission in the near future.

China

Back in Goa in 1551-1552, Xavier learned that he was the head of the newly-created province of India. But his mind was on China. After settling certain domestic troubles in Goa, he helped arrange an embassy to the Chinese sovereign and obtained from the Portuguese viceroy in India the appointment of a friend as ambassador. After many difficulties, Xavier finally departed for China by way of Malacca. In the last week of August 1552, his ship reached the desolate island of Shang-ch'uan, off the coast of China, not far from Canton. Since the Chinese had nothing but contempt for foreigners, whom they considered to be barbarians, the doors to the fabled Middle Kingdom were firmly barred against Xavier and all Westerners. For his part, Xavier was obsessed with the notion that the way to the Chinese was through the emperor. Yet, while awaiting an audience and permission to preach in November 1552, he was seized by a fever, grew daily weaker, and finally died on the morning of December 3, his last desire unfulfilled and the name of Jesus on his lips.

Xavier was buried the day after his death, but his body was exhumed two months later in order for it to be taken to Goa for final disposition. According to those present, it was found to be fresh and incorrupt. In any event, Francis Xavier is now enshrined in the Church of the Good Jesus in Goa – except for his right arm, which baptized so many thousands of converts. It was taken to Rome and is now preserved in the Church of the Gesù, near the tomb of his beloved leader Ignatius Loyola.

Francis Xavier's work

Francis Xavier left his mark on Christian history in at least three ways: as a prime exemplar of the Ignatian ideal, as one of the greatest missionaries in the history of the faith, and as an inspiration for modern Catholic missions. The Ignatian ideal was to serve the Roman Catholic church with complete devotion and unquestioning obedience, revivifying its teachings and devotional practices, applying them with renewed fervor and intelligence, "for the greater glory of God." The main means for doing this was to follow the admonition of Paul, who taught that good sons of the church should become "all things to all men that [they] might by all means save some" (1 Corinthians 9:22). Xavier fully exemplified this ideal and method.

In particular, Xavier preached the Word smoothly rather than boldly. With "the greater glory of God" in mind, he adapted his methods to suit the situation, utilizing holy craftiness to accomplish pious ends. For example, when he first came to Goa in 1542, he made an estimate of the situation that allowed him to accomplish his goal of rejuvenating the spiritual life of the Portuguese colony. While the other priests of Goa lived in splendid houses, he, the papal nuncio, took up residence in a modest little room in the local hospital. There he came into contact with people from all classes and

became acquainted with them in an environment in which they were most prepared to listen to spiritual counsel. Most of them recovered and remembered Xavier's kindnesses and edifying words. The Jesuit missionary who came to them in simple dress, spoke to them with gentle, homely words, and who sympathized fully with their smallest troubles soon seemed to them like one of themselves. By the same token, Xavier had a superb opportunity to obtain accurate information about the life, character, interests, and peculiarities of the people to whom he wished to minister. In the end they became so accustomed to telling him their hopes and fears, that they were soon willing to confess their sins to him as well. Under the guidance of Loyola, he had become all things to all men that he might win some.

Later, in Japan, he realized that the Goan approach would not work with the proud and more sophisticated Japanese people. In India he had won the poor and humble lower castes by impressing them with his humility and by appearing as one

The Grand Canal, Venice. Xavier prepared here before departing on his mission.

of them in his torn cassock and shabby cowl. In Japan humility was no virtue, and poverty was despised. So, Xavier put on the most magnificent apparel he could obtain and went about with an imposing retinue. Most importantly he drew upon his splendid university education in order to cope with the Japanese insistence that he explain reasonably the Christian faith before they would accept it. Therefore in Japan he spent considerable time expounding the compatibility of the existence of evil with God's omnipotence and the necessity of the incarnation.

The Ignatian ideal

Xavier's experience also demonstrates how the Ignatian ideal, used in moderation, could help Westerners adjust to foreign cultures. More quickly than many modern Protestant missionaries, Xavier recognized that as long as theological essentials are maintained, much of the native culture can be preserved in the process of conversion to Christianity. He noticed that people in all cultures share the same vices and virtues and that their philosophy reveals the presence of natural law, reason, and emotion. Moreover, their commitment to Christ can be as genuine and admirable as that of any devout Western Christian, so much so that Xavier often felt humbled in the presence of his Japanese Christian brothers. Thus, as the Jesuit missionary preached the true God and the true faith, he did it in the cultural context of the people as he found them.

This is not to say that Xavier's method was without fault. He sometimes used Portuguese might to facilitate the conversion of native peoples, and he always used it to help him gain entry into foreign societies. In addition, he sanctioned the use of the Inquisition and apparently approved the persecution of Nestorian Christians in India.

Greatest Catholic missionary

Francis Xavier has served as the inspiration for modern Catholic missions. Most historians consider him the most gifted and successful missionary ever produced by the Roman Catholic church. There is no doubt that he was one of the most courageous figures in Christian missionary history. For example, Xavier was once told of some islands – the Moro group, located on the fringes of present-day Indonesia – where the inhabitants were mostly cannibals and head-hunters. Accounts of that time claimed that they were such barbarians that if an individual wished to have a great feast, "he will ask his neighbor for the loan of his father, if he is very old, in order to serve him up as a dish." Undaunted by those reports, Xavier spent three months among the people of those islands, preaching much and converting a few. Twenty years later, his Jesuit brethren, entering by the door he had opened, turned all of the reputed cannibals into fervent Christians.

Moreover, there are the many inspirational miracles attributed to the Jesuit missionary. Xavier himself, far from laying claim to miraculous powers, invariably denied that he possessed them. On the other hand, he was the kind of man who made it easy for people to believe that he had extraordinary powers. However, in the end, there is no need to stress his ability to work wonders because his faith, hope, and charity testify to his special relationship to God more eloquently than the most stupendous miracle.

Menno Simons
1496-1561

Menno Simons (1496-1561) gave his name to a body of evangelical believers in the Reformation period whose direct descendants are still with us today. The various Mennonite and Baptist denominations, along with some others, currently represent that aspect of Protestantism typified by the distinctively Anabaptist, free, or believers' churches.

Menno was not an original founder of this free church, Anabaptist/Mennonite movement, because he was converted about ten years after its birth in Zurich, Switzerland. Nevertheless, at the time when the movement was in grave danger of being exterminated elsewhere and totally discredited by the excesses of some in the

Netherlands, he deserves much credit in that at great sacrifice he personally gathered together, redirected, and reinvigorated the surviving remnant of the Dutch branch of Anabaptism. He provided it with stable, long-term leadership, fulfilling ably and simultaneously the roles of itinerant evangelist, teacher, theologian, and bishop-at-large. He carefully led the Dutch back to an approximation of the more balanced and moderate teachings of the original Swiss founders of evangelical Anabaptism.

To the outside world, Simons was an able, articulate spokesman for and apologist of

the renewed movement. As a result, those Dutch Anabaptists and their north German counterparts not only survived but grew and significantly influenced both Dutch Protestantism's openness to religious toleration and the rise of the English Baptists. The English in turn have played a major role in creating the distinctively pluralistic character of American Christian society.

Right: Anabaptist martyrs in Amsterdam, 1549.

Below: An Anabaptist ferryman held secret services in his boat.

The Life of

Menno Simons

1496	Birth in Friesland, Netherlands.
1524	Ordained as a Roman Catholic priest.
1525	January: first Anabaptist baptisms, Zurich.
1526-1530	Serves as popular evangelical Catholic preacher.
1527	First Anabaptist "Confession of Faith," the Schleitheim Articles.
1531	Provoked to Bible study by martyrdom of Siche Snijder.
1534-1535	The Münster episode.
1535	April: slaughter of 300 Anabaptists at Old Cloister; shock of this leads to conversion.
1536	January: leaves the Roman Catholic church.
1536	Baptism as an Anabaptist.
1537	Ordination as an Anabaptist elder by Obbe Philips.
1539	Publication of *The Foundation of Christian Doctrine*.
1543	Flees to North Germany.
1561	January 31, death.

Menno Simons

and the Radical Reformation

Kenneth R. Davis

Magisterial and radical reformers

Through the fifteenth century, in both the Roman Catholic church and European Christian society, the call for reform was widespread and urgent. Some reformers wanted theological reform. The Christian faith was thought to have become too impersonal, rational, and speculative. It seemed to be too divorced from personal piety, the simple teachings of Jesus, and the ordinary person. Some other reformers focused more on the need for correcting the institutional abuses provoked by the secularization and materialism of church officialdom.

Others were deeply disturbed by the rampant moral laxity, sexual license, drunkenness, superstitions, and general lack of discipline of some clergy and religious orders as well as of society at large.

When a Europe-wide movement for reform broke loose in the early sixteenth century, it built upon the reform concerns from the previous century. It also found new impetus and strength through the emergence of an improved text of the Bible and of a new system for studying the text. Moreover, the Bible was being printed and translated into the languages of the people and widely distributed. Consequently, a massive reform impulse spread across Catholic Europe like a prairie fire.

Although initially unified in its support of Martin Luther's challenge of 1517 to the abuses of the indulgence system, the movement's expectations, as one might suspect from its diverse roots, were not one but many. Indeed, after 1521 it began to separate into several major components: Roman Catholic reform (with several sub-groupings and differing perspectives), magisterial Protestant (Lutheran, Reformed, and, somewhat later, Anglican), and also a miscellany of diverse groups dissenting from both the Roman church's and magisterial Protestant's visions of reform. These dissenters were, and often still are, lumped together as radicals or Anabaptists.

Magisterial Protestants were biblically and evangelically reformed Roman Catholics who became schismatic by breaking with the papacy. However, they retained the state church ideal, the medieval view of the essentialness of ecclesiastical and civil cooperation to create and sustain a unitary Christian society. But the dimensions of this Christian society were reduced from an Imperial/Roman European Christendom to each new emerging state.

The only significant unity clearly found thus far within radical dissent is that for a variety of reasons its various groups rejected both magisterial Protestant and Roman Catholic versions of reform as adequate options. Nevertheless, following Luther's example, most historians have persisted in assuming some kind of basic unity (theological, psychological, or sociological) to legitimize binding them all into one movement, as even the designation "radical" suggests. As a result, the evangelical Anabaptists (Brethren), forerunners of the modern believers' churches in Protestantism, have been lumped indiscriminately with, and by implication identified with, the revolutionery and fanatical sects that also existed on the fringes of both the magisterial and evangelical Anabaptist reform movements.

One can distinguish at least four major divisions within radical dissent. First, there were the *rationalists*, who saw reform as an intellectual emancipation, permitting the Bible to be interpreted in rationalistic, and even non-Trinitarian terms. They were the forerunners of Unitarianism.

Second, the *spiritualists*, by adopting a moderate mysticism that stressed the internality, immediacy, and individuality of Christian experience, weakened all the external aspects of Christian life and practice. Indeed, if necessary they could stay within the established denominations. Some aspects of this spiritualist emphasis found renewed expression in seventeenth-century pietism.

Third, the *evangelical brethren* (Anabaptist/Mennonite) branch, began in Zurich as an offshoot of Zwinglian Protestantism. These Swiss brethren and their related variants, by instituting believers' baptism (rebaptism) in January 1525 and establishing the first believers' church in Zollikon, were the first true Anabaptists in Reformation times. While drinking deeply from the theological fountains of Zwingli, Erasmus, Luther, and Karlstadt, they created a new synthesis around a vision of reform that centered more on the necessity for a personal commitment to Jesus Christ, direct obedience to the Scriptures, and practical piety than seemed to be emerging from the more theological and institutional emphases of Luther and Zwingli. Indeed, combining moralistic, pietistic, and spiritualistic insights from Erasmus and Karlstadt with their own intense Bible studies, a number of Zwingli's associates (such as Felix Mantz, Conrad Grebel, and Simon Stumpf) concluded that the magisterial Reformation was deficient and incomplete. Doctrine needed to be personalized and productive of a holy life-style through real repentance. Faith to be truly saving must be a working, regenerating faith, if reform was to lead to the restitution of New Testament Christianity. Believers' baptism, in contrast to infant baptism, and the practice of brotherly discipline became the appropriate, concomitant, and distinctive institutionalized practices. Also,

Menno Simons, Anabaptist leader.

the new believers' community was no longer to be necessarily identified or coterminous with the civil society at large.

This evangelical Anabaptist branch of radical dissent began the emergence of the modern free or believers' church tradition within contemporary Protestantism, as currently reflected in Mennonite, Baptist, Brethren, and such like denominations.

A fourth group within radical dissent, the *eschatological revolutionaries*, helped form the direct backdrop for the remarkable ministry of Menno Simons. Regrettably, the revolutionaries gave a violent, militant twist to their convictions about the imminence of Christ's return and its relation to reform. The opposing ungodly faced destruction by the sword wielded by the elect. With the death of its principal leader, Thomas Münzer, and the failure of an associated peasants' revolt in 1525, this frightening movement was largely discredited.

Also with the fiasco of Anabaptists' behavior in the small German town of Münster in 1534-1535, it looked as if Anabaptism might not survive. But a leader of remarkable stature and capability arose. His name was Menno Simons.

Menno Simons

Menno Simons was born in Friesland in 1496. As a newly ordained priest in the Roman church, he was assigned to his first charge in 1524, the village church in Pingjum in Friesland. According to his own testimony, he soon began to have doubts whether the bread and wine in the mass really became the flesh and blood of the Lord. These nagging doubts drove him to a study of the New Testament (a hitherto unread book). What he found there seemed both to confirm his doubts and to relieve his conscience.

Thereafter, new ideas drawn from the New Testament increasingly entered his preaching. Such change greatly increased his popularity and reputation as a Catholic evangelical preacher. Menno noted, however, that his evangelicalism had little impact on his rather frivolous lifestyle, which he described as "full of gambling and drinking."

Shortly after, Menno was shocked into a further study of the Bible when he heard the news of the beheading of an apparently pious Christian, named Sicke Snijder, for being rebaptized. Menno had never before heard of a second baptism, so he again turned to an examination of the Scriptures. This time, his study led him to question the validity of infant baptism. When he turned to the writings of the Fathers, Luther, Bucer, and Bullinger, he found they did not agree among themselves and were of little help. Finally he concluded that he had been deceived about infant baptism also. But nothing changed. He continued primarily to promote his own career as a Catholic priest. He sought and received a transfer to Witmarsum, an upward move in terms of recognition and fame. He admitted that, personally, he still was not taking Christianity very seriously.

The Anabaptists

It was at Witmarsum that Menno had his first direct contact with Anabaptists and then with several emissaries from Münster. After conferring with the latter, he opposed them vigorously for their fanaticism, though he was apparently impressed by their zeal for truth and for piety of life. Menno's conscience began to trouble him with reference to his intemperate life-style and his own motives of personal advancement and material gain.

The slaughter of 300 Anabaptists (in April 1535) who had sought refuge in the Old Cloister, including Menno's own brother, was the final step in a spiritual struggle that had been going on in him for at least four years. Some of those who died had apparently initially been led away from the Roman church by his own preaching. Menno eloquently describes as follows the impact of the Old Cloister events on his life:

After this had transpired, the blood of these people although misled fell...so hot on my heart that I could not stand it nor find rest in my soul. I reflected upon my unclean, carnal life...I saw that these children, although in error, willingly gave their lives and their estates for their doctrine and faith ... But I myself ... acknowledged abominations simply in order that I might enjoy physical comfort and escape the Cross of Christ.

Finally Menno confessed his hypocrisy, earnestly sought God's mercy and forgiveness, and was converted. But, to what? Not to Anabaptism, not yet, but to a more personally sincere and pious expression of biblical Christianity and ministry. It was an ascetic conversion not unlike Augustine's or Paul's.

After nine months of attempting to preach his new faith from the old pulpit, on Sunday, January 30, 1536, he publicly renounced his Roman faith and office and sought out the fellowship of some peaceful Anabaptists. He began also an attempt to correct and reclaim some who had been involved with the Münster error. Although he apparently was baptized at this time and identified himself somewhat with the nonviolent Anabaptists associated with Obbe Philips, Menno was unsure of his role and perhaps even uneasy about some aspects of peaceful, Melchiorist Anabaptism.

Shortly after, he left the area and retired to eastern Friesland to think through his conversion.

Anabaptist elder

Menno's active ministry of reconstruction began when a delegation of Anabaptists came to him in Friesland and urged him to take up a leadership role among them. After a time of earnest prayer and because he was burdened with their critical need, he heeded the call. Menno was ordained in Groningen early in 1537, as an Anabaptist elder by the laying on of hands of Obbe Philips and at the request of the brotherhood.

His teaching, evangelizing, and pastoral ministry-at-large lasted for twenty-four years and aimed at reconstructing from the remnants of Melchiorite Anabaptism a new, peaceful, united Anabaptism that was much closer to the earlier, moderate evangelical Anabaptism of the Marpeck group in Strasbourg. The defection of Obbe Philips in 1540 and Menno's publication of *The Foundation of Christian Doctrine, 1539,* outlining the essential character of his brand of Anabaptism, firmly established Menno's leadership.

Because of the charges of heresy levelled against him, Menno's ministry required ceaseless travel, often just ahead of the authorities, in spite of which he continued to find time to write. It is amazing that he survived. Many of his converts were martyred. The authorities offered numerous inducements to abet his capture because they realized that Anabaptism could not be stamped out while he remained at large – but to no avail. His wife and children also suffered much personal discomfort and fear, especially in the earlier years.

North Germany

After an extensive and fruitful ministry in Groningen, Friesland, and Amsterdam, late in 1543 Menno finally left Holland for the less hostile environment of northern Germany. There he spent the final eighteen years of his life and ministry, years that were comparatively peaceful. After a brief illness, he died in his own home on January 31, 1561.

Menno sought to unify and rebuild Dutch Anabaptism by delineating a balanced, moderate, mediating evangelical Anabaptist theology. As the most prolific Anabaptist writer in the first thirty-five years of the movement (he wrote about twenty-five books and tracts), and even though much more a pastoral and apologetic theologian than a systematizer, Menno was in many ways to Anabaptism what John Calvin was to magisterial Protestantism. He reasserted and expounded on virtually all basic teachings and practices of the earlier evangelical Anabaptists (Grebel, Mantz, Sattler, Hubmaier, and Marpeck). His writings remained dominant in the development of the movement that became the bearer of his name – the Mennonites.

Menno always saw true, biblical Christianity in terms of his own dramatic, ascetic, and very personal conversion, and of his earnest commitment to the recovery of churches who faithfully reflected

Menno Simons; a modern woodcut.

a biblical life-style. In stark contrast, Menno and most Anabaptists viewed the nominal Christianity around them as artificial and hypocritical.

Biblical transformation

The strength of the positive response to the Anabaptists' message lends credence to their criticisms. Accordingly, Menno again and again emphasized that the Christian church would be renewed and reformed to biblical standards only by the reestablishment of churches composed exclusively of personally committed believers in Jesus Christ as Savior and Lord – ones whose lives individually gave outward evidence of having been transformed by the Word and the Spirit, in response to sincere repentance and faith. These believers are then by the same Spirit gathered together into mutually supportive, holy, disciplined, separated from worldly society's norms and values witnessing, loving, and caring brotherhoods.

Church discipline

The use of the ban in the practice of church discipline (an essential doctrine) created the most difficulty for Menno's generally moderate stance. His loyalty to his colleagues, Dirk Philips, a strong-willed ex-Franciscan, and Leenaert Bouwens, apparently led him to adopt a rather harsh stance that weakened his unifying efforts. Should the shunning of unrepentant, erring brethren break even conjugal bonds? Initially Menno sided with the Swiss and south German Anabaptists' moderate stance, but later he supported the sterner views of his colleagues, a decision that eventually split the Dutch Mennonites. The more moderate group, called the Waterlanders, in reaction rejected the name Mennonite, preferring to be called *Doopsgezinden* (Baptists).

Contribution

Rarely has one man reconstructed, reestablished, and revived a movement as successfully as Menno Simons did. His re-markable success and the love his followers had for him indicates the spiritual strength of his dedication, the quality of his vision, and above all the greatness of his pastoral heart. In general Menno preserved Dutch Anabaptism by bringing it back to the central biblical tenets of earlier evangelical Anabaptism with which it had had some founding ties at Strasbourg. Virtually all direct survivors of sixteenth-century Anabaptism bear his name to this day.

Under Menno's leadership, Dutch Anabaptism not only recovered its unity but took on renewed evangelistic fervour. "By around 1550 approximately one quarter of the population of the Northern Netherlands were considered to be Mennonites... [Indeed,] they prepared the basis on which the subsequent Reformation – although after 1550 under Calvinist leadership – prevailed."

Nearly all aspects of what Durnbaugh has laid out as the essential elements of the modern believers' church kind of Christianity (as typified also by the modern Baptists, Brethren, and others) are clearly expounded by Menno. How much these later believers' church denominations indirectly drew upon him is debatable, but recent research seems to indicate that it is probably much more than has hitherto been recognized. Menno Simons deserves a place among the great leaders of Christianity.

Hymns of the Faith

From the earliest days of the church, hymn-singing has been a vital feature of Christian worship. At first it was eastern Christians, in the Syrian, Byzantine and Armenian churches, who laid greater emphasis on the singing of hymns.

Early hymnwriters in the western church include Hilary, bishop of Poitiers, who died c. A.D. 367, and Ambrose of Milan, a number of whose simple hymns are still sung in translation.

Hymns of the Reformation

Martin Luther, the great German reformer, devoted much energy to hymnwriting; he wanted to ensure that all believers joined in worship, and not merely those who understood Latin, the traditional language of church worship in the west. Luther caused offence to some more hidebound Christians by setting some of his new Christian lyrics to popular lovesongs – one example is his Easter hymn, "O Sacred Head, Sore Wounded."

Luther also broke away from medieval church music by deliberately using simple tunes, in contrast to the complex polyphony of medieval worship. This too was part of his struggle to make worship accessible to the ordinary person. Many of the tunes to these Lutheran hymns were later elaborated by J.S.Bach in his series of almost 300 church cantatas, composed for solo singers, choir and small orchestra, for performance at different times in the church year.

The English hymnwriters

England's first hymn-tune composers were Thomas Tallis and Orlando Gibbons, in the later sixteenth century. Scotland, following Calvin's tradition, restricted singing in church to the psalms.

The great period of English hymnwriting was the eighteenth century. Influenced particularly by the German Moravians, Isaac Watts wrote many hymns, including the classic, "When I Survey the Wondrous Cross". John Newton, the converted slave-owner, wrote many famous hymns, most notably "Amazing Grace". But above all, John and Charles Wesley wrote thousands of hymns in this period, among them "Love Divine, All Loves Excelling," and "Hark, the Herald Angels Sing".

Hymn-singing invariably accompanies periods of revival and awakening. Just as the Awakening of the eighteenth century was matched by the hymns of the Wesley brothers, so the rise of the Salvation Army in nineteenth century urban England had its own stirring hymns, and the campaign revivals of D.L.Moody and Ira D.Sankey in the U.S.A. and Britain their characteristically lively hymns.

Congregational hymn-singing in an English church.

John Knox
*c.*1514-1572

John Knox (*c.* 1514-1572) was an ordained minister successively of the Roman Catholic church, the Church of England (he declined a bishopric), and the Church of Scotland. The Reformation came late to Scotland (1560), but fourteen years before that, John Knox was carrying a sword in defense of George Wishart (*c.* 1513-1546), who was spreading Protestant doctrines. After the archbishop of

St. Andrews had Wishart burned at the stake, Knox became in turn tutor, preacher in St. Andrews, (the ecclesiastical capital), galley-slave in French bondage, and chaplain to the young English king Edward VI.

During Mary Tudor's reign (1553-1558), when England reverted to the church of Rome, Knox was in exile on the European mainland. There he helped originate the Puritan

tradition and worked on the English version of the Bible, but to spread the gospel in his native land was his burning concern.

When he did return to Scotland in 1559, the queen regent, a zealous Roman Catholic, had him proclaimed an outlaw, but he was not subdued. English ambassador Randolph reported to his superiors in London: "The voice of one man is able in one hour to put more life in us than five hundred trumpets continually blustering in our ears."

When the Reformation did triumph in his backward little northern kingdom, it was Knox who laid the church on right foundations. He aimed at support for the poor, equality of all men before God, and the advancement

Edinburgh, center of Knox's Scottish Reformation.

The Life of
Knox

c. 1514	Birth.
c. 1536	Ordained priest in the church of Rome.
1546	By this time a supporter of the Reformation.
1553	In exile on the European continent.
1555	Revisits Scotland.
1559	Final return to Scotland.
1560	Triumph of the Reformation in Scotland. The Scots Confession drafted, followed by the First Book of Discipline.
1567	Preaches at coronation of infant James VI.
1572	Death in Edinburgh.

Scotland
St Andrews
● Edinburgh

of education by a school in every parish. He and his colleagues went to great pains to establish sound doctrine in their "Reformed Kirk."

All this was done despite savage attacks by powerful vested interests. To John Knox, compromise was anathema. He saw politics only through religious eyes, and (unusually for his era) he headed a revolution that was bloodless.

John Knox: a portrait in stained glass.

John Knox

and the Scots Reformation

J. D. Douglas

John Knox, the Scots Reformer.

Exile

The best evidence available suggests that John Knox was born about 1514, was ordained priest perhaps in 1536 after studies at St. Andrews University, and in 1543 was still signing himself "minister of the sacred altar" under the archbishop of St. Andrews.

Then, after a dramatic and inexplicable turnaround, he is found acting as a bodyguard to George Wishart. When the latter was executed, Knox's subsequent activities included a chaplaincy to Edward VI of England, in whose church he declined advancement because he foresaw "evil days to come."

When the Roman Catholic Mary suppressed Protestantism in England for a time, Knox went into exile, first in Frankfurt, then in John Calvin's Geneva. He studied Greek and Hebrew, participated in Bible translation work, and, having arranged for his recent bride, Marjory, and her mother to join him, lived for several years a peaceful life.

Even then, however, he was looking ahead. He consulted Calvin about the right of the civil authority to prescribe religion to subjects, and whether the godly should obey a magistrate who enforced idolatry and condemned true religion. In 1555, with the Reformation still five years off, he revisited Scotland, where the widow of James V was regent during the minority of her daughter (Mary Queen of Scots).

For six months Knox preached privately in southern Scotland, where he was welcomed far beyond his expectations. Everywhere he went he dispensed the Lord's Supper in the simple Reformed manner that so attracted those long accustomed to the tedious repetition of the mass in a strange tongue. He dissuaded people from attending mass, and such absenteeism became the mark of a thoroughgoing religious decision.

Although condemned to death and burned in effigy, Knox, before leaving Scotland, issued a "Wholesome Counsel," reminding heads of families that they were bishops and kings, and recommending the institution of something similar to the early advisor of the Protestant lords, who repeatedly urged him to come home.

Return

Knox did return finally in May 1559 and was promptly outlawed by royal decree.

When the cause was in jeopardy because of the French intervention and English fickleness (the new queen, Elizabeth I, looked on him with a jaundiced eye for writing against women rulers), Knox in a memorable sermon revived his wilting supporters.

Victory for the Reformation was at last secured in 1560. The Auld Alliance with France was revoked, and Scots, for the first time in their history, cheered the advent of an English army that crossed the border to help them.

Knox and five others soon produced the Confession of Faith, and this remained authoritative until superseded in 1647 by the Westminster Confession. Then came the First Book of Discipline, which aimed at uniformity in doctrine, sacraments, election and sustenance of the ministry, church discipline, support of the poor, equality of all before God, and advancement of education (the book, unhappily, was to be rejected by the state). Knox produced also the Book of Common Order, compiled earlier by him in Geneva to guide ministers in carrying out their functions.

Knox's teaching

What had been achieved? Knox and his colleagues taught four positive principles:

Holy Scripture is the sole and sufficient rule of faith and practice. Claiming to be the sole disburser of religious knowledge, Rome obscured such knowledge in a dead language and stressed those utterances of Fathers, councils, and popes that furthered the old church's ends. The Reformers declared such things to be of value only if they coincided with Scripture, and that even the poorest and plainest of persons should have free access to God's Word in the vernacular.

Man is justified by faith alone. Although Rome did not completely disregard the work of Christ as the ground of forgiveness and salvation, human merit was so presented as to depreciate our Lord's sacrifice and to sell heaven and eternal life for money ("nae penny, nae paternoster"). The new-old proclamation of Jesus Christ as an all-sufficient and all-justifying Savior offered the free gift of eternal life against Rome's merchandise of souls.

The minister is simply teacher of the gospel, servant, and steward. The priest professed to repeat Christ's sacrifice, to stand between God and man, and to forgive or retain sins. Ignorance was exploited, the vision of Christ obscured. The Reformers taught that the function of Christ's pastors and teachers was to preach the gospel, expound Scripture, tend the flock, and administer the laws that Christ appointed.

The people have a voice in electing pastors and office-bearers. Rome expected the surrender of judgment, reason, and conscience to priests (some of whom were of outrageous reputation). The Reformers held that Christian people are Christ's flock, that offices and ordinances are appointed for their good, and are effective only as they promote the

John Knox's house, Edinburgh.

instruction, spiritual welfare, and prosperity of the people, who were to be consulted in electing ministers and lay readers.

Then came trouble. Few of the top nobility had identified themselves with reform. Many opportunists, having "greedily gripped to the possessions of the kirk," refused to acquiesce in Knox's idealistic schemes and shattered his plan that church revenues should pass to the ministers, the schools, and the poor.

Two-thirds of the income in fact remained with the former owners; the remainder was to go partly to the Reformed clergy, partly to the crown. Thus no new state arose to partner the new church in a Christian commonwealth: Mary's Catholic monarchy was not Calvin's Protestant republic.

The Scots Reformation
Nonetheless a revolution had triumphed over incredible odds. Knox's life had often been in danger. He was shot at, ambushes were laid for him, and he had "need of a good and assured horse." His *Historie* shows how provocative he could be. Thus one bishop was "blind of one eye in the body, but of both in his soul." Of an archbishop's avarice Knox commented dryly, "As he sought the world, it fled him not." His churlishness toward Mary Queen of Scots was reflected in his singleminded philosophy: "To me it is enough to say that black is not white, and man's tyranny and foolishness is not God's perfect ordinance."

John Knox seemed an improbable leader: an apostate priest of undistinguished appearance and obscure origin; an undiplomatic, socially graceless man; a reluctant crusader resolved to go only when and where summoned by the God who had divided the waters of the Red Sea and tumbled the walls of Jericho. He saw to the heart of things, undergirded by the assurance that he fought not for fleeting advantage, but for the everlasting truth of God. "What I have been to my country," he said as his life was closing, "albeit this unthankful age will not know, yet the ages to come will be compelled to bear witness to the truth."

Knox's treatise on prayer and his letters, lesser known as they are, reveal a gentler, more compassionate side, as does that sensitive, moving rubric in which he begins, "Be merciful unto me, O Lord, and call not into judgment my manifold sins; and chiefly those whereof the world is not able to accuse me."

Knox was essentially, like Luther, a man of his time; yet the tendency now is to judge him by modern standards and to forget the pressures and demands of the mid-sixteenth century. It is never the way of the world to flee those that seek it. It is extraordinary, though, that those who regard Knox as a gloomy bigot, whose legacy to Scotland inhibits innocent enjoyment and the tourist trade, have never considered what he did, say, for the civil rights movement.

The Reformer died in Edinburgh on November 24, 1572. At his funeral the Regent Morton, no friend of ministers, said, "Here lies one who neither flattered nor favoured any flesh." It might leave a lot unsaid, but one is left with the impression that Knox himself would have approved the wording.

Even more enthusiastically, however, would he have endorsed the inscription on the Reformation Monument in Geneva, Switzerland: *"Un homme avec Dieu est toujours dans la majorité"* ("One man with God is always in the majority"). Four centuries later, we need that word more than ever.

Teresa of Avila
1515-1582

Teresa of Avila (1515-1582) was a major figure in the sixteenth-century movement of Roman Catholic reform. With the restoration of the spirit of radical poverty in the monastic system, she had begun a reform of the regular religious orders that was equal to the introduction of the seminary system for priests in the secular orders. The vivid passion of her mysticism, brilliantly portrayed in Bernini's *Saint Teresa in Ecstasy*, caught the imagination of the age and deeply influenced the artists of the sixteenth and seventeenth centuries. El Greco's intimate portraits of the suffering of the crucified Christ is a primary example.

In addition, Teresa's life and writings helped to restore many of the religious institutions of Spain. In 1617 the Spanish parliament named her the Patroness of Spain. In 1622 Pope Gregory XV proclaimed her a saint.

The Life of
Teresa

1515	Birth.
1538	Enters the Carmel of Avila.
1563	Opens reformed Carmelite convent of St. Joseph.
1565	Writes *The Way of Perfection*.
1577	Begins work on *The Interior Castle*.
1582	Death.

The town walls of Avila, Spain, home town of Teresa.

Teresa of Avila

and Catholic Mysticism

Caroline T. Marshall

Renaissance Spain

The Spain into which Teresa of Avila was born in 1515 was violent and restless, expansive and wealthy. Less than twenty-five years earlier, Isabelle, the Catholic queen of Castile, and her husband, Ferdinand of Aragon, had completed the seven-hundred-year-old reconquest of Christian Spain. Moors and Jews were expelled. At the same time, the royal couple had, by their sponsorship of exploration, initiated the expansion of Spain overseas.

The intense religious nationalism of the Reconquesta dominated Spanish culture for centuries thereafter. Its most signifi-

cant expressions in Teresa's lifetime were a prolonged struggle against the Protestant Reformation and the effort to Christianize Spain's new American colonies. The rulers of Teresa's Spain, Charles V, Holy Roman emperor, and Philip II, king of Spain, were deeply committed to the defeat of the Protestants and to the restoration of the one Catholic faith in Europe. Teresa of Avila was equally devoted to those causes.

She was the daughter of Alonso de Capeda and Beatriz de Ahumada. Her father was not noble, but succeeded in marrying his children into the upper classes. They were a deeply religious

Bernini's famous sculpture of the "Ecstasy of Saint Teresa", Rome.

family. Indeed, Teresa shared all the religious enthusiasms of her age. As a child she attempted to escape, with her young brother, to the Holy Land; there they hoped to be martyred by the Turks. Thwarted by her family, she continued to play at religious games in which she was the heroine.

Teresa's youth
Teresa was educated at home under the guidance of her father, but unlike many young ladies of her class, was not taught Latin. At sixteen she was sent to Our Lady of Grace, an Augustinian convent, in order to complete a finishing school education. While there she was deeply touched by the lives of the nuns but did not immediately contemplate entering a convent. On the other hand, marriage did not appeal to her. The times required that she choose one or the other. She chose the convent but remained confused about her choice. Ultimately, this lack of true vocation led her to become quite ill.

Finally, a relative presented Teresa with a copy of the *Letters* of Jerome of Bethlehem, the fourth-century patriarch who had been deeply interested in the lives of Christian women. Jerome's strong advocacy of the monastic life for women inspired Teresa to begin again. Her health improved.

Carmel of Avila
In 1538 she entered the Carmel of Avila, but the relaxed rule of the Carmelites offended her. In their lives she encountered practices that were alarming and disappointing. She fell ill again in 1539, still distressed and unsure of her religious calling. Above all, she was disappointed in her prayer life.

After a prolonged sickness that almost led to her death, Teresa was introduced to the *Third Spiritual Primer*, by Francisco de Osura, a Franciscan. De Osura followed a tradition of Christian mysticism that had been deeply influenced by the Sufi mystics of Islam. In this system emphasis is placed on prayer in which the worshiper detaches himself from every-

thing except God. A sort of spiritual intuition, which is combined from memory, will, and understanding, enables the supplicant to receive a direct experience of God, who then illumines the soul with knowledge of Himself. De Osura's inspiration was to be the foundation of Teresa's mystical and spiritual life. By 1540 she was ready to resume convent life. However, she was partly paralyzed. For twelve more years she struggled to achieve that perfect love of God that would set her free from illness and uncertainty.

Transfixion
Teresa was helped by a new Jesuit confessor (advisor) and by a new Catholic emphasis on the personal and emotional experience of God. In 1555 she saw a picture of Christ that highlighted His terrible suffering for the salvation of men. Teresa was struck to the heart with sorrow and with love. She felt she had experienced some sort of second conversion. Following this, her mystical life developed rapidly. Suddenly, the local *Index* listed her favorite mystical treatises, and she was forced to abandon them. However, she found new help in a succession of spiritual advisors, and in 1559 she had the "transfixion," an experience in which a cherub pierced her heart with an arrow, leaving Teresa with a burning love of God and an unquenchable desire for His presence.

Teresa's advanced spiritual state led her into reform. In 1563, with the blessing of Pope Paul IV, she opened the reformed Carmelite convent of St. Joseph's of Avila. There the Discalced (Shoeless) Carmelites would live under a strict rule through which Teresa sought to correct the laxness and corruption which had so upset her as a young nun. In 1562 she wrote the first draft of the *Life*, her spiritual autobiography, and in 1565 wrote *The Way of Perfection*, a guide to the mystical and contemplative life. She also initiated the expansion of her reformed convent system with the establishment of sister houses throughout Spain. In 1567 she met the most famous of her "spiritual children," John of the Cross, a mystic and a poet. John, who became a Carmelite monk, was her rival in mystical experience and her devoted helpmate in reform.

The Interior Castle

After an active life as a reformer, she settled briefly in 1577 to write an account of the higher spiritual state she had achieved since the *Life*. The result was *The Interior Castle*, her most important literary achievement and a classic of Christian mystical thought. In addition to her *Life, The Interior Castle*, and *The Way of Perfection*, Teresa wrote a constitution for her order, *The Book of Foundations*, and many other works of spiritual importance, not the least of which were her own *Letters*.

The Way of Perfection was written for Teresa's nuns. Its central theme is the salvation of souls. In it Teresa stresses her conviction that it is the primary obligation of her nuns to save the church from Protestants, especially in France. It must be noted that she did not understand the theology of the Reformers, and she badly confused Lutherans and Calvinists in her writing.

In *The Way of Perfection*, Teresa also explains the social needs of her church. She instructs the nuns not to pray for their own salvation or for the wealth and well-being of their order, but for the salvation of all men. She stresses radical poverty and declares that money and worldly rewards destroy humility, which trait is the chief characteristic of the Christian. She concludes with a teaching exercise on ways in which the Lord's Prayer may be used as a vehicle of contemplation.

In *The Interior Castle* Teresa reaches the most sophisticated level of her mystical thought. The castle is a crystal fortress composed of seven apartments. It represents Teresa's soul. In the central apartment of the fortress or castle is God Himself. Through the stages of prayer she moves through the apartment as her soul searches for the Deity. At last she progresses from vocal prayer to pure contemplation, and, as she does, her soul is united with its Maker in the heart of the castle. Thus she finds both her true self and God.

This mystical union is what she hoped for her nuns. However, as the *Life* was written for her spiritual advisor in order that he might help her spiritual progress and *The Way of Perfection* was given as practical advice for her nuns, *The Interior Castle* was written as a theological treatise. Although Teresa was untrained, *The Interior Castle* is a successful theological statement.

Blaise Pascal
1623-1662

Blaise Pascal (1623-1662) is to France what Plato is to Greece, Dante to Italy, and Shakespeare to England. The Bibliothèque Nationale in Paris guards none of its manuscripts more jealously than those of Pascal. Though he died before he was forty and suffered continually from ill-health, Pascal won a fame in the seventeenth century that is still increasing today. At the age of sixteen he began contributions to geometry, physics, applied mechanics, and mathematical theory that were of great importance. Reared as a Roman Catholic, he became a devout and committed Christian, always conscious of his sinful nature and need of the grace of the Lord Jesus.

Pascal's *Provincial Letters*, written anonymously as part of a major controversy, were described by Voltaire as "the first work of genius to appear in France." He planned to write a "Defence of the Christian Religion" but did not live to complete it; however, the notes he made for it, published after his death as Pascal's *Pensées*, are to be placed alongside such great works as Augustine's *Confessions*. The story of his life is moving, and its setting is the fascinating period of France in the Thirty Years War, the Fronde, and the beginnings of the glittering society that found its symbol at Versailles. However, his Christian faith and hope is more moving and became supremely important to him, as his *Pensées* abundantly testify.

Sculpture of Blaise Pascal by Augustin Pojou, 1785.

The Life of
Pascal

1623	Birth.
1627	Mother's death.
1651	Father's death; his sister Jacqueline enters the Convent of Port Royal.
1654	His definitive conversion experience, November 23.
1656-1657	The eighteen *Provincial Letters* appear.
1658-1662	Bad health.
1662	Death.

● Paris

France

Clermont-Ferrand ●

Blaise Pascal

Christian Thinker

Peter Toon

Precocious scholar

Born at Clermont-Ferrand of good Auvergnat stock in 1623, Blaise Pascal became a man of wealth and position by reason of parentage and a man of extraordinary scientific achievement through the use of a brilliant and precocious mind. Following the death of his mother when he was four, his father, Etienne, took him with his two sisters, Gilberte and Jacqueline, to Paris where he personally guided their education. From there the family moved to Rouen in 1639, when Etienne was appointed as royal commissioner of finance for Normandy. In this city Blaise continued the scientific interests he had already developed in Paris. His treatise on conic sections, written when he was only sixteen, was received with amazement by the scientific community; later his work on the pressure of the atmosphere, based on research he did at Rouen, was also to startle his elders.

But it was also in the cultural center of Rouen that Blaise was to experience what has been called his "first conversion," an experience that caused him to take his Catholic faith much more seriously and to do so as a "Jansenist." It happened in this way. In January 1646 his father fell down and broke his thigh. Two men were called in to care for him, and they turned out to be keen Jansenists. That is, they took the profession of Christianity seriously and followed the general teaching on grace and morality that Cornelius O. Jansen (1585-1638) had taught, arising from his profound study of Augustine of Hippo. In turn, this meant that they were opposed to the Jesuits, who appeared to them to make Christianity too easy and accessible. It also

meant that they looked to the Convent of Port Royal in Paris as the center of this teaching, for not only did it contain the nuns of this persuasion, but around it lived men who were wholly committed to Jansenism.

Conversion

Blaise was attracted to this Augustinian approach to grace and its strict view of morality, and he persuaded all the family to adopt it. Jacqueline was later to enter the Convent of Port Royal and Blaise himself to become a close friend of the community in and around the convent. Yet this "conversion" was basically to right theology, and it was not as yet a conversion of the heart to the love of God. That was to come later in Pascal's "second conversion."

The family returned to Paris in 1650, and so Blaise was able to join in the parties of polite society as well as attend the clubs of the scientists. His father died in 1651, and immediately afterwards his sister entered the Convent of Port Royal. It was around 1653 that Blaise began his earnest study of human nature. "When I began the study of man I found that the abstract sciences were not suited to humanity, and that I was drifting further from my proper condition by my knowledge than other men were by their ignorance....I did at least expect to find companions in the study of man....but there I was mistaken. Even fewer study human nature than those who study geometry....They may be right. May it not be better for a man's happiness that he should not know himself?" But he did pursue this study, as his observations and comments in the *Pensées* reveal.

Panorama of Clermont-Ferrand, France, birthplace of Blaise Pascal.

Second conversion

While his own fame as a savant increased, Pascal also felt a deep spiritual hungering after the reality behind the doctrine and morality of Jansenist Catholicism. His scientific achievements and inventions (including the first calculating machine) did not satisfy him. Then on November 23, 1654, he experienced his "second conversion." His account, written immediately afterwards and always carried around by him, begins in this way: "From about half-past ten in the evening until about half-past twelve....FIRE....God of Abraham, God of Isaac, God of Jacob, not of the philosophers and savants. Certitude. Certitude. Feeling. Joy. Peace. God of Jesus Christ. My God and Thy God. 'Thy God shall be my God'...." In a mystic vision, there was revealed to him in a light of fire the living God, who purged him of his sins and brought him assurance, joy, peace, and love. Henceforth he knew that he must live for God and for God alone; to Him everything else must take second place. His life-style changed, and he gave much more to the poor. His scientific studies were not abandoned, but they took second place. He became a man who lived for fellowship with God.

Pascal maintained his contacts with the men and women of Port Royal and shared many thoughts with his sister there. In loyalty to them, he rose to the defense of a leading Jansenist, Antoine Arnauld (1612-1694), who had been condemned by the Sorbonne in 1655. At the request of the members of Port Royal he not only defended Arnauld but moved on, in his eighteen *Provincial Letters* (1656-1657), to criticize the moral teaching and advice given to penitents by the Jesuits. The *Letters*, published anonymously in order to avoid imprisonment, were not only brilliant in argument but also in French literary style; they are prized as a leading example of French prose at its best. Pascal's sister, Gilberte, provides an insight into the reasons for his admirable style: "He had a natural eloquence which gave him a marvellous facility for saying what he wanted to say, but to this he added certain rules which he had worked out for himself, which served him so well that not only could he say what he meant to say but he would say it in the very manner of his choice, and so that his discourse produced just the effect he intended." Even Voltaire, who disliked Pascal's theology, had to agree with this evaluation of his ability.

The *Pensées*
Toward the end of his life, Pascal's great interest was to produce an "Apology for the Christian Faith," which would speak directly to the agnostics and atheists of Paris and Rouen, whom he knew well. This would not be of the traditional intellectual type, based on various arguments for the existence of God and of logical structure. Instead, he would use proofs drawn from morality and history in order to appeal to the heart and to personal experience. He would place before his readers an accumulation of probabilities, independent of each other, that would by their total, general impression point to the existence of the living God and truth of the Catholic religion. So he wrote down his mature thoughts on a variety of topics and kept the papers by him, ready for the time when they would form the material for the "Apology."

Regrettably that time never came. When he died, Pascal left behind nearly 1,000 fragmentary writings alongside his finished treatises on the weight of air and the equilibrium of liquids. From these fragmentary writings various editors, with differing degrees of accuracy, have produced editions of them known as the *Pensées*. As French literature, they are highly valued by the French as an example, perhaps the best example, of the French genius. As personal confession and experience they rank alongside Augustine's *Confessions* as one of the great Western books on Christian spirituality. Here is an example of one thought: "Every religion is false which, as to its faith, does not worship one only God as the origin of all things, and, to its morality, does not worship one only God as the goal of all things" (No. 478).

There is much in the *Pensées* that can

only be appreciated against the background of his "second conversion" when he came to know God in his heart. "The heart has its reasons which reason does not know." "Reason acts slowly and with so many views, on so many principles, which it must aways keep before it, that it constantly slumbers and goes astray from not having its principles to hand. The heart does not act thus; it acts in a moment, and is always ready to act. We must then place faith in the heart or it will always be vacillating." "We know truth, not only by the reason but also by the heart, and it is from this last that we know first principles" (Nos. 278, 252, 282).

The God of miracles
Another important factor in his approach was his belief that God does really perform miracles. This was confirmed for him by the miraculous healing of his niece in 1656 from a lachrymal tumor. When this was touched by a spine from what was believed to be the crown of thorns of Jesus, healing began immediately, and no scientist could offer any naturalistic explanation. The God whom he portrays is thus the God of miracles, especially of the great miracle of the resurrection.

Pascal's scientific achievements had much to do with rigorous experimentation, leading to experimental knowledge; and his great thoughts have also much to do with experience, the experience of the heart before the living God. Pascal, who loved the truth above all else, looked beyond truth to the source of truth, even to God Himself, the source of wisdom and knowledge, the One who orders all things and of whom and through whom all things proceed and to whom they return.

John Owen
1616-1683

John Owen (1616-1683) became the outstanding theologian of those who espoused the "Congregational Way" in seventeenth-century England; also he was among the most learned and active of those who expounded and defended Reformed, Calvinistic theology in Europe. For both these reasons, he was used by Oliver Cromwell during the period of the English Civil War and especially in the period of the Protectorate, when he held senior positions in Oxford University and advised Cromwell on national affairs.

However, with the return of the monarchy in 1660, Owen had to leave Oxford. He then became pastor of a gathered, Congregational church in London. There he devoted much time to the production of books that helped secure his reputation as a great British theologian. He wrote a massive exposition of the letter to the Hebrews, defenses of orthodox theology, treatises on such topics as the Holy Spirit, and practical works dealing with the growth of holiness in the believer. His collected works are a theological treasure house for those who are willing to make a determined effort to master his demanding literary style.

Engraving of John Owen, Congregationalist theologian.

The Life of
Owen

1616	Birth.
1628-1637	Queen's College, Oxford.
1637	Adopted into the Church of England.
1643	Vicar of Fordham, Essex.
1646	Adopts the Congregational Way.
1649-1651	Chaplain with Cromwell's armies.
1651-1660	At Oxford University.
1660-1683	Nonconformist minister.
1683	Death.

England

Oxford • Coggeshall •

John Owen

Puritan Theologian

Peter Toon

Congregationalist Puritan

The son of a clergyman, John Owen studied at Queen's College, Oxford, taking his B. A. in 1632 and M.A. in 1635. By that time he had acquired a thorough training in the Greek and Latin classics and so could pursue the study of theology. He did that in a university where an English form of Arminianism (high-church Arminianism) was the dominant theology. Owen's sympathies were in a different direction – toward Augustine and the theology of Calvin and the English Reformers of the sixteenth century. After ordination, he left the university to become a chaplain in private homes, before he was offered the parish of Fordham, Essex, in 1643. His first book, *A Display of Arminianism*, also appeared at that time. Owen had nailed his colors to the mast: in the struggle between king and Parliament he had chosen to support the latter; and in the controversy between Reformed and Arminian theology he had chosen to accept the former.

His next step was to adopt the Congregational Way as the biblical form of church polity. Thus his aim became to purify the national church by the Word of God and encourage the creation of gathered congregations in every parish. He was a Congregationalist (in contrast to a Presbyterian) Puritan; but he longed to see all the Puritans cooperating to find a way to defeat the king's armies and to settle the question of the religion of the national church, to which structure he was committed.

From Fordham Owen moved to Coggeshall, also in Essex, in 1648 where he put his principles into practice and formed a gathered church in the parish.

But his stay in Coggeshall was soon interrupted by calls to act as chaplain with the Parliamentary armies, and so he went with them first to Ireland and then to Scotland. Following those expeditions and the defeat of the royalist cause, he was sent by Oliver Cromwell to bring godliness, good order, and learning to Oxford University.

Cromwell's advisor

So began in 1651 the busiest period of Owen's life, when he was wholly involved not merely in the affairs of Oxford University but also in national affairs, as a trusted advisor to Cromwell. He had the vision of a nation seeking after godliness and a national church accommodating within its parishes godly and learned men of both Congregational and Presbyterian principles, teaching the nation the content of the gospel. He sought to put into effect plans for the reform of the university and the national church, but time was too short to accomplish what he desired.

Following the death of Oliver Cromwell, the short rule of his son, Richard, and the return of Charles II to England, Owen was removed from the Deanery of Christ Church. He joined nearly 2,000 other Puritan ministers in leaving the ministry of the national church (which now became Episcopalian again) in order to become Protestant Nonconformists/ Dissenters.

During the remaining twenty-three years of his life, Owen served as a Nonconformist pastor, worked diligently for the improvement of the lot of ejected ministers, and produced an array of top-class theological literature. It is for the latter that Owen is remembered. There were

Queen's College, Oxford, John Owen's *alma mater*.

books written in defense of classic Christian orthodoxy (for example on the Trinity, 1669), in defense of the principles of Nonconformity and Congregationalism and against the conformity required within the national church, and in the defense of Protestantism and against Roman Catholicism.

The books, however, that show his own deep spirituality and grasp of both biblical and historical theology are those that expound the Scriptures (commentaries on Psalm 130 and the letter to the Hebrews), set forth the working of the Holy Spirit upon Christ and within the people of God (discourse on the Holy Spirit), explain the state of the sinful soul and its need for holiness and communion with God, and provide meditations upon the glory of the exalted Lord in heaven.

Once Owen had come to clear views on the nature of the gospel and of the church, he steadfastly held to those views. Adherence to them first brought him high positions between 1649 and 1660 and then caused him to be among the despised and maltreated Nonconformists until his death. Throughout his ministry he actively opposed Arminian, Socinian, and Catholic "errors" and wholeheartedly commended the Reformed faith, which for him was much more than a sound systematic doctrine. It was a way of life in humble dependence upon the sovereign grace of God, mortifying sin and seeking to be holy; and it was a way of life that included the fellowship of the saints within the gathered church. Though he married twice (Mary Rooke in 1644; Dorothy D'Oyley in 1676), he left no children, and his name has been passed on solely through his writings.

Theologian's theologian

Regrettably Owen has never gained that position in literature to which his learning and abilities entitle him. In comparison with other, less able, seventeenth-century writers, he has been neglected. This is because his style, in contrast to the lively style of Richard Baxter and John Bunyan, is heavy and not easy to follow. Thus he

Statue of Oliver Cromwell outside Westminster Hall, London.

has become very much the theologian's theologian rather than a theologian of the people.

The fullest description of John Owen provided by someone who knew him is by Robert Asty in his brief *Memoir* published in 1721. He writes:

As to his person, his stature was tall, his visage grave and majestic and withal comely: he had the aspect and deportment of a gentleman, suitable to his birth. He had a very large capacity of mind, a ready invention, a good judgment, a great natural wit which, being improved by education, rendered him a person of incomparable abilities. As to his temper he was very affable and courteous, familiar and sociable: the meanest persons found an easy access to his converse and friendship. He was facetious and pleasant in his common discourse, jesting with his acquaintance but with sobriety and measure: a great master of his passions especially that of anger; he was of a serene and even temper, neither elated with honor, credit, friends or estate, nor depressed with troubles and difficulties.

Surviving portraits confirm his majestic appearance; his natural wit is more obvious in his personal letters (see *Correspondence*) rather than his published books. His serene and even temper well fitted him for the intellectually demanding task of theological reflection and writing.

John Bunyan
1628-1688

John Bunyan (1628-1688) was an English Puritan author and preacher best known for his allegory of the Christian life *The Pilgrim's Progress* which remains a classic of Christian popular literature. Among his approximately fifty other books are his conversion narrative, *Grace Abounding to the Chief of Sinners*; the semi-fictional dialogue, *The Life and Death of Mr. Badman*; *The Holy War*, another allegory of salvation; and a collection of children's poems,

A Book for Boys and Girls. Because he was imprisoned for twelve years for refusing to stop preaching, after the Restoration of Charles II, he is at once a sign of the extent to which Puritan ideas penetrated to the less educated, much to the discomfiture of the establishment. He is also a representative of the new, less political, Nonconformity that succeeded Puritanism toward the end of the seventeenth century.

Bunyan's direct, even fierce, accounts of Christian experience mingle biblical theology and imagery with a vigorous folk idiom. Characters like Mr. Valiant-for-Truth and Mr. Worldly Wiseman, and images like the Slough of Despond and the House Beautiful retain their power, even if *The Pilgrim's Progress* is no longer as current in Nonconformist circles as it once was.

Statue of John Bunyan, Bedford, England.

The Life of

Bunyan

1628	Birth in Elstow, near Bedford, England.
1644-1647	In Parliamentary army, but sees no active service.
1653	Becomes member of Bedford congregation.
1656	First of 59 books.
1658	Death of first wife.
1659	Marries Elizabeth.
1660	Imprisoned for preaching.
1666	*Grace Abounding to the Chief of Sinners*.
1672	Appointed pastor of the Bedford Nonconformist church; released from prison.
1676	Imprisoned for six months.
1678	*The Pilgrim's Progress*.
1680	*The Life and Death of Mr. Badman*.
1682	*The Holy War*.
1684	The second part of *The Pilgrim's Progress*.
1688	Death in London.

England

• Elstow

London •

John Bunyan

and The Pilgrim's Progress

Roger Pooley

Mechanic preacher

John Bunyan was born in Elstow, near Bedford, in 1628. His education was meager, like that of many "mechanic preachers" thrown up by the Puritan movement at the height of its influence. Perhaps his real education began in 1644, at the age of sixteen, when he was mustered to the Parliamentary army to garrison Newport Pagnell. Though he saw no action, he was part of the regiment of Sir Samuel Luke, where listening to preaching was common.

Bunyan's real religious crisis, as described in *Grace Abounding*, did not begin until the 1650s, when he was working as a tinker. Helped by the converted Royalist John Gifford, pastor of the Bedford congregation (at that time part of the Cromwellian state church), he felt called to the lay ministry and brought out his first book in 1656, a defense of the Incarnation against the new Quaker group. In 1659 he remarried, a year after his first wife, whose name we do not know, but whose

dowry of two books of popular piety is recorded in *Grace Abounding*, died.

Other books followed, but in 1660, with the restoration of Charles II, he was arrested by a zealous magistrate and spent twelve years in jail for refusing to stop preaching. Shortly before his release (his imprisonment was not continuously severe) in 1672 Bunyan was called to be pastor of the Bedford church, which we must view as Nonconformist rather than Puritan.

Puritanism

Puritanism was, in essence, a movement for "a more godly thorough Reformation" in the English church and English society, beginning essentially in 1560 and briefly victorious in the 1640s and 1650s. But after the Restoration the Clarendon Code of the 1660s (which effectively ejected from the Church of England Puritan clergy who refused to conform to the Prayer Book) meant that their doctrines and their largely anti-episcopal and anti-hierarchical church structures could only be carried on in a minority church of uncertain legal status. And of course Puritanism as a political force – an extremely radical one in its last days – was virtually finished.

The village green, Elstow, Bunyan's birthplace.

Inset: The Moot Hall, Elstow; today devoted to a Bunyan museum.

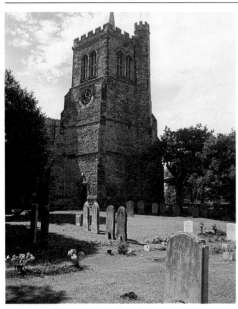
The belfry, Elstow abbey church.

Although their doctrines were similar, John Bunyan refers to the Puritans in the past tense in *Mr. Badman*, and in any case there was a less political and apocalyptic cast to the movement in Bunyan's later years. *The Holy War* contains many battle scenes around the town of Mansoul, but there is no call for another New Model Army to arise. Bunyan became well-known as a preacher in London – still a center of loyalty to Puritan ideas – as well as Bedford from this time on, and especially after the success of *The Pilgrim's Progress*. In 1688 he died in London as the result of a fever caught during a journey attempting to reconcile a father and son.

The Pilgrim's Progress
Bunyan's major contribution to Christianity can be summed up in three words, *The Pilgrim's Progress*. Bunyan had been writing, mostly sermon treatises and poems, for about twenty years when the first part of his masterpiece appeared in 1678. Immediately it was clear to him and his audience that he had found something special, an allegory of the Christian life that incorporated the Reformation emphases on justification by faith and the

Bible's availability to all, yet which had the vigour and immediacy of the folk tale. Huckleberry Finn's verdict – "interesting, but tough" – catches it exactly.

In a journey from the City of Destruction to the Celestial City, the man Christian meets many obstacles, from the recognizably hostile like Apollyon to the subtle threats of the false pilgrims whose doctrine is misleading and whose homes are "as empty of religion as the white of an egg is of savour." But there can never be compromise in "the wilderness of the world;" all he meets is either help or hindrance, and "there is a way to hell, even from the gates of heaven."

Grace Abounding
The fierce Puritan either/or viewpoint that structures *The Pilgrim's Progress* is not the rule-bound moralism of popular caricature. In fact Bunyan attacks those of the Anglican establishment in his day – satirized in the figure of Mr.Worldly Wiseman – whom he saw as reducing Christianity to ethical precepts. *Grace Abounding to the Chief of Sinners* (1666), Bunyan's spiritual autobiography, describes how he arrived at such a position. In some ways it follows the pattern of many Puritan conversion narratives; he is convicted of sin and attempts to appease God and his conscience by "legal righteousness" (religious observances without a true dependence on Christ). But he is thrown into despair and, finding most who offer advice strangers "to much combat with the devil," goes through an agonized, long-drawn-out period of temptation before finding some assurance of salvation by reading Luther on Galatians and grasping the message of John 6:37.

Like most Puritans, Bunyan read the Bible through the eyes of Paul, and the contrast between the terrors of the law and the freedom and joy brought by grace is complete. Texts from the Bible fall with a palpable "weight" on Bunyan's mind; indeed its effect on Bunyan's imagination led C.H. Spurgeon to conclude that his blood was "Bibline." Modern readers might find elements of neurosis in the account, for instance in Bunyan's fear that the bell of Elstow church would fall on him as a punishment for his un-Christian delight in bellringing. But this should serve to emphasize Bunyan's heroism, rather than to dismiss him as abnormal; and it certainly points to one of the key themes in his work, the importance of fear.

Godly fear

Fearful, a character in Part II of *The Pilgrim's Progress*, has "the heart of the matter" in him, and in the impressive ending to Part II, where the pilgrims cross the river of death, Much-Afraid "went through the river singing." In one of his less well-known works, *A Treatise of the Fear of God* (1679), Bunyan draws a distinction between godly fear, which causes one to rely entirely on God for salvation, and slavish fear, which causes one to doubt God. Part of the genius of *The Pilgrim's Progress* is the way that Bunyan manages to give physical reality to psychological states; and so in Doubt-

ing Castle the pilgrims are fiercely beaten with a club by Giant Despair before they escape with the key of Promise.

In general there is more danger to the pilgrims in Part I than in Part II (1684), where Christian's wife, Christiana, journeys with her friend Mercy and a number of others in Christian's footsteps. Part II has even been characterized, rather unkindly, as a church outing because of its collective, even leisurely mode. But this change may reflect that Part I is based on Bunyan's own conversion experience in the early 1650s and his experience of religious persecution in the 1660s; whereas Part II may come from a growing feeling of assurance, fellowship, and security in his later Christian life.

The original follow-up to the first part of *The Pilgrim's Progress* was *The Life and Death of Mr. Badman* (1680), a dialogue between Wiseman and Attentive, narrating the fall of a comprehensive sinner. It is much more episodic than *The Pilgrim's Progress*, with stories from popular compendia about the judgment of

Half-timbered cottages in the village of Elstow, Bedfordshire.

John Bunyan's tomb, Bunhill Fields, London.

God on sinners interspersed with the main narrative. But literary critics have seen it as more influential for the development of prose fiction than were Bunyan's more strictly allegorical works. And it contains some forthright statements about social ethics, particularly honesty in trading, a sensitive issue for Bunyan's congregation.

The Holy War

The Holy War (1682) is Bunyan's attempt at an epic, a history of the salvation, apostasy, and restoration of the town of Mansoul. There is a richness of invention and structural precision about the book, though it is less immediately personal than his other imaginative works. Bunyan's poems are also important; though even the best-known, such as "Who Would True Valour See," are not in the same league as those of George Herbert (1593-1633) or those of John Donne (1573-1631).

Bunyan's *Book for Boys and Girls*, later known as *Divine Emblems* (1686), is important for the history of children's literature as one of the earliest collections of verse for children and the precursor of an eighteenth-century tradition of such collections by Christian poets such as Isaac Watts, Charles Wesley, and Philip Doddridge. Bunyan used emblems (essentially miniature allegories, images, or short narratives with explicit, worked-out moral or spiritual significance) in a number of his works, for instance in the House of the Interpreter episodes in *The Pilgrim's Progress*, but *Divine Emblems* is his most sustained, ingenious, and amusing collection. The tunes to some of them may possibly be by Bunyan – we know he played fiddle and flute though hymn singing was not permitted in his congregation.

Bunyan is representative of a flowering of popular piety, soaked in the teaching and imagery of the Bible, doctrinally sophisticated, and emotionally intense. This piety demonstrates how far down the social scale Puritanism, originally a university-inspired movement, penetrated. Bunyan demonstrates the strength of the lay leadership of early Nonconformity. But examples of his kind of strength under persecution, even his ability to construct a sophisticated religious treatise without benefit of much formal education, could be multiplied. However, *The Pilgrim's Progress* is a unique synthesis. Its central image, with many resonances in the Bible, particularly the Exodus story, also has a provenance in the popular romances which, Bunyan confesses, were once his favorite reading. Bunyan knew the hostility of the real-life Judge Hategoods, yet he could also twit the religious hypocrites with ironic humour. And, like many of the great Christian writers of the period, he constructs a distinctively Christian heroism that is vulnerable, prone to mistakes, and yet ultimately victorious through grace.

George Fox
1624-1691

George Fox was the leader of a seventeenth-century Christian awakening from which came the Quaker movement (now known as the Society of Friends or the Friends Church). Beginning in England at the time of the Civil War between Royalist and Parliamentary forces, the movement spread rapidly across England and the American colonies, in spite of harassment under Commonwealth and Restoration governments that brought property loss, imprisonment, and death. By the end of the century, there were 100,000 Quakers, an American colony (Pennsylvania), and a strong public witness to Christian holiness, peace, religious freedom, business integrity, and social justice.

Many early adherents were drawn from Seeker communities of northern England. Those Christians, disillusioned with monopolistic state religion, whether Catholic, Anglican, Presbyterian, or Independent, had been meeting informally for Bible study and prayer. George Fox (1624-1691) forcefully articulated their criticism of the institutional church for its second-hand faith, sin-excusing doctrines, hireling ministry, and ecclesiastical compromise with political powers. They responded eagerly to his prophetic proclamation of a new Day of the Lord, in which the true church is recovered and kingdom righteousness effected through Christ's power.

After the Toleration Act of 1689 granted limited freedom to Quakers, the movement gradually took shape as a denomination. Quakers share the Puritan legacy with Baptists, Congregation-alists, and Presbyterians. In 1986 approximately 350,000 persons (half of them African) identified themselves as Quakers.

George Fox, founder of the Quakers.

The Life of

Fox

1624	Birth at Fenny Drayton, in the English Midlands.
1643	Leaves home to engage in religious search.
1647	Spiritual awakening and beginning of itinerant ministry.
1652	Pendle Hill vision of the gathered church.
1655-1657	Meetings with Oliver Cromwell to urge religious liberty.
1660	First official Quaker peace statement; Restoration.
1664-1666	Imprisonment, Scarborough Castle (longest of eight).
1667-1668	Reorganization of the churches shattered by persecution.
1669	Marriage to Margaret Fell.
1671-1673	American visits to Quaker families and meetings.
1674	Imprisonment and serious illness, Worcester and London.
1677-1678	Travels in Europe.
1691	Death in London.
1694-1706	Publication of Fox's *Journal* and other doctrinal and pastoral writings.

George Fox

and the Quakers

Arthur O. Roberts

Seeker

"There is one, even Christ Jesus that can speak to thy condition." This discovery of Christ in present reality turned George Fox from frustrated seeker to joyous finder and initiated a Christian awakening in England. George was twenty-three years old at the time (1647) and already a discerning critic of his culture. When human counselors could not fill his spiritual void, he turned to Bible reading and prayer, often in the sanctuary of "hollow trees and lonesome places." On some of those occasions he received "openings," such as that attending a university does not make a minister, that the people not the steeple is the church, and that the same Spirit who inspired the Scriptures is their true interpreter.

Even as a lad, Fox had been unusually sensitive to God, having been well taught by godly parents. He remembered experiencing the "pureness" of Divine presence at the age of eleven. This vision of the world as God wants it contrasted starkly with the world of political violence and ecclesiastical hypocrisy into which he entered as a youth. He worked first as a cobbler and then as a partner with a wool and cattle dealer. His integrity brought him commercial success. But the spiritual conflict raged furiously within him until his experience of Christ brought peace.

Fox made Swarthmore Hall, Cumbria, the headquarters of his mission.

Artist E. Wehnert's view of George Fox preaching in a tavern.

From his spiritual illumination until 1652 Fox engaged in itinerant ministry, preaching at the close of Puritan meetings, or outdoors before crowds. He exhorted seekers to heed the voice of Christ within, to be honest in business, compassionate to the needy, and to share in the free ministry of the true church. Large numbers of persons were "convinced" (converted) through his preaching, and opposition intensified. Fox was thrown down church steps, beaten with sticks, and even with a brass-bound Bible. He refused to be intimidated, and his courage and physical stamina gave credibility to a central theme of his preaching: the power through Christ to live a holy life. For such preaching Fox spent six months in Derby jail. Offered release if he would accept a commission in Cromwell's army, Fox refused, saying Christ had brought him into the "covenant of peace." For this he was jailed another six months.

The Quaker movement
Historians mark 1652 as the beginning of the Quaker movement. Up desolate Pendle Hill (believed to be a haunt of demons)

George Fox climbed one day and saw "a people in white raiment, coming to the Lord." The vision signified that proclaiming Christ's power over sin would gather people to the kingdom. And it did. By 1660 there were 50,000 followers. Zealous young men and women ("the valiant sixty") joined Fox in preaching at fairs, market places, in the fields, in the jails, in the courts, and through the printing press. Gervase Benson, Edward Burrough, John Audland, Mary Fisher, Francis Howgill, and William Dewsbury gave significant ministry. Some of them had left Cromwell's army to join what James Naylor termed "the Lamb's war."

At first they called themselves "children of the Light," "publishers of Truth," or "the camp of the Lord." Gradually they came to prefer the term "Friends," in accord with Jesus' words found in John 15:14. Critics, looking at early displays of religious emotion, had dubbed them "Quakers," in response to which Fox, with more fire than tact, had bid a tormenting judge to tremble at the Word of the Lord.

The restoration of monarchy did not

bring relief from harassment as Quakers had hoped. In fact, the Clarendon Code of 1661-1665 put thousands of Quakers in prison for illegal assembly and refusing test oaths. Three were hanged in Boston for their witness to religious liberty, one a grandmother, Mary Dyer, whose statue on Boston Common testifies to the price paid for religious freedom.

George Fox

After release from prison in 1666, Fox visited British Friends to set up a system of local and regional meetings, which diffused authority in what Fox believed was the gospel order. In this way the cult of personality was resisted. In 1669 Fox married a widow, Margaret Fell. Her home in Swarthmoor had served for many years as a headquarters, and her own public ministry (including long imprisonments) added strength to the Friends. Their marriage was a loving one, and her children honored Fox and cared for him in London during his later years. During the 1670s Fox traveled extensively in Europe, the West Indies, and America, and sustained the movement through widely circulated pastoral letters and doctrinal writings. At George Fox's death in 1691, Friends numbered 100,000, mostly in England, Scotland, and the American colonies.

George Fox's personal dynamism, anointed by the Spirit, made him a powerful preacher, a penetrating seer, a gentle pastor, and occasionally a healer. He led into ministry servants such as Mary Fisher and aristocrats such as William Penn and Isaac Penington. Fox could be devastating to critics; but also persuasive, as when he pled with a burdened, tearful Cromwell, "Lay your crown at Jesus' feet!" To those who longed for a more authentic Christianity his sermons, rich in biblical metaphor and common speech, brought hope in a dark time. His oft reprinted Journal is a Christian classic, and the aphorisms of his letters continue to inspire, for example, "Truth can live in the jails," "Be valiant for Truth upon the earth and tread upon deceit," and "Keep on the mountain of holiness."

Fox's achievement

George Fox recovered to Christians a confidence in immediate revelation. Fox believed spiritual revelation had been obscured by liturgy or closeted within the Bible. The leadings of the Holy Spirit, he said, are not contrary to Christ nor to the Scriptures, which testify of Him. Persons can experience Christ. They can be guided by His Spirit, individually and corporately. They can do the will of God in the common ventures of life. They can, as Fox said, "walk cheerfully over the earth," responding sensitively to what God is saying to those whom they meet. John Woolman's ministry in quickening the Christian conscience against slavery exemplifies such trust in spiritual guidance.

George Fox restated a logos theology about Christ. In this he followed John's gospel, with its "word" and "light" metaphors for Christ. Christ is the Light who reaches all people, first in judgment of sin and then, for those who heed, in salvation from that sin and victory over it. Christ is the Word whose coming in the flesh, glorified by the passion and resurrection, confirms the inner "voice of the true shepherd." Christ died for all people and His atonement is unlimited. The early Quaker scholar Robert Barclay elaborated this theology, using the term "the universal and saving light." By refusing to separate the Christ in the heart from the Christ whose blood was shed on Calvary, Quakers walked a narrow road between a doctrine of universalism, which renders Jesus' death unnecessary, and a doctrine of election, which renders it arbitrary. Joseph John Gurney restated this theology in the nineteenth century, but the road proved slippery for Quakers. A major separation occurred, the group following Elias Hicks emphasizing the inward, and the group following Gurney emphasizing the outward, manifestations of Christ.

George Fox taught the sanctifying power of Christ's atonement. It seemed to

A contemporary satirical print of a seventeenth-century Quakers' meeting.

the Quakers that an overemphasis upon grace turned Christ's death into what William Penn scorned as "a securer way of sinning then before, because at his cost." Fox said Christian leaders promise to "build up Adam and Eve's fallen house and when they have taken the people's money tell them it cannot be done." This teaching about victory over sin included both an inward change of the heart and an outward change in actions. Christians are to live by the ethics of Christ's kingdom, not waiting for a better situation or

the Second Coming. This emphasis upon practical holiness prompted in Quakers a confidence in Christian leavening. They initiated certain reforms, such as the just price in commerce, equitable banking, just dealings with the Indians, and remedial actions on behalf of the mentally-ill, war victims, and the oppressed.

George Fox challenged the church to reclaim its pacifism. Christians do not kill, Fox said, because Christ takes away the occasion for war. Neither evangelism nor social order requires a military shield.

Bedroom, Swarthmore Hall, Cumbria.

Covenant church. The church is the people of God, not the building in which they worship. Although Quakers distinguished between the general ministry of all Christians and the particular ministry of some, they expected meetings for worship to be open and participatory, with messages voiced by men or women upon whom the Lord laid the burden of message-bearing. For them, as for earlier and later seekers, silence is a means of centering down to hear the voice of Christ in their midst.

In company with Baptists such as Roger Williams, Fox asserted that the kingdom is hindered by state control and priestly hierarchy. Fox and his followers respected God's witness to persons outside Christendom, such as the American Indian, believing that missionary proclamation is truly "good news" when it honors that inward Light in everyone. George Fox believed faithful witness to the kingdom by word and deed would speed the gathering of the world's peoples to Christ. The colony of Pennsylvania stands as an historic seed plot for the peaceable kingdom, so artistically portrayed by the painter Edward Hicks.

Puritan piety had asserted that God puts the sword of Reformation into soldiers' hands. They drew parallels between Cromwell's cause and ancient Israel's. The Quakers denounced this as apostate Christianity. Fox and other Quakers drew up this 1660 Declaration, a public statement of Christian pacifism: "The spirit of Christ, which leads us into all Truth, will never move us to fight and war against any man with outward weapons, neither for the kingdom of Christ, nor for the kingdoms of this world." Quakers have not always found it easy to live by it (or to suffer for it), but this statement embodies a central Christian conviction, shared historically with persons in the Anabaptist traditions and increasingly by others also.

George Fox reemphasized the church's witness to the kingdom. Christ is present with His people in worship and in work, baptizing them with His Spirit. Outward sacraments (special holy means) belong to pre-Christian times, not to the New

Philipp Jakob Spener
1635-1705

Philipp Jakob Spener (1635-1705) has often been singled out as the founder of German Pietism. His *Pia Desideria* (Pious Longings) became the manifesto of the Pietist movement. First published in 1675, the volume advocates a program of six principles to reform the lifeless Protestantism only too evident to Spener's sensitive spirit. The influence of the little book extended far beyond the confines of the author's homeland.

First there is a plea for regular Bible study on the part of laity and clergy alike. This, reinforced by regular fasting and prayer, became the hallmark of Pietism.

Second, there is a renewed stress on the priesthood of all believers, which is the ideology underlying the *collegia pietatis* (house-group).

Third was Spener's emphasis on true faith, consisting not in intellectual assent to creeds and formulae, but in active deeds of love: faith manifesting itself in works.

Fourth, Pietism had an ecumenical thrust. Spener saw his ideas helping to break down the ecclesiastical barriers between the Lutheran and Reformed churches, cutting through the "territorialism" of the Reformation settlement and putting an end to arid theological controversy.

Fifth, Spener pleaded for an entire reshaping of the ministry and a recovery of the sense of clerical vocation. Pastors, thoroughly trained themselves, should undertake their duties in their parishes with great seriousness, establishing schools where the young would be taught the catechism and be led to confirmation. The deepening of the spiritual life through devotional literature was to be the basis of such a program.

Finally, Spener pleaded for a rediscovery of "vital" preaching that should cut to the heart, inspire repentance, kindle faith, and so lead to consecrated service.

Founded largely on these six principles, the Pietistic movement was to mark the life of Christian churches, not only in Spener's Germany, but in many other lands.

The Life of
Spener

1635	Birth in Alsace.
1666-1668	Ministers in Frankfurt-am-Main.
1675	Publication of *Pia Desideria*.
1686	Chaplain of the elector of Saxony in Dresden.
1691	Rector of the Nicolaikirche in Berlin.
1698	Renounces all controversy.
1705	Death.

Philipp Jakob Spener

and Pietism

Ian Sellers

Spiritual deadness

Philipp Jakob Spener was born to pious parents in Rappoltsweiler, Alsace, in 1635. He lived during the age of Protestant scholasticism in the Lutheran world, when a cold, dry formalism often reigned and the church had sometimes become little more than a department of state. At the University of Strasbourg, where he was a student, Spener revolted against this spiritual deadness and tried to rediscover for himself the springs of genuine Christian piety.

He ministered first of all in Strasbourg and then (after 1667) in Frankfurt am Main. There he founded among the laity a number of *collegia pietatis* or house groups for the deepening of the spiritual life. In 1675 he set out his views very clearly in his tract *Pia Desideria*. When some of his groups, to Spener's dismay, seceded from the church, he became the object of suspicion and mild persecution.

In 1686 Spener removed to Dresden as chaplain to the elector of Saxony. Again controversy dogged his path, and in 1691 he moved to Berlin as rector of the Nicolaikirche. There he enjoyed the protection of the first king of Prussia, Frederick I, who shared many of his views. In 1698 Spener renounced all controversy and published his collected correspondence in four volumes. By the time of his death, in 1705, Pietism was firmly established in Würtemburg and in Halle, where Hermann Francke (1663-1727) had founded his theological school at the new university in 1694 and published his *Pietas Hallensis* in 1701. Pietism was also evident at Berthelsdorf where under its influence Zinzendorf, Spener's godson, was led to found a Moravian community at Herrnhut. It was less securely planted at Dresden and Leipzig.

Spener was a curious character: enthusiastic, yet as ponderous as the state churches that he sought to reform; by nature timid, yet bold in his defense of his ideals; naive, yet forced to assume a political role that did not suit him. He remains one of the greatest of German Protestant leaders.

Pietism

As the Pietist movement spread, its proponents were seen as "enthusiasts," devotees of heart-religion (*Herzensreligion*) in that they stressed the awfulness of sin and the need for the conversion experience. They developed a deep love for Jesus of a mystical variety. They became distinguished, too, for their missionary zeal. From the Halle School evangelistic work was begun first among the Jews. Then in 1705, under the auspices of the Halle-Danish mission, the first two missionaries departed for the Far East. Later Henry Mühlenberg (1711-1787) sailed to North America to reorganize the churches in that continent. The Moravians in particular drew from Pietism a vision of a world to be won for Christ. Again Pietism encouraged a revived interest in the second advent and the Millennium, an emphasis not unconnected with its missionary zeal.

Pietism became noted also for its hymnwriters (though never particularly for its preachers): the hymns of Paul Gerhardt (1607-1676), Joachim Neander (1650-1680), and Gerhard Tersteegen (1697-1769) whether in German or in English translation, became one of the most precious legacies to the church.

Finally, the Pietist stress on good works took positive form in the founding at Halle of the famous orphanage. Other beloved institutions followed, here and elsewhere throughout the German states. These ranged from workhouses for the unemployed, shelters for unmarried mothers, hospitals and dispensaries, to homes for the deaf, dumb, blind, and mentally ill. To Spener, social work (*Fürsorge*) and the "cure of souls" (*Seelsorge*) were complementary.

Two controversies surrounding Pietism concern its origins and its impact on subsequent developments. Some historians would argue that Pietism really began among the Reformed rather than the Lutheran churches: it was mediated to Germany from Holland through the influence of Theodore Unterlyk and from Switzerland, where the youthful Spener paid a visit to Jean de le Badie (1610-1674) and came away deeply impressed. Nor should the influence on Spener of English Puritan writings, especially Lewis Bayly's *Practice of Piety*, be overlooked.

Other historians would emphasize that Pietism was not only a reaction against formalized state religion but a world-weary response to the horrors of the Thirty Years War (1618-1648), which had left Germany devastated. Others would point to its evocation of many of the features of medieval piety, for example a particular devotion to the wounds of Jesus, taken up by Moravians and passed on by them to Methodists. Pietism could then be seen as a regressive movement, a retreat from modernity, which was the argument of Albrecht Ritschl (1822-1889) in his *History of Pietism* (1880-1886). Perhaps, like Methodism, it should be seen as the product of several different forces operating in different places over widely differing periods of time.

Philipp Jakob Spener.

Pietism and the Enlightenment
Similar arguments surround the fruits of the Pietist movement, its contribution to German and, indeed, European history. In so far as Pietism had passed its peak by 1750, its mantle having fallen on the shoulders of Methodists and Moravians, its connection with the rationalist Enlightenment of the latter half of the eighteenth century is a fascinating problem. There certainly was a connection, but whether the Enlightenment arose out of Pietism or, as is more likely, in reaction to it, remains a moot point.

Pietism enjoyed a marked revival in the Napoleonic period in Germany, and it spilled over in later years into other lands. It inspired the work of the Haldane brothers in Scotland and of the Monods in Switzerland, and it fueled the idealism of that strangest of Russian Czars, Alexander I, and his Holy Alliance (1816). The leading German representatives of this renewed Pietism were the Baroness von Krüdener (1764-1824) and J. A. W. Neander (1789-1850), a Jewish convert to Lutheranism whose childlike religious faith made a deep impression on his contemporaries.

Nineteenth-century Pietism
Through Friedrich Tholuck (1799-1877), a pupil of Neander, whose warmth and devotional spirit Tholuck inherited, Pietism

became a marked feature of the "Old Lutheranism" of the later nineteenth century in Germany. It inspired much that was best in the evangelistic, devotional, and charitable life of the churches. But it did not align with the confessional orthodoxy and political conservatism of the "New Lutherans," whose spokesman was Ernst Hengstenberg (1802-1869), and of the liberal rationalist school, whose main exponent, Albrecht Ritschl, denounced Spener and his successors. Pietism nevertheless continued to flourish in both Germany and the Scandinavian countries, where it contributed greatly to evanelistic enterprise. Norway was especially affected, but there Pietism went back to the days of Spener and the great popular hymnwriter Hans Bronson.

Meanwhile in Britain, Pietism was an important strand in the teaching of George Müller of Brethren and orphanage fame, of the great Baptist preacher C. H. Spurgeon, of the Keswick Convention movement, and, more remotely, of William Booth and the Salvation Army.

In America, the influence of Pietism is more checkered and diffuse. It was present among the Reformed churches in the 1730s, especially in the person of Theodore Frelinghuysen (1691-1747). It influenced Jonathan Edwards and the Great Awakening, and it was a powerful force behind the holiness and revivalist movements of the nineteenth century, especially the work of Charles Finney. Many of the experiments in communitarian living also owed something to Pietism. But it was only a minor strand in the rise of fundamentalism, from which it differed in being largely postmillennial, sacramental, dedicated to social reform, and preferring devotional literature (*Erbauungsliteratur*) to systematic theology and apologetics.

In the twentieth century, Pietism fed the Pentecostal revival, and in more recent years it will be obvious that many of the characteristics of the neo-pentecostal and house church movements are basically Pietist. Spener's legacy is a long-lasting one.

The legacy of Pietism

Every movement of living faith that protests against a lifeless ecclesiastical formalism is bound on the one hand to produce in some of its followers an unbalanced emphasis, an unhealthy introversion, a contemptuous dismissal of all learning not specifically religious, and a carping, censorious spirit. But on the other hand it tends to attract more than its fair share of critics. From the first, Pietism was used as a term of abuse, and Pietists were derided as fanatics and kill-joys. The spirited attacks of literary men probably harmed them more than the heavy assaults of the theologians, such as J. Deutschmann of the Wittenberg theological faculty, who in 1695 charged Spener with heretical teaching under 283 heads.

Remarkably, the kinds of gibes targeted at Spener are still hurled at contemporary evangelicals by some of the spokesmen of the major liberalized denominations, for whom Pietism is a frightened, world-renouncing deviation, politically obtuse, morbidly introspective, and contemplating the violent end of the present world order with secret anticipation. These charges may be true of some small groups of extremists, but if mainstream evangelicals hold firmly to the Pietist inheritance of Spener and Francke, especially in their missionary and charitable concerns, they are able to bear such misinformed reproaches with equanimity.

Jonathan Edwards
1703-1758

Jonathan Edwards (1703-1758) is a key figure in the intellectual history of New England and of American theology. A person of precocious intelligence and a major Calvinist theologian and philosopher, he was converted when he was seventeen. From the time when he became pastor of the church at Northampton, Massachusetts, until his untimely death from the aftereffects of a smallpox injection, he played a dominant role in leading and guiding the Great Awakening (1735-1737, 1740-1744) and in defending historic Calvinism against the attacks of Deists and Arminians, often by using their own intellectual weapons against

them. During his ministry at Northampton, Edwards published a large number of sermons and works of practical piety, most notably *The Religious Affections* (1746).

Following disagreements with the church over, among other issues, the terms of Communion (Edwards held that the Lord's Supper was not a "converting ordinance" and that only professing Christians should attend), he became a missionary to the Indians at Stockbridge, Massachusetts, in 1750. It was there that he published *The Freedom of the Will.* In 1757 he agreed, somewhat reluctantly, to be appointed as president of the

College of New Jersey, hoping to find time to write what was to have been his *magnum opus, The History of Redemption.* But it was not to be. He died in 1758 at age fifty-five.

Jonathan Edwards is important not only for his pastoral insight, personal saintliness, and commanding intellect; he is one of only very few in the history of the church who seems to have been granted an almost perfect integration of "the heart" and "the head." His writings in expounding and defending of the evangelical and Reformed faith are of lasting value to the Christian church.

Jonathan Edwards.

The Life of

Edwards

1703	Birth; the only son of Timothy Edwards, pastor at East Windsor, Connecticut.
1720	Graduates from Yale College.
1724	Tutor at Yale.
1728	Marries Sarah Pierrepoint.
1729	Pastor of the church at Northampton, Massachusetts.
1735-1737	Active in spiritual awakening in Northampton and elsewhere in New England.
1750	Termination of the Northampton pastorate. Becomes a missionary at Stockbridge, Massachusetts.
1757	Invited to become president of the College of New Jersey.
1758	Arrives at Princeton (January); dies there (March).

Jonathan Edwards

New England Theologian

Paul Helm

Influences on Edwards

The American historian Perry Miller says justly of Jonathan Edwards that he is "the greatest philosopher-theologian yet to grace the American scene." Edwards was born into a prominent New England Puritan family in 1703 and, despite considerable intellectual isolation, showed astonishing early maturity both in making scientific observation and in philosophical speculations ("Notes on the Mind.") Some of those show a close affinity to the outlook of the British idealist philosopher George Berkeley (1685-1753), who though he lived briefly in Rhode Island, never met or influenced Edwards. ("Strictly speaking there is no proper substance but God himself.") It is probable that the similarity is partly because both Berkeley and Edwards had a common philosophical starting point: the philosophy of John Locke. Locke's writings, Edwards says, gave him more pleasure "than the most greedy miser finds, when gathering up handfuls of silver and gold, from some newly discovered treasure."

Although Locke remained a lifelong influence on Edwards, his importance is marginal in comparison with that of the Bible and of the Reformed and Puritan theologians whose writings Edwards grew up with. "However the term 'Calvinist' is in these days, amongst most, a term of greater reproach than the term 'Arminian'; yet for distinction's sake: though I utterly disclaim a dependence on Calvin, or belief in the doctrines which I hold, because he believed and taught them." Many of Edwards's more practical writings abound with approving quotations from John Flavel, Thomas Manton, John Owen, Theophilus Gale, and Samuel Rutherford. And Jonathan Edwards said of the Reformed theologian van Mastricht that his writings were better "than any other book in the world, excepting the Bible, in my opinion."

Conversion

After being educated at home he entered the Collegiate School of Connecticut (which afterwards became Yale College) in 1716, graduating in 1720. It was around this time that he was converted, remarking that as he read 1 Timothy 1:17, "There came into my soul, and was as it were diffused through it, a sense of the glory of the Divine Being; a new sense, quite different from anything I had ever experienced before... from about that time I began to have a new kind of apprehension and ideas of Christ, and the work of redemption, and the glorious way of salvation by him." From this time until his death, Edwards devoted his considerable powers to proclaiming and defending the gospel whose power he had experienced, the gospel of his Puritan and Calvinistic forbears.

After two years' further study of divinity and a short period as a supply minister in New York he became a tutor at Yale in 1724, and two years later he became a minister of the gospel at Northampton (first assisting and then, in 1729, succeeding his grandfather, Solomon Stoddard, to the pastorate). Under his powerful preaching, born out of personal sense of sin as an affront to the sovereign majesty of God and of the need of divine grace through Christ, the church at Northampton and other churches wider afield in New England were visited with revival from 1735 – "the work of God" as Edwards called it.

In several notable sermons, such as "God Glorified in Man's Dependence" and "Sinners in the Hands of an Angry God," Edwards stressed that sinners are *immediately* dependent upon God for His grace. In the wake of the excesses and disappointments of the revival, Edwards employed his analytic powers as well as his spiritual discernment to distinguish between the spurious and the beneficial, lasting effects of revival. A series of important writings, *Narrative of Surprising Conversions* (1737), *The Distinguishing Marks of a Work of the Spirit of God* (1741), *Thoughts on the Revival* (1742), culminated in *The Religious Affections* (1746). Edwards's characteristic method, drawing on the wealth of Puritan experiential divinity with which he was familiar, was to distinguish accidental from essential features of religious experience and to characterize true experience in terms of its character and fruit. In the diary of the missionary David Brainerd (1718-1747), which Edwards published in 1749 after Brainerd's early death (Brainerd was to have married one of Edwards's daughters), Edwards believed he had found an ideal case-study exhibiting precisely those features of true religion that he had highlighted in the *Religious Affections*.

The half-way covenant

Edwards's pastorate at Northampton ended in 1750, following a prolonged controversy over the qualifications for Communion. During the pastorate of his grandfather the church had adopted the "half-way" covenant position, the view that those could attend Communion who, though baptized, had made no personal profession of faith. The Lord's Supper came to be regarded as a "converting ordinance." Edwards attempted to return to the original Congregational position, according to which the church was composed of only those who were "visible saints," for Edwards saw the half-way covenant as a device for dulling the

sinner's awareness of his need of God's sovereign mercy at once. "To profess the covenant of grace, is to profess it, not as a spectator, but as one immediately concerned in the affair, as a party in the covenant professed."

Edwards's sermons do not accord with the customary idea of revival preaching. He did not rant. The sermons were carefully written-out, reasoned, doctrinal statements based upon solid biblical exegesis and with the characteristic Puritan "application" to conscience and practice. By all accounts Edwards delivered them in a dry, matter-of-fact monotone. Many of them came from the substance of his books, for example *Charity and Its Fruits*, an exposition of 1 Corinthians 13, posthumously published in 1852.

If in his preaching and church discipline Edwards strove to preserve the awareness of man's immediate dependence upon God for salvation and also to guard against psychological excess, he also wished to safeguard his immediacy from attack from another quarter, the rationalizing theology of the Arminians and of the Deists. In Edwards's judgment, both of these movements had a common, deadly effect, that of "distancing" God from human affairs in general and from the application of salvation in particular. For Arminianism made the reception of divine grace to depend upon an allegedly free choice of the human will, turning a gospel of grace into moralism. And Deism had a similar effect, claiming that the laws of nature have an inherent power or necessity. According to Deism, having set the globes in motion God retreats into the shadows.

It was wholly characteristic of Edwards that he was prepared to use philosophical argument not to establish biblical doctrine – Edwards trusted the authority of Scripture for that – but to show the reasonableness of that doctrine and to rebut philosophical objections to it. He had a confidence in the powers of human reason, which was more characteristic of the eighteenth century than of his Puritan forebears, greatly as he revered them.

New Park Street Church, Boston, U.S.A.

God at a distance, to make Him await their pleasure. "The Arminian doctrine ... concerning habits of virtue being only custom, discipline, and gradual culture, joined with the other doctrine, that the obtaining of these habits in those that have time for it, is in every man's power, according to their doctrine of the freedom of the will, tends exceedingly to cherish presumption in sinners while in health and vigor, and sends them to their utter despair, in insensible approaches of death by sickness or old age." Rather "the power, and grace, and operation of the Holy Spirit, in, or towards, the conversion of the sinner, is immediate (and not mediated by the concurring action of the will)."

But Edwards was not a fatalist. Men are accountable to God because, though they are *naturally* able to do what is good (that is, they have the necessary physical and psychological powers), they are *morally* unable (that is, they cannot bring themselves) to do what is good because of their inherently depraved nature.

The liberalizing and rationalizing theologians found an opponent armed with weapons they were used to wielding themselves.

The Freedom of the Will

Despite the considerable duties and distractions in his work among the Indians at the frontier post of Stockbridge, where he settled in 1750, Edwards found time to begin his assault on Arminianism. His most famous book, *The Freedom of the Will* (1754), was the fruit of years of sustained theological and philosophical reflection, to which his voluminous notebooks, many of them still unpublished, bear testimony. In the book Edwards uses arguments of unsurpassed, relentless power, the result of his ability to reason things out for himself, to show the logical incoherence of the idea that men have free will, the power to choose indifferently between alternatives.

If men really have the metaphysical power to choose or to refuse Christ, as they please, then they are able to hold

Original Sin

On occasion Edwards carried his philosophical defense of orthodox Calvinism to extremes. In his *The Great Christian Doctrine of Original Sin Defended* also written at Stockbridge and published posthumously (1758), Edwards argues that the imputation of Adam's sin to his posterity is not improper. For, he argues "that God does, by his immediate power, *uphold* every created substance in being, will be manifest, if we consider that their present existence is a *dependent* existence, and therefore is an *effect* and must have some *cause*; and the cause must be one of these two – either the *antecedent existence* of the same substance, or else the power of the Creator." He argues that it cannot be the antecedent existence of anything, because what is past has ceased to be, and hence cannot be the cause of anything. "Therefore the existence of created substances, in each successive moment, must be the effect of the *immediate* agency, will and power of God." God's arrangement between Adam and his posterity was no less "natural" than the idea of a continuous personal identity, since the persistence of a person through time is in reality a moment by moment new creation by God of a series of momentary individuals. Once more, Edwards insists upon the immediacy of the divine control. Yet it is hard to see how Edwards's doctrine of continuous creation is consistent either with his own causal determinism defended in *The Freedom of the Will* or with the facts of self-consciousness.

Despite the implausibility of this view it was of considerable importance for Edwards. He was the intellectual and the theologian of New England Calvinism and of the Great Awakening. Truth revealed in abstruse reflection of the metaphysics of personal identity, the immediate dependence of the soul on God, was the same truth propounded in some of his most famous words in "Sinners in the Hands of an Angry God":"The Observation from the words that I would now insist upon is this – There is nothing that keeps wicked

men at any one moment out of hell, but the mere pleasure of God. I mean his *sovereign* pleasure, his arbitrary will, restrained by no obligation, hindered by no manner of difficulty, any more than if nothing else but God's mere will, had in the least degree, or in any respect whatsoever, any hand in the preservation of wicked men one moment." Edwards's thought, whether expressed in the reason ing of a treatise or the measured language of the pulpit, was all of a piece.

Princeton

The seven years of "exile" in Stockbridge, which proved to be a period of great theological fruitfulness, were brought to an end in 1757 when Edwards received an invitation to become president of the College of New Jersey. Edwards was not attracted. "I have already published something on one of the main points in dispute between the Arminians and Calvinists; and have it in view, God willing (as I have already signified to the public), in like

Yale College, Connecticut. Edwards graduated from Yale in 1720.

manner to consider all the other controverted points." But he was persuaded. In January 1758, he moved to Princeton, but died of smallpox on March 22.

By his writings and his personal example of saintliness and his influence as a church leader Jonathan Edwards may be said to have exercised a threefold influence. His able defense of historic Calvinism held back the oncoming rationalizing and romanticizing influences in New England and to a lesser extent in the wider American theological scene. Edwards also came to be regarded as the inspiration of "New England Theology." Theologians such as Jonathan Edwards, Jr.; Joseph Bellamy; Samuel Hopkins; and Nathanael Emmons adopted a "governmental" theory of the atonement and developed a characteristic anthropology according to which holiness is the choice of the greatest good, moral character lies in the will, regenerating grace brings moral power to do what a person has physical power to do but would never otherwise do. Much of this is taken from Edwards's distinction between natural and moral ability and inability, but it is likely that the New England theologians systematized this distinction in a way that Edwards would not have wholly endorsed. That is particularly true of the Pelagianizing theology of N.W. Taylor (1786-1858), who, though claiming to be an Edwardsean, defended positions clearly contrary to those Edwards had devoted his life to maintaining.

The Princeton theology

It is interesting to note that although Edwards became the president of the College of New Jersey shortly before his death, the theology of that college (what later came to be called "Princeton theology"), although being wholly in theological harmony with Edwards's Calvinism, looked for its philosophical and metaphysical underpinnings not to Edwards but to the Scottish "Common Sense" philosophy of Thomas Reid (1710-1796), brought to the New World by John Witherspoon (1723-1794). This held to a realistic rather than idealistic view of the external world and to a view of personal identity that stressed its numerical unity through time.

A second major influence exerted by Edwards was upon British evangelical theology of his day. Edwards's long years of intellectual isolation were to some extent broken by voluminous correspondence with a number of Scottish theologians, for example John Erskine, who also sent him books. During the troubles with the church at Northampton, Edwards even expressed a willingness to emigrate and to minister in the Church of Scotland. More important, Edwards's call to prayer for revival, *A Humble Attempt to Promote Explicit Agreement and Visible Union of God's People in Extraordinary Prayer for the Revival of Religion* (1749), was widely circulated among evangelical ministers in the British Isles. Perhaps more significantly it was Edwards's *Freedom of the Will* that provided one of the means by which the spell of hyper-Calvinism, which had hung over English Particular Baptists, was broken. Andrew Fuller's *The Gospel Worthy of All Acceptation* (1784) is heavily influenced by Edwards. It is out of that emancipated circle of Baptists that William Carey was sent to India, the first modern Protestant missionary.

Finally Jonathan Edwards's writings have always exerted an influence upon those who value a robust and penetrating defense of the Reformed faith by an original and remarkable mind.

John and Charles Wesley

1703-1791; 1707-1788

than 250,000 miles in all weathers. "I offered them Christ" was his own repeated summary of his aim as he faced congregations drawn from all classes of society.

The Methodist church today, numbering more than 23,500,000 in membership, with a community of some fifty million from many countries, is in one sense the least of the Wesleys' legacies. Methodism has left its mark on the whole church and indeed much of the world.

John Wesley on horseback; the New Room, Bristol, England.

The story of Methodist origins is largely a tale of two brothers. John and Charles Wesley were together responsible, under God, for the new movement. It started as a society within the Church of England, and the Wesleys wanted it to stay like that. But soon after their deaths Methodism separated from the establishment and became a church in its own right. The name *Methodist* had first been applied to members of the Holy Club at Oxford University; it included the Wesleys and George Whitefield.

The Wesley brothers were sons of Samuel and Susanna Wesley. Their father was the Anglican rector of Epworth in Lincolnshire where they were both born. It was in May 1738 that the Wesleys each received assurance of salvation in a momentous experience of evangelical conversion. It lit the fire of evangelistic zeal in their hearts and sent them out, like Whitefield, on a mission to Britain in which they were involved until toward the close of the eighteenth century.

Charles (1707-1788) was less active after the 1750s but John (1703-1791) kept going tirelessly to the end. He had spent a lifetime in the saddle as a gospel outrider and only toward the end took to a chaise or a coach. He must have covered more

Lives of the

Wesleys

1703	June 17, birth of John Wesley.
1707	December 18, birth of Charles Wesley
1720	June 24, John Wesley at Christ Church, Oxford.
1726	March 17, John Wesley a fellow of Lincoln College, Oxford.
	June 13, Charles Wesley at Christ Church, Oxford.
1738	May 21, Charles Wesley's evangelical conversion.
	May 24, John Wesley's evangelical conversion.
1744	June 25, first Methodist conference, London.
1784	September 1, ordinations for North America.
1788	March 29, death of Charles Wesley
1791	March 2, death of John Wesley.

England

Epworth •

• Oxford
Bristol • London

John and Charles Wesley

and Methodism

A. Skevington Wood

"The world... my parish"
Visitors to Westminster Abbey in London often pause in the south choir aisle to look at a striking memorial. In the second bay approaching Poet's Corner, not far from a tablet recording the contribution of William Tyndale to Bible translation, there is a sculptured medallion showing profiles of the two Wesley brothers. Below it are inscribed some words spoken by John on his deathbed: "The best of all is God with us." Another now well-known saying – "I look upon all the world as my parish" – accompanies a reproduction of the

scene when John preached on his father's tombstone at Epworth after being refused permission to use the church. The memorial is rounded off with a proverb quoted by Charles in one of his letters: "God buries his workmen, but carries on his work."

It was A. P. Stanley, then dean of Westminster, who unveiled the tablet in 1876 and who had suggested a joint commemoration. That reflected shrewd insight. John and Charles Wesley were partners in the task of mission and in the shaping of Methodism. In his correspondence John regularly assumed that they were in harness. "My brother and I"

was his invariable expression. Their gifts were complementary. John with his genius for improvisation was the chief architect of the emerging movement. Charles was not only its songwriter but also exercised an inspirational, and at times restraining, influence, especially so far as relationships with the Church of England were concerned. Both were notably effective preachers and shared the pastoral oversight of the newly-formed societies, although John was regarded as the undisputed leader. When the early Methodists referred to "Mr. Wesley" it was him they meant.

The Wesleys were sons of the established church and themselves took Anglican orders. Their father was staunch in his allegiance, but he, like his wife, had been brought up as a Nonconformist and that strain was to be reflected in John's independent outlook. The spartan discipline of the family home left its mark on the brothers and became a feature of the Methodist societies.

Lord Soper, a veteran Methodist, preaching at Tower Hill, London.

The Old Rectory, Epworth, site of John Wesley's rescue from the fire.

Childhood

A disastrous fire destroyed the rectory in 1709 and endangered the lives of all the residents. John Wesley was the last to be snatched from the flames by two brave villagers, as his face was seen at an upstairs window. It was a scenario he never forgot. He thought of himself as "a brand plucked from the fire" (Zechariah 3:2). After his evangelical conversion he realized that he had been rescued spiritually in an even more crucial experience. When later he sat for his portrait by the artist George Vertue, a blazing house formed the background, with the text from Zechariah beneath. The latter reappeared in his self-composed epitaph when, at the age of fifty, it was feared he might die of consumption.

Charles Wesley was also rescued from the Epworth fire; as the youngest child he was the first concern of the nursemaid. But his life had almost been snuffed out before it began. He was born prematurely and seemed to be more dead than alive. He was wrapped in soft wool in the hope that he would survive which, with a

struggle, he did. Thus both brothers were aware that they had been spared for a purpose – a purpose that became clear to them when, within the space of three memorable days in 1738, they each discovered the reality of saving faith and knew that God had raised them up to do a work for Him in evangelizing Britain.

Although they were sent to different schools in London, John and Charles both studied at Oxford University. Charles entered Christ Church as John finished his course there and, with a fellowship at Lincoln College, had been appointed as a lecturer in Greek. Both were members of an earnest, questing group known as the Holy Club. Charles had been its originator, but John assumed the leadership when he returned to Oxford after serving briefly as his father's curate. The club met for Bible study, prayer, and self-examination, as well as caring for the sick, the poor, and those in prison.

Georgia

The Wesley brothers were soon to exchange the religion of a hermit for that of a frontiersman, as one writer has phrased it. In 1735 they sailed for the North American colony of Georgia. They left with high hopes of missionary success but soon came back disappointed and disillusioned. "I went to America to convert the Indians," exclaimed John, "but, oh, who shall convert me?" Without an authentic experience of salvation by grace through personal faith in Christ it was hardly to be expected that positive results would follow.

The Georgia venture had brought the Wesleys into contact with some Moravian Christians who challenged them concerning their lack of assurance of salvation. Back in England another Moravian, Peter Boehler (1712-1775), was instrumental in leading both John and Charles not only to an understanding but also even more important to actual experience of justifying faith. On Whit Sunday, May 21, 1738, after reading Luther's commentary on Galatians, Charles could testify: "I now found myself at peace with God, and rejoiced in hope of loving Christ ... I saw that by faith I stood; by the continual support of faith." Next morning he composed his conversion hymn, after meditating on Psalm 107.

Salvation!

Three days later John shared the same experience. It was at a little meeting in Aldersgate Street, London, as he listened to someone reading from Luther's preface to Romans. In classic words of his *Journal* he described what happened to him: "I felt my heart strangely warmed. I felt I did trust in Christ, Christ alone for salvation; and an assurance was given to me that he had taken away *my* sins, even *mine*, and saved *me* from the law of sin and death." John Wesley said he now had the faith of a son rather than simply that of a servant. He immediately testified to what the Lord had done for him and then went to the house where his brother was staying to announce to him jubilantly, "I believe!"

Even a rationalist such as W.E.H. Lecky has claimed that it is scarcely an

exaggeration to conclude that the scene in Aldersgate Street forms an epoch in English history. It set in motion a chain of events that was to transform the face of society. Fired by their own experience of saving grace, the Wesleys were to travel the length and breadth of the land with unquenchable zeal to offer Christ to all. Their vision and goal was nothing less than a mission to the nation. Whereas other evangelical clergy might further the cause by faithful ministry in their own parishes, the Wesleys, with Whitefield, saw the need to journey incessantly as itinerants in order that God's message for the people might reach them where they were. And, as the churches were increasingly closed to the Wesleys because their teaching was unfashionable, they resorted to the open air and preached in the fields, the market places, the parks, at the mines – indeed, wherever a congregation could be mustered. Not since the days of

Charles Wesley; the New Room, Bristol.

Wyclif and his Lollards had such a strategy been so extensively and effectively deployed.

Methodist societies

John Wesley was not only a master planner of national mission. He also devised a follow-up program that actually worked. He realized the urgent need to conserve the gains of evangelism. The Methodist societies provided the essential framework of pastoral care. "I determined by the grace of God," John declared, "not to strike one stroke in any place where I cannot follow the blow." He had found that when he failed to do that, "almost all the seed had fallen by the wayside." Unless the converts were properly nurtured he feared he might be merely "weaving a rope of sand." He was determined to leave a more permanent legacy, and the organization of Methodism was the outcome.

The basic Methodist unit, the society, was subdivided into fellowship classes and more confidential bands. The societies were gathered in circuits or preachers' rounds, which in turn were included in districts. Together they formed the Methodist connexion, over which John Wesley exercised personal control. From 1744 onward he invited others to advise him in a yearly conference which, after his death, was invested with legal authority. John was supported not only by a few Anglican clergymen but also by his assistants who were stationed in the circuits as he appointed them. Those itinerants, the forerunners of the Methodist ministry, were supplemented by local preachers and together were responsible for services on the circuit plan as assigned by the superintendent. This "wheels within wheels" structure was adopted as a model when Methodism developed into a separate denomination.

It must not be forgotten, however, that the blueprint for the Methodist organization was not produced in the calm of some quiet retreat but under the incessant

City Road Chapel, London, first opened November 1, 1778.

pressures of intensive evangelism. In the formative years the brothers were engaged in the thick of the battle and the structures outlined above were not the outcome of some theoretical pipe dream but rather represented a practical response to what the ongoing situation demanded. John Wesley was no armchair idealist. His scheme of oversight was hammered out on the anvil of evangelistic experience.

Preaching the gospel

Although others since his day have recognized his unusual organizing ability, John himself saw his calling as being primarily that of a gospel preacher. The means employed in winning back a nation to its lost faith in God was the proclamation of the Word. The Wesleys were no innovators. John repeatedly insisted that they preached only the fundamental principles of Christianity. When pressed to identify what these were, he encapsulated them in "these two – the doctrine of justification, and that of the new birth; the former relating to that great work God does *for us*, in forgiving our sins; the latter to the great work of God *in us*, in renewing our fallen nature." The difference between the Wesleys' preaching of these truths and the formal recognition of them as part of the church's doctrine lay in the power of the Holy Spirit to apply the truths with conviction as vital to the conversion of unbelievers.

John Wesley's caliber as a teacher and theologian has been reassessed in recent years. In the past he has too often been dismissed as something of a lightweight in this respect. But it is now being conceded that, although he lacked the leisure to compile a systematic compendium, his preaching, writing, and organizing were nevertheless undergirded and directed by a keen theological appreciation. He was indebted to the Fathers of the primitive church, but his overall approach was determined by the biblical principles of the Reformation. He laid particular stress on the doctrines of assurance and holiness. In resisting the more extreme forms of

eighteenth-century theological determinism, his stance was that of an evangelical Arminian.

Although hundreds of books have been written about John Wesley – in itself a tribute to his continued importance – we know him best through his own writings, and especially the more personal disclosures to be found in his lengthy *Journal* and many letters. The former has been commended by the poet Edward Fitzgerald as "one of the most interesting books in the language." It provides a blow-by-blow account of John's evangelistic journeys covering more than fifty years. His clear, simple, and direct prose style has been admired by literary experts, contrasting so sharply as it does with the florid, artificial products of his contemporaries. His mastery of logical argument is apparent in his controversial treatises and in his powerful appeals to the nation at large to reconsider the case for Christianity.

John Wesley's influence

Historians have not hesitated to hail John Wesley as one of the foremost social reformers of his century. When the *Gentleman's Magazine* reported his death, the feature of his achievement singled out for special commendation was his doing "infinite good to the lower classes of the people." The obituary went on to explain that "by the humane endeavours of him and his brother Charles a sense of decency in morals and religion was introduced to the lowest classes of mankind; the ignorant were instructed, the wretched relieved, and the abandoned reclaimed."

John Wesley ensured that collections for the poor were regularly taken up in Methodist services. He was concerned for the unemployed and devised schemes to find work for them. He launched a lending fund to assist those who were hoping to start a business. The Stranger's Friend Societies were designed to provide relief for the poor. Nor was poverty the only social evil John sought to counter. In his *Thoughts on Slavery* (1774) he was among the first to protest against what

John Wesley's house, Moorfields, London.

later, in a letter to William Wilberforce, he called "that execrable villainy, which is the scandal of religion, of England, and of human nature." His denunciation of war in his treatise on original sin was equally trenchant. His advocacy of prison reform anticipated the efforts of John Howard.

This, then, was John Wesley. Though small in physical stature he was undoubtedly great in achievement and influence. His stated desire was "to be on full stretch for God." Sir Leslie Stephen graphically, if rather irreverently, dubbed him "a human gamecock." That sums him up. His single aim is expressed in the words of his brother Charles:

To serve the present age,
My calling to fulfil;
O may it all my powers engage
To do my Master's will.

Charles Wesley's legacy

In what on the surface appears to be a curious piece of understatement John de-clared after Charles's death that his brother's "least praise was his talent for poetry." This was not intended to be a disparagement of what Charles had achieved as a hymn writer. It simply recognized his other outstanding gifts and attainments. As we have seen, Charles was something more than John's shadow. He exercised a distinctive ministry of his own as an evangelist, a counselor, and a shepherd of souls. For almost twenty years Charles covered the country in his travels until he found that he was unable to stand the pace as could his more resilient brother. But first from Bristol, and later in London, he continued to support and supplement the cause that John so relentlessly pursued.

It is, however, as a composer of Christian hymns that Charles Wesley is now mostly remembered. There was scarcely a day in the fifty years following his evangelical conversion in which he did not set down some lines in verse. His last hymn was dictated from his deathbed when he was too weak to hold a pen. Along with Isaac Watts he was a major pioneer in hymn writing, for until the eighteenth-century revival, congregational singing was confined to somewhat stilted metrical versions of Scripture. Charles anticipated the outburst of lyrical poetry early in the next century and interpreted biblical themes in the language of the heart.

The plaque on Charles Wesley's house in Bristol claims, without exaggeration, that "his hymns are the possession of the Christian Church." "Jesu, Lover of My Soul," "Love Divine, All Loves Excelling," "O Thou Who Camest from Above," "Hark the Herald Angels Sing," "Christ the Lord Is Risen Today" – these and many more are now sung around the world by Christians of every communion. The psalmist could rejoice that God's statutes had been his songs in the house of his pilgrimage (Psalm 119:54). It was through Charles Wesley that the doctrines of salvation he and his brother preached throughout the land were articulated in the voice of praise.

George Whitefield
1714-1770

George Whitefield (1714-1770) was an Englishman whom many consider the greatest evangelist since the apostle Paul.

Although he was an ordained Church of England clergyman, most of Whitefield's preaching was done out of doors. In those days, before the electrical amplification of sound, his congregations were numbered in the thousands.

Whitefield preached three and four times a day from the time he was twenty-two until his death at fifty-five. This ministry took him to almost every county in England, often to Wales, fifteen times to Scotland, and twice to Ireland. But he was particularly devoted to the American colonies,

George Whitefield preaching.

visiting seven times and repeatedly evangelizing from New Hampshire in the north to Georgia in the south.

His accomplishments were many. He erected an orphan house in Georgia and in herculean labor supported it throughout his lifetime. He built two large churches in London and, as far as his traveling would allow, served as their pastor. He was the first leader of the Evangelical Revival that transformed Britain and was the chief figure of the Great Awakening in America. He preached so as to be understood by the poor and unlearned, but he also ministered to audiences composed of the aristocracy of

England and was gladly heard by many great ones in America.

Whitefield's essential message to all mankind was, "Ye must be born again!" This brought upon him the wrath of many, but he met their opposition only with kindness. Whitefield's earthly remains are entombed beneath the pulpit of the First Presbyterian Church at Newburyport, Massachusetts.

The Life of
Whitefield

1714	December 16, birth at Bell Inn, Gloucester, England.
1735	March, converted at Oxford University.
1736	Graduates, is ordained a deacon, and begins ministry.
1739	Begins open-air preaching; influences John and Charles Wesley to adopt the practice too.
1740	Preaches throughout the American colonies.
1741	Marries.
1743	Elected moderator of Calvinistic Methodists.
1748	Begins regular ministry to the nobility in London.
1753	Opens tabernacle in London.
1768	Death of Mrs. Whitefield; opens Trevecca College.
1770	Makes his seventh visit to America, dies at Newburyport, Massachusetts.

England

● Gloucester
London ●

George Whitefield

English Evangelist

Arnold A. Dallimore

Early Training

On December 16, 1714, George Whitefield was born into an upper middle class home. His parents were the proprietors of the Bell Inn at Gloucester, but when he was a child of two his father passed away. Until she remarried, his mother succeeded well in the operation of the business.

As a boy George revealed a very lively spirit and yet a deep sensitivity. He had an excellent memory and was chosen to make speeches before the town fathers. But he was especially fond of reading plays and of imagining himself as playing all the parts. At the age of fifteen he left school and worked in the inn, but he soon returned to school and proved a very diligent student.

Several of Whitefield's father's forebears had attended Oxford University, and at the age of eighteen he followed them, entering Pembroke College. He soon became a member of the Holy Club, a group led by Charles and John Wesley. He surpassed all the other members in his search for salvation. In March 1735, after months of desperate striving, he cast himself on the mercy of God, trusted Christ, and received the forgiveness he had so earnestly sought. His soul was flooded with joy.

In 1736 he received his B. A. degree and was ordained to the ministry of the Church of England. He preached his first sermon in the church he had attended as a boy, and he was so earnest that a report was made to the bishop he had driven fifteen people mad. In the many churches to which Whitefield was immediately invited in Bristol and London crowds that overflowed the buildings gathered to hear him. People surged into his lodgings seeking spiritual counsel until he hardly had time to eat or sleep, and many sought to touch his garments as he walked the street.

Georgia

Had merely earthly success been his aim, Whitefield could have continued to enjoy such popularity all his days. But he willingly forsook the acclaim and sailed for America, to take up the work begun by the Wesleys in Georgia. The passage across the ocean was slow and dangerous in those times. Whitefield served as chaplain to all on board, and, although many mocked when the journey began, before the vessel reached America he was lovingly accepted and life on board was transformed.

He was received in the colony with an enthusiasm like that shown in London. Seeing, however, the need for an orphanage in Savannah, he soon returned to England to raise the money to establish it.

Open-air preaching

In 1739 Whitefield resorted to open-air preaching. This was first to a company of degraded coal miners, and in a few days he had congregations of some thousands. He wrote:

> The first discovery of their being affected was to see the white gutters made by their tears which plentifully fell down their black cheeks .... Hundreds and hundreds of them were soon brought under deep convictions, which, as the event proved happily ended in a sound and thorough conversion.

Whitefield took to himself the liberty of

preaching anywhere opportunity afforded. If a church was allowed, he used it, but if not, he stood on whatever might be available – a stone wall, a horse block, a pile of turf, or a table placed at the roadside. He was driven with a passion to reach mankind with the gospel. He also persuaded other ministers to take up the open-air ministry, and prominent among those men were his friends Charles and John Wesley.

Before long, however, it became evident there were differences in the doctrinal positions of Whitefield and John Wesley. They had each vowed in ordination that they accepted the doctrinal Articles of the Church of England with their strong Calvinistic emphasis. From the time of his conversion Whitefield had held to the Calvinistic theology, but Wesley had been brought up to accept the Arminian views. In turn, in addressing a company of the people Whitefield had gathered in Bristol, John Wesley preached a severe sermon "against Predestination." Whitefield, who had not brought the subject into his preaching, wrote to John and urged him not to publish his discourse.

Despite Wesley's action, being about to leave again for America, Whitefield turned his thousands of followers over to Wesley, that he might lead the work until Whitefield himself should return. Very shortly after Whitefield's departure Wesley published the Bristol sermon, and he and his brother preached everywhere against the Calvinistic doctrines. This meant the beginning of a sad division in the movement.

After he reached America in 1740 for the second time at the age of twenty-four, Whitefield established the orphan house in Georgia. He also preached throughout the colonies and was everywhere heard by thousands.

Whitefield and Franklin

Benjamin Franklin became one of his most interested listeners. Franklin reports that all of Philadelphia seemed to become religious under Whitefield's influence, but he especially tells of his persuasive powers. Upon attending one of his services, feeling the orphan house should have been built in Pennsylvania rather than in unpopulated Georgia, Franklin had refused to contribute toward it. But upon hearing Whitefield present the need, Franklin began to soften and decided to give his copper money. But with another stroke of persuasion he planned to put the silver in the collection dish, and when it finally came around Franklin emptied his pocket, gold and all. And he heard a friend who sat near, who in his determination not to give had come without money, now trying to borrow from others around him.

Franklin and Whitefield became close friends, but the philosopher always withstood the evangelist's efforts to lead him to Christ.

Whitefield's ministry was probably never more powerful than during his visit at this time to New England. A deep spiritual work had been begun under the preaching of Jonathan Edwards, and

The Bell Inn, Gloucester, Whitefield's birthplace.

under Whitefield it continued and expanded. It spread throughout several colonies and remained in power for several years. It revived the work of God in America, richly establishing the nation's spiritual heritage, and has been termed by historians the Great Awakening.

Upon returning to England in March 1741, Whitefield was confronted by several difficulties. He found that during his absence Wesley had turned the people against him. He began to preach in his favorite locations in London – Kennington Common and Moorfields – and soon won back a congregation. Friends also built a large wooden shed (he called it a tabernacle) for him at Moorfields, and it was filled regularly beyond capacity. It became his headquarters until replaced by a fine brick structure some years later. In the doctrinal controversy, though he stood firmly for what he believed, he ever regarded the Wesleys as his bosom friends, and in later years they each remarked on the kindness he showed them during this episode.

Scotland and Wales

During 1741 Whitefield also made his first visit to Scotland. Here, where Calvinism was the theology of the land, he was received with joy. Such doctrines, however, had become little more than theories to many people; but under his ministry they were brought to life and began to be preached by many a pastor with new power and fervor.

Upon leaving Scotland he went to Wales. There he married a widow, eleven years his senior. Their life together was not unhappy, as some have supposed, but he spoke many times of the enjoyment and help she was to him. Indeed, Mrs. Whitefield accompanied him on his second trip to Scotland. The remarkable feature of this visit were the two tremendous Communion services at Cambuslang, one of them with twenty thousand persons present and the power of the Spirit manifest upon a multitude of hearers.

Whitefield now remained in Britain for three and a half years, and during that time a movement grew up around him. Men and women in large numbers were converted wherever he went, and, although most were members of the Church of England, they also continued to meet as a local spiritual fellowship. Men arose in their midst to lead those companies, and several proved capable and godly preachers. Whitefield had been known since his first coming before the public as a Methodist, and as these several groups came into being, they too were termed *Methodist* and throughout his lifetime Whitefield was known as "the leader and founder of Methodism."

Calvinistic Methodism

Under other leaders a similar work was being done in Wales. In 1743 Whitefield met with those men at their request and the conference resulted in the organization of the Calvinistic Methodist Association. Whitefield largely planned the form of structure on which this body was built, and when, eighteen months later, Wesley organized his work, he largely adopted the plan Whitefield had used.

But Whitefield was again urged to return to America. Fanaticism had entered the work in New England, and he was being blamed for it. He was a very sick man when he reached shore, and as he began to preach he was thought to be dying. But he forced himself on, and although he ministered with the greatest of zeal, he also conducted himself in a manner that set the example of common sense to the several "exhorters" who had proved extremists. He remained in the New World for more than three years on this trip and then spent two and a half months preaching in Bermuda on the way home.

When he arrived in England, Whitefield determined to relinquish the leadership of his branch of Methodism. He did this for two reasons: first, he could see he would need to devote almost half of his time to America; and second, he knew that to continue in the prime position would mean to face constant opposition from Wesley. To the followers who urged him

George Whitefield's school, Gloucester, England.

to remain in the foremost position and enjoy the prominence which was rightfully his he replied, "Let the name of Whitefield perish, but Christ be glorified! And let me be but the servant of all!" This important fact of his history has never been fully recognized, and it deserves to be known and emphasized.

The servant of all

At this time (1748) Whitefield became and remained throughout the rest of his life, as he said, "the servant of all." He assisted any thoroughly evangelical cause without the least regard to denomination. The evangelical movement in the Church of England was richly revived and expanded under his influence; he assisted Presbyterians, Congregationalists, and Baptists, and he very frequently preached in the assistance of Wesley's cause. He ministered regularly to a number of the proud and wealthy aristocrats as they gathered to hear him in Lady Huntingdon's drawing room. He built a fine new brick tabernacle to replace the old wooden structure in Moorfields and also

erected a large new chapel in Tottenham Court Road, London. Each year, whenever he was not in America, he made a visit to Scotland, and twice he went to Ireland, largely assisting John Wesley's work there.

The fact that he was no longer building his own organization based on the Calvinistic beliefs, and especially that he was helping Wesley, was not liked by many of his followers. In the feeling against Wesley one of them once asked Whitefield if they would see Wesley in heaven. To this he replied, "No! He will be so near the throne and we so far from it that we won't even be able to see him."

Whitefield's achievement

Whitefield lived at a tremendous pace. He arose at four in the morning, spent an hour with God and His Word, and preached at five. Hundreds gathered at that early hour to hear him, and John Newton stated, "I have seen Moorfields as full of lanterns at these times as I suppose [the theater district] is full of flambeaux on an Opera night." He often preached twice again during the day, besides his traveling, his letter writing, and his being interviewed by spiritual seekers. He generally closed the day by preaching to any who were in the house wherever he might be and endeavored to be in bed by ten o'clock.

But having begun this style of life at the age of twenty-two, by the time he was forty-five he was worn out. Nonetheless, Whitefield drove himself on, made five more trips to Scotland and two more to America. For the larger part of one year he was too sick to preach with anything like the usual frequency, and although he went to Holland to recuperate he preached there through an interpreter. As Sir James Stephen says, he undoubtedly preached more than 30,000 times.

Whitefield's sermons

The sermons that are published as his provide a very poor representation of George Whitefield's ministry. He published one sermon each week when he was twenty-three, and these are far better than people suppose. But during the last year of his life seventeen sermons were taken in shorthand by a man standing in the crowd, and because there was immediate sale for anything professing to be by Whitefield, that man published them. Upon seeing the first, Whitefield declared it was a totally false representation of what he had said. Yet those sermons went forth and served for a century as the chief product by which he was remembered. Likewise the pictures of Whitefield are in the main regrettable. The best is a profile medallion produced by Wedgwoods; it manifests something of the strength that characterized him.

Most of the ministers in America at that time kept slaves and entirely condoned the custom. Sad to say, Whitefield endorsed the practice and kept slaves for the support of his orphanage. That was his worst and almost only fault, for he was a truly holy man. More than almost any other man he was constantly conscious of living under the eye of God and sought so to live as to be unashamed in the great

day when he would stand before Him.

And as Whitefield had begun so he continued. He held tenaciously to the fundamentals of the faith – the inerrancy of Scripture, the lost condition of fallen man, the atonement made by Christ, and salvation to all who will believe on Him. He labored only with true evangelicals and opposed all who denied the faith. In this work he maintained an unswerving course, and Sir James Stephen summed up his life and his character by saying:

If ever philanthropy burned in the human heart ... embracing the whole family of a man in the spirit of universal charity, it was in the heart of George Whitefield .... He had no preferences but in favor of the ignorant, the miserable and the poor. In their cause he shrank from no privation, and declined neither insult nor hostility. To such wrongs he opposed the weapons of an all-enduring meekness and a love which would not be repulsed. The springs of his benevolence were inexhaustible and could not choose but flow.

Whitefield's ministry had a lasting effect in each of the lands in which he labored. With regard to America it must be stated that Methodism in the colonies, in its beginnings, was built from hundreds of persons who had been converted under his preaching. The Presbyterian church made striking growth, particularly in the central colonies under his influence. At the time of his first arrival in America the Baptist work was small and was lacking in zeal, but moved by his example a number of men began to labor with a grand new fervor, especially in the South. Indeed, each of these denominations is deeply indebted to him, and America has since been very different from what it would have been had there been no George Whitefield.

William Wilberforce
1759-1833

William Wilberforce's parish church, Clapham, London.

Since the sixteenth century the European maritime nations had traded in slaves bought from West African chiefs. The Atlantic slave trade effected the largest enforced migration in history and had an adverse influence on West Africa.

By the eighteenth century, the slave trade was highly important to the European economy. Ships sailed from Bristol, Liverpool, or the Continent laden with cheap goods, alcohol, and arms to trade for slaves. Men and women were shipped across the Atlantic ("the Middle Passage") lying naked and chained in holds below deck, and were usually exercised once a day. The mortality rate was high, and the crews also suffered many casualties, mainly from disease; the moral effect on young sailors was further evil. The slaves were unloaded and sold in the West Indies or continental America, where they spent the rest of their lives in hard labor. The ships reloaded with sugar, rum, or cotton and returned with the trade winds to their ports of origin.

With all Europe, the British believed that the slave trade, though deplorable, was an economic necessity and honorable to those engaged in it. Then Anthony Benezet, a French-born Quaker of Philadelphia, wrote a devastating pamphlet. Meanwhile a British surgeon and chaplain from the West Indies, James Ramsay, had begun to protest against slavery. British Quakers agitated for abolition, followed by John Wesley in a strong pamphlet published in 1766.

Nothing could be done except by Parliament, and no Member of Parliament (M.P.) seemed ready to lend his name and effort. Then a new name appeared on the scene – William Wilberforce, the young M.P. for York.

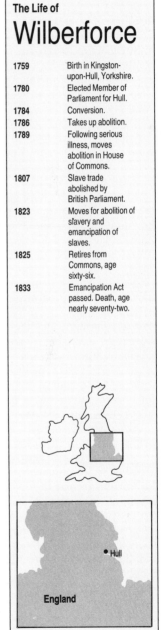

The Life of

Wilberforce

1759	Birth in Kingston-upon-Hull, Yorkshire.
1780	Elected Member of Parliament for Hull.
1784	Conversion.
1786	Takes up abolition.
1789	Following serious illness, moves abolition in House of Commons.
1807	Slave trade abolished by British Parliament.
1823	Moves for abolition of slavery and emancipation of slaves.
1825	Retires from Commons, age sixty-six.
1833	Emancipation Act passed. Death, age nearly seventy-two.

• Hull

England

William Wilberforce

and the Abolition of Slavery
John C. Pollock

Opposite:
William Wilberforce.

Member of Parliament

William Wilberforce was an unlikely leader in an aristocratic age, for he was the son of a rich merchant. Born in the great northern seaport of Hull on August 24, 1759, he lost his father at the age of eight and went to live with an uncle and aunt who had been influenced by George Whitefield and the early Evangelical Revival. They were friends of John Newton, the ex–slave trader and sailor who had become a much loved hymn-writer.

Newton became a hero to young Wilberforce; but his mother, seeing him a fervent little "Methodist," took him away. She gradually scrubbed his soul, sending him to boarding school and to Cambridge University, until nothing was left of his boyhood faith except a more moral outlook then usual among carefree young men of fashion.

At Cambridge his cheerful, amusing character made him popular, though physically he was an ugly little man. His bosom friend was William Pitt, the future prime minister, his exact contemporary. Both were intent on a political career. Wilberforce, the indolent amateur, entered the House of Commons before the more serious-minded Pitt, at the age of twenty-one in 1780. Four years later, with Pitt already prime minister, Wilberforce won the important seat of Yorkshire on Pitt's behalf and became a man of political consequence. He was a good parliamentary speaker with an exceptionally attractive voice, his tones "so distinct and melodious that the most hostile ear hangs on them delighted."

Conversion

The following winter of 1784-1785, during a journey to the south of France and back,

Wilberforce underwent a long, drawn out, but very deep, conversion (or rededication) to Christ through discussions with Isaac Milner, his former schoolmaster, and their reading together a celebrated religious book and the Bible. Inner conflict between ambition and the claims of Christ sent him nearly out of his mind until he sought John Newton again and received counsel. Newton also urged him to stay in politics, believing that God might have raised him up for a purpose. At that time there were only two other fervent Christians in the House of Commons.

Newton was one of the influences, in the next two years, which convinced Wilberforce that he must take up the cause of the slaves – Newton was thoroughly ashamed of his own early part in the slave trade. He, James Ramsay, Thomas Clarkson, and like-minded friends, especially among the Quakers, were trying to rouse the nation's conscience, but only Parliament could effect abolition. In 1787, horrified by the mortality rate on the Middle Passage, Wilberforce agreed to bring in a bill. From the start he expected that slavery itself would disappear once the slave trade was abolished.

He was already interested in other reforms, especially in improving the morals (or "manners") of the British people. In 1787 he wrote in his diary: "God has put before me two great objects: the Abolition of the Slave Trade and the reformation of manners." He drove these crusades in tandem; but abolition, as the greater evil, consumed most of his time, thought, and energy, and it ended any hope of high office.

At first he was expecting quick victory. The evidence, amassed by Clarkson,

Wilberforce himself, and a committee of the Privy Council appointed by Pitt, showed overwhelmingly the evil effects of the trade upon human lives and on the African continent. Wilberforce aimed for an international convention, but that proved impossible; he then planned for unilateral British abolition. By now the opposition was thoroughly aroused. The strain induced a serious illness in 1788, and Pitt had to move the question in the House of Commons on his behalf. The doctors cured Wilberforce by opium, which was then considered a "pure drug;" he was obliged to take it for the rest of his life. No moral issue was involved, but the drug weakened his eyesight and increased a natural tendency to muddle and to indolence – temptations he strenuously resisted without realizing their cause.

The slaving lobby

By 1789 he had recovered and made his first great parliamentary speech for abolition. The Commons, however, took the matter no further than the appointment of another inquiry. Less than a month later the French Revolution began, followed in a few years by the outbreak of war between France and Britain. Pitt became immersed in prosecuting the war and lost the edge of his zeal for abolition, unless it were gradual, which Wilberforce could not accept. The slave trade lobby used every act and subterfuge, but threats, fears, and personal abuse failed to dissuade Wilberforce, who said that in this matter, "where the actual commission of guilt is in question, a man who fears God is not at liberty" to hold back. The agent of one of the West Indian islands complained that the more Wilberforce was knocked down the more strongly he recovered.

Wilberforce led a remarkable team of M.P.s, lawyers, and propagandists. His own character was an important factor. He had optimism, charm, and friendliness: it was difficult for opponents to dislike such a delightful character. He worked hard when in good health and took endless trouble. He had wide sympathies, especially with the oppressed or those helping them, and was a great encourager.

He also was an active personal evangelist in his circle, writing a long book with an immense title, generally shortened to *A Practical View*, to expound the heart of the Christian faith. Gradually he gathered round him a growing number of political friends who were committed Christians, nicknamed "The Saints" by contemporaries and the "Clapham Sect" by posterity. Wilberforce lived for some years in Clapham, then a village south of London, at first in the house of his cousin, Henry Thornton, and then, after both married, in one nearby. Wilberforce's marriage, when nearly forty, to Barbara Spooner was happy, but she was little help to his work. One of their sons became a well-known bishop.

Abolition

Early in 1806 Pitt died. The change of government and the fortunes of war offered a new opportunity to the abolitionists. One, James Stephen, a brilliant maritime lawyer who had worked in the slave-owning islands, spotted a way of "bringing in Abolition by a sidewind" by a bill that apparently was designed to further the war effort. It passed through Parliament in 1806 and suddenly made abolition an immediate possibility. On February 23, 1807, the climax of more than twenty years, the House of Commons voted for abolition by 267 votes, amid scenes of unparalleled enthusiasm and admiration for Wilberforce. The United States of America also abolished her slave trade in 1807.

Wilberforce's triumph brought him immense prestige and enabled him to pursue his schemes for improving the quality and morality of life in Great Britain. He was making goodness fashionable and laying the foundations of Victorian England. More than any other man, he helped to end the venality of political life and encourage probity in commerce. He was untiring in pushing reform, directly or by aid to other pioneers

The Houses of Parliament, London.

attend personally) agree on universal abolition. France agreed early in the 1820s, but Spain and Portugal proved obdurate.

Emancipation

Wilberforce had expected slavery in the British West Indies to wither away, the slaves being transformed into free peasantry, as a result of the extinction of the slave trade. By 1823 he had given up hope and launched his last great crusade, for emancipation and the abolition of slavery forever. He was already sixty-four years old and brought in Thomas Buxton, a younger M.P., to act as helper and successor "if I am unable to finish it."

Wilberforce was heavily attacked, not only by slave owners fearing ruin but by the radicals, who alleged that he cared nothing for the "white wage slaves" toiling in poor conditions in English factories, mills, mines, and gravel pits. In fact he cared deeply but believed that the hopelessness of the slave mattered more. He recognized that the libel was a part of the campaign to preserve slavery. William Cobbett, whose attacks on Wilberforce became famous, supported slavery in the belief that emancipation in the West Indies would bring distress to the factory workers of England. William Ewart Gladstone, the future prime minister, also voted against emancipation.

Wilberforce, old and ill, retired from Parliament in 1825, highly honored except by the radicals. He remained the moral force behind Buxton's parliamentary efforts. Wilberforce was the "conscience of England," and the virtual leader of the evangelical Christians. He lived just long enough to hear that the House of Commons had voted to emancipate all slaves in the British dominions. He died a few days later on August 6, 1833 and was buried in Westminster Abbey.

such as Elizabeth Fry, Jeremy Bentham, and Samuel Romilly in their work for prisoners; Sir Thomas Bernard and Count Romford in care for the poor; or Hannah More in schools. He was involved in more than sixty societies working at home and abroad and was a co-founder of the Bible Society and of the Church Missionary Society.

Wilberforce's chief concern continued to be the slaves and the "sorrows of Africa." He helped to found and direct the African Institute to promote civilization and offset the evil done by the slave trade; and he took a large share in establishing the settlement of Sierra Leone for liberated slaves. The slave trade did not end with its abolition by Britain and America; illicit trading had to be suppressed, and the Continental powers persuaded and pushed toward abolishing their own slave trades. Wilberforce failed to make the Congress of Vienna (which he did not

William Carey
1761-1834

William Carey (1761-1834) has been aptly designated the "Father of Modern Missons" for his role in initiating a movement that has had extraordinary impact on the Christian church. Indeed, the modern missionary movement has been one of the most extensive global movements ever to occur in human history, one that was instrumental in transforming Christianity from a faith limited primarily to Western Europe into the world's largest religion. The part that one obscure artisan played in this massive missionary endeavor is one of the truly inspiring stories of Christian humanitarian service.

Carey became a missionary at a time when independent mission boards were nonexistent and at a time when recruits were not required to be ordained or seminary trained. But his lack of basic qualifications was outweighed by his enthusiasm for missions, his dependence on God, and his determination to succeed in a high-risk venture.

Carey's accomplishments as an evangelist, church-planter, teacher, translator, and field director were enormous; and as a forty-year veteran missionary to India who never took a furlough, Carey set a powerful example of sacrifice and fortitude for generations of foreign missionaries who were to follow him.

He was a true pioneer in missions at a time when there was very little support for cross-cultural evangelism. He had no established guidelines, no patterns of success and failure upon which to draw for his own course of action. Yet, his all-encompassing program involving social, educational, and evangelistic activities set a pattern for a well-rounded missionary endeavor that is still a model today.

Opposite: William Carey with his Brahmin teacher; below: Carey Memorial church, Moulton, England.

The Life of

Carey

1761	Birth.
1781	Marriage to Dorothy.
1785	Begins full-time ministry at the Baptist church in Moulton.
1792	Publication of *Enquiry*
1793	Voyage to India.
1795	Founding of a tiny Baptist church in Malda.
1800	Move to Serampore.
1807	Death of Dorothy.
1808	Marriage to Charlotte Rumohr.
1812	Warehouse fire.
1817	Split of Baptist Missionary Society.
1819	Founding of Serampore College.
1821	Death of Charlotte.
1823	Marriage to Grace Hughes.
1830	Reunification of Baptist Missionary Society.
1834	Death.

William Carey

Father of Modern Missions

Ruth Tucker

Shoemaker

Like so many other outstanding figures in history, William Carey was an unlikely candidate for greatness. The son of an English weaver, he had limited formal schooling and as a teenager was apprenticed to a shoemaker. His interests, however, were far broader than merely perfecting a skilled craft. He began studying the New Testament and Greek during his apprenticeship, and by his early twenties he was utilizing his biblical knowledge in the pulpit of a tiny Nonconformist church – a two-hour walk from his home.

It was as a young, impoverished pastor-shoemaker that Carey's interests became focused on foreign missions. His concern developed naturally out of his personal interests in travel and geography. He was intrigued with accounts of exploration and read with fascination the volumes of *Captain Cook's Voyages*. Later, when he began supplementing his income by teaching school, he was sometimes moved to tears during his geography lessons as he presented statistics of the unchristianized nations.

It was Carey's association with other Baptist pastors that provided him with the opportunity to articulate his concern for foreign missions. In a Baptist ministerial meeting at Northampton, England, in 1786, Carey raised the issue of the Great Commission and its application for modern times. The reaction was immediate and harsh. The very suggestion that these ministers were in some way responsible to "teach all nations" was ridiculed as the fantasy of an enthusiast. It was widely held among eighteenth-century Christians that the apostles alone had been obligated to carry out the Great Commission. The Particular Baptists, with whom Carey was associated, generally believed that God would use supernatural means for the evangelism of the unreached tribes and nations. So Carey's remarks were not well received. Indeed, he was publicly rebuked.

An Enquiry

What Carey had hoped could be accomplished in a serious discussion with his peers became a personal project in the months that followed, a project that resulted in an eighty-seven-page apology for foreign missions. His treatise, entitled *An Enquiry into the Obligations of Christians to Use Means for the Conversion of the Heathens* (that being the shortened title), opened with a concise scriptural defense of missions and proceeded to cite mission work that had been accomplished throughout church history from the earliest apostles to the Moravians and John Wesley. He then went on to present statistical tables surveying the countries of the world – their populations, land size, and religions – and to answer the arguments against the practicality of foreign missions to the "heathens": "Their distance from us, their barbarous and savage way of living, the danger of being killed by them, the difficulty of procuring the necessaries of life, or the unintelligibleness of their languages." In the final chapter, he outlined a strategy for missions and dealt with such issues as prayer support, denominational cooperation, finances, and the quality of recruits.

As significant as the *Enquiry* has become in missionary literature, it was not widely read or circulated when it first was printed. Its very plain literary style and the general lack of interest in foreign missions combined to ensure its relative obscurity. Carey's hope that profits from its sale would help underwrite a foreign mission venture were not realized, and many copies remained unsold. What gave the work credibility, more than any other factor, was Carey's personal demonstration of his concern for missions, his example as a volunteer for the inaugural operation of the Baptist Missionary Society.

The Baptist Missionary Society was formed in 1792, some months after the publication of the *Enquiry*, though not as a direct result of Carey's personal influence. In a sermon from Isaiah, he had challenged his fellow pastors of the local Baptist Association to broaden their horizons of ministry, to "expect great things from God; attempt great things for God." It was a moving sermon, but most of the pastors in the association lacked vision and were impoverished (as was Carey himself). The challenge would have gone unheeded but for the support of Andrew Fuller, an influential pastor, whose commitment to the cause led to the official organization of the new mission society.

A willing recruit

After Fuller agreed to serve as the secretary of the mission, the first major item of business was to find a willing recruit – a matter quickly resolved when John Thomas, a physician who had already served in India with the East India Company, offered himself. The most startling turn of events occurred when Carey volunteered to be a "suitable companion" and was accepted on the spot. How much thought Carey had given to the decision is not known, but his announcement proved to be shocking news to his family and church. His wife, Dorothy, was pregnant with her fourth child and did not share her husband's vision for foreign missions. She had served as a dutiful pastor's wife and accepted his "eccentric" views on foreign missions without ever imagining the end result – that his passion for a lost world would suddenly disrupt the only family stability she had ever known.

Her refusal to leave the security of her home and neighborhood and embark on a perilous voyage to a land of uncertainties (except for its menacing climate and primitive living conditions) did not deter Carey. After a hectic speaking and fundraising tour with John Thomas, he left his pregnant wife and two youngest children behind and set sail for India with his eight-year-old son (Felix) and the Thomases. Before they actually left the country, however, Thomas was detained by his creditors. This caused several weeks' delay – enough time for Dorothy to have her baby and be persuaded to accompany her husband. After a five-month voyage through violent storms, they arrived in India to launch their mission venture.

As significant as this event was to become in dating the inauguration of the modern missionary movement, it was not highly acclaimed at the time, and it was not the first significant Protestant missionary endeavor. More than a century earlier John Eliot (1604-1690) had conducted very effective evangelistic work among the Algonquin Indians of North America. There had likewise been some notable missionary endeavors carried out by German Pietists under the Danish-Halle Mission, particularly through the ministry of Bartholomaeus Ziegenbalg (1682-1719) and Christian Friedrich Schwartz (1726-1760). And by the time Carey set sail, the Moravians, under the leadership of Count Nicolaus von Zinzendorf (1700-1760), had already begun circling the globe in a laudable effort to plant Christianity abroad through the witness of artisans and tradesmen.

Yet despite the impressive missionary careers of those great men, the impact of those earlier mission endeavors paled in comparison to the impact of William Carey's endeavor. The implications of his theology and methodology would have a monumental impact on all future generations, not because he was the first to introduce new ideas and methodology, but because he so effectively articulated a biblical philosophy of mission and so thoroughly integrated the various facets of missionary work into a cohesive program of cross-cultural evangelism.

The first years

The Careys' early years in India were very trying. Initially, the family lived in a malaria-infested marsh outside Calcutta, while Thomas and his family lived in relative affluence in the city. Housing was utterly inadequate, as was the food supply and health care. None of the family was spared the severe effects of tropical diseases, and in 1794, a year after they arrived, five-year-old Peter succumbed to dysentery. It was a trauma that Dorothy was unable to endure. Her already unstable mental condition deteriorated, and she was later described by a missionary as being "wholly deranged."

Only the overpowering sense that he was accomplishing the will of God provided the staying power for Carey during his early years in India. After seven years of struggling to establish a ministry – which included language study, itinerant preaching, and secular employment at an indigo factory – Carey was unable to claim even one Indian convert. Yet, that period of apprenticeship was a fruitful time for him. He had acquired a remarkable grasp of the language, had translated large portions of the New Testament into Bengali, had planted a tiny non-Indian church, and had made the name of Christ known throughout much of Northern Bengal. A new era of mission work would begin for Carey at the turn of the nineteenth century with a crucial move to Serampore, a Danish colony out of reach of the troublesome East India Company.

Serampore

The decision to move to Serampore in 1800 was a difficult one for Carey. It meant leaving the people and area he had grown accustomed to, but Serampore was the only location that offered a mission base to the first new party of missionaries to arrive from England. Here, instead of being rebuffed by the East India Company, they were warmly welcomed by the Danish officials. It was a decisive move that multiplied the ministry opportunities for the struggling Baptist Missionary Society. Serampore was a more densely populated area than was Northern Bengal, and in less than a year Carey and his colleagues were able to report the conversion of two Indian nationals. By 1803 there were twenty-five baptized converts. The move to Serampore and the help of additional missionaries contributed to the increase, but equally significant was the change in Carey's style of preaching and his emphasis on Bible translation. He discovered (after seven barren years of evangelistic preaching) that focusing on the death and resurrection of Christ was considerably more effective than pointing out the evils of Hinduism. Still, the work was slow. After a quarter of a century the number of baptized converts did not exceed seven hundred.

The centrality of Scripture to world evangelism was powerfully demonstrated throughout Carey's long mission career. The emphasis he placed on Bible translation set the style for the Protestant missionaries in the century that followed. He was not the first missionary to translate the Bible for the people for whom he was ministering, but he was the first to turn his mission base into a widely-recognized linguistic center.

Yet Carey has traditionally been overrated as a linguist. It is true that the quantity of translation work that he accomplished was unparalleled. With the help of Indian teachers, he made six translations of the entire Bible (Bengali, Sanskrit, Oriya, Hindi, Assamese, and Marathi) and translated the New Testament and portions of Scripture into nearly thirty additional languages; but in many instances the quality was sorely lacking, and complete revisions were later necessary.

An indigenous church

The necessity of establishing an indigenous church was another priority of Carey's that was closely associated with his Bible translation work. He was convinced that the availability of the Scriptures would stimulate the spontaneous growth of Christianity in India and pave the way for a strong indigenous church. His optimistic hopes for church growth were never realized, but he did place great emphasis on training nationals. Indeed, his first convert, Krishna Pal, served as an effective evangelist in Calcutta and Assam.

In many ways Carey was far ahead of his time in his emphasis on training nationals and in contextualizing the gospel. The nineteenth century – that "Great Century" of foreign missions – was a century of Western expansion and imperialism, and it seemed only natural for missionaries to impose Western civilization on people. African tribal dances, Tahitian floral leis, and Indonesian communal dwellings were regarded as evidence of a decadent "heathen" life-style and were replaced by activities, fashion, and housing that more closely resembled that in the West.

Carey's leatherworking equipment.

Carey, however, had a profound respect for Indian culture and went out of his way to impress this upon the minds of his converts. He studied and translated Indian scriptures and literature and even offered courses in them at Serampore College, a Christian school that he established in 1819. He was heavily criticized by some of his colleagues for his emphasis on Eastern literature, but he regarded it as an essential ingredient in developing an indigenous Indian church. Equally significant was the fact that the college was ecumenical in its orientation – much to the despair of some of Carey's Baptist associates, who were eager to expand the Baptist denomination in India.

Although Carey was a strong supporter of Indian culture, he did not find it inconsistent to be at the forefront of social reform. There were some Indian customs on which he voiced strong opposition. For example, he loudly protested the practice of infanticide, child prostitution, and sati (widow burning): in so doing he aided the cause of Hindu reformers, who were able to influence legislation banning these deplorable practices.

Carey's concept of mission entailed many facets of social, intellectual, spiritual, and even economic life. He believed that missionaries should be as economically self-sustaining as possible. During his early years in India, Carey worked as a factory foreman; later he was a well-paid language professor at Fort William College in Calcutta. In addition, the Serampore mission was supported by funds received from its boarding school. The mission operated on a communitarium basis, which allowed for funds not needed for living expenses to be used for expansion of the mission work.

The enormous task of evangelizing India prompted Carey to maximize the efforts of anyone who could be helpful to the task. As a teacher at Fort William College, he was aided in his translation work by non-Christian students and colleagues. Nor were children outside the scope of mission work. His son Jabez (born only

William Carey's cottage, Moulton, England.

weeks before the Careys sailed to India) at the age of thirteen began learning Chinese in order to help translate the Bible into that language, and Felix was actively involved in preaching at the age of sixteen. His teenage son, William, was stopped by authorities for distributing literature, and other missionary children were equally active in the cause.

Carey also recognized the need for women missionaries, particularly in reaching Indian women, who were secluded from the outside world and entirely out of reach of male missionaries. Women were an essential part of the ministry at Serampore, and he pleaded for more women to join in the work. Such insight was rare during a period when missionary women were generally not viewed as having a ministry in their own right.

The Serampore trio

Carey was above all a team player. The early work in India was not identified so much with Carey as it was with the "Serampore Trio." Joshua Marshman and William Ward worked alongside Carey, and together they formed the backbone of the mission. Carey had a unique ability to see the good qualities in an individual when others tended to look at the bad. He praised his fellow workers for their dedication and spoke of the warm harmony that existed at Serampore. That harmony, however, was eventually shattered when young missionaries arriving on the field balked at the practice of communitarianism and at the authoritarian control by the senior missionaries. The result was a temporary split in the mission that deeply grieved the self-sacrificing and peace-loving Carey.

Carey's personality and character, above all else, contributed to his success as a missionary. "I can plod," he wrote. "I can persevere in any definite pursuit. To this I owe everything." This quality was demonstrated vividly when a warehouse fire destroyed not only valuable paper and equipment but also irreplaceable manuscripts. Carey stoically accepted the tragedy as the will of God and immediately began the arduous task of redoing some of the translations that had been lost.

Father of modern missions

His monumental contribution to missions, and the one factor above all others that warrants him the title "Father of Modern Missions" was the role he played in turning the tide of Protestant thought in favor of foreign missions. But the time was right for William Carey. The missionary movement that arose in the nineteenth century was part of an era of reform. During his four decades of ministry in India, many new mission boards were organized and great missionary pioneers were penetrating the barriers of civilizations that were virtually unknown to the West: Robert Morrison in China, Adoniram Judson in Burma, Robert Moffat in southern Africa, and John Williams in the South Seas. Yet, among all the other "greats," it was to be Carey who would be most remembered as an outspoken apologist for the cause of missions and for demonstrating that ideological position through forty years of effective cross-cultural ministry.

Elizabeth Fry
1780-1845

Elizabeth Fry reading in prison.

In the unreformed prisons of early nineteenth-century Britain, women as well as men received little or no help to renounce a life of crime. Elizabeth Fry (1780-1845) dared to visit unruly female prisoners and devised a scheme for giving them practical help. It proved strikingly effective in improving life behind bars. Her inspiration for the work was the Quaker conviction that all human beings, even the most degraded, should be treated with respect.

As a Quaker minister, Fry traveled widely, spreading her ideas in continental Europe and gaining international acclaim. Part of her fame stemmed from the fact that she, as a woman, had taken a successful initiative in a sphere of public policy. She believed that it was important for women to play a leading part in philanthropic enterprise. Her exemplary dedication made many other women, both in her own day and afterwards, realize that large-scale charitable ventures were within their capacity. Elizabeth Fry was one of those Christians who were fired by their faith to inject greater humanity into a largely inhumane system.

The Life of

Fry

1780	Birth; the daughter of John Gurney in Norwich, England.
1798	Becomes impressed by the reality of God.
1800	Marries Joseph Fry, London merchant.
1811	Acknowledged as Quaker minister.
1813	First visits Newgate Prison.
1817	Organizes ladies' committee to visit Newgate.
1821	Establishes British Society for Promoting Reformation of Female Prisoners.
1827	Publishes Observations on the Visiting, Superintendence and Government of Female Prisoners.
1828	Fry's bank stops payments.
1840	Founds Protestant Sisters of Charity.
1845	Death.

England

Norwich •

• London

Elizabeth Fry

and Prison Reform

David W. Bebbington

Quaker heritage

The girl who became Elizabeth Fry was born in 1780, the daughter of John Gurney, a prosperous merchant and banker of Norwich, England. Although the family was steeped in the tradition of the Society of Friends – Elizabeth's great-great-grandfather, Robert Barclay, had been a leading early exponent of Quaker principles – its members attended meetings only once a week and moved without qualms in Norwich society. They were what contemporaries called "gay Quakers," who held relatively loosely to their inherited convictions. The young Elizabeth suffered from ill health and nervous self-doubt, especially after the death of her mother when she was twelve.

By the age of seventeen Elizabeth confided to her diary that she had no religion; but in the following year she was powerfully affected by the ministry of a traveling Quaker from America, William Savery. A sense of the presence of God began to grow, a process helped by a visit to the stricter Friends of Coalbrookdale in Shropshire. Elizabeth started to observe Quaker ways more conscientiously, assuming the distinctive plain Quaker cap in 1799. Although in later years she was quite prepared to co-operate with other Christians in joint enterprises such as the Bible Society, Elizabeth Fry remained until her death a devoted member of the Society of Friends.

After twice declining his proposals, when she was twenty Elizabeth married Joseph Fry, a London merchant in tea, coffee, and spice. He was a loyal husband, but Elizabeth found his Quaker devotional life too shallow and his dedication too weak. Eventually, in 1828, his banking enterprise stopped payments and the shame of business failure hung over the

family. He was excluded from membership by the Society of Friends, though subsequently readmitted. Much of Elizabeth's time was occupied in looking after her eleven children. In 1808 she feared she was not proving "a useful instrument in the Church militant" and was "a careworn wife and mother." In the following year, however, her father died, and from his funeral onwards she began to play a much fuller part in Quaker worship. In 1811 she was recognized by Barking Monthly Meeting as a minister, an unpaid post among Friends that neverthless frequently entailed traveling to serve other meetings. Her ministry, which was greatly appreciated on account of her musical voice, seems to have become more evangelical in tone over the years, a general trend among the Quakers of her day. She delighted to dwell, like John Wesley, on the theme of the availability of the grace of God to all.

Newgate

It was in 1813 that Elizabeth Fry's attention first turned to prisons. She visited Newgate, the notorious jail near her London home, with clothes for the children of female prisoners. The state of Britain's prisons at that time was appalling. Locally administered, they were staffed by inefficient jailers who frequently supplemented their poor incomes by performing favors for the better-off inmates. There was acute overcrowding, because prison construction had not kept pace with population growth. Prisoners were normally idle and dissipated, loud in their oaths, violent in their ways, and living in filthy conditions. There was no separation between those whose cases had not yet come to trial (often to be proved innocent) and hardened offenders. Women fared no better than men, and sometimes, as at Newgate, kept children with them in jail.

Elizabeth's relatives were already trying to press for improvements, but it was her achievement to realize that direct action could transform conditions. From Christmas 1816 she visited the female prisoners regularly, and in the following year she organized a scheme whereby at least one of a team of twelve ladies would enter Newgate daily to read the Bible to women while they were trained in sewing. A key element was the appointment of monitors to supervise small classes of fellow-prisoners, an idea recently applied to children's education by another Quaker, Joseph Lancaster. The scheme was adopted only after the women gave their unanimous consent, a central feature of Quaker decision-making. Life behind bars was transformed. Glad of some useful occupation, the women changed from a furious rabble to an orderly community. A grateful Corporation of London rapidly assumed responsibility for paying for clothes and a resident matron. A nation alarmed by the problem of public order in the economic dislocation that followed the Napoleonic Wars acclaimed Elizabeth Fry as a heroine.

Reforming female prisoners

Her fame enabled Elizabeth to create a number of ladies' committees elsewhere for prison visiting, linked from 1821 through the British Society for Promoting Reformation of Female Prisoners. On a journey to Scotland with a brother, in 1818, she observed conditions in the provincial jails and, by giving publicity to them, ensured improvements. She secured better arrangements for women taken on board convict ships for transportation to the colonies, obtained reprieves for a number of women sentenced to death (though not for all of them), and held discussions with Sir Robert Peel before, as Home Secretary, he introduced his reforming Prison Act of 1823. She set down many of her conclusions on penal policy in a book published in 1827, stating, for instance, her opposition to capital punishment.

Already she was being consulted by prison reformers abroad. From 1838 onward, she made a number of continental tours on which, apart from addressing Quakers, she tried to persuade the authorities to imitate her methods. She earned the esteem of the king of Prussia, who, when in England in 1842, insisted on visiting her at home. In Britain, however, opinion veered during the 1830s in favor of a harsher penal policy. Elizabeth was dismayed at the spectacle of the new Pentonville Prison whose dark cells, she declared in 1843, "should never exist in a Christian and civilized country." Although she had accepted solitary confinement as an occasional form of punishment for disobedience, she believed that its increasing introduction as the standard policy for all offenders during the whole of their imprisonment would prevent them from being prepared for a useful life after discharge. Well before her death in 1845, the vogue for her particular remedies in her homeland had passed.

Nevertheless Elizabeth Fry remained an example of the scope for philanthropy among Christian ladies. She insisted that the female role was not restricted to the home but that it also encompassed practical care, especially for women in need. She had promoted various other charitable schemes herself; a shelter for destitute children in London, a district visiting society at Brighton, collections of improving books for isolated coastguards, and training for a small nursing order, the Protestant Sisters of Charity. But it is for prison reform that she is most remembered. She stood in a line of Christians who pioneered methods of caring for prisoners that included the Congregationalist John Howard, who in 1777 had urged more humane treatment for offenders, and the Baptist F. B. Meyer, who in the 1870s offered help at the prison gate to those released. Elizabeth Fry contributed a distinctively Quaker way of acting on the words of Jesus: "When in prison, you visited me."

Timechart 1700-2000

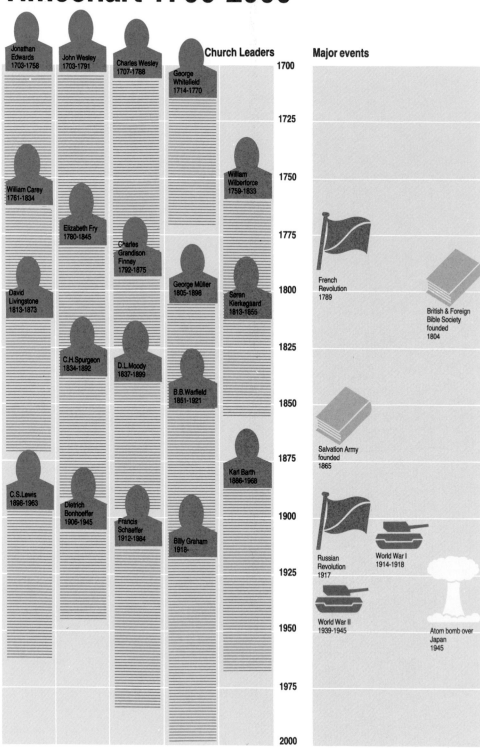

Church Leaders

Jonathan
Edwards
1703-1758

John Wesley
1703-1791

Charles Wesley
1707-1788

George
Whitefield
1714-1770

William
Wilberforce
1759-1833

William Carey
1761-1834

Elizabeth Fry
1780-1845

Charles
Grandison
Finney
1792-1875

George Müller
1805-1898

David
Livingstone
1813-1873

Søren
Kierkegaard
1813-1855

C.H.Spurgeon
1834-1892

D.L.Moody
1837-1899

B.B.Warfield
1851-1921

Karl Barth
1886-1968

C.S.Lewis
1898-1963

Dietrich
Bonhoeffer
1906-1945

Francis
Schaeffer
1912-1984

Billy Graham
1918-

Major events

French
Revolution
1789

British & Foreign
Bible Society
founded
1804

Salvation Army
founded
1865

Russian
Revolution
1917

World War I
1914-1918

World War II
1939-1945

Atom bomb over
Japan
1945

1700

1725

1750

1775

1800

1825

1850

1875

1900

1925

1950

1975

2000

Charles Grandison Finney
1792-1875

Although also a lawyer, pastor, professor, and college president, Charles Grandison Finney (1792-1875) is most often remembered as a revivalist. It is only right that this should be so, for, despite the fascinating diversity of his career, religious revivals clearly remained the organizing center and motivating passion of his life. An "immensely important man in American history by any standard of measure," as Sydney Ahlstrom has phrased it, Finney introduced literally thousands in his own generation and since to that kind of evangelical Christianity that is united by a common authority (the Bible), drawn together by a shared experience (conversion), and committed to the same duty (obedience to Christ in worldwide mission and benevolence).

The first half of the nineteenth century in the United States is often called the Age of Jackson. Yet historians have commented, "In a very special sense, the age was as much Finney's as it was Jackson's." Indeed, the very persuasiveness of Finney's influence, the fact that persons of widely divergent religious traditions continue to read and appreciate Finney, seems to suggest that his life and thought cannot be made to conform easily to the standard theological and ecclesiastical categories. Perhaps this is why some have called him a Calvinist, whereas others have called him an Arminian. In

actuality, Finney is best seen as a "bridge figure," seeking to guard his listeners (as he himself commented in his *Memoirs* "against hyper-Calvinism" on the one hand and "low Arminianism" on the other. Such a stance allowed him to link together in active ministry both Presbyterians and Wesleyans, Congregationalists and Baptists.

His fundamental concern throughout life remained that of getting sinners converted and then setting them to work preparing for the coming of the millennial kingdom. In the diligent pursuit of that task, he had no peer.

The Life of Finney	
1792	August 29, birth in Warren, Connecticut.
1818	Enters law office in Adams, New York.
1821	October 10, converted.
1824	Ordained by the Oneida Presbytery; married.
1824-1826	Labors in upstate New York; revivals in Jefferson and St. Lawrence Counties.
1825-1826	Western revivals in Oneida County.
1827	New Lebanon convention.
1827-1830	Conducts revivals in Wilmington, Philadelphia, Lancaster, etc.
1830	*New York Evangelist* founded.
1830-1831	Revival in Rochester, New York.
1832	Accepts pastorate of Chatham Street Chapel, New York City.
1835	Appointed professor of theology at Oberlin Collegiate Institute, Ohio; *Lectures on Revivals of Religion* published.
1836	Accepts pastorate of the Broadway Tabernacle, New York City.
1837	Accepts pastorate of the Oberlin Congregational Church.
1846	*Lectures on Systematic Theology* published.
1851-1866	Is appointed president of Oberlin College.
1875	August 16, death.
1876	*Memoirs* published.

Charles Grandison Finney

and Revivalism

Garth Rosell

Childhood

Charles Grandison Finney, the "Father of Modern Revivalism," was born on August 29, 1792, in Warren (Litchfield County), Connecticut, the seventh child of farming parents, Sylvester and Rebecca (Rice) Finney. With land increasingly scarce and costly in Connecticut, in 1794 the Finneys joined with many other young families in the great westward migrations of post-Revolutionary America. Settling in Hanover (now Kirkland), Oneida County, New York, following a brief stay in the village of Brothertown, Charles first attended a nearby common school, then the Hamilton Oneida Academy in Clinton. While there he came under the influence of Principal Seth Morton, who taught the popular, six-foot-two-inch Finney the basics of classical education, singing, and the cello.

In 1812 Finney returned to Connecticut to attend the Warren Academy in preparation for further studies at Yale College. Persuaded against attending Yale, Finney then spent two years teaching in New Jersey. In 1818 his mother's illness forced him to return to New York where he began the study of law, entering the office of Judge Benjamin Wright in Adams as an apprentice. Although it is uncertain as to whether or not Finney was actually admitted formally to the bar, he did regularly argue cases in the local justices court of Adams.

Conversion

Finney's remarkable religious conversion on October 10, 1821, however, dramatically changed the direction of his life. Leaving a promising legal career, claiming he had been given "a retainer from the Lord Jesus Christ to plead his cause," he sought entry into the Presbyterian ministry. Taken under care by the St. Lawrence presbytery (June 25, 1823), he studied theology with George Gale, his Princeton-trained pastor in Adams, was licensed to preach on December 30, 1823, and subsequently ordained on July 1, 1824. Hired by the Female Missionary Society of the Western District, he began his labors as a missionary to the settlers of upstate New York in the spring of 1824.

Under his preaching, a series of revivals broke out in a number of little villages throughout Jefferson and St. Lawrence counties, places such as Evans Mills, Antwerp, Brownville, and Gouverneur. By 1825 his work had spread to the towns of Western, Troy, Utica, Rome, and Auburn. These so-called western revivals (centered in Oneida County), in which Finney used such "new measures" as the anxious seat, protracted meetings, allowing women to pray in public, and the like, brought Finney national fame.

Revivalism

Not all were pleased with his success. Yale-trained revival leaders such as Lyman Beecher and Asahel Nettleton, troubled by false reports of alleged excesses, joined with other evangelical leaders from the Northeast at the village of New Lebanon in the summer of 1827 to discuss their differences. It was at that meeting that Finney emerged as the new leader of evangelical revivalism. This leadership was consolidated, during the years between 1827 and

1832, as Finney's revivals swept urban centers such as New York City, Philadelphia, Boston, and Rochester. Although Finney was involved in promoting revivals throughout his lifetime, even traveling to England for that purpose in 1849-1850 and again in 1859-1860, these early years were the high watermark of his revival career.

Forced in 1832 to curtail his travels, having contracted cholera in addition to the recurrent respiratory illnesses that troubled him throughout most of his lifetime, he became pastor of the Chatham Street Chapel (Second Free Presbyterian Church) in New York City. He subsequently held pastorates at the Broadway Tabernacle of New York City (1836-1837) and the First Congregational Church of Oberlin, Ohio (1837-1872). In 1835 he accepted an appointment as professor of theology at the newly-formed Oberlin Collegiate Institute in Ohio (now Oberlin College). He later served as president of Oberlin College from 1851 until 1866.

Theology

Theologically, Finney can best be described as a New School Calvinist. His preaching and teaching, always pointed and dramatic, stressed the moral government of God, the ability of people to repent and make themselves new hearts, the perfectability of human nature and society, and the need for Christians to apply their faith to daily living. For Finney, this included the investment of one's time and energy in establishing the millennial kingdom of God on earth by winning converts and involving oneself in social reform (including anti-slavery, temperance, and the like).

Throughout his lifetime, Finney produced a variety of books, sermon collections, and articles. Among the more important were his *Lectures on Revivals of Religion* (1835), a kind of manual on how to lead revivals. He wrote: "It [a revival] presupposes that the church is sunk down in a backslidden state, and a revival consists in the return of the church from her backslidings, and in the conversion of sinners. ... A revival is nothing else than a new beginning of obedience to God." His *Lectures on Systematic Theology* (1846) reflect his special brand of

"arminianized Calvinism." And his *Memoirs* (1876) recount his remarkable involvement in the great revivals of the first half of the nineteenth century.

Finney was married three times: to Lydia Andrews, Elizabeth Ford Atkinson, and Rebecca Rayl. He lost the first two by death. He had eight children, all by his first wife, and was a devoted father and husband. On August 16, 1875, a quiet Sunday in Oberlin, Ohio, Charles Finney, the great revivalist, died.

Charles Grandison Finney.

George Müller
1805-1898

Opposite: George Müller, founder of a Christian orphanage.

One of George Müller's orphan houses.

faith. For Müller's challenge to conventional Christians was that they should open themselves in prayer to God's leading and trust Him for every neèd as it arose. Though he never made any public appeals for funds, all his needs were met, sometimes literally at the last moment. He was able to assert that God had never failed him. In the same way, by faith, he maintained schools, distributed literature, and supported missionaries overseas.

A member of the "Open" Brethren, Müller was widely respected for his character, his work, and his evangelical witness. His influence spread far beyond his own denomination and his adopted country, and lasted long after his death.

George Müller (1805-1898), a German who lived and worked in England for almost seventy years, stands out as one of the most remarkable "men of faith" of his century.

Religion was part of the European social structure in the nineteenth century, with well-filled, "respectable" churches. World mission, like the British Empire, was expanding and exciting. Yet amidst middle-class affluence the poor remained appallingly deprived, as Charles Dickens's novels so clearly show. George Müller helped to expose Victorian complacency (it was that rather than mere hypocrisy) and did much to stir a new spirit of caring and faith.

His astonishing achievement was primarily the creation of orphan homes in Bristol, England, where 2,000 destitute children were surrounded with Christian love and given sound education. Before his death the homes had cared for more than 8,000 children, educated them, and found them work – and all by

The Life of	
Müller	
1805	Birth in Kroppenstadt, Prussia.
1825	Converted at Halle University.
1829	Goes to London to train as a missionary to the Jews.
1832	Moves to Bristol.
1834	Founded the Scriptural Knowledge Institution.
1835	Inaugurates his first orphan home in Bristol.
1870	Transfers the oversight of Ashley Down Orphanage to son-in-law.
1875-1892	World-wide speaking and preaching tours.
1898	Death in Bristol.

George Müller

Brethren Philanthropist

Cyril J. Davey

Bristol ministry

George Müller, born September 27, 1805, at Kroppenstadt in Prussia, was the son of a government tax-collector. As a youth he was wild and drunken. Still undisciplined, he began training for the Lutheran ministry at the University of Halle. Then, at the age of twenty, in a students' prayer meeting, he was converted. With a strong call to evangelism, he left Halle and went to London to train as a missionary to the Jews. But he fell ill and was sent to Devon to recuperate. There, though very much a foreigner, he took pastoral charge of a small Independent chapel, preached widely in the area, and the pattern of his future ministry began to take shape.

Müller started his lifelong association with the Brethren and married Mary Groves, of a leading Plymouth Brethren family. Giving up a small church salary, the couple committed themselves to live by faith alone. In 1832 they moved to Bristol, and, under Müller's forthright evangelical ministry, the rundown Bethesda chapel was transformed. Lydia, their daughter, was born the next year.

Müller, with an unshakable belief in the Bible, was convinced that if Christians took Scripture seriously there were no limits to what they could achieve for God. He began the Scriptural Knowledge Institution (S.K.I.) two years after arriving in Bristol. All four of its aims were practical and evangelical. These were: to organize schools on a scriptural foundation; provide education for poor children; circulate the Scriptures; and support missionaries. The response to the S.K.I. ensured that Müller would launch his next and greatest venture with complete confidence.

By the time the Müllers arrived in Bristol, cholera had swept through the city and the wealthy fled to the country from their splendid homes in Clifton. The poor lived – and died – in squalid, narrow streets where children groveled for food in the garbage heaps.

The first orphanage

In 1834 a fifth aim was added to S.K.I. – "to feed, clothe and educate destitute orphan children." Believing that this was God's will, Müller was certain the Lord would provide what was necessary – 1,000 pounds to begin a home and the right people to run it. In April 1836 Müller opened a home for thirty orphaned girls. The expenses were 240 pounds for the year, the income that came in amounted to 840 pounds. In December he opened another home for infants and nine months later a third for boys. Altogether he then had nearly one hundred children under care.

This was the beginning of one of the most astounding stories of prayer and faith – what most people regarded as a story of miracles. By 1870 the orphan homes, transferred to Ashley Down, had 2,000 resident children. Their life included a good general education, a great deal of practical work, a healthy diet, and daily worship and prayers.

By the 1880s S.K.I. had received more than one million pounds for its projects, of which 700,000 pounds was for the orphanages. But if the cost in money was high, the demands on faith were higher still. Müller never made an appeal for money. The children never went hungry or ill-dressed. Never a debt went unpaid. Yet there was never any security – except the faith that God knew and would provide. God did so, though often at the very last moment, when there was not a penny in the purse and no food on the tables. Müller's homes existed by a never-ending succession of miracles of faith. Their history is largely page after page of answered prayers.

After 1870, things changed. Mary Müller died. Two years later George married Susannah Sanger, who equally shared his whole way of life. He also handed over the running of the homes to James Wright, a widower who married his daughter Lydia.

New departures

Far from retiring, however, Müller began a new stage of life. From 1875 to 1892 he traveled extensively. Fluent in several languages, he ministered not only in Europe but throughout the world, preaching, speaking, and conducting Bible-teaching missions. He encouraged Christians to love and use the Bible, to listen to God and to trust Him. His expositions were compelling because they were filled with the things that had happened to him, his homes, and his children.

In those seventeen years he toured the United States, Australia, and New Zealand three times each, and India twice; preached in forty-two countries; traveled a quarter of a million miles; and addressed some three million people.

In 1898, at the age of ninety-two, George Müller died. Bristol had seldom, if ever, seen such a funeral with the streets so deeply lined with silent people paying tribute to a man everywhere known and respected. Through S.K.I. he had raised 1,453,153 pounds. God had kept all His promises. George Müller himself kept his own promise to ask only for what he needed. He died with 160 pounds.

The work has continued, though today, with radical changes in childcare, the

Orphan babies from George Müller's homes in Bristol, England.

huge old orphanages have been sold and far fewer children live in ten modern residential houses. Yet, despite changes, the need and the love, faith and response, remain the same.

George Müller's work was influential in social action, education for the poor, and world evangelization. But there was something else of far greater significance that characterized the man – his conviction that God as revealed in the Bible would answer prayers and keep all His promises. The Bible was the foundation of everything he believed, preached, and did. He was shocked that Christians, even the Brethren at Bethesda, were afraid to live by "dependence on God." S.K.I., with its four aims, was established to prove the reliability of God's promises.

The 1832 cholera epidemic highlighted the desperate plight of Bristol's "waifs and strays." But although the fifth aim of S.K.I., to serve the orphans, was the outcome of Christian compassion, for Müller compassion was only a secondary motive. His primary intention was to prove without doubt or contradiction that God would keep His promises. He believed that if he could demonstrate this through his work with the orphans, then Christians everywhere would be led to deeper and more effective faith. It certainly touched many of those who heard the remarkable and continuing story, even if not to the depth Müller had hoped. In particular it became a force in the lives of many of his own "children."

Thirty years after Müller's homes were established, similar work was begun in London and elsewhere, notably by Dr. Barnardo (1866), the Rev. Dr. T. B. Stephenson (Methodism's National Children's Home, 1868), and later still the Church of England's Waifs and Strays Society. They all owed a great deal to Müller's pioneering inspiration and example.

Evangelism and education

Though in the 1830s "education for the poor" was minimal, Müller was always committed to it as an adjunct to evangelism and as a matter of social justice. Even before he accepted his first orphans, S.K.I. had begun two Sunday schools, two adult schools, and six day schools. By 1880 it was responsible for seventy-two day schools with more than 7,000 children, mainly in the Bristol area, but also in Italy and Spain and in South America, where it continued until the 1970s.

Müller's homes provided a general education that developed discipline, idealism, and Christian character; but its quality was so high that he was attacked for "educating the poor above their station." Equally, because he kept boys at school until they were fourteen and girls until they were seventeen he was accused of robbing factories and mines of their proper source of cheap labor. But none of his children left without work to go to – the boys usually to trade apprenticeships and the girls to domestic service, teaching, and, later, nursing. Müller opened his own teacher training institution in Gloucestershire, where he sent his most promising pupils before appointing them to his own schools.

S.K.I. always gave valuable impetus to evangelism through literature and the free distribution of Scriptures and tracts. The Christian bookshop opened in Bristol is still in operation, despite being destroyed in World War II.

Müller, of course, was committed to world evangelization from the time of his conversion, and S.K.I. always supported missionaries. Hudson Taylor was entertained at the orphan house in 1866 before he sailed for China, where he organized the China Inland Mission on the same faith basis as Müller ran S.K.I. and the homes. In the early years all of China Inland Mission's twenty-one missionaries with wives and families were almost entirely dependent on support channeled through George Müller.

"And all this by faith!" On this fundamental was based the whole life work of a man who influenced generation after generation and whose commitment still challenges us today as it did his own time.

Søren Kierkegaard
1813-1855

Søren Kierkegaard, "father of existentialism".

in Christian Denmark was automatically a Christian. The second obstacle was the speculative, liberal reinterpretation of historic Christianity, particularly that inspired by philosophical idealism. Against both of those Kierkegaard urged that Christianity is a decisive way of *existing*, rooted in the authority of Jesus, not based on any philosophical system.

The Life of
Kierkegaard

1813	May 5, birth.
1838	Reconciled to his father and returns to the Christian faith.
1840	September 10, engaged to Regine Olsen.
1841	Publishes *The Concept of Irony* and breaks with Regine Olsen.
1843	Begins work on *Either-Or* and *Edifying Discourses*.
1846	Publishes *Concluding Unscientific Postscript* and is targeted by satirical attacks in the *Corsair*.
1848	Easter, undergoes a deeper experience of the Christian faith; writes *The Sickness unto Death* and *Training in Christianity*.
1854	December 18, begins open attack on the established church in *Attack on Christendom*.
1855	October 2, collapse on street and is paralyzed.
1855	November 11, death; near riot ensues at his funeral.

Denmark

Copenhagen •

Søren Kierkegaard (1813-1855), today renowned as the "father of existentialism," is a man who has had a pivotal influence on existential philosophy, theology, and psychology. His imprint can be clearly seen in the works of such people as the early Karl Barth, Paul Tillich, Martin Heidegger, and Rollo May. More or less unknown outside Denmark in his lifetime, Kierkegaard burst upon the European scene about the time of World War I, although his full influence was not felt in the United States until World War II.

Within the fourteen large volumes that make up his collected published writings (Danish edition) can be found works that fall under the categories of literature, philosophy, and theology, in addition to a large volume of writings that are sermonic or devotional in form but which the author called "discourses," because he was not ordained to preach.

It is likely that Kierkegaard himself would have rejected most of what passes for existentialism in the twentieth century. His own goal was not to found a philosophical movement, but to try to renew the possibility of authentic Christian faith among his contemporaries. There were two main obstacles to this, he thought. The first was the illusion of "Christendom," that everyone

Søren Kierkegaard

and Existentialism

C. Stephen Evans

A troubled youth

Søren Kierkegaard was reared in the wealthy home of Michael Pedersen Kierkegaard, who was a devout, but strict, father. There he absorbed Lutheran orthodoxy, laced with a strong pietistic influence. Young Søren was an extremely reflective person, who from an early age struggled with feelings of guilt and depression. The causes for that seem to have stemmed in large measure from his relation with his father, who also struggled with guilt and with what was then termed "melancholy." His depression was aggravated by a series of deaths in the family; five of Søren's brothers and sisters died within a relatively short time.

As a young man Søren became engaged to Regine Olsen and then broke the engagement (1841), partly because he felt he was unfit for marriage. He continued to love the girl, however, and interpreted his sacrifice as religious in character. That experience marked the beginning of his "authorship," much of which concerned the necessity of "dying to self" acquiring a willingness to sacrifice any earthly good if necessary – in order to achieve a genuine "God-relationship."

One other external event also shaped his work: a conflict (1846) with the *Corsair*, a Danish satirical magazine, in which Kierkegaard became convinced that "the crowd is untruth." The person who wishes to stand firm for the truth must be prepared to be "the individual" who does not fear the laughter or seek the accolades of the public.

True Christianity

Kierkegaard wrote in an attempt to help the individual acquire the inward personal concern, or "subjectivity," that he believed was essential to become a true Christian. He saw Christianity as the final and most adequate answer to the question, How should I *exist*? Basically, he believed there were three major ways of answering this question. These three answers made up what Kierkegaard termed the three "spheres of existence" or "stages on life's way."

The first stage he termed the esthetic stage; this is the life-view in which a person is urged to enjoy life by developing his natural drives and abilities. The esthete lives "for the moment." This life is symbolized by the casual love affair, and it culminates in despair.

The second stage is the ethical life a life of duty and commitment, which is symbolized by marriage. A truly earnest attempt to live such a life culminates in the discovering of a person's own moral shortcomings and, therefore, the recognition of guilt.

The final and highest state is the religious, which involves a recognition that man is unable to become a whole person on his own and must seek the help of God. Kierkegaard sees Christianity as differing from all other religions, however, in that Christianity alone says that man is not even able to establish a relationship with God on his own. Since man is sinful, it was necessary for God to take the initiative by Himself becoming a man. Man can know God only through a revelation, which must be accepted as authoritative.

Kierkegaard stresses that Christianity sees the incarnation as an actual historical event; thus a Christian acquires salvation not through trying to live a moral life (as many liberal theologians who were

Kierkegaard's contemporaries said) but through faith in the Jesus of history. Kierkegaard believed that God's loving self-sacrifice in Christ could not be understood by finite, sinful human beings. He thus opposed any attempts to understand philosophically the incarnation or scientifically "prove" the truth of Christianity. For Kierkegaard, one becomes a Christian only through faith, which is produced by the consciousness of sin through the work of God. The incarnation was and remains a paradox to *human* reason, which is competent only to ascertain its own incompetency with respect to the content of Christianity. For the proud man who will not acknowledge his sinful limits, the incarnation will necessarily be an offense.

Indirect communication

A significant feature of Kierkegaard's writing is his attempt to utilize "indirect communication." He believed that moral and religious truth could be acquired only by an individual through personal appropriation, unlike mathematical and scientific truth, which can be directly and objectively given by one person to an-

other. To help stimulate his readers to concern themselves personally with the "three stages on life's way," Kierkegaard wrote a series of books that are attributed to pseudonymous authors who actually embody the life-views they represent. Thus, Kierkegaard's audience not only reads *about* the esthetic, ethical, and religious ways of life, but also *encounters* these views. People are thereby forced to reflect about their own lives.

When reading Kierkegaard it is important not to attribute all the opinions of these pseudonymous characters to Kierkegaard himself. Kierkegaard's own deepest beliefs are contained in the series of "discourses," in those he termed "edifying" but more especially in those he termed "Christian." The beginning reader of Kierkegaard is well advised to start with these latter works, such as *Purity of Heart Is to Will One Thing, Works of Love*, or *The Sickness unto Death*, before reading such pseudonymous works as *Either-Or* and *Fear and Trembling* or his philosophical masterpieces, *Philosophical Fragments* and *Concluding Unscientific Postscript.*

Frederiksborg Castle, Copenhagen, Denmark.

Sunset at Nyhavn, Copenhagen.

Christianity and Christendom

Kierkegaard's life culminated with his attack (1854) on the Danish state church, which he saw as an embodiment of Christendom. In Christendom, Christianity is abolished by being made into a triviality. Nobody can *become* a Christian because it is assumed that everybody *is* a Christian. Being a Christian has been reduced to being a "nice person" who conforms to the established human order. Kierkegaard saw his task as that of "reintroducing Christianity into Christendom" by helping his contemporaries see that being a Christian requires a radical, courageous decision to follow Christ. This is a decision that must be continually renewed and that may bring the individual into conflict with the established order, which is permeated by worldly values.

Kierkegaard is a controversial figure among evangelicals. Although everyone concedes the value of some of his edifying writings, many have criticized Kierkegaard as too fideistic and subjective in his understanding of religious knowledge. This is primarily because of his attack on apologetics; for Kierkegaard, faith stems solely from the consciousness of sin, and rational evidence plays no positive role. Suspicion of Kierkegaard is also due to his strong emphasis on subjective, inward appropriation of truth.

However, if Kierkegaard sees faith as unsupported by reason, it is not because faith is in itself irrational or absurd. Rather, he claims that faith appears absurd to human reason because our reason is permeated by sin. And when one of his pseudonyms says "truth is subjectivity," his purpose is *not* to deny that there are objectively true propositions, but to affirm that these propositions cannot really make a person's life true until they are inwardly, subjectively appropriated.

David Livingstone
1813-1873

David Livingstone (1813-1873), the Scottish missionary and explorer, exercised a greater influence on the history of central Africa than any other person, Christian or non-Christian, in the nineteenth century. As an evangelist or church planter his achievements were minimal; as a crusader against the cruelties of the East African slave trade his success was limited; yet as an explorer his record is unparalleled. Some would therefore dispute his right to the title "missionary," and Livingstone's missionary service in the employ of the London Missionary Society was indeed restricted to the years 1841 to 1856.

However, Livingstone himself regarded all his activities, geographical exploration included, as part of his missionary commission. He believed they were a part of the purpose of God to "open up" the African interior to the gospel and its attendant blessings of freedom and prosperity. Livingstone's travels did, in fact, open up large areas of central Africa both to later missionary work and to European commercial and imperial penetration. The beginnings of Protestant missions in what are now Malawi, Uganda, Tanzania, and Zaire were all to a greater or lesser extent a consequence of the impact made by his life and death. It may appear ironical that the man whose selfless devotion to the welfare of the African peoples has become legendary should also be remembered by some modern writers as a

pioneer of the age of European colonial rule in Africa. His life and work remain the subject of argument and conflicting interpretations, but no modern reassessment has dislodged his position as one of the most remarkable Christians of the nineteenth century.

The Life of

Livingstone

1813	Birth in Blantyre, Scotland.
1840	Sails for South Africa as a missionary of the London Missionary Society.
1854-1856	Crosses Africa from west to east.
1856-1858	Receives a hero's welcome on first visit home to Britain.
1858	Returns to Africa as British consul and leader of Zambezi expedition.
1864-1865	Second visit home to Britain.
1866-1873	Last journeys in central Africa.
1873	Death at Chitambo, in what is now Zambia.

David Livingstone, missionary and explorer

Scotland

Blantyre• •Edinburgh

David Livingstone

Explorer and Missionary

Brian Stanley

Opposite: Livingstone and Stanley meet in Africa.

Medical student

David Livingstone was born in 1813 into the harsh environment of the British Industrial Revolution. The one-room home in which he grew up in Blantyre, Scotland, overlooked the cotton mill where, from the age of ten, he worked a fourteen-hour day. His early education consisted of night school supplemented by reading books supported on the spinning frame at which he worked. His appetite for hard work and thirst for knowledge were reinforced from the age of twenty by a strong personal Christian faith. After reading an appeal for medical missionaries for China by the German missionary Karl Gutzlaff, Livingstone determined to train as a doctor for missionary service. Medical and theological studies in Glasgow led to his acceptance in 1838 by the London Missionary Society (LMS) for further training. China proved an impossible destination owing to the outbreak of the first Opium War, and contact with Robert Moffat (1795-1883), the celebrated LMS missionary in South Africa (and Livingstone's future father-in-law) induced the young Scot to volunteer for service in southern Africa.

Livingstone began his missionary career on Moffat's station at Kuruman in July 1841, but soon moved farther into the interior in search of peoples unreached by missionary influence. From 1843 to 1853 he worked among the Tswana people, but with only a single conversion – that of the Bakwena chief, Sechele – to show for his labors. Increasingly Livingstone's aspirations focused on the territory farther to the north on either side of the Zambezi River. Here the country was more populous and out of reach of the Boer farmers from the south; above all the Zambezi offered the prospect of a route for "legitimate" trade, which Livingstone believed to be the only force capable of driving the slave trade from the region. He decided first to push northwestward to the Atlantic coast in the hope of finding an alternative route to central Africa that would avoid hostile Boer territory. After a journey of astounding courage, Livingstone reached the coast at Luanda in May 1854. Disappointed with the west coast route, he then proceeded not merely to retrace his steps but to follow the course of the Zambezi to its mouth on the Indian Ocean, where he arrived in May 1856 after a journey of nearly 2,500 miles.

National hero

Livingstone returned to Britain in December 1856 to find himself fêted as a national hero. His geographical achievement was unprecedented, and it had been accomplished in the name of a cause dear to the heart of the evangelical conscience in Britain – the elimination of the hated slave trade from the African continent. However, the public applause concealed serious divergences of view between Livingstone and the LMS, which had surfaced long before his return. Livingstone spoke of going back to Africa "to try to make an open path for commerce and Christianity." Knowing that the LMS would not give him a free hand to engage in exploration and trade, Livingstone had allowed negotiations to proceed with the British government regarding an appointment as a British consul. In October 1857 he informed the LMS that his return to Africa would not be under its auspices, and in March the Zambezi expedition

David Livingstone's birthplace, Blantyre, Scotland.

sailed under Livingstone's leadership.

The expedition was a disaster. On his trans-African journey Livingstone had jumped to the erroneous conclusion that the Zambezi would be navigable virtually in its entirety. He had gravely underestimated the Cabora Bassa Rapids. Their impassability to steamer traffic destroyed Livingstone's vision of the Zambezi as a highway for Christianity and commerce into the heart of Africa. He turned instead to the Shire River, which stretched northward from the Zambezi, and to Lake Malawi, which he discovered at its end. The land at the southern end of the lake appeared well populated and favorable to cotton cultivation; a Christian commercial presence there might cut off a large proportion of the east African slave trade at its source. Before this vision could find any fulfillment, the British government recalled the expedition, in 1863. So ended one of the saddest episodes in Livingstone's life, marked by constant wrangling between Livingstone and his companions and by the crowning blow of the death of his wife, Mary, in April 1863.

Livingstone's reception in Britain on his second visit home in 1864-1865 was noticeably cooler than in 1856-1858. The British government had lost its former enthusiasm for his plans. He returned to Africa for the last time in 1866 as an unpaid consul, with merely nominal authority. His final years were spent exploring the uncharted territory between Lakes Malawi and Tanganyika. For years at a time his whereabouts and very survival were unknown to the rest of the world. Expeditions were dispatched to find Livingstone. The one led by the journalist H. M. Stanley was merely the best publicized and the most successful. Stanley's discovery of Livingstone in November 1871, followed in January 1874 by the poignant news of his death at Chitambo on May 1, 1873, ensured that Livingstone was once again a legend, a heroic symbol of the driving sense of mission that lay at the heart of Victorian Christianity.

Puncturing the myth

Recent biographies of Livingstone have taken some pleasure in puncturing the "Livingstone myth" and exposing some of the less attractive personality traits revealed in his journals and correspondence. As a missionary, he found the yoke of society control almost unbearable; the

LMS certainly had cause to complain in 1857 about the way Livingstone kept the society in the dark about his negotiations with the British government, at a time when the society was counting on his continued services. As a husband and father, Livingstone must bear some of the responsibility for the sadnesses that afflicted the members of his family; his wife, Mary, strained by years of separation from her husband and inadequate financial support, became prey to bouts of depression and drinking. As a leader of men, Livingstone was often dictatorial and unreasonable. But his failings were the obverse of his strengths, the product of his obsession with the service of Africa in the name of Christ. Any assessment of David Livingstone's significance in Christian history ought to focus not on the rough edges of his personality but on the issues that his missionary theory and practice raised for later generations.

Some of Livingstone's ideas seem dated and eccentric. His hopes of eliminating the slave trade by the introduction of legitimate commerce in African raw materials and European manufactures reflected the intellectual influences of his youth and in particular the ideas of the Scottish economic philosopher Adam Smith. The attempts of Livingstone and his immediate successors to ally missionary work in central Africa with European trade were counter-productive. After his death, confidence in the early Victorian missionary prescription of "commerce and Christianity" gradually evaporated.

Livingstone believed that God was at work in every area of human activity – in geographical discovery or commercial intercourse as much as in the strictly Christian sphere – moving history to a "glorious consummation" when the rule of Christ would be supreme. His was a Christian vision typical of the Victorians in its rational optimism. Nonetheless, the breadth of his missionary understanding reminds the church in a less confident age that conversion to Christ does indeed have implications for the economic and cultural life of a society.

Missionary expansion

Of more immediate relevance today is Livingstone's unchanging insistence that the watchword in missionary strategy ought to be not consolidation but expansion. He criticized the LMS for concentrating its missionary resources in the well-established churches of the Cape Colony while ignoring the mass of unevangelized peoples to the north. He warned that the prevailing policy of consolidation was producing missionary-dominated churches: "perpetual tutelage and everlasting leading strings would enfeeble angels." The rates of growth of the African churches were, he argued, in inverse proportion to the number of missionaries stationed among them.

In some respects, indeed, Livingstone anticipated modern church growth theory. He justified his own policy of pushing ever onward beyond the Tswana people to evangelize the surrounding tribes as "the only way which permits the rational hope that when the people do turn to the Lord it will be by groups." Recognizing that the level of receptivity to Christianity among most African peoples at the time was extremely low, he urged that missions should concentrate, not on obtaining isolated conversions within a well-worked, limited area, but rather on the widest possible diffusion of Christian truth and principles so that the conditions might be created for whole peoples to turn to Christ.

According to David Livingstone, there could be no substantial missionary reaping without a prior commitment to widespread sowing, and his own career was wholly consistent with this maxim. The Protestant churches of sub-Saharan Africa, many of them born in the aftermath of Livingstone's explorations, are today among the strongest in the world. Livingstone believed himself to have been led by God to "open up" Africa for the gospel. More than a century after his death, it seems that he may, after all, have been right.

C.H.Spurgeon
1834-1892

In the late nineteenth century, an age of great preachers, the greatest was Charles Haddon Spurgeon (1834-1892). Others attracted large audiences or published occasional collections of pulpit addresses, but Spurgeon outdid them all. In 1865 his sermons sold 25,000 copies weekly. Deeply rooted in the strong Puritan traditions of East Anglia, Spurgeon had a firm grasp of what he believed and a remarkable ability to communicate his convictions. His

ministry at the Metropolitan Tabernacle was a major tourist attraction in south London. As pastor of the largest Baptist church in the world, he exercised a powerful sway over his own denomination.

In his later years, concern at an apparent dilution of central evangelical truths by certain fellow-ministers led him to separate from the mainstream of Baptist life in Britain. His reputation as a preacher made him a redoubtable champion of

orthodoxy. Spurgeon's influence was perpetuated by the many ministers trained at the college he founded, both in his own lifetime and afterwards, and even more so those trained by his writings. Apart from his sermons, he composed a large number of books that achieved an extensive international circulation. Spurgeon was a robust character who clearly spoke plain common sense. Yet he also enlivened all he said with a playful humor. He was a profoundly effective preacher of the gospel of Jesus Christ.

The Metropolitan Tabernacle, South London, built to house the huge crowds attracted by C.H.Spurgeon's preaching.

The Life of
Spurgeon

1834	Birth at Kelvedon, Essex, England.
1850	Converted and subsequently baptized.
1851	Pastor of Waterbeach Baptist Church, Cambridgeshire.
1854	Pastor of New Park Street Baptist Church, London.
1855	Preaches at services in Exeter Hall.
1856	Begins preaching at services in Surrey Gardens Music Hall.
1861	Metropolitan Tabernacle opened.
1864	Criticizes evangelical clergymen in Church of England.
1869	Establishes orphanage.
1887	Leaves Baptist Union during Down-Grade Controversy.
1892	Death at Mentone, France.

Spurgeon's birthplace, Kelvedon, Essex.

C.H.Spurgeon

Prince of Preachers

David W.Bebbington

Conversion

Charles Haddon Spurgeon was born on June 19, 1834, the oldest son of a coalyard clerk and minister of the Independent denomination, John Spurgeon. When the baby was ten months old, the family moved within the county of Essex (England) from the village of Kelvedon to the ancient market town of Colchester. About eight months later Charles was transferred to the care of his grandfather, another Independent minister, who served in the village of Stambourne for fifty-four years. Charles spent six years and many subsequent delightful holidays there, precociously exploring the library of Puritan works that had once belonged to the first Independent minister of the village in the seventeenth century.

At the age of fifteen Spurgeon was converted in Colchester, under the ministry of a Primitive Methodist local preacher. He joined the Independent church in Newmarket (Suffolk), where he had gone in the previous year as a student schoolteacher, but, four months after his conversion, was baptized in the River Lark near the village of Isleham. Moving to a school in Cambridge, he joined St. Andrew's Street Baptist Church and became a village preacher. For three years he regularly served the small church of Waterbeach, near Cambridge, until his growing fame as a preacher brought him to the attention of the New Park Baptist Church in south London, once the congregation of John Gill, the greatest of eighteenth-century theologians among the Baptists, and of John Rippon, their leading figure at the turn of the nineteenth century. He accepted a call to its pulpit while he was still under twenty years old.

New Park Street

Spurgeon soon created a stir. The unsophisticated country lad preached so powerfully that congregations, previously at a low ebb, grew rapidly. Elaborate sentences replete with poetic phraseology had become fashionable in the London pulpit in recent years, but Spurgeon spoke with a pithy directness that startled his audience. He possessed a happy knack of embodying Puritan theology in homely words and was prepared to use humor to press home his message. A powerful but melodious voice was supplemented by a gift for dramatic gesture. Dwelling on central evangelical themes, his ministry was rewarded with many conversions. Although some criticized him for irreverence, his popularity meant that the building size had to be extended less than a year after his settlement at New Park Street.

Meanwhile, services were held in the Exeter Hall, the setting for the annual meetings of the great evangelical societies in the heart of London. Soon the hall could not contain the crowds that flocked to hear him, and Spurgeon secured the Surrey Gardens Music Hall for his services. He was censured for occupying a place dedicated to worldly amusement, but on the first evening, October 19, 1856, 10,000 people packed the building. A false cry of fire caused panic in which seven died and many were injured. Spurgeon was temporarily downcast, but, boldly resuming services in the Music Hall, consolidated his position as the leading preacher of the day.

In 1861 the congregation moved to its permanent home, the Metropolitan Tabernacle. On Spurgeon's insistence, its architecture was Grecian in style, for Greek was the language of the New Testament. The new building had permanent seating for 3,600, but at least 2,000 others normally squeezed in. Over the next thirty years many would-be hearers were turned away on Sunday evenings. The church grew in membership from 232 on Spurgeon's arrival in 1854 to 5,311 at the end of 1891. During that period 14,460 were baptized and added to the church. Spurgeon's fame as a preacher gathered huge congregations when he traveled the country. Sermon preparation was rarely difficult for him. He would defer choosing a topic for Sunday morning until Saturday evening and that for Sunday evening until the preceding afternoon. Sufficient notes would occupy about one side of a sheet of paper, and many illustrations were improvised during delivery. Each Monday a sermon was revised for publication. One was issued weekly from 1856 until a quarter of a century after his death, at first as *The New Park Street Pulpit* and later as *The Metropolitan Tabernacle Pulpit*. The sermon that proved to have most converting power was "Compel Them to Come In," delivered in 1859, but probably his greatest pulpit compositions where those of the years around 1870, when he was at the height of his abilities.

C.H.Spurgeon in 1854.

Spurgeon's theology

Calvinism remained the framework of Spurgeon's theology throughout his life, but his beliefs were modified over time. He came to embrace the idea that funds for Christian work should be sought primarily through prayer, unsuccessfully urging this "faith mission" principle on the Baptist Missionary Society in 1863. He objected to ordination, dropping the title Reverend in 1864. In the same year he gained some notoriety by charging evangelical clergymen with bad faith in remaining within the Church of England despite the teaching of baptismal regeneration that was to be found in its formularies. At this point, with typical bravado, he erected a baptismal font in his garden as a birdbath. Although he never joined the committee of the Baptist Union, he frequently preached under its auspices and in 1865 took a leading part in the formation of the London Baptist Association.

By the 1880s, as new intellectual currents ran through English Nonconformity, he felt increasing alarm at lax theological opinions in his own denomination. In 1887 he publicly withdrew from the Baptist Union in the so-called Down-Grade Controversy. It was not a protest against the views of John Clifford, the most prominent of the General Baptists, nor against the Arminian convictions that Clifford shared with the Methodists; Spurgeon had a Methodist preach for him immediately afterwards. Rather, Spurgeon criticized younger men "who are giving up the atoning sacrifice, denying the inspiration of Holy Scripture, and casting slurs upon justification by faith." Bound by a private promise not to state names,

Victorian London, by Gustave Doré.

Spurgeon felt wounded when the Baptist Union council criticized him for making general and unsubstantiated charges. Although there was no possibility of reconciliation, Spurgeon's action strengthened the position of more conservative opinion in the denomination.

The last years

In his last years Spurgeon suffered from a sense of isolation, accentuated by political differences with previous friends. His earlier support for the Liberal Party terminated in 1886 when he feared that William Ewart Gladstone's policy of Home Rule for Ireland would threaten the welfare of the island's Protestants. Rheumatic gout had brought on Bright's disease, and Spurgeon was frequently forced to rest, especially at Mentone in the south of France, where he died in 1892. Yet his masterful personality had achieved a great deal in his lifetime. The Pastor's College, begun in the late 1850s, trained nearly 900 men before his death. His *Lectures to My Students*, a classic for those preparing for the ministry, was the first publication issued through the Book Fund, a charitable agency for Christian workers run by Spurgeon's wife. He also edited a widely circulating monthly church magazine, *The Sword and Trowel*, founded a colportage society, and created a successful orphanage. His telling wit was deployed to good purpose in several books, particularly the best-selling *John Ploughman's Talk* and *Sermons in Candles*. His most substantial literary work was a six-volume commentary on the Psalms, *The Treasury of David* (1870-1885). But it was the published sermons more than anything else that attracted a vast international audience even beyond the Protestant world. Spurgeon justly remains an enduring influence on preaching in the late twentieth century.

D.L.Moody
1837-1899

By the second half of the nineteenth century, steamships had brought the continents nearer. Railways had spread across America and Britain. Horse tramways eased access within cities, which were growing vast through increased mobility, high birthrate, and multiplying industries.

All this made mass evangelism possible. The Wesleys and George Whitefield had preached to huge crowds in the open air,

but that, however effective, was spontaneous and haphazard, not in organized campaigns. Evangelism in the earlier nineteenth century was the work of circuit riders or individual pastors and teachers such as Charles G. Finney.

Population movement and industrialization had tended to weaken the churches, especially in the big cities, where people from the countryside or small townships often lost close touch

D.L.Moody as a young man.

with religion, though almost all were Christians in name and background.

There was, therefore, a need as well as an opening for a man who could proclaim the name of Christ to many thousands together, in such a way that the churches would be revived.

The man who emerged was Dwight Lyman Moody (1837-1899). He came from an unlikely background – a small farming community in New England. He was only semi-educated, but of such stature that he could land in Britain in 1873 utterly obscure, and leave in 1875 with Scotland, England, and Ireland at his feet. His story – and above all his personality – command attention: rugged, delightful, compassionate : a man of total integrity, with a supreme gift for bringing New Testament Christianity before the whole range of contemporary hearers and putting them to work for God.

The Life of
Moody

1837	Birth at Northfield, Massachusetts.
1855	Conversion in Boston.
1860	In Chicago, abandons business career to be children's worker, then evangelist.
1870	Recruits Ira D. Sankey as singer.
1871	Chicago fire.
1873-1875	First British campaign.
1875-1876	Brooklyn, Philadelphia, New York campaigns.
1879,1881	Founds schools: Northfield (girls) and Mount Hermon (boys).
1882-1884	Second British campaign.
1885	Sponsors movement for world evangelization.
1886	Founds Moody Bible Institute.
1899	Death at Northfield, age sixty-two.

D.L.Moody

and Revival

John C.Pollock

Conversion

D. L. Moody, who seldom used his first name, was born in 1837, fifth son of a smallholder and mason in Northfield, Massachusetts. His father died of too much whiskey when D. L. was four. The family of eight was reared in poverty by its strong-willed mother, and Moody's education was erratic because he was needed on the farm (all his life he could never spell). He disliked farming, and, at the age of seventeen, he went to Boston and got a job in the shoe store of his uncles, the Holtons.

His mother was a Unitarian, but her brothers were Trinitarian. Attendance at the Sunday school of their Boston church led D. L. Moody to a very definite conversion to Christ on April 21, 1855, through the influence of his teacher.

Moody was muscular and well built, a hard worker, ambitious, and full of fun. In 1856 he migrated to Chicago, the new and thrusting city of the Great Plains, and quickly found work in a shoe store. His happy ways and delightful manner, his keen business sense and unbounded energy might have made him a millionaire. However, he became more and more absorbed in Christian work among the roughest boys and girls in Chicago's slums. At first he felt himself too uneducated to preach or teach, but soon developed a breezy gift of making the Bible come alive. His desire to win souls became so strong that in 1860 he gave up his business career to run his children's mission, and the new YMCA, without salary. During the Civil War he served in the war zones and in Chicago as a lay chaplain. He was never ordained. By 1865, age twenty-eight, he had become a highly effective if homespun evangelist, though ridiculed in Chicago as "Crazy Moody" for his unrestrained zeal.

In 1862 he had married Emma Revell, English-born of Huguenot descent. She was self-effacing, yet her culture, sense, sweetness, and faith were vital factors in polishing Moody for the great work ahead. They had two sons and a daughter. Supremely happy family life gave Moody the firmest base for his work and travels.

Moody meets Sankey

In 1867 the Moodys visited the British Isles. An ex-pickpocket, Harry Moorhouse, whom he met in Dublin, later came to Chicago and taught Moody to preach the *love* of God: "I had thought," Moody said, "that God hated sinners as well as sin." In 1870 he met Ira D. Sankey, a young civil servant with an untrained but exceptionally fine voice. Moody persuaded Sankey to join him to lead the singing at the independent church on Chicago Avenue which, in a rather haphazard way, had grown up around his mission in the city's slums.

Moody was becoming a figure of some importance in the Christian life in the Middle West, and he would probably have spent his life there had it not been for the Chicago fire of October 1871. All he had built up was destroyed with the city. While in New York that winter, raising funds to rebuild the churches, he underwent a profound spiritual renewal. In 1872 he revisited Britain briefly. He had not intended to preach, but his effectiveness and freshness led to three independent invitations to return for a prolonged mission. It was on this visit also that he heard an ex-butcher, Henry Varley, remark: "The world has yet to see what God will do with a man fully consecrated to him." Moody resolved to be that man.

In June 1873 Moody and Sankey landed in Liverpool, England, to find no arrangements, organization, or funds, partly through Moody's own neglect. They therefore took up a half-answered invitation from a druggist in York, where they began an entirely unprepared mission in a most unlikely city, with such success that they were invited to the great industrial town of Newcastle. The real breakthrough came at Edinburgh, capital of Scotland, at the turn of the year. Moody's unconventional preaching and Sankey's singing reached right to the rather frozen heart of a strongly religious nation.

Revival

All Scotland was stirred by Moody and Sankey during 1874; their own evangelism inspired many lesser campaigns. Moody developed the "after meeting" or inquiry room, worked closely with the churches, and emphasized the need for pastoral care of converts. His strong social concern sparked off new movements for the relief of distress and for the bodily and spiritual welfare of the young. Later in 1874 the two evangelists moved to England.

Moody, now in his later thirties, was physically large, though quick in movement. He had a huge chest, short neck, a rather round face with a full black beard, and gray eyes. His voice was not attractive and his English often ungrammatical, but while he seemed to chat to someone in the eighth row he could be heard by 12,000 or more, with no aid except sounding boards. An Englishman wrote that he never could listen to Moody "without feeling the strongest desire to love and know Christ."

The British campaign reached its climax in London from March to July 1875. Moody and Sankey reached poor and rich alike and brought thousands to Christ, giving fresh impetus to the strong evangelicalism of the Victorian age. Moody's plain, urgent message was backed by his integrity, his skill in bringing out the best in the hundreds of clergy and laity who worked with him, and by his refusal to answer critics or indulge in controversy.

D. L. Moody was now famous. The United States opened up, and Moody and Sankey campaigns took place throughout the later 1870s and after. In New York City Moody preached in Barnum's Hippodrome, future site of the first Madison

Moody preaching in London, 1874.

Square Garden, where Billy Graham would hold his great 1957 crusade.

Moody transformed revival from its old pattern of camp meetings, single church affairs, or spontaneous happenings. Clergy and laity of many denominations would cooperate with Moody in preparation and follow-up. His revival services would continue nightly for many weeks with great effect; as a spicy Boston paper complained, "The masses are undoubtedly becoming permeated with piety." And, as in Britain, the social influence of Moody was enormous.

The vast sale of Sacred Songs and Solos could have made Moody and Sankey rich, but they refused to touch the profits, which they put in a trust fund, out of which Moody founded the Northfield School for girls who were too poor to obtain good education (1879), followed by Mount Hermon (1881) for boys, nearby across the Connecticut River. Mount Hermon was partly endowed by an eccentric manufacturer of alarm clocks, for Moody loosened many purses for good causes.

Aerial view of the main campus of Moody Bible Institute, downtown Chicago, Illinois.

Second London campaign

From 1882-1884 the evangelists were again in Britain. By the close of the second London campaign the aged Lord Shaftesbury, the great evangelical social reformer, could speak of an unprecedented movement among the very poor "towards a knowledge of the Word of God." At the opposite end of the scale, Moody held a mission in Cambridge University, overcoming ridicule and barracking to win an unprecedented response. A direct result was the "Cambridge Seven," seven young men of wealth, social position, and athletic prowess who gave up their careers and sailed in 1885 to be missionaries in China, a sacrifice that made an immense impact on the Western world, especially in universities.

Moody had recently started, by a typically last-minute decision, the summer Northfield Conferences where Christians could meet for prayer and Bible teaching. The enthusiasm generated by the Cambridge Seven inspired at Northfield the formation of the Student Volunteers with the goal of world evangelization. Through this, and his constant encouragement to overseas missions, Moody was one of the strongest influences in the expansion of Christianity, though he never traveled beyond America and Britain.

Moody Bible Institute

In 1886 Moody founded the Moody Bible Institute (MBI) in Chicago, securing the brilliant R. A. Torrey as first president. Down the years many hundreds of men and women who lacked college education were able to train for full-time Christian service at MBI, which pioneered the concept of Bible institutes. As Moody said: "When I am gone I shall leave some grand men and women behind." MBI (and Moody's Chicago Evangelization Society from which it grew) also started a colportage enterprise, the origin of Moody Press.

Despite heart trouble in his later years, Moody refused to let up. He was taken ill during a campaign at Kansas City in November 1899 and died on December 22 at the age of sixty-two.

No man had ever done more for the Christian cause in his generation. He had recruited for Christ many who were leaders in the next. And Moody's character, dedication, and faith had set a standard in evangelism by which those who come after are judged.

B.B.Warfield
1851-1921

Within nine months, between November 12, 1920, and July 29, 1921, three outstanding leaders of the revival of Calvinism – Abraham Kuyper, Benjamin Breckinridge Warfield, and Herman Bavinck – died, to the great loss of Reformed thought in the whole world. Kuyper was most notable for the range of his endeavors, for his activity as a journalist, and later as prime minister of the Netherlands.

Bavinck is especially remembered for his Reformed Dogmatics sold in four large volumes. B. B. Warfield was perhaps the most accomplished scholar of the evangelical church, capable of producing intensive studies on detailed points of doctrine and also of penning general birds-eye surveys of whole areas of theology. The productions of Warfield have scarcely aged, and new editions of his works have

been excellent sellers.

Besides the doctrine of biblical inspiration, the themes of predestination, the Person and work of Christ, and perfectionism, Warfield paid particular attention in his studies to the theology of Augustine, Calvin, and the Westminster Confession. In these areas he scarcely had any rival in his own time in the range and depth of his scholarship. Surrounded as he was by a galaxy of men with similar convictions teaching at Princeton Theological Seminary and sharing his approach to Scripture, Warfield caused the Princeton Theological Review to be one of the most significant influences of his own time and to remain a monument of massive evangelical scholarship.

Benjamin Breckinridge Warfield, Reformed theologian.

The Life of
Warfield

1851	November 5, birth near Lexington, Kentucky.
1871	Graduates from the College of New Jersey [Princeton University].
1876	Graduates from Princeton Theological Seminary.
1878	Begins teaching at Western Theological Seminary, Allegheny, Pennsylvania.
1881	Publishes famous article "Inspiration" with A. A. Hodge.
1887	Begins teaching at Princeton Theological Seminary.
1915	His wife, Annie Pierce, dies.
1921	February 16, 1921, death in Princeton, New Jersey.

B.B.Warfield

and the Calvinist Revival

Roger Nicole

Youth

Benjamin Breckinridge Warfield was born at "Grasmere" near Lexington, Kentucky, on November 5, 1851. His father was a farmer, especially interested in the breeding of short-horn cattle. The ancestors of the family had immigrated from southern England to Virginia and from there to Maryland. Warfield's mother was the daughter of Robert J. Breckinridge, well-known preacher and educator, who wrote two important works on theology and was an advocate of the emancipation of slaves.

After attending private schools in Lexington under the tutelage of gifted teachers, Benjamin Warfield matriculated in 1868 at the College of New Jersey, now called Princeton University. He graduated in 1871 with highest honors. He had shown special interest in mathematics and physics. He then pursued further work in Europe and announced his decision to prepare himself for the Christian ministry in mid-summer 1872. He therefore entered Princeton Theological Seminary in 1873 and graduated in May 1876.

The same year he married Annie Pierce Kinkead and journeyed with her through Germany. While on their honeymoon, they were caught in a fierce storm, and she was struck by lightning and permanently paralyzed. The continued care and love that Warfield devoted to his invalid wife throughout the remainder of her life have often been mentioned by those who knew them well as a notable manifestation of the work of the Holy Spirit in his life. Because of her needs, Professor Warfield very seldom left home for more than two hours at a time. In spite of his great concern for the church, he did not attend the annual meetings of the General Assembly of the Presbyterian Church of the U.S.A. Mrs. Warfield died in November 1915, and her husband survived her for only a little more than five years.

After a brief period of ministry as assistant pastor in the First Presbyterian Church of Baltimore (1877-1878), Warfield was called to become instructor in New Testament language and literature at Western Theological Seminary, Allegheny, Pennsylvania in 1878. He stayed there for nine years, until 1887. During that period his attention was centered particularly on the *Didache*, which had been recently recovered to Christian scholarship. He also published an important work on textual criticism of the New Testament, which passed through many editions, perhaps more than any of his other writings. As a contributor, with A. A. Hodge, to the *Presbyterian Review*, he made a notable mark as a champion of a strict doctrine of the inspiration and inerrancy of Scripture. This was articulated in an article, "Inspiration," published in the *Presbyterian Review* for April 1881 and reprinted with notes and appendixes by Baker Book House in 1979. This article presented basically the position that Warfield was to defend and elaborate for more than forty years.

Princeton

In 1887 Warfield transferred to Princeton Theological Seminary, where he was called to succeed A. A. Hodge, who had died in 1886. It is in this capacity that his major contributions were made, both by virtue of his teaching and in his publications. In Princeton Seminary the teaching of theology was recognized to be central to the whole curriculum, and Warfield

The library, Princeton College, in the nineteenth century.

manifested his comprehension of the theological enterprise by a continual interaction with the whole range of theological disciplines. In that way he came to occupy a pivotal position in the seminary and also in the Presbyterian Church in the U.S.A.

In a controversy started in the late 1880s, Warfield strongly opposed a revision of the Westminster Confession of Faith, which was intended to broaden it. This was carried on later with reference to the discussion on inspiration precipitated by the positions of professors Charles A. Briggs, Llewelyn Evans, and Henry P. Smith. The effect of the controversy was the dismissal of Briggs and Smith from the ordained ranks in the Presbyterian Church in the U.S.A. (Professor Evans died before a similar fate could befall him.) This controversy resulted in a monumental book by Warfield on the subject of inspiration, a theme that remained of strong concern to him even long years afterwards.

From 1890 to 1902 Warfield was the editor of the *Presbyterian and Reformed Review*, a successor to the *Presbyterian Review*, and he contributed indefatigably to its pages both by articles and book reviews. This kind of activity continued after the name of the journal was changed in 1903 to the *Princeton Theological Review*.

A renewal of the controversy about revising the Westminster Confession of Faith occurred in 1903, particularly with reference to a proposed union between the Presbyterian Church in the U.S.A. and the Cumberland Presbyterian Church. Warfield resolutely opposed both the revision and the union, but his influence did not prevail, and he was constrained to take a minority stance in the church in which he had earlier had a dominant influence.

Warfield's writings

Warfield's output in complete volumes during his lifetime was relatively small. Undoubtedly, his greatest volume is *The Lord of Glory* (1907), a systematic study of the various titles given to Christ in the New Testament. A thin volume on *The*

Plan of Salvation appeared in 1915, outlining the place of Reformed thought in the general spectrum of Christian views. His Thomas Smyth lectures at Columbia Theological Seminary entitled *Counterfeit Miracles* (1918), emphasized strongly his view of the cessation of special charismata after the death of the apostles. Three volumes of sermons or biblical meditations entitled respectively *The Power of God unto Salvation* (1903), *The Saviour of the World* (1914), and *Faith and Life* (1916) complete the roster of his major publications.

The major substance of his work and thought was to be found in his articles and critical reviews, which his editors reproduced in part in ten large volumes released by Oxford University Press between 1927 and 1932. These have been recently reprinted (1983). Many of the more important contributions have been brought back into circulation in the five volumes published at the Presbyterian and Reformed Publishing Company: *The Inspiration and Authority of the Bible,* (1948); *The Person and Work of Christ,* *(1950); Biblical and Theological Studies,* (1952); *Calvin and Augustine,* (1956); *Perfectionism,* (1958). Two new editions of his shorter works were produced in 1970 and 1973.

On Christmas Eve 1920, Warfield was struck with a severe attack of angina pectoris, which obliged him to suspend his activities at Princeton. He had recovered enough to resume his classes by February 16, 1921, but the effort may have been too great for him, and he died under the onslaught of a new attack that very night.

One aspect of Warfield's thought concerning which some caution is needed is his tendency to present our recognition of the authority of the Bible as based on a rational demonstration of its credentials. In this area, Warfield stands in contrast to Bavinck and Kuyper and particularly to Cornelius Van Til of Westminster Theological Seminary. Reason, however, was not viewed by Warfield as the source of theology or as its norm, but rather the Scriptures.

Karl Barth
1886-1968

By any reckoning Karl Barth (1886-1968) ranks as the outstanding theologian of the twentieth century. Born in Switzerland, he came from a conservative Reformed background. In student days he fell under the sway of the German liberal Protestantism of such thinkers as Harnack and Herrmann.

Barth achieved prominence when the demands of parish work and the trauma of World War I on the Swiss borders forced him back to the Bible and brought about the explosion of his *Epistle to the Romans* (1919, 1922). Revolting against historico-literary criticism, he refocused here on the great themes of the otherness of God, the miracle of grace in Christ, and the paradox of judgment and justification. Response to the commentary opened the door to a renewal of biblical, historical, and dogmatic work in which Barth, now a theological professor in Germany, played a dominant part.

With the rise of Hitlerism and its "German Christianity," Barth became a leader in the theological opposition that found confessional expression in the *Barmen Declaration* (1934). Dismissed to Switzerland (1935), he combined his massive efforts at dogmatic reformulation with an extensive teaching ministry at Basel and an active role in important church developments, from the formation of the World Council of Churches to Roman Catholic renewal during and after Vatican II.

Although Barth derided the term *neo-orthodoxy* and differentiated himself from its acknowledged representatives (e.g., Rudolf Bultmann, Friedrich Gogarten, Emil Brunner, and Paul Tillich), he gave stimulus to the movement as an attempt to present older doctrines in new modes. Neo-orthodoxy soon lost its original impetus, but Barth, although suffering some decline in personal influence, decisively shaped the agenda of church life and theology by his varied contributions, and his impact will undoubtedly be felt for decades to come.

Karl Barth.

The Life of
Barth

1886	Birth.
1908	Ordained.
1908-1909	Marburg.
1909-1911	Geneva.
1911-1921	Safenwil.
1913	Marries Nelly Hoffmann.
1919,1922	*Romans.*
1921-1925	Teaches at Göttingen.
1925-1930	Teaches at Münster.
1930-1935	Teaches at Bonn.
1932-1968	*Church Dogmatics.*
1934	Barmen Declaration.
1935-1962	Basel.
1948	Addresses Amsterdam Assembly.
1962	Trip to America.
1966	Rome.
1968	Death.

Karl Barth

and Neo-Orthodoxy
Geoffrey W. Bromiley

Theological earthquake

Born at Basel on May 10, 1886, the eldest son of Fritz and Anna Barth, Karl Barth was educated at Bern, where his father taught New Testament and church history from 1889. He also studied theology in Berlin, Tübingen, and Marburg. Ordained in 1908, he spent a year in Marburg, took up an assistantship in Geneva (1909-1911), then pastored the small industrial parish of Safenwil in Aargau (1911-1921). At Safenwil he plunged into trade union matters, wrestled with the demands of preaching God's Word, and saw his liberalism collapse under the pressure of World War I on the Swiss border.

Turning to Scripture, he wrote his commentary on Romans, which in its revised second edition rocked European theology like an earthquake, challenging its critical methods and stressing God's transcendence and grace in startling paradoxes. The impact made even by the 1919 edition opened up a new sphere for Barth, with his call to a professorship at Göttingen (1921), then at Münster (1925), and later Bonn (1930).

Although provoking opposition, Barth gained an enthusiastic student following and found more mature supporters who would form the nucleus of what is often called *neo-orthodoxy*. Emil Brunner of Zurich (1899-1966) was perhaps closest to Barth, but made bigger apologetic concessions to liberal positions, for example, in the matter of evolution, the virgin birth, or natural theology. Rudolf Bultmann of Marburg (1884-1976) shared certain convictions but engaged in more radical criticism, existentialized the gospel, and finally pressed on to demythologizing.

Friedrich Gogarten (1887-1967) combined the attack on the older liberalism with the new subjectivism and also with a Lutheran view of the orders that set him for a time among the German Christians.

Paul Tillich (1886-1965), who was never close to Barth, veered off in a wholly different direction with his attempted correlation of theology and the human situation. The Niebuhr brothers, Reinhold (1893-1971) and Richard (1894-1962), represented a distinctly American brand of neo-orthodoxy, which had little in common with Barth but might not have been possible without his earlier writings. In general, the leaders of neo-orthodoxy were closest to Barth in their reaction against liberalism. For the rest they developed most strongly the existential element, which Barth himself would quickly transcend, and little theological sympathy existed between the mature Barth and their more detailed positions.

At Göttingen and Münster, Barth extended his influence with *The Word of God and the Word of Man* (1924), commentaries on 1 Corinthians (1924) and Philippians (1927), and *Theology and Church* (1928). He also took up historical and dogmatic study that found expression in his *Protestant Theology* (1947), *Christian Dogmatics* (1928), *Anselm* (1931), and *Church Dogmatics I*, (1932).

Barth and Nazism

By 1933, however, Barth had to give much attention to the church conflict with Hitlerism. His lasting contribution was his drafting of the *Barmen Declaration* (1934) with its clear commitment to Christ's lordship and consequent opposition to the allying of Christianity with

National Socialism. Barth's stand led to his dismissal from Bonn (1935). The issues were his resistance to an unqualified oath of loyalty to Hitler and his refusal to open classes with the Hitler salute instead of a hymn and prayer. A timely vacancy at Basel enabled him to spend his remaining years in his native land and city.

At Basel, Barth continued his opposition to Nazism with courses on the confession (for example, *Credo* [1935] and *The Knowledge and Service of God* [1938]), discussion of the political service of God, sponsorship of relief for refugees, and vocal support for the Allies in World War II (in defiance of Swiss neutrality).

After the war, however, he gladly taught again in Bonn (*Dogmatics in Outline* [1947]) and arranged for emergency supplies to Germany from Switzerland. He had little sympathy with Adenauer's regime and incurred criticism with his advice to East European Christians to work with communist governments, although he had no commitment to Communism (or doctrinaire socialism) as such.

Barth did not let political concerns claim his main energies. Playing a role in the forming of the World Council of Churches, he gave a leading address at the crucial Amsterdam Assembly (1948). His Roman Catholic contacts (for example with Balthasar and Küng) made him an indirect force at Vatican II. Through his many students he also had a wider influence on church affairs both at home and abroad. Visits to other countries, culminating in journeys to America (1962) and Rome (1966), added a personal voice by means of lectures, discussions, and interviews.

Nevertheless, Barth's chief ministry lay in the study and classroom. From Basel issued the steady stream of the *Church Dogmatics* from I, 2 in 1939 to IV, 4 Fragment in 1968. To these volumes one must also add the *Shorter Romans* (1941), *Rudolf Bultmann* (1952), *Christ and Adam* (1952), *The Humanity of God* (1956), *Evangelical Theology* (1962), and various sermon collections and shorter pieces. Physical infirmities hampered Barth after his 1962 retirement, but he continued to write, teach, and preach as health permitted. On the eve of his death, December 9, 1968, he had broken off in mid-sentence. He died peacefully, hands folded for prayer, confident that God would reign and that by God's promise he would stand as a justified sinner.

Barth's achievement

The merits of Barth's theological contribution are plain. He shattered the tyranny of higher criticism, allowing it a servant role but insisting on exposition *with* the biblical authors and not *about* them. He also destroyed the older liberalism with its belief in human progress, its dilution of doctrine, its focusing on religious experience, and its wedding of faith and culture. He rejected an exclusive divine immanence, an imaginary historical Jesus, an elimination of miracle, and a secularized eschatology.

Barth's new biblical approach opened the door to biblical theology and theological exegesis. It involved a strong commitment to the authority of Scripture as the normative text through which God speaks His Word by the Spirit. Barth's first biblical insight was that God is truly God (not man writ large), although in the light of the incarnation he would modify his earlier stress on God's total otherness and perceive also His humanity. The centrality of Christ figured large in Barth's ongoing *Dogmatics*. In Christ he found the key to election, creation, covenant, and anthropology as well as atonement; he even explored sin in Christological antithesis. Christ's finished work for us formed for Barth the necessary basis of the Spirit's work *in* us. The facticity of this work (resurrection as well as death) was essential; hence he sharply opposed Bultmann's demythologizing existentialism. Equally essential was Christ's deity as well as His humanity. As he commented in this regard, he had "to acknowledge that orthodoxy is right on almost all points."

Romans

Nevertheless, especially through his earlier writings, Barth helped to introduce neo-orthodox emphases that he would later deplore. In *Romans* he almost dualistically exaggerated the divine/human distinction, fatefully differentiated the historical and the non-historical, and outrageously pressed the category of paradox, which later, in contrast to divine *doxa* (glory), he would reserve for the sphere of evil, for example, the impossible possibility. With his stress on the element of decision and the "moment," he left an opening for the existentialism he would quickly have to resist.

Yet, even in *Romans*, his statements carried a plain implication of universalism that would cut the root of true evangelicalism. Paradoxically, the younger Barth was also at pains to struggle against any false sense of assurance, replacing it with the demand for a constant renewal of faith in face of the unheard-of nature of the divine message and the lack of any possibility of ordinary verification.

Barth outgrew the forceful exaggerations of *Romans* with further biblical and historical study, but his mature theology still raises problems. He slides over the objective inspiration of Scripture and concedes too readily a capacity for error. He cavalierly ignores natural revelation and hence the possibility of authentic apologetics. His handling of election leaves many loose ends, and his Christological account of creation, notwithstanding valuable insights, hardly does full justice either to the Father and Spirit or to creation as such. The relation between static and dynamic command raises complications in ethics. As regards reconciliation, the extreme stress on objectivity almost invites an inference of automatic salvation for all (although Barth rejected this). Furthermore, the endorsement of facticity suffers from the denial of any possibility whatever of historical verification. Barth's account of evil has also called for criticism, partly because it is more speculative than biblical, partly because it presents evil in too negative terms, and partly because evil seems to lose its threat in view of the definitiveness of God's victory over it in Christ (although again Barth denied any such implication).

The defects in Barth's theology hardly negate its significance. Breaking the older liberalism, as the older conservatism had been unable to do, Barth facilitated a restoration of genuine theology and preaching on a biblical basis. He strenuously resisted the perversions of existentialism and demythologizing that reintroduced liberalism in new guise. He offered a provocative reconstruction and placed it squarely under the judgment of the scriptural norm. Above all, he displayed in all his work a pastoral concern, a prayerful spirit, a confidence in God, a commitment to Christ, and a trust in God's Word and Spirit that set him in the Reformation tradition and provide a model for all who succeed him, whether or not they accept his detailed teachings.

Dietrich Bonhoeffer
1906-1945

Dietrich Bonhoeffer (1906-1945), German Lutheran theologian and pastor, is a landmark figure in twentieth-century Christian thought. His theological understanding was shaped by the Scriptures and by his education and experiences in various countries. His focus was especially placed upon Christology and ethics. He manifested a deep concern for racial justice, the pursuit of world peace, and the development of Christian community. His book *The Cost of Discipleship* has left an indelible imprint on the thinking of many Christians.

Bonhoeffer quickly perceived that the National Socialists' (Nazis') announced intention to bring about Germany's moral and spiritual renewal was a sham, even though most of his fellow churchmen embraced the new order with boundless enthusiasm. He openly criticized Hitler and the Nazi anti-Jewish policy and identified with the Confessing Church, the group opposing the nazification of the Protestant church organization.

Bonhoeffer's brother-in-law, Hans von Dohnanyi, drew him into the plot against Hitler in 1940. The conspirators in the military intelligence service employed him as a courier because of his foreign contacts, especially in ecumenical circles. Although he had no direct role in the assassination attempt on Hitler in July 1944, Bonhoeffer's connection with the conspirators was discovered, and Hitler ordered his execution, which took place at the Flossenburg concentration camp on April 9, 1945.

Bonhoeffer's life and ideas on resistance have deeply influenced the South African anti-apartheid movement, Latin American liberation theology, and other Christians who struggle against tyranny, in whatever form or wherever it may be. The secular and death-of-God theologies that claimed him were mere passing fads, but the political ethic and emphasis upon discipleship are Bonhoeffer's abiding legacies.

Dietrich Bonhoeffer.

The Life of **Bonhoeffer**	
1906	Birth.
1928-1929	Student pastorate in Barcelona.
1930-1931	Studies in the United States.
1933	Criticizes abuses of the Hitler regime.
1937	Publication of *The Cost of Discipleship*.
1939	Publication of *Life Together*.
1940	Becomes actively involved in resistance movement against Hitler.
1943	April, imprisoned in Berlin.
1945	April 9, death by execution.

Dietrich Bonhoeffer

The Struggle against Hitler

Richard V. Pierard

Studies

Dietrich Bonhoeffer was born in 1906. He came from a distinguished family, his father being a noted neurologist. He studied at both Tübingen and Berlin, receiving a doctorate in theology at the University of Berlin, and taught at Berlin for several years.

A student pastorate in Barcelona (1928-1929), study in the United States (1930-1931), and attendance at the Cambridge conference of the World Alliance for Promoting International Friendship Through the Churches (1931) awakened him to a wider world of faith. Named the latter's Youth Secretary for Germany and Central Europe, he plunged wholeheartedly into ecumenism. He insisted that the movement must seek to understand what the church is and to speak about matters of doctrine and heresy where the church had betrayed Christ, such as the treatment of Jews and the false church government in Germany. It should not be a council of theologians but an assembly of the church of Christ witnessing to the world. Although he resigned his youth post in 1937, he deepened his ecumenical ties even as he became implicated in the conspiracy against Hitler.

Bonhoeffer's role in the resistance to Nazism flowed from his understanding of the church, which for him was a unity in Christ, a divine community composed of people who are simultaneously sinful and holy, judged and forgiven, and its authority rests upon the Word of God. His conception of the church as unity underlay his commitment to ecumenism, whereas the church as the presence of God in the world was the reason it must exercise political responsibility. To be sure, the church would sin when it entered politics, but it lived by forgiveness.

Resistance to Hitler

From 1933 on, Bonhoeffer criticized the abuses of the Hitler regime. He categorically rejected the "Aryan clauses," which provided for removing those of Jewish descent from public office, including church posts, whether or not they were Christians. In April he declared that the church may criticize an unjust action of the state, assist the victims of this injustice, and even "take direct political action" if it is convinced that the state has failed in its duty to keep law and order. He belonged to the group opposing the takeover of the Protestant church by the pro-Nazi "German Christians," helped write the Bethel Confession (a forerunner of the *Barmen Declaration* of May 1934), and joined Martin Niemöller's Pastors' Emergency League.

Then he left for a pastorate in London (1933-1935) but remained in close contact with the opposition, now known as the Confessing Church. Through his friend George Bell, bishop of Chichester and president of Life and Work, Bonhoeffer gained ecumenical sympathy for the Confessing position. At a major ecumenical youth conference in Fano, Denmark, in August 1934, he delivered a powerful sermon on peace and persuaded that body to denounce ecclesiastical nazification as "incompatible with the true nature of the Christian church."

Yet he grew increasingly dissatisfied with the Confessing Church's apolitical stance and exclusive concern with internal church matters. Also, it did not share his pacifistic views and would not speak out against the Nazi persecution of the Jews.

Since Nazis now controlled the theological faculties, the Confessing Church opened some alternative schools known as preachers' seminaries, and in April 1935 Bonhoeffer was called back to Germany to direct one situated in the remote Pomeranian village of Finkenwalde. Here he developed his ideas of the church as a confessing community. After the police closed the seminary in 1937, he used the device of "collective pastorates" (ministerial students apprenticed to parish pastors) to operate underground. The students were placed in churches in the area, and he met with them regularly for instruction. With the coming of war most of them were drafted, and in March 1940 the Gestapo abolished the last collective pastorate. In 1939 he was invited to teach at Union Theological Seminary, New York City, but returned home after one month. Realizing that war was imminent, he felt his responsibility was to minister to fellow Christians in Germany.

A military coup
In 1938 Hans von Dohnanyi, Bonhoeffer's brother-in-law, had told him about plans for a military coup against Hitler, but it was aborted because of the Munich agreement. When the police slapped a preaching ban on him in 1940, Bonhoeffer's brother-in-law secured him a job on the staff of military intelligence (the *Abwehr* department). He was to travel abroad and gather news, pass on information about the progress of the German resistance movement, and use his ecumenical connections to gain credibility and support in the West for their planned overthrow of Hitler. Meanwhile, a jurisdictional dispute over intelligence operations arose between the SS-controlled Main Security office and the *Abwehr*, and Bonhoeffer was among those arrested. In April 1943 he was placed in Tegel military prison in Berlin but was allowed some freedom to write and see friends.

Because he was not involved in the July 20, 1944 attempt on Hitler's life, he es-caped the reprisals that followed, but two months later the Gestapo uncovered *Abwehr* documents that implicated him in the ongoing conspiracy. After lengthy interrogations, Bonhoeffer and the other *Abwehr* figures were removed to various concentration camps. On April 5, 1945, Hitler ordered their execution, and four days later the thirty-nine-year-old pastor went to the gallows.

In the late 1930s Bonhoeffer had abandoned the "Christian pacifism" that hitherto had marked his thought (he had even planned to visit Gandhi) and decided that the only way to secure peace would be to eliminate Hitler. For him, treason had become true patriotism; but Lutheran theology with its emphasis on the two kingdoms offered no support to one who embarked on the path of armed resistance.

Yet, as Bonhoeffer maintained in *Ethics*, one must carry out his moral responsibility to serve Jesus Christ and his fellow men, even though this may require the breaking of laws. The man who acts on his personal responsibility is the one who sees his action committed to the guidance of God and is in obedience to Him. "There is now no law behind which the responsible man can seek cover," and thus he entrusts his decision and action to the divine governance of history. By acting responsibly he may incur guilt, but Jesus took upon Himself the guilt of all men.

Writings
Athough an extensive body of literature has grown up around Bonhoeffer, he still remains an enigma. His principal scholarly works, *Sanctorum Communio* (1930), *Act and Being* (1931), and *Creation and Fall* (1933), went virtually unnoticed in his own lifetime. The ones that were well-received, *The Cost of Discipleship* (1937) and *Life Together* (1939), are more tracts on Christian living than serious theological treatises. His early postwar popularity in the West was based on these and two fragmentary works pieced together from his papers, *Letters and*

Papers from Prison (1951) and *Ethics* (1949). The full range of his thought became available only with the publication in German of his *Collected Works* (6 vols., 1958-1974), large portions of which have been translated into English. His death at such an early age precluded a systematic exposition of his ideas, and thus his tantalizing statements and flashes of insight lend themselves to a variety of interpretations.

Bonhoeffer brought a new dimension to Christian discipleship by distinguishing between "cheap" and "costly" grace. For him the cheap variety is "the preaching of forgiveness without requiring repentance, baptism without church discipline, communion without confession." It is grace without discipleship, the cross, and the living, incarnate Jesus Christ. Because even the best Christians remain sinners, cheap grace justifies living a life of sin, and any attempt to engage in a serious life of discipleship is labeled as "legalism" or "enthusiasm."

Costly grace

Costly grace, on the other hand, calls us to follow Jesus Christ. It condemns sin and justifies the sinner, and it cost God the life of His Son. It requires us to renounce sin and turn over our lives to Him. Grace is not an encouragement to live a sinful life on the grounds that all will be forgiven anyway. Rather, the Reformation doctrine of justification by faith alone comforts us and fosters discipleship because we know our striving is not in vain.

More controversial are his concepts "religionless Christianity," "the world come of age," "Jesus the man for others," and "the church for others." Secular and death-of-God theologians extracted these and other catch phrases from his later works and made him into the herald of their new theology. What he meant, however, was something rather different than these interpreters of the 1960s led people to believe. Bonhoeffer recognized that, since the thirteenth century, man has moved steadily from God and now he runs his affairs without reference to the deity. However, the church is still trying to reach secular man with "religion" and is getting nowhere. The answer is a "religionless" Christianity that involves participation in the suffering of God in the secular world. The church is not to preoccupy itself with "religious concerns" (that is, confining Christianity to limited areas of life, making salvation into a drop-out situation where one escapes to another realm, engaging only in religious activities off in a corner, and seeing the world as the source of recruits for the religious sphere), but rather it must serve the world.

Bonhoeffer calls on the church to follow the pattern of Jesus, the Man for others who is active in the whole of people's lives, not just in their weaknesses and dark times. Christianity is a life to be lived, and faith must be translated into action, not in a narrowly pietistic sense, but in a way that touches every aspect of existence. He believed Christ and His church should not be separate from the world but situated in its midst and ministering in every way to modern man who thinks he can live without God. Contrary to the impression left by the secularists, Bonhoeffer did not want to abolish God or the rites of the church. Rather the Lord's Supper, worship, and prayer were central experiences in his own life.

C.S.Lewis
1898-1963

is the best-selling Christian author of all time. Although he has been dead since 1963, his books continue to evangelize non-Christians, instruct new converts, and edify the faithful of all ages. His range of influence is manifested in that, next to Jesus Christ and the apostle Paul, he is one of the most quoted spokesmen for biblical Christianity.

During the first week of September 1947 thousands of people all over the English-speaking world pulled their issue of *Time* magazine from the mailbox: on the cover they saw a color portrait of a handsome man enframed by angel wings on one side and Satan on the other. The caption for this striking cover read: "Oxford's C.S. Lewis; his heresy: Christianity."

C.S. Lewis's picture and its caption focused international attention on an increasingly renowned and remarkable man. Not yet forty-nine, Lewis had been a Christian only sixteen years. Already, however, he was one of the most popular Christian authors in Great Britain and America. A staunch defender of orthodox Christianity, Lewis had reached wide audiences with his radio broadcasts in World War II, as well as with two important books, *The Problem of Pain* and *The Screwtape Letters* which appeared during the early 1940s. Lewis's conservatism, manifested in a high view of the Bible and an adherence to orthodox doctrine, delighted beleaguered evangelicals but repulsed the fashionable liberals. In brief, Lewis was at once celebrated and reviled. Nevertheless, his fame as the brilliant university don who ably defended and explained Christianity continued to grow. Despite opposition from a skeptical academic world, the Oxford Christian eventually published nearly forty books, many of which were written in a popular style. Today more than 40 million of his books are in print in numerous languages. He

Magdalen College, Oxford.

The Life of
C.S.Lewis

1898	November 29, birth in Belfast, N.Ireland.
1908	Mother dies and leaves him his first Bible.
1913-1914	Studies at Malvern College, England.
1917	Begins studies at University College, Oxford.
1917-1919	Serves in the British Army in France; wounded in action.
1920-1923	Returns to Oxford, earns firsts in Honor Mods, Greats, and English.
1929	Becomes a theist.
1931	Becomes a Christian.
1933	Publishes first Christian book, *The Pilgrim's Regress*.
1936	Publishes first scholarly book, *The Allegory of Love*.
1940	Publishes *The Problem of Pain*.
1942	Publishes *The Screwtape Letters*.
1945	Publishes *The Great Divorce*.
1947	Publishes *Miracles*.
1950	Publishes *The Lion, the Witch and the Wardrobe*, the first of seven Narnia Chronicles.
1952	Publishes *Mere Christianity*.
1956	Marries Joy Davidman Gresham on April 23 in Oxford.
1960	Joy dies from cancer in Oxford on July 13.
1963	November 22, death at The Kilns, Oxford.

C.S.Lewis

Defender of the Faith

Lyle W. Dorsett

This man of enormous influence was born in Belfast, Northern Ireland, on November 29, 1898 to parents who were nominal members of the Church of Ireland. Clive Staples Lewis was baptized and confirmed in the established church, and he and his only sibling, a brother named Warren Hamilton (1894-1973), were educated in English boarding schools. Warren eventually became a career officer in the British army and Jack (as C.S. Lewis became known to family and friends) went to University College, Oxford, where he took highest honors in honor moderations, greats, and English in 1920, 1922 and 1923, respectively.

The first quarter century of C.S. Lewis's life was full of momentous events. Among those were the death of his mother in 1908, three years of private tutorials in Surrey with the brilliant W.T. Kirkpatrick, and combat service in France during World War I. His mother's death made him doubt the existence of God; his atheist tutor taught him to think critically and become even more wedded to materialism; and the ravages of war (he was wounded and his best friend killed) left him believing there was nothing worth pursuing besides things of the mind and pleasures of the flesh.

Following World War I, Lewis returned to Oxford to pursue a life of teaching and writing. The academic life suited this man with an unusually gifted intellect. He enjoyed teaching, feeding his intellectual curiosity, and writing for publication and posterity. His first book, a cycle of lyrics entitled *Spirits in Bondage*, appeared in 1919 under the pseudonym Clive Hamilton. As philosophy tutor at Magdalen College, Oxford, he published a second volume of poetry, *Dymer*, in 1926.

Conversion

Lewis did not write another book for several years because he was riddled with self-doubt and inner turmoil. His firm grip on materialism began to slip. Two close friends went from agnosticism to Christianity, and Lewis became puzzled that his own favorite authors, among them John Milton, Edmund Spenser, George MacDonald, and G.K. Chesterton, were Christians themselves. At one point Lewis declared that a man cannot be too careful about his reading. He was correct. By 1929 he was persuaded that there is a God; by 1931 he had surrendered his life to Jesus Christ.

From 1931 until his death thirty-two years later, C.S. Lewis's life had new meaning. He resumed writing with renewed vigor, and his work in general had a clear focus. Much like the apostle Paul nearly two thousand years before, Lewis's life was strikingly changed. Everything he did had new purpose. To be sure he continued as a fellow and tutor at Magdalen College, Oxford, until 1955, when he assumed a professorship of medieval and Renaissance literature at Magdalene College, Cambridge. And it is true that he consistently published scholarly and well-received books on literary history and criticism, beginning with *The Allegory of Love: A Study in Medieval Tradition* (1936). This was followed by *Rehabilitations and Other Essays* (1939), *A Preface to Paradise Lost* (1943), *English Literature in the Sixteenth Century, Excluding Drama* (1954), *Studies in Words* (1960), and An Experiment in Criticism (1961). The bulk of his work, on the other hand, was designed to point unbelievers to Christ, to explain Christianity to seekers, and to instruct those who were

young in the faith toward spiritual maturity. In response to one liberal critic Lewis admitted, "Most of my books are evangelistic." (See *God in the Dock*, p. 181.)

Christian writer

Soon after his conversion Lewis began publishing decidedly Christian books. Twenty-four months after his Damascus Road experience he published *The Pilgrim's Regress: An Allegorical Apology for Christianity, Reason and Romanticism* (1933). For the next three decades he turned out a stream of books on Christian apologetics, discipleship, and *praeparatio evangelica* (pre-evangelism). It is not too strong to say that he became a literary evangelist. Indeed, many of his Oxford colleagues were disappointed even irritated by his determination to spread the good news of Jesus Christ. Furthermore, it is widely believed that Lewis's transparent faith and his evangelistic outreach engendered so much hostility and created so many enemies that he was never elected to a professorship at Oxford. Consequently, it was at Cambridge University where a professorship was created for him in 1955.

Among his writings that still sell well and touch lives are the novels in his space trilogy entitled *Out of the Silent Planet* (1938), *Perelandra (Voyage to Venus)* (1943), and *That Hideous Strength* (1945). These works of imaginative literature help prepare the minds of adults for the truth of the gospel in the same way that the Chronicles of Narnia awaken the imagination and spiritual awareness of children. This latter series, consisting of seven books published in as many years, comprises these books of fantasy: *The Lion, the Witch and the Wardrobe* (1950); *Prince Caspian* (1951); *The Voyage of the 'Dawn Treader'* (1952); *The Silver Chair* (1953); *The Horse and His Boy* (1954); *The Magician's Nephew* (1955); and *The Last Battle* (1956).

Lewis wrote other works of fiction that have profoundly influenced people in the decades since they were published.

Kings's College, Cambridge, England.

C.S. Lewis's home, The Kilns, Headington, Oxford.

Among these are *The Screwtape Letters* (1943), *The Great Divorce* (1945), and *Till We Have Faces* (1956). Besides these works of the imagination, he wrote nonfiction that grows in popularity with each passing year. *The Problem of Pain* (1940); *The Abolition of Man* (1943); *Miracles: A Preliminary Study* (1947); *Mere Christianity* (1952); and two autobiographical novels, *Surprised by Joy: The Shape of My Early Life* (1955) and *A Grief Observed* (1961) still sell extremely well and change lives.

Debater

Lewis, of course, did more than write books, give lectures, and tutor undergraduates. He helped form the famous Socratic Club in Oxford. This was a debating society, originated by Stella Aldwinckle and designed to point people to Christ, by hosting debates on such topics of philosophy and religion as "Is there a God?" Members of the club sought the most effective speakers for the Christian side they could find, and encouraged atheists

and pagans to bring out their best guns. Socratic Club members believed that truth would win out in a fair debate, so they brought in such luminaries as Dorothy L. Sayers, Austin Farrer, and Lewis himself to lift the Christian banner.

Evidently many university students became professing Christians because of the Socratic Club. There also is evidence that C.S. Lewis's speaking tours among Royal Air Force personnel during World War II, his radio broadcasts on the basis of Christian faith and doctrine during the same years, and his many preaching engagements in the 1940s all helped to point unbelievers to Jesus Christ and encourage the faithful in bolder discipleship.

Marriage

Lewis spoke less, wrote more, and stayed closer to home in the 1950s. He told one friend that he had so many demands on his time that he was forced to establish priorities. Speaking was enjoyable, he admitted, but it tended to puff him up. Furthermore, he believed his writing

The tomb of C.S. and W.H. Lewis.

reached a larger audience. It is also true that his volume of correspondence increased with his growing popularity by the 1950s, and it took an extraordinary amount of time to answer the mail. Likewise an aged woman (the mother of a friend who was killed in World War I) who lived in his home required much more time. Finally, the long-time bachelor married Joy Davidman Gresham in 1956, and with her he acquired an instant family, complete with two stepsons.

His wife died a premature death from cancer in 1960. She was only forty-five years old. Lewis lived until November 22, 1963, when he died from heart and kidney failure. His passing was overlooked in the news because his end came the same day President John F. Kennedy was assassinated in the United States. Nevertheless, Lewis is not forgotten. Several months after he was buried, *Letters to Malcolm: Chiefly on Prayer* (1964), in the press before he died, came out and has remained in print. Other post-humously published collections of his works continue to appear. Among the most important are *Poems* (1964); *Narrative Poems* (1969); and his extremely popular *Letters of C.S. Lewis* (1966), edited by his brother W.H. Lewis; *Letters to an American Lady* (1967), edited by Clyde S. Kilby; *C.S. Lewis: Letters to Children* (1985), edited by Lyle W. Dorsett and Marjorie Lamp Mead; and *They Stand Together: The Letters of C.S. Lewis to Arthur Greeves, 1914-1963* (1979), edited by Walter Hooper.

A quarter century has passed since C.S. Lewis's death. His popularity is greater than ever; his books continue to sell in record-breaking numbers. The secret of his influence is manifold, but among the keys to his success in reaching ever-wider audiences are his timeless, Christ-centered themes. And not only was Lewis Christ-centered, he also avoided using the phraseology and jargon of cultural Christians. Instead, he wrote with clarity, boldness, and urgency to a post-Christian world. He used the everyday language of intelligent people, and he applied his teaching and stories to practical issues. In brief, he was a master communicator. He knew his audiences, and he pointed them to the theme of themes, Christ.

Francis A. Schaeffer
1912-1984

Francis A. Schaeffer (1912-1984) was the noted founder of L'Abri Fellowship and among the most influential conservative evangelical leaders in recent decades. He was the author of twenty-three books that were translated into more than twenty-five languages. He lectured throughout Europe and the United States at major secular and Christian universities, while three film series based on his books introduced him to a wider general audience.

Francis Schaeffer's unique gift was his ability to proclaim biblical truth and the gospel of Jesus Christ in a way that combined spiritual and intellectual integrity with practical, loving care. This was especially evident in the work of L'Abri Fellowship, founded by Schaeffer with his wife, Edith, in Switzerland in 1955.

During most of the last thirty years, the work of L'Abri (French for "The Shelter") was centered largely in the Schaeffers' own home. Thousands of people came to L'Abri from all walks of life and from all around the world.

Dr Francis Schaeffer.

Many of these were young people searching for truth and reality in their lives. In the Schaeffers' home, and in the larger work of L'Abri, they found someone who cared for them personally, who listened carefully to their questions, and who gave them answers based on an uncompromising commitment to biblical truth. L'Abri now includes branches in Switzerland, England, the Netherlands, Sweden, and two in the United States.

The Life of
Schaeffer

1912	Birth in Philadelphia.
1930	Becomes a Christian at age eighteen.
1935	Marries Edith Seville; enters Westminster Theological Seminary.
1937	Faith Theological Seminary founded, following split with Westminster; Schaeffer involved in its foundation.
1948	Moves to Lausanne, Switzerland, as a missionary.
1951	Spiritual crisis results in renewal.
1955	L'Abri Fellowship established.
1958	Beginnings of L'Abri in England.
1968	Publishes first book, *The God Who Is There*.
1979	American L'Abri founded.
1984	Death in Rochester, Minnesota.

U.S.A.
Philadelphia ●

Francis Schaeffer

and L'Abri
David Porter

Student days

Born in the Germantown section of Philadelphia, Pennsylvania, Francis Schaeffer was the only child of working-class parents. Although his parents were from a nominally Christian background, Schaeffer was not raised as a Christian. On his own he attended a liberal Presbyterian church, but he was unable to find satisfying answers there and became an agnostic during his high school years. In search for answers, Schaeffer began to read widely in philosophy. Out of curiosity, however, he thought he should also read the Bible. After six months he was convinced that the Bible is truth and the only adequate source for the answers to life's basic questions.

Schaeffer's conversion in 1930, at the age of eighteen, changed the direction of his life in a decisive way. He left trade school to complete college preparatory studies at night while working full time during the day. Although he had done poorly in school, his grades improved markedly. Over the strong opposition of his father, Schaeffer began studies in 1931 at Hampden-Sydney College, Hampden-Sydney, Virginia, where he graduated *magna cum laude* in 1935 and was selected as the outstanding Christian in his class.

During Schaeffer's college and seminary years the modernist-fundamentalist controversy within American Protestantism reached the point of crisis. Schaeffer's own denomination, the Northern Presbyterian Church, was torn by bitter conflict as theological liberals took control of the denomination's leadership. The conflict was played out dramatically in his local church, which on one occasion, in the summer of 1932, sponsored a youth speaker who preached on why the Bible is not God's

Word and why Jesus is not the Son of God. During the discussion time, Schaeffer rose to defend the orthodox Christian view as best he could, even though still a young Christian. Immediately following, a young woman also stood and gave an articulate defense based upon the Scriptures and the view of the renowned evangelical scholar and apologist J. Gresham Machen. Schaeffer hastened to meet the young woman, Edith Seville, after the meeting. Three years later in the summer of 1935 they married, and the life they shared over the next forty-nine years was characterized by the common defense of the faith, which was the occasion of their first meeting.

In the fall of 1935 Schaeffer entered Westminster Theological Seminary to prepare for the ministry. Founded in 1929 by Machen and other leading Presbyterian scholars, Westminster sought to provide a conservative alternative to theological liberalism (and one that also reflected rigorous academic standards). In addition to Machen, Schaeffer also studied under the distinguished scholar Cornelius Van Til, who provided a lasting influence on Schaeffer's own theology, though their approaches to theology reflect some major differences.

By 1936 the theological crisis in the Northern Presbyterian Church had reached breaking point. Machen was defrocked and put out of the ministry for his firm stand for orthodoxy in belief and practice. Conservatives were thus faced with a dilemma – either stay in and try to change the denomination they believed had strayed seriously from orthodoxy, or separate and associate in a new denominational fellowship that defended the historic

Christian faith. Schaeffer was among those who felt compelled to separate, although he later regretted the bitterness that ensued among many who left.

Pastoral ministry
Schaeffer graduated from Faith Theological Seminary in Wilmington, Delaware, and in 1938 began a series of pastorates. He served as pastor of the Covenant Presbyterian Church in Grove City, Pennsylvania. Three years later he was elected moderator of the Great Lakes Presbytery of the Bible Presbyterian Church, and also became associate pastor of the Bible Presbyterian Church in Chester, Pennsylvania.

Schaeffer's pastoral ministry proved valuable as it helped shape the course of his life's work. He learned that no matter what their vocation or strata of life, people were asking the same basic questions. He attempted to present truth in terms that were understandable to all those in his congregation, whether they were working-class or intellectuals.

In 1943 the Schaeffers were called to the Bible Presbyterian Church in St. Louis, Missouri. It was during this pastorate that they began a youth ministry as an outreach of their local church. This led them to an interest in international youth ministry.

A turning point in Schaeffer's life came in 1947. Europe was still recovering from the effects of World War II, and Schaeffer was granted special leave from the denomination to tour Europe and represent the Independent Board for Presbyterian Foreign Missions and the Foreign Relations Department of the American Council of Christian Churches. While traveling in Europe for three months he had opportunity to observe first-hand the spiritual needs that existed in the church there. Schaeffer's concern for the spiritual condition of the European church was soon followed by a calling from God.

The Schaeffers moved to Lausanne, Switzerland, in 1948 and established Children for Christ, a missionary work to boys and girls. Schaeffer continued to minister throughout Europe preaching on the dangers of liberalism, which included the existentialism taught by theologian Karl Barth.

Spiritual crisis
In 1951 Schaeffer faced a spiritual crisis that forced him intensely to reexamine his Christianity. It was during that time that he "felt a strong burden to stand for the historical Christian position, and for the purity of the visible church." However, he saw little of what should be the results of Christianity.

The problem unfolded to Schaeffer in two parts. First, the reality of Christianity was not evident among those who held the orthodox position. Second, he saw a lack of spirituality in his own life; his faith was not the vibrant and joyful experience it once was. This caused him to rethink his whole position. He spent much time searching the Scriptures, praying, walking the mountains, and pacing the hayloft of their chalet. His conclusion: "As I rethought my reasons for being a Christian, I saw again that there were totally sufficient reasons to know that the infinite-personal God does exist and that Christianity is true." Those kinds of struggles and questions about Christianity became the basis for the L'Abri work.

L'Abri
In 1954 the Schaeffers turned their chalet into a shelter for men and women who were searching for help. It was a faith venture that operated on four principles: (1) they would not ask for money, but would rather make their needs known only to God; (2) they would not recruit staff but depend on God to send the right people their way; (3) they would plan only short-range, to allow for God's sovereign guidance; and (4) they would not publicize themselves but trust that God would send them those in need.

A year later a major crisis threatened the Schaeffers' ministry and tested their faith. In February 1955 the local government decided that foreigners' residence permits were to be canceled. The Schaeffers believed that God had planned for them to be in Switzerland, and they relied heavily on the power of prayer. By means of unsolicited gifts God provided the money they needed to buy a new residence, the Chalet les Melezes in the village of Huemoz. Eventually, permission to stay in Switzerland was granted by the federal government, and the real work of L'Abri began.

L'Abri would become a "shelter" for thousands in the decades to come. People from all walks of life would travel to Chalet les Melezes to hear the message of Christ and receive direction for their lives.

Apologetic and cultural critique

Francis Schaeffer's apologetic method shared aspects of Cornelius Van Til's, notably his discussion of presupposition in religious thought, though in many other ways he diverged sharply from Van Til. He argued that philosophy is not an academic compartment, but that everybody holds to some world view or other. By urging inquirers to follow through the implications of their religious presuppositions he compelled them to face up to the world view they were (often unconsciously) holding.

Schaeffer's critique traced an accelerating divergence in the history of Western thought between the world of the empirical and the known, and the world of the metaphysical and that which is to be held by faith. Modern man, he argued, has engaged in a "leap of faith" to unite the two, thereby abandoning reason and denying his "mannishness." He argued the necessity of biblical Christianity as the one adequate answer to the problems raised by the fact of human personality and the nature of the external world – and the failure of humanist atheistic philosophies to provide such an answer.

This analysis formed the basis of several influential books, notably *Escape from Reason* and *The God Who Is There* (both 1968). He developed the theme further in the ten-part film series *How Should We Then Live?* (1977), and in an accompanying book of the same title.

Much of Schaeffer's later thinking derives from his insistence on a personal universe in which men and women live who are created in the image of a personal God. He claimed that "history is going somewhere" and that the existence of a personal God bestows meaning and significance to time and space. For example, his cultural analysis included extensive treatment of the arts, in which he benefited from the friendship and teaching of Dutch art historian Hans Rookmaaker. His view of the arts had much in common with the tradition of scholars such as Ernst Gombrich and Erwin Panofsky, who gave critical significance to meaning and truth in painting. In *Art and the Bible* (1973) Schaeffer suggests as criteria for evaluating art both the artist's faithfulness to his own world view and also the absolute validity – or otherwise – of that world view.

Schaeffer never formulated a philosophy of art but taught a strong doctrine of creativity, which was reinforced by his wife, Edith, in several of her books dealing with the family, domestic life-style, and similar topics. He was responsible, in substantial sectors of evangelicalism, for a new awareness that the arts and cultural involvement were legitimate, even desirable, areas for the Christian to engage in.

An expanding ministry

In the 1970s, Schaeffer's teaching became much more sociological and political. His critique of the modern quest for personal peace and affluence underpinned a series of analyses of a wide range of subjects such as ecology, church and doctrinal purity, abortion, euthanasia, war and peace, and civil rights.

Schaeffer's books were translated into many languages, and invitations to speak abroad multiplied. In 1974 he addressed the International Congress on World Evangelization at Lausanne, where he received a standing ovation from delegates. From that time, however, his uncompromising defense of biblical inerrancy – "the watershed that divides" – and his critique of contemporary evangelicalism made him an often controversial figure.

With the making of his films, Schaeffer's ministry entered a new phase, especially when the second, *Whatever Happened to the Human Race?* (1979) caught the attention of the medical profession and provided opportunities to discuss abortion and related topics with concerned doctors. Schaeffer and other L'Abri workers spoke at seminars arranged to coincide with showings of the films.

Pastoral and church influence

Central to Schaeffer's pastoral ministry was personal compassion, based on careful and sympathetic listening. Most frequently seen in his personal counseling at L'Abri, compassion also characterized his whole apologetic system. He was prepared to "weep real tears," whether it was for an individual wounded by contemporary problems or for a society that was so lost that it was prepared to abort thousands of children.

Schaeffer saw pre-evangelism as a necessary prelude to confronting people with the gospel, holding that only by listening to what the questions are can one give adequate answers. But though L'Abri was sometimes thought of as a mission to intellectuals, Schaeffer taught that the scholar and the illiterate must come to faith in exactly the same way: by faith in the work of God in Christ. The purpose of pre-evangelism is to bring men to recognize that need.

Though his early church life was lived in a climate of separation, Schaeffer was bitterly distressed by schism. He never ceased his striving for the visible purity of the church, however, and in later life vigorously criticized contemporary evangelicalism. In the early 1950s his denominational experiences precipitated a major spiritual crisis, which is documented in *True Spirituality* and elsewhere in his writings. His posthumously published letters, written in that period, show an awareness of many mistakes made by the separatists and a growing sense of spiritual reality in his life. He counseled his fellow separatists to show love as well as to defend the truth and, particularly after hearing Hugh Alexander speak in Switzerland, entered into a new understanding of the relationship between combating for the faith and depending on the leading of the Holy Spirit.

Schaeffer had considerable influence upon the conservative Presbyterian churches in America and was involved in a number of significant developments. *The Church Before the Watching World* (1971) offers "a practical ecclesiology," and in *The Church at the End of the Twentieth Century* (1970) he examines the future of the institutionalized church. A volume of sermons, *No Little People*, was published in 1974. Publication of his *Letters* began in 1985.

Schaeffer's achievement

Perhaps the most prominent theme in Francis Schaeffer's life and work was his emphasis on "the Lordship of Christ in the totality of life." For Schaeffer, life could not be divided into a "spiritual" part and a "nonspiritual" part. If Jesus Christ is indeed Lord, he must be Lord of all, in every area.

In the early years of L'Abri, Schaeffer emphasized the lordship of Christ, especially in intellectual matters and the arts. But with the rapid breakdown of our Western culture, he directed his concern increasingly toward the lordship of Christ over the critical issues of the day. On these issues he spoke with a prophetic voice – concerning the family, religious freedom, opposition to tyranny, and especially the sanctity of every human life.

Schaeffer helped untold thousands find Jesus Christ as Savior and as the Lord of all of life. Many have gone on to become intellectual leaders and accomplished artists. But in addition to this, the lives of countless unborn children have been saved in response to his militant prolife activism.

Billy Graham

1918-

By the mid-twentieth century, theological liberalism dominated the mainstream churches. The authority of the Bible was discounted, and a belief in the upward march of humanity was still in fashion, though the upheaval of two world wars had brought it seriously into question.

The countries of Eastern Europe, with their historic churches, had come under the control of militantly atheist regimes, which had discouraged or actively persecuted Christians. In Asia and Africa the colonial empires, which had favored Christianity, were being dismantled.

Although the faith was spreading in South Korea, liberated from the Japanese and soon to be rescued from communist invasion, and in parts of Africa and South America, it was in decline in Britain and North America. Evangelicals had tended to retreat into a fortress mentality. There were plenty of evangelists, but since Billy Sunday's last great campaign in 1917, none of them had their nation's ear.

Back in May 1940 a small Bible institute in Florida was holding its graduation ceremony. Before the guest of honor delivered his oration, the class valedictorian rose to make her address. Her mind was on the war already raging in Europe and on the spiritual darkness of the times; she was not thinking of any particular individual.

She said that at each critical epoch of the church, God had "chosen a human instrument to shine forth His light in the darkness. Men like Martin Luther, John and Charles Wesley, Moody and others who were ordinary men, but men who heard the voice of God. It had been said that Luther revolutionized the world. It was not he but Christ working through him. The time is ripe for another Luther, Wesley, Moody. There is room for another name in this list."

Sitting in the hall, one of the class of 1940, was a young man from North Carolina, aged twenty-one: Billy Graham.

Billy Graham.

The Life of	
Billy Graham	
1918	Birth, in Charlotte, North Carolina.
1934	Conversion.
1943	Graduates from Wheaton College; marries Ruth Bell.
1945	Becomes Youth for Christ's first full-time evangelist.
1949	Los Angeles campaign: national fame.
1954	Greater London crusade: world fame.
1956	Founds *Christianity Today* and (1960) *Decision* magazines.
1957	New York crusade (sixteen weeks). Start of television ministry.
1959	Australia-New Zealand crusade.
1974	Convenes Lausanne Congress for World Evangelization and (1983) Amsterdam World Conference.
1977	First preaching tour in Eastern Europe.
1982	First preaches in U.S.S.R.
1984-1985	Mission England.
1986	Second Amsterdam Conference.

Billy Graham

and Modern Evangelism

John C. Pollock

Billy Frank

Like D. L. Moody, William Franklin Graham came from a rural background. He was born on November 7, 1918, near Charlotte, North Carolina, eldest of the four children of a dairy farmer having land on the outskirts and a milk route in the city. Both grandfathers had fought for the Confederacy and were descended from Scots-Irish Presbyterian families who settled in the Carolinas before the Revolution.

Billy Frank, as he was known to his family, grew up tall, fair-haired, and very high spirited and energetic. He reveled in the farm work but was not too attentive to the rather indifferent schooling that was available during the Depression; his special love was baseball. He was reared in a happy, united home with plenty of humor and a strong moral outlook, accompanied by regular church-going. Billy was passing through a period of mild rebellion when, in 1934, soon after his sixteenth birthday, he underwent a profound experience of conversion to Christ during a campaign led by Mordecai Ham, a fiery Southern evangelist.

One passion

Encouraged by his parents, Billy Graham entered Bob Jones College at Cleveland, Tennessee, in the fall of 1936, but neither the climate nor the system suited him. He transferred in January 1937 to the small, rather unusual Florida Bible Institute at Tampa (now Trinity College, Clearwater). The family atmosphere and the emphasis on individual nurture was just what was needed to foster his native intelligence and spiritual ambitions. He believed he had no aptitude for preaching; but he be-

came overwhelmingly conscious of an inner call, which at length he accepted. A personal crisis came when the girl he hoped to marry chose another; Billy turned singlemindedly to the service of Christ, training himself to get the message across. "I had one passion," he said many years later, "and that was to win souls. I didn't have a passion to be a great preacher. I had a passion to win souls."

In 1940, aged nearly twenty-two, already ordained as a Southern Baptist minister and particularly effective as an evangelist to youth, Graham accepted an opportunity for higher education. He entered Wheaton College near Chicago. He had an insatiable desire to learn. He majored in anthropology, as he expected to proceed to seminary, and might have made the honor roll had he not been appointed a student pastor.

At Wheaton he fell in love with Ruth McCue Bell, daughter of a Presbyterian missionary surgeon in China, Nelson Bell. Ruth and Billy married in 1943, shortly after his graduation.

Full-time evangelism

A brief pastorate near Wheaton proved to be a springboard. First, Graham was invited by a busy Chicago pastor and seminary professor, Torrey Johnson, to take over his weekly Sunday evening radio program, "Songs in the Night." This brought George Beverly Shea, the bass-baritone singer, and Graham together. Then Johnson founded Youth for Christ, aimed specifically at servicemen. He chose Graham as preacher for the opening rally. Early in 1945 Graham became Youth for Christ's first full-time evangelist and traveled all over North

America.

Graham and Youth for Christ, brash and inexperienced though they might have been, brought a freshness, urgency, and total loyalty to Christ and to biblical Christianity, which began to dispel the gloom and negative attitudes that had settled on the churches and their youth work. Early in 1946 Johnson took Graham and three others for a whirlwind preaching tour in war-weary Britain, where Graham returned for a five-month's tour (1946-1947) with young Cliff Barrows and Cliff's wife as musicians. Aimed at youth, the tour taught Graham much and led eventually to a wider invitation. At this time also Graham's vision of a worldwide return to evangelical Christianity was deepened by attending conferences in Europe.

In the later 1940s, in American "city-wide" campaigns with Cliff Barrows and Bev Shea, he laid the foundations of co-operative evangelism; unlike most evangelists of the day, Graham welcomed the help of ministers who did not necessarily agree with all the message he preached. Meanwhile he had become the reluctant and part-time president of a small college and seminary in Minneapolis, Minnesota, at its founder's dying request. Northwestern was a diversion, but it provided experience in administration and leadership and brought in several of his future evangelistic team. It also made Minneapolis his natural working base, though his home was at Montreat in North Carolina.

Los Angeles crusade

Billy Graham's breakthrough into the consciousness of the nation came late in 1949 with the extraordinary effect of his seven-weeks' Los Angeles crusade (the term he adopted a little later) in a large tent. Attendance, and the numbers who came forward for counseling, were small compared with later years, but they seemed fantastic in 1949.

Thereafter Boston and other crusades quickly established Graham as the leading evangelist in the United States, though he was still only in his early

Billy Graham in Seoul, 1974; 2,700,000 people were present.

thirties. He formed his methods, drawing on the expertise of others such as Dawson Trotman, founder of the Navigators, who molded the follow-up system. Graham started, with some hesitation, the weekly "Hour of Decision" broadcast; he founded the Billy Graham Evangelistic Association which, with his own integrity, helped banish the rather tarnished image acquired by mass evangelism since D. L. Moody's death a half century before; and he began to have an influence on public figures and became the friend of President Eisenhower. Graham also wrote a best-seller, *Peace with God*, and launched evangelistic feature films.

Greater London Crusade

In 1954 the Greater London Crusade made Graham an international – indeed, world-famous – figure. The crusade began amid press uproar that was none of his making and ended three months later with the Archbishop of Canterbury and the Lord Mayor of London on his platform; a few days later Graham was received by the prime minister, Sir Winston Churchill, greatest man of the age. With a respectful press, thousands of lives profoundly changed, and a new atmosphere, the country was wide open to evangelism: Graham later believed he should have stayed in Britain throughout that summer. Next year his all-Scotland campaign was equally effective. Afterwards, an invitation to preach before the queen at Windsor was not only the beginning of a true friendship with the British royal family but caused many doors to open overseas.

Graham was tall and good-looking, with an engaging personality and strong sense of humor and a marked ability to lead and organize as well as to preach. He had a humility that made him always eager to learn and listen to advice and new ideas, yet with a clear perception of the unalterable truths of the biblical gospel. In the United States he was attacked by fundamentalists for refusing to reject support from liberals, and by liberals for refusing to preach salvation by a social gospel; but he avoided religious and political controversy and would not hit back at critics. He was also attacked by both sides on the race question, but, as was eventually recognized, he contributed substantially to the improvement of race relations.

By the end of the 1950s Graham had held a long, exhausting, but strong crusade in New York. He had found a way to use television for the gospel, long before the rise of the "electronic church," and had thus greatly widened his audience. He had preached in India and the Far East and held crusades in New Zealand and in Australia, which came near to national religious revival in the crusade of 1959. He was about to tour Africa, the Caribbean and South America; and his crusades in North America were drawing ever larger audiences. During all this frequent traveling, his wife, Ruth, had strengthened his base by sacrificing her own wishes and staying at home to raise their family of two sons and three daughters, all of whom grew up to follow their parents in Christian service. Ruth Bell Graham, and the happy home she made, played an important part in bringing Graham to greatness.

Billy Graham, more than any single churchman, was demonstrating that the biblical gospel spoke to the needs of the later twentieth century, in contrast to the theological liberalism that dominated the leadership of the mainstream churches. To deepen the intellectual base of evangelical Christianity, Graham and his father-in-law, Dr. Nelson Bell, founded (1956) a journal, *Christianity Today*, which quickly established itself as a powerful voice. On a more popular level he founded (1960) *Decision* magazine.

Reaching everyone

By now Billy Graham and his team (for it was always a team effort) had transformed mass-evangelism. "Operation Andrew" ensured that a very large number of the uncommitted were brought to his crusades. Preparation, always church-centered, was as thorough and widely based as the follow-up, and many thousands of church people had a part, drawn from entire regions rather than merely the city of the crusade stadium. Thus his audiences were always enormous, and Graham, like Moody before him, had the gift of reaching a very wide range of ages, types, and classes by the same sermon.

By the 1970s, when he was in his fifties, Graham had become much more than an evangelist; he was a world Christian statesman, recognized as the unofficial leader of evangelical Christianity. Many who were now in positions of responsibility had come to conversion or commitment through his ministry. His Schools of Evangelism, held in conjunction with crusades, had brought fresh vision and skill to tens of thousands of clergy and laity throughout the world.

In 1966 Billy Graham had sponsored (nominally through *Christianity Today*) an international congress of evangelism at Berlin, followed by regional congresses on different continents. In 1974 his great congress at Lausanne drew Christian leaders of all races and most churches; and though Lausanne refused to set up a rival organisation to the World Council of Churches, it confirmed biblical evangelism as a mighty force in world Christianity; evangelicals had recovered the initiative that they had lost in the first half of the century. Lausanne, and Graham personally, also helped them to recover the strong social conscience that had been one of the glories of their nineteenth-century forebears.

Graham had always taken a close interest in political affairs, without endorsing one party or particular policies. Overseas he had met many heads of state, always putting the gospel before them; in the United States his counsel was sought by successive presidents and public figures. Richard Nixon had been one of his close friends, and at the Watergate crisis, although deploring wrongdoing, Graham refused to abandon his friendship with a president in deep trouble.

In 1983 Graham fulfilled a long-cherished dream of encouraging itinerant evangelists worldwide, by bringing several thousand together at Amsterdam to learn from an impressive panel of speakers and experts. Thousands more wished to come, and in 1986 a second world conference was held. Many of these evangelists had been helped by his crusades in their own countries, such as South Africa, Korea, Brazil, Taiwan, the Philippines, and Japan.

Graham also entered a new area of ministry: the communist-ruled states of Eastern Europe. In the course of eight years he preached in all but one. His first preaching tour in an officially atheist state was in Hungary (1977), followed by Poland (1978), where the Roman Catholics opened their great cathedrals to him. His first official visit to the Soviet Union, to Moscow in 1982 at the invitation of the Russian Orthodox and the Baptist churches, brought controversy, mainly created by the Western press, but it was followed by a wider tour to six Soviet cities in 1984. By the following year he had preached in every country of Eastern Europe except Bulgaria and during his third visit to Hungary, for the first time in a communist land, was able to use a public stadium.

He returned to Britain in 1984 for "Mission England with Billy Graham" in six regions, and a seventh in 1985. Mission England was honoured by the queen when she invited the Grahams to stay at Sandringham, her country home, and Billy to preach in her village church. A very successful mision to France followed in 1986.

By Billy Graham's sixty-ninth birthday in 1987, he had preached in most countries of the world, to 100 million individuals in person and countless millions by television, radio, and films. Nearly 2 million individuals had come forward at his crusades. He had put new heart and depth into biblical Christianity, found new ways and strategies to promote the cause of Christ, and had fostered a whole new generation of leaders. None of this would have happened without his personal example as a man of God.

Further Reading

Peter

Brown, Raymond E., Karl P. Donfried, and John Reumann, eds. *Peter in the New Testament*. Minneapolis: Augsburg, 1973.

Carson, D. A. *Matthew*. In *The Expositor's Bible Commentary*, vol. 8. Edited by Frank E. Gaebelein. Grand Rapids: Zondervan, 1984; passim, esp. pp.363-78.

Cullman, O. *Peter: Disciple, Apostle, Martyr. A Historical and Theological Essay*. 2d ed. Philadelphia: Westminster, 1962.

Walls, Andrew F. "Peter," *IBD* 3:1199-1202.

Paul

Allen, R. *Missionary Methods: St. Paul's or Ours?* Grand Rapids: Eerdmans, 1962.

Bruce, F. F. *Paul: Apostle of the Heart Set Free*. Grand Rapids: Eerdmans, 1977.

Munck, J. *Paul and the Salvation of Mankind*. Translated by F. Clarke. London: SCM Press, 1959.

Ridderbos, H. *Paul: An Outline of His Theology*. Translated by J. R. DeWitt. Grand Rapids: Eerdmans, 1975.

John

Culross, James. *John Whom Jesus Loved*. London: Morgan and Scott, 1910.

Filson, F. V. "Who Was the Beloved Disciple?" *Journal of Biblical Literature* 68 (1949): 83-88.

Fowler, Harlan D. *Behold the Flaming Sword: A Biography of John and Jesus*. New York: Vantage, 1983.

Parker, P. "John the Son of Zebedee and the Fourth Gospel." *Journal of Biblical Literature* 81 (1962): 35-43.

Smalley, Stephen S. *John: Evangelist and Interpreter*. Nashville: Thomas Nelson, 1984.

Thomas, W. Griffith. *The Apostle John: His Life and Writings*. Grand Rapids: Kregel, 1984.

Titus, E. L. "The Identity of the Beloved Disciple." *Journal of Biblical Literature* 69 (1950): 323-28.

Turner, G.A. "John, the Apostle," *The Zondervan Pictorial Encyclopedia of the Bible,* vol. 3. Edited by Merrill C. Tenney. Grand Rapids: Zondervan, 1975, pp. 637-41.

Ignatius of Antioch

Corwin, V. *St. Ignatius and Christianity in Antioch*. New Haven, Conn.: Yale U., 1960.

Grant, R. M. *Ignatius of Antioch*. Camden: Thomas Nelson, 1966.

Musurillo, H. "Ignatius of Antioch," *Theological Studies* 22 (1961): 103-10.

Schoedel, W. R. *Ignatius of Antioch*. Philadelphia: Fortress, 1985.

Yamauchi, E. *Pre-Christian Gnosticism*. Grand Rapids: Baker, 1983.

Justin Martyr

Barnard, L. W. *Justin Martyr: His Life and Thought*. Cambridge: Cambridge U., 1967.

Dods, M., G. Reith, and B. Pratten, trans. *The Writings of Justin Martyr and Athenagoras*. Edinburgh: T. & T. Clark, 1892.

Goodenough, E. *The Theology of Justin Martyr*. Amsterdam: Philo, 1968. Reprint of 1923 ed.

Osborn, E. F. *Justin Martyr*. Tübingen: J. C. B. Mohr, 1973.

Van Winden, J. C. M. *An Early Christian Philosopher*. Leiden: Brill, 1971.

Irenaeus

Lawson, John. *The Biblical Theology of St. Irenaeus.* London: Epworth, 1948.

Nielsen, J. T. *Adam and Christ in the Theology of Irenaeus of Lyons.* Assen: Van Gorcum, 1968.

Smith, Joseph P. *St. Irenaeus: Proof of the Apostolic Preaching.* New York: Paulist/ Newman, 1952.

Wingren, G. *Man and the Incarnation: A Study in the Biblical Theology of Irenaeus.* Philadelphia: Muhlenberg, 1959.

Tertullian

Barnes, T. D. *Tertullian. A Historical and Literary Study.* Oxford: Clarendon, 1971.

Bray, G. L. *Holiness and the Will of God. Perspectives on the Theology of Tertullian.* Atlanta: John Knox, and London: Marshall, Morgan & Scott, 1979.

Origen

Crouzel, H. "Origen and Origenism," in *The New Catholic Encyclopedia,* vol. 10. New York: McGraw-Hill, 1967, pp. 767-74.

Fathers of the Third Century. Vol. 4 of *The Ante-Nicene Fathers.* Reprint. Grand Rapids: Eerdmans, 1976.

Greer, Rowan A., trans. and ed. *Origenes, An Exhortation to Martyrdom, on Prayer, First Principles, Prologue to the Commentary on the Song of Songs, Homily XVII on Numbers.* New York: Paulist, 1979.

O'Meara, John J. *Origen, Prayer, Exhortation to Martyrdom.* No. 19 of *Ancient Christian Writers.* New York: Newman, 1954.

Richardson, Cyril. *Alexandrian Christianity.* Vol. 2 of *The Library of Christian Classics.* Philadelphia: Westminster, 1953.

Trigg, Joseph Wilson. *Origen,*

The Bible and Philosophy in the Third Century Church. Atlanta: John Knox, 1983.

Cyprian

Benson, E. W. *Cyprian His Life, His Times, and His Work.* London: Macmillan, 1897.

Hinchcliff, P. *Cyprian of Carthage and the Unity of the Christian Church.* London: Geoffrey Chapman, 1974.

Athanasius

Athanasius *Contra Gentes and De Incarnatione.* Edited and translated by Robert W. Thomson. Oxford: Clarendon, 1971.

———. *The Life of Antony and the Letter to Marcellinus.* Translated and introduced by Robert C. Gregg. Classics of Western Spirituality Series. New York: Paulist, 1980.

———. *Letters Concerning the Holy Spirit.* Translated and introduced with notes by C.R. B. Shapland. New York: Philosophical Library, 1951.

Dragas, George D. *Athanasiana: Essays in the Theology of Saint Athanasius.* London: n.p., 1980.

Basil the Great

Clark, William Kemp Lowther. *St. Basil the Great, A Study in Monasticism.* Cambridge: Cambridge U., 1913.

Frend, W. H. C. *The Early Church.* London: Hodder and Stoughton, 1965; Philadelphia: Lippincott, 1965, 1966.

Selected writings in Stevenson, James, ed. *Creeds, Councils and Controversies.* New York: Seabury, 1966. pp. 104-19.

Jerome

Campenhausen, Hans von. *Men Who Shaped the Western Church.* New York: Harper, 1964. Pages 129-82.

Kelly, J. N. D. *Jerome: His Life, Writings, and Controversies.* London: Duckworth, 1975.

Murphy, Francis X., ed. *A*

Monument to Saint Jerome. New York: Sheed and Ward, 1952.

Sparks, H. F. D. "Jerome as a Biblical Scholar." In *The Cambridge History of the Bible.* Vol. 1, *From the Beginnings to Jerome.* P. R. Ackroyd and C. F. Evans. Cambridge: Cambridge U., 1970. Pages 510-41.

John Chrysostom

Baur, J.C. *John Chrysostom and His Time.* 2 vols. London and Glasgow, 1959, 1961 (the best account).

Neill, Stephen. *Chrysostom and His Message.* London: Lutterworth, 1962 (including selections).

Pelikan, J., ed. *The Preaching of Chrysostom: Homilies on the Sermon on the Mount.* Philadelphia: Fortress, 1967.

Quasten, J. *Patrology.* Vol. 3, Utrecht/Antwerp and West-minster, Md.: Paulist/ Newman, 1963 (for catalogue of works).

Stephens, W. R. W. *St. John Chrysostom, His Life and Times.* London, 1872 (sympathetic older account).

Augustine

Bonner, Gerald S. *St. Augustine of Hippo, Life and Controversies.* Philadelphia: Westminster, 1963.

Brown, Peter. *Augustine of Hippo* Berkeley, Calif.: U. of California, 1967.

Gilson, Etienne. *The Christian Philosophy of St. Augustine.* New York: Random House, 1961.

Nash, Ronald H. *The Light of the Mind: St. Augustine's Theory of Knowledge.* Lexington, Ky. U. of Kentucky, 1969.

Portalie, Eugene. *A Guide to the Thought of Saint Augustine.* Chicago: Henry Regnery, 1960.

Leo the Great

Feltoe, C. L. *The Letters and Sermons of Leo the Great.*

Nicene and Post-Nicene Fathers. Ed. by Philip Schaff and Henry Wace. 2d Ser., vol. 12. Grand Rapids: Eerdmans, 1956. Reprint.

Jalland, T. G. *The Life and Times of St. Leo the Great.* London: SPCK, 1941.

Murphy, F. X. "Leo I, Pope, St." *New Catholic Encyclopedia.* Vol. 8. New York: McGraw-Hill, 1967. Pages 637-39.

Ullman, W. "Leo I and the Theme of Papal Primary." *Journal of Theological Studies* n. s. 11 (1960): 25-51.

Patrick

Bury, J. B. *The Life of St. Patrick and His Place in History.* London: Macmillan; New York: Macmillan, 1905.

Chadwick, Nora. *Studies in the Early British Church.* Hamden, Conn.: Shoe String, 1973.

Hanson, Richard Patrick Crosland. *The Life and Writing of the Historical Saint Patrick.* New York: Seabury, 1983.

———. *St. Patrick: His Origins and Career.* Oxford: Clarendon, 1968.

Hughes, Kathleen. *Early Christian Ireland.* Ithaca, N.Y.: Cornell U. 1972.

O'Rahilly, Thomas F. *The Two Patricks: A Lecture on the History of Christianity in Fifth-Century Ireland.* Dublin: Dublin Institute for Advanced Studies, 1942.

Ryan, John, ed. *Saint Patrick.* Dublin: published for Radio Eireann by the Stationery Office, 1958.

Columba

McNeill, John T. *The Celtic Churches: A History,* A.D. 200 to 1200. Chicago: U. of Chicago, 1974.

Menzies, Lucy. *St. Columba of Iona.* Glasgow: Iona Community, 1949.

St. Adomnan. *Life of Columba.* Ed. Alan Orr Anderson and Marjorie Ogilvie Anderson.

London: Thomas Nelson, 1961.

Simpson, W. Douglas. *The Historical Saint Columba.* Edinburgh: Oliver and Boyd, 1963.

Gregory the Great

Batiffol, Pierre. *St. Gregory the Great.* Trans. John L. Stoddard. London: Burns, Oates and Washbourne, 1929.

Dudden, Frederick H. *Gregory the Great.* 2 vols. New York: Russell & Russell, 1905, 1967.

Gregorius I. "Pastoral Care." Ed. and trans. Henry Davis. In *Ancient Christian Writers,* vol. 11. Westminster, Md.: Newman, 1950.

Richards, Jeffrey. *Consul of God: The Life and Times of Gregory the Great.* Boston: Routledge & Kegan Paul, 1980.

Sharkey, Neil. *St. Gregory the Great's Concept of Papal Power.* Washington, D.C.: Catholic U., 1956.

Bede

Bede *Opera Historica.* Trans. and introd. J. E. King. 2 vols. 1930 (reprint 1962).

Blair, Peter Hunter. *The World of Bede.* New York: St. Martin's, 1970.

Bonner, Gerald. "The Christian Life in the Thought of the Venerable Bede," *Durham University Journal* 63 (December 1970): 39-55.

———. *Famulus Christi: Essays in Commemoration of the Thirteenth Centenary of the Birth of the Venerable Bede,* London: SPCK, 1976.

Boniface

Boniface *The Letters of Saint Boniface.* Trans. Ephraim Emerton. New York: W. W. Norton, 1976.

Greenaway, George William. *Saint Boniface.* London: Adam & Charles Black, 1955.

Laux, John Joseph. *Der Heilige Bonifatius, Apostel der Deutschen.* Freiburg im Breisgau and St. Louis: Herder, 1922.

Lampen, Willibrord. *Winfried-Bonifatius.* Amsterdam: D. N. van Kampen, 1949.

Neill, Stephen. *A History of Christian Missions.* New York: Penguin, 1979.

Talbot, C. H. "St. Boniface and the German Mission." In *The Mission of the Church and the Propagation of the Faith,* ed. G. J. Cuming. Cambridge: Cambridge U., 1970.

Alcuin

Alcuin. *The Life of St. Willibrord.* In *The Anglo-Saxon Missionaries in Germany,* Trans. and ed. Charles H. Talbot. New York: Sheed and Ward, 1954.

Almedingen, E. M. *Charlemagne* London and Sydney: Bodley Head, 1968.

Duckett, Eleanor Shipley. *Alcuin Friend of Charlemagne, His World and His Work.* New York: Macmillan, 1951.

Einhard and Notker the Stammerer. *Two Lives of Charlemagne.* Trans. Lewis Thorpe. Baltimore: Penguin, 1969.

Gaskoin, C. J. B. *Alcuin: His Life and Work.* New York: Russell and Russell, 1966.

Wallach, Luitpold. *Alcuin and Charlemagne: Studies in Carolingian History and Literature.* Ithaca, N. Y.: Cornell U., 1959.

Anselm

Church, Richard William. *Saint Anselm.* London: Macmillan, 1913.

Eadmer *The Life of St. Anselm.* Ed. and trans. R. W. Southern. London and New York: Thomas Nelson, 1962.

Hopkins, Jasper. *A Companion to the Study of St. Anselm.* Minneapolis: U. of Minnesota, 1972.

Bernard of Clairvaux

Bernard of Clairvaux, *Life and Works of Saint Bernard, abbot of Clairvaux*. Ed. Dom. John Mabillon. Trans. and ed. with additional notes by Samuel J. Eales. 4 vols. London: J. Hodges, 1889–1896.

Coulton, George Gordon. *Two Saints: St. Bernard and St. Francis*. Cambridge: Cambridge U., 1932, reprint ed. Folcroft, Pa: Folcroft Library, 1974.

Gilson, Etienne. *The Mystical Theology of St. Bernard*. Trans. A. H. C. Downes. London: Sheed & Ward, 1940.

Scott-James, Bruno. *Saint Bernard of Clairvaux*. Chicago: Henry Regnery, 1953.

Williams, Watkin W. *St. Bernard of Clairvaux*. Westminster, Md. Newman Press, 1953.

Peter Abelard

Abelard, Peter. *The Cruel Tragedy of My Life: The Autobiography of Peter Abelard*. Albuquerque, N.M.: Foundation for Classical Reprints, 1985.

Compayre, Gabriel. *Abelard and the Origin and Early History of Universities*. New York: Greenwood, 1969.

Luddy, A. J. *The Case of Peter Abelard*. Dublin: M. H. McGill, 1947.

Luscombe, David E. *The School of Peter Abelard: The Influence of Abelard's Thought in the Early Scholastic Period*. London: Cambridge U. 1969.

Weingart, Richard. *The Logic of Divine Love: A Critical Analysis of the Soteriology of Peter Abelard*. London: Clarendon, 1970.

Williams, Paul, "The Abelardian Perspective: A Moral View of Christ's Work." Ph.D. diss., Drew University, 1976; microfilm edition, Ann Arbor, Mich.: University Microfilms, 1981.

Thomas Becket

Duggan, Anne. *Thomas Becket: A Textual History of His Letters*. New York: Oxford, 1980.

Knowles, David. *Thomas Becket* London: A.C. & C. Black, 1970.

Smalley, Beryl. *The Becket Conflict and the Schools: A Study of Intellectuals in Politics*. Oxford: Basil Blackwell, 1973.

Warren, Wilfred L. *Henry II*. London: Eyre Methuen, 1973.

Innocent III

Packard, Sydney R. *Europe and the Church under Innocent III*. New York: H. Holt, 1927.

Renna, Thomas J. *Church and State in Medieval Europe, 1050-1314*. Dubuque, Ia.: Kendall/Hunt, 1974.

Ullman, Walter. *A Short History of the Papacy in the Middle Ages*. New York: Methuen, 1974.

Francis of Assisi

Esser, Cajetan. *Origins of the Franciscan Order*. Chicago: Franciscan Herald, 1970.

Englebert, Omer. *St. Francis of Assisi. A Biography*. Trans. Eva Marie Cooper. Chicago: Franciscan Herald, 1965.

Fleming, John V. *An Introduction to the Franciscan Literature of the Middle Ages*. Chicago: Franciscan Herald, 1977.

Habig, Marion A., ed. *St. Francis of Assisi, Writings and Early Biographies*. 3d rev. ed. Chicago: Franciscan Herald, 1973.

Thomas Aquinas

Chesterton, Gilbert Keith. *Thomas Aquinas*. Garden City, N. Y.: Image, 1956.

Copleston, Frederick Charles. *Aquinas*. London: Search, 1976. New York: Barnes and Noble, 1976.

Foster, Kenelm. *The Life of St. Thomas Aquinas*. London: Longmans, Green, 1959; Baltimore: Helicon, 1959.

Gilson, Etienne. *The Christian Philosophy of St. Thomas Aquinas*. Trans. Edward Bullough; ed. G. A. Erlington. St. Louis and London: B. Herder, 1937.

Grabmann, M. *The Interior Life of St. Thomas Aquinas*. Trans. Nicholas Ashenbrener. Milwaukee: Bruce, 1951.

John Wyclif

Buddensieg, Rudolf. *John Wyclif, Patriot and Reformer*. London: T. Fisher Unwin, 1884. Reprint ed., Darby, Pa.: Arden Library, 1979.

Carrick, J. C. *Wycliffe and the Lollards*. New York: Gordon, 1977.

Kenny, Anthony. *Wyclif*. Oxford: Oxford U. 1985. (A good introduction to his thought.)

Spinka, Matthew, ed. *Advocates of Reform, from Wyclif to Erasmus*. London and Philadelphia: Westminster, 1953. (Includes parts of two of his writings.)

Wyclif, John. *Wyclif: Select English Writings*. Ed. Herbert E. Winn. London: Oxford U., 1929.

Catherine of Siena

Catherine of Siena. *Catherine of Siena: The Dialogue*. Trans. and introd. Suzanne Noffke. Mahwah, N. J.: Paulist, 1980.

Curtayne, Alice. *Catherine of Siena*. London: Sheed & Ward, 1935. Reprint ed. Rockford, Ill.: Tan, 1980.

Levasti, Arrigo. *My Servant Catherine*. Trans. Dorothy M. White. Westminster, Md.: Newman, 1954.

John Hus

Leff, G. *Heresy in the Later Middle Ages.* Vol. 2., chap. 9. Manchester: Manchester U., 1967; New York: Barnes and Noble, 1967.

Spinka, Matthew *John Hus. A Biography.* Princeton: Princeton U., 1968.

———. ed. *Advocates of Reform. From Wyclif to Erasmus.* London: SCM; Philadelphia: Westminster, 1953. (Includes Hus's *Simony.*)

Martin Luther

Althaus, Paul. *The Theology of Martin Luther.* Philadelphia: Fortress, 1966.

Bainton, Roland. *Here I Stand: A Life of Martin Luther.* Nashville: Abingdon, 1950.

Edwards, Mark U., Jr. *Luther and the False Brethren.* Stanford, Calif: Stanford U., 1975.

Kittelson, James M. *Luther the Reformer: The Story of the Man, and His Career.* Minneapolis: Augsburg, 1986.

Spitz, Lewis W. *The Protestant Reformation, 1517-1559.* New York: Harper & Row, 1985.

Ulrich Zwingli

Bromiley, Geoffrey W., ed. and trans. *Zwingli and Bullinger.* Vol. 24 of *The Library of Christian Classics.* Philadelphia: Westminster, 1953.

Potter, G. R. *Zwingli.* Cambridge and New York: Cambridge U., 1976.

Rilliet, J. *Zwingli: Third Man of the Reformation.* Trans. Harold Knight. Philadelphia: Westminster, 1964.

Zwingli, Ulrich. *Commentary on True and False Religion.* Ed. S. W. Jackson and Clarence Neville Heller. Durham, N. C.: Labyrinth, 1929, 1981.

William Tyndale

Bruce, F. F. *History of the Bible in English: from the Earliest Versions.* New York: Oxford U., 1978. Chaps. 3-6.

Tyndale, William. *The Work of William Tyndale.* Ed. and introd. G. E. Duffield. Appleford: Sutton Courtenay, 1964.

Williams, Charles Harold. *William Tyndale.* London: Nelson, 1969.

John Calvin

Calvin, John. *Institutes of the Christian Religion.* Trans. F. L. Battles. 2 vols. Philadelphia: Westminster, 1967.

McNeill, John T. *The History and Character of Calvinism.* New York: Oxford U., 1954.

Parker, T. H. L. *John Calvin.* London: J. M. Dent, 1975.

Reid, W. Stanford, ed. *John Calvin: His Influence in the Western World.* Grand Rapids: Zondervan, 1982.

Wendel, François. *Calvin: The Origins and Development of His Religious Thought.* London: Collins; New York: Harper & Row, 1963.

Thomas Cranmer

Bromiley, Geoffrey W. *Thomas Cranmer, Theologian.* London: Lutterworth, 1956.

Cox, J. E., ed. *Miscellaneous Writings and Letters of Thomas Cranmer.* Cambridge: Cambridge U., 1946.

Packer, J. I. Introduction to *The Work of Thomas Cranmer.* Ed. Gervase E. Duffield. Appleford: Sutton Courtenay, 1964.

Pollard, A. F. *Thomas Cranmer and the English Reformation, 1489-1556.* New York and London: Putnam's, 1905. Reprint ed., Hamden, Conn.: Archon, 1965.

Ridley, Jasper. *Thomas Cranmer,* Oxford: Clarendon, 1962.

Ignatius Loyola

Brodrick, James. *The Origin of the Jesuits.* New York: Longmans, Green, 1940.

Donnelly, John Patrick. "For the Greater Glory of God: St. Ignatius Loyola." In *Leaders of the Reformation,* ed. Richard L. DeMolen. Selinsgrove, Pa.: Susquehanna, 1984.

Dudon, Paul. *St. Ignatius of Loyola.* Milwaukee: Bruce, 1949.

Foss, Michael. *The Founding of the Jesuits, 1540.* London: Hamish Hamilton, 1969.

Loyola, Ignatius. *St. Ignatius' Own Story.* Trans. W. I. Young. Chicago: Regnery, 1956.

———. *Spiritual Exercises.* Trans. Anthony Mattola. Garden City, N. Y.: Doubleday, 1964.

Francis Xavier

Brodrick, James. *St. Francis Xavier, 1506-1552.* New York: Wicklow, 1952.

Diehl, Katherine Smith. "Catholic Religious Orders in South Asia, 1500-1835," *Journal of Asian Studies* 37, no. 4 (August 1978): 699-711.

Farley, M. Foster. "The Jesuits in Asia," *Mankind* 6, no. 10, (February 1981): 8-13, 32-34.

Schurhammer, Georg. *Francis Xavier: His Life, His Times.* Trans. M. J. Costelloe. 4 vols. Chicago: Jesuit Historical Institute, 1973-1982.

Skoglund, Herb. "St. Francis Xavier's Encounter with Japan," *Missiology* 3, no. 4 (October 1975): 451-67.

Menno Simons

Bender, H. S. *Menno Simons.* Scottdale, Pa.: Herald, 1956.

Davis, K. R. *Anabaptism and Ascetism.* Scottdale, Pa.: Herald, 1974.

Estep, W. R. *The Anabaptist Story.* Grand Rapids: Eerdmans, 1975.

Goertz, Hans-Jurgen, ed. *Profiles of Radical Reformers.*

Scottdale, Pa.: Herald, 1982.

Wenger, J. C., ed. *The Complete Writings of Menno Simons.* Trans. L. Verduin. Scottdale, Pa.: Herald, 1956.

John Knox

McEwen, J. S. *The Faith of John Knox.* Richmond, Va.: John Knox, 1961.

Reid, W. Stanford. *Trumpeter of God: A Biography of John Knox.* New York: Scribner's, 1974.

Whitley, Elizabeth. *Plain Mr. Knox.* London: Skeffington, 1960; Richmond Va.: John Knox, 1960.

Teresa of Avila

Dicken, E. W. T. *The Crucible of Love: A Study in the Spanish Mysticism of Santa Teresa and St. John of the Cross.* 1963.

Hamilton, Elizabeth. *The Great Teresa, A Journey to Spain.* 1960.

Hatzfeld, Helmut. *Santa Teresa of Avila.* 1969.

Peers, Edgar A. *A Handbook of the Life and Times of St. Teresa.* 1954.

Rees, A., ed. *Teresa of Avila and Her World.* 1981.

Teresa of Avila. *The Complete Works of Saint Teresa of Jesus.* Ed. Silverio de Santa Teresa and Edgar A. Peers. 3 vols. 1946.

Blaise Pascal

Pascal, Blaise. *The Provincial Letters.* Harmondsworth: Penguin, 1967.

———. *Pensées.* Harmondsworth: Penguin, 1966.

All the books of H. F. Stewart on Pascal are worth reading, as also is the study by Jean Mesnard.

John Owen

Owen, John. *The Collected Works of John Owen.* Ed. W. H. Gould. 24 vols. Edinburgh, 1850-1853. Reprint ed., 16 vols. London: Banner of Truth, 1965-1968.

———. *The Correspondence of John Owen.* Ed. Peter Toon. Cambridge: James Clarke, 1970.

Toon, Peter. *God's Statesman: The Life and Work of John Owen,* Exeter: Paternoster, 1971; Grand Rapids: Zondervan, 1973.

John Bunyan

Bunyan, John. *The Pilgrim's Progress.* Many editions.

———. *The Whole Works of John Bunyan.* Grand Rapids: Baker, 1977.

Brown, John. *John Bunyan, 1628-1688: His Life, Times and Work.* Ed. Frank M. Harrison. Reprint of 1928 ed. Hamden, Conn.: Shoe String, 1985.

Froude, James A. *Bunyan.* Ed. John Morley. Reprint of 1888 ed., New York: AMS, 1985.

Greaves, Richard. *John Bunyan* (2 vols). Grand Rapids: Eerdmans, 1969.

George Fox

Barbour, Hugh, and Arthur O. Roberts, eds. *Early Quaker Writings.* Grand Rapids: Eerdmans, 1973.

Fox, George. *The Journal of George Fox.* Ed. John L. Nickalls. Cambridge: Cambridge U., 1952.

Vipont, Elfrida (Foulds). *The Story of Quakerism.* London: Bannisdale, 1954.

Trueblood, D. Elton. *The People Called Quakers.* 2d ed. Richmond, Ia: Friends United, 1971.

Philipp Jakob Spener

Schmidt, Martin, and Wilhelm Jannasch, eds. *Das Zeitalter des Pietismus.* Bremen: C. Schunemann, 1965.

Spener, Philipp Jakob. *Pia Desideria.* Trans. Theodore G. Tappert. Philadelphia: Fortress, 1964.

Stoeffler, Fred Ernest. *The Rise of Evangelical Pietism.* Leiden: E. J. Brill, 1965.

Jonathan Edwards

Cherry, Conrad. *The Theology of Jonathan Edwards.* Garden City, N. Y.: Anchor Books, 1966.

Edwards, Jonathan. *Works.* Ed. Perry Miller. Vol. 1. New Haven, Conn.: Yale U., 1957.

Works. Memoir by Sereno E. Dwight. Rev. and corr. Edward Hickman. Edinburgh and Carlisle, Pa.: Banner of Truth, 1834, 1974.

Winslow, Ola Elizabeth. *Jonathan Edwards.* New York: Collier, 1941, 1961.

John and Charles Wesley

Davies, R. E. *Methodism.* London: Epworth, 1963; Baltimore: Penguin, 1963.

Gill, F. C. *Charles Wesley, The First Methodist.* London: Lutterworth, 1964.

Snyder, H. A. *The Radical Wesley.* Downers Grove, Ill.: InterVarsity, 1980.

Tuttle, R. G. *John Wesley: His Life and Theology.* Grand Rapids: Zondervan, 1978.

Wood, A. Skevington. *The Burning Heart. John Wesley, Evangelist.* Grand Rapids: Eerdmans, 1967.

George Whitefield

Dallimore, Arnold A. *The Life and Times of George Whitefield.* Vol. 1. London: Banner of Truth, 1970; vol. 2. Westchester, Ill.: Cornerstone, 1980. Edinburgh: Banner of Truth, 1980.

Ryle, J. C. *Christian Leaders of the Eighteenth Century.* London: T. Nelson, 1869. Reprint ed., Carlisle, Pa.: Banner of Truth, 1978.

Seymour, Aaron. *The Life and Times of Selina, Countess of Huntingdon.* 2 vols. London: W. E. Painter, 1840.

Whitefield, George. *The Works of George Whitefield.* 6 vols. London: E. and C. Dilly, and

Kincaid and Creech, 1771.
———. *George Whitefield's Letters*. Edinburgh: Banner of Truth, 1976.

William Wilberforce
Furneaux, Robin. *William Wilberforce*. London: Hamish Hamilton, 1974.
Pollock, John. *Wilberforce*. Tring: Lion Publishing, 1977; New York: St. Martin's, 1978.
Wilberforce, William. *Real Christianity*. (Abridged and paraphrased version of *A Practical View*, 1797.) London: SCM, 1958.

William Carey
Carey, William. *An Enquiry into the Obligation of Christians to Use Means for the Conversion of the Heathen*. London, 1792.
Drewery, Mary. *William Carey: A Biography*. Grand Rapids, Zondervan, 1979.
Smith, George. *The Life of William Carey: Shoe-maker and Missionary*. New York: Dutton, n.d.
Walker, F. Deauville. *William Carey: Missionary Pioneer and Statesman*. Chicago: Moody, n.d.

Elizabeth Fry
Kent, John. *Elizabeth Fry*. London: B. T. Batsford, 1962.
Rose, June. *Elizabeth Fry: A Biography*. London: Macmillan, 1980.
Whitney, Janet P. *Elizabeth Fry: Quaker Heroine*. London: Harrap, 1937.

Charles Grandison Finney
Cross, Whitney R. *The Burned-Over District*. New York: Harper & Row, 1965.
Charles G. Finney: An Autobiography. Old Tappan, N. J.: Revell, 1876.
Finney, Charles Grandison. *Lectures on Revivals of Religion*. Ed. William G. McLoughlin. Cambridge, Mass.: Belknap, Harvard U., 1960.

McLoughlin, William G., Jr. *Modern Revivalism: Charles Grandison Finney to Billy Graham*. New York: Ronald, 1959.
Rosell, Garth M. "Charles G. Finney: His Place in the Stream of Evangelicalism." In *The Evangelical Tradition in America*. Ed. Leonard I. Sweet. Macon, Ga.: Mercer U., 1984.
Wright, George Frederick. *Charles Grandison Finney*. Boston and New York: Houghton Mifflin, 1891.

George Müller
Pierson, A. T. *George Müller of Bristol*. London, 1905; Grand Rapids: Zondervan, 1984.
Steer, Roger. *George Müller: Delighted in God*. London: Hodder and Stoughton, 1975.

Søren Kierkegaard
Besides *Kierkegaard's Writings*, which are steadily becoming available from Princeton U., and *Søren Kierkegaard's Journals and Papers*, Bloomington Ind. (Indiana U., 1967-1978), the following are recommended:
Eller, Vernard. *Kierkegaard and Radical Discipleship*. Princeton, N.J.: Princeton U., 1968.
Evans, C. Stephen. *Kierkegaard's Fragments and Postscript: The Religious Philosophy of Johannes Climacus*. Humanities P., 1983.
Lowrie, Walter. *A Short Life of Kierkegaard*. Princeton, N.J.: Princeton U., 1942.
Swenson, David. *Something About Kierkegaard*. Reprint. Macon, Ga.: Mercer U. 1984.

David Livingstone
Jeal, Tim. *Livingstone*. London: Heinemann, 1973; New York: Putnam, 1973.
Pachai, Bridglal, ed. *Livingstone, Man of Africa: Memorial Essays 1873-1973*. London: Longman, 1973.
Schapera, I., ed. *Livingstone's Missionary Correspondence*

1841-1856. London: Chatto & Windus, 1961.
Seaver, George. *David Livingstone: His Life and Letters*. London: Lutterworth, 1957; New York: Harper, 1957.

Charles Haddon Spurgeon
Fullerton, W. Y. *Charles Spurgeon*. Chicago: Moody, 1966.
Kruppa, P. S. *Charles Haddon Spurgeon: A Preacher's Progress*. New York: Garland, 1982.
Payne, E. A. "The Down Grade Controversy: a Postscript," *The Baptist Quarterly* no. 4 (Oct. 1979).
Spurgeon, C. H. *The Early Years, 1834-1859*. London: Banner of Truth, 1962.
———. *The Full Harvest, 1860-1892*. Edinburgh: Banner of Truth. 1973.

D.L.Moody
Findlay, J. F. *Dwight L. Moody, American Evangelist, 1837-1899*. Chicago: U. of Chicago, 1969.
Pollock, John. *Moody: A Biographical Portrait*. New York: Macmillan, 1963; Grand Rapids: Zondervan, 1963; Chicago: Moody, 1984.

B.B.Warfield
No extensive biography is available.
See: Statement by Ethelbert Warfield, *Revelation and Inspiration*, pages v-ix; *Princeton Theological Review*, volume 19 (1921), 329, 330, 369-91; account by Samuel G. Craig in *Biblical and Theological Studies*, xi-xviii; *The Banner of Truth* (February 1971) was devoted to Warfield.
Hoffecker, W. Andrew. "Benjamin B. Warfield." In *Reformed Theology in America: A History of Its Modern Development*, ed. David Wells. Grand Rapids: Eerdmans, 1985, pp. 60-86.
——— *Piety and the Princeton Theologians*. Grand Rapids: Baker, 1981.

Meeter, John E, and Roger A. Nicole. *A Bibliography of Benjamin Breckinridge Warfield, 1851-1921.* Nutley, N. J.: Presbyterian and Reformed, 1974.

Noll, Mark A., ed. *The Princeton Theology, 1812-1921.* Grand Rapids: Baker, 1983.

Karl Barth

Barth, Karl. *Evangelical Theology.* Grand Rapids: Eerdmans, 1963.

Bolich, G. C. *Karl Barth and Evangelicalism.* Downers Grove, Ill.: InterVarsity, 1980.

Bromiley, Geoffrey W. *An Introduction to the Theology of Karl Barth.* Grand Rapids: Eerdmans, 1979.

Busch, E. *Karl Barth.* Philadelphia: Fortress, 1976.

Dietrich Bonhoeffer

Bethge, Eberhard. *Dietrich Bonhoeffer, Man of Vision, Man of Courage.* New York: Harper, 1970.

———. *Costly Grace: An Illustrated Biography of Dietrich Bonhoeffer.* San Francisco: Harper & Row, 1979.

Bonhoeffer, Dietrich. *The Cost of Discipleship.* New York: Macmillan, 1959.

Godsey, John D., and Geoffrey B. Kelly, eds. *Ethical Responsibility: Bonhoeffer's Legacy to the Churches.* New York: E. Mellen, 1982.

Godsey, John D. *The Theology of Dietrich Bonhoeffer.* Philadelphia: Westminster, 1960.

Klassen, A. J., ed. *A Bonhoeffer Legacy: Essays in Under-standing.* Grand Rapids: Eerdmans, 1980.

Rasmussen, Larry. *Dietrich Bonhoeffer: Reality and Resistance.* Nashville: Abingdon, 1972.

C.S.Lewis

The best selection of Lewis's books and papers is in the Marion E. Wade Collection, Wheaton College, Wheaton, Illinois.

Green, Roger Lancelyn, and Walter Hooper. *C. S. Lewis: A Biography.* New York: Harcourt Brace Jovanovich, 1974.

Lewis, C. S. *The Pilgrim's Regress.* London: G. Bles, 1950; Grand Rapids: Eerdmans, 1977.

———. *Surprised by Joy.* New York: Harcourt Brace, 1955; London: G. Bles, 1955.

Francis Schaeffer

Dennis, Lane, ed. *Francis A. Schaeffer: Portraits of the Man and His Work.* Westchester, Ill.: Crossway, 1986.

Parkhurst, Louis G. *Francis Schaeffer: the Man and His Message.* Wheaton, Ill.: Tyndale, 1985.

Ruegsgegger, Ronald, ed. *Reflections on Francis Schaeffer.* Grand Rapids: Zondervan, 1986.

Schaeffer, Edith. *L'Abri.* London: Norfolk, 1969; Wheaton, Ill.: Tyndale, 1972.

———. *The Tapestry.* Waco, Tex.: Word, 1981. (An extended autobiography of Edith and Francis Schaeffer.)

Schaeffer, Francis. *The Complete Works of Francis A. Schaeffer: A Christian World View.* Westchester, Ill.: Crossway, 1982.

Billy Graham

Pollock, John. *Billy Graham.* New York: McGraw-Hill, 1966; Grand Rapids: Zondervan, 1966.

———. *Billy Graham: Evangelist to the World.* San Francisco: Harper & Row, 1978.

———. *To All Nations: The Billy Graham Story.* San Francisco: Harper & Row, 1985.

Index

Picture credits

The Ancient Art and Architecture
Collection 87, 107, 155, 179, 191,
207, 223, 257
B.B.C. Hulton Picture Library 39, 85,
139, 143, 273, 285, 306, 314, 321,
325, 337, 338, 357
The Banner of Truth Trust 343
Cedok (London) Limited 186
The Danish Tourist Board 327, 328
Tim Dowley 77, 93, 156, 160, 162,
163, 164, 178, 181, 182, 238, 254,
284, 287, 290, 291
Mary Evans Picture Library 49, 63,
121, 127, 185, 187, 197, 232, 233,
271, 275, 281, 329, 331, 345
French Government Tourist Office
43, 146, 206, 259
Sonia Halliday Photographs 11, 23,
31, 69, 81, 91, 95, 111, 147, 161, 166
Italian State Tourist Office 79
A.N.S.Lane 9, 17, 19, 37, 46, 88, 105,
109, 133, 135, 141, 171, 176, 188,
189, 192, 193, 204, 205, 209, 211,
224, 225, 227, 229, 297, 299
The Mansell Collection 45, 55, 59,
261, 279
London Mennonite Centre 35, 240,
241, 243, 245
Moody Bible Institute 339, 341, 342
National Portrait Gallery, London
217, 295, 303
National Tourist Organisation of
Greece 31
Northern Ireland Tourist Board 97, 98
Planet Earth Pictures 51, 53, 61
Chris Pipe 183
S.C.M. Press 347, 351
Claire Schwob 363
Scripture Union 44, 65, 73
Jamie Simson 21, 28, 71, 83
Spanish National Tourist Office 253
Swiss Government Tourist Office
199, 215
Tunisian National Tourist Board 49
Peter Wyart 13, 14, 16, 25, 33, 57, 66,
68, 74, 75, 99, 100, 101, 103, 104,
112, 113, 114, 115, 117, 118, 120,
123, 124, 125, 126, 129, 131, 132,
137, 148, 149, 151, 153, 154, 165,
167, 172, 173, 175, 177, 201, 202,
203, 219, 220, 248, 249, 250, 251,
263, 264, 265, 266, 267, 268, 269,
270, 272, 276, 288, 292, 294, 301,
305, 307, 311, 312, 333, 334, 335,
355, 358, 359, 360